THE CHINESE IN BRITAIN

About the Author

Barclay Price is the author of numerous articles for journals and magazines, and is the author of *Running a Workshop*, published by the Crafts Council, which sold over twenty thousand copies. Before retiring he was a senior arts administrator and served on the board of Creative Scotland, Scotland's arts council. This book came from discovering that the first Chinese immigrant lived in Edinburgh and expanded to cover other stories from across the United Kingdom.

THE CHINESE IN BRITAIN

A HISTORY OF VISITORS AND SETTLERS

BARCLAY PRICE

AMBERLEY

This edition published 2024

Amberley Publishing
The Hill, Stroud
Gloucestershire, GL5 4EP

www.amberley-books.com

Copyright © Barclay Price, 2019, 2024

The right of Barclay Price to be identified as the Author of this work has been asserted in accordance with the Copyrights, Designs and Patents Act 1988.

All rights reserved. No part of this book may be reprinted or reproduced or utilised in any form or by any electronic, mechanical or other means, now known or hereafter invented, including photocopying and recording, or in any information storage or retrieval system, without the permission in writing from the Publishers.

British Library Cataloguing in Publication Data.
A catalogue record for this book is available from the British Library.

ISBN 978 1 3981 1951 2 (paperback)
ISBN 978 1 4456 8665 3 (ebook)

Typesetting and Origination by Amberley Publishing.
Printed in India.

Contents

Introduction — 6

Part One: 1687–1900
1 The Most Beautiful Kingdom — 10
2 Britain's First Chinese Gentleman — 17
3 Manning British Ships — 29
4 Domestic Service — 38
5 The Origins of Chinatown — 45
6 Astonishing Acts — 51
7 Wealth and Poverty — 60
8 Missionary Connections — 68
9 A Chinese Gentleman Farmer — 80
10 Celestial Displays — 89
11 Studious Endeavours — 99
12 Delicate Diplomacy — 109
13 Ambassadorial Engagements — 118
14 The Revolutionary — 134

Part Two: 1901–1987
15 Below Decks — 138
16 Chinatown — 146
17 Sweat and Steam — 160
18 Changing Taste — 167
19 Unwelcome Action — 177
20 One Immigrant's Story — 189
21 Portraying China — 195
22 Academic Achievements — 212
23 Diplomacy in Troubled Times — 224
24 Taking up the Pen — 240
25 Other Travellers — 249
26 Portraying Britain — 275

Index — 283

Introduction

> If the stranger or traveller be firm and correct as he ought to be,
> there will be good fortune.
> *I-Ching*, 56, Lu Hexagram (Stranger, Traveller), translated by
> James Legge and Wang Tao in Dollar, Scotland, 1869

Today more than 400,000 Chinese live in Britain, substantial numbers of Chinese attend British universities, and an increasing number of Chinese visit Britain on business and as tourists. Yet it is not so long ago that the sight of a Chinese person in Britain was a remarkable event. This book examines the history of Chinese travellers to Britain over the 300 years from the first recorded visitor in 1687. Those who came included seamen, students, cooks, brides, diplomats, jugglers, servants, sportsmen, bureaucrats, writers and 'curiosities'. Some visited for just a few days, others stayed many years, while a number became permanent residents.

The Lu Hexagram.

Introduction

Accounts of some who decided to live permanently in Britain are included, in particular the earliest settlers, but this is not a history of Chinese migration to Britain. That subject is fully and admirably covered by *The Chinese in Britain, 1800–Present* (see below). The foreword to that book states: 'This book magnificently fills a puzzling gap: until now, there has been no full, historically grounded study of one of Britain's most important, if smaller, migrant communities: the Chinese.' The research and writing of this book came through accidentally stumbling across a mention of William Macao. Fascinated, I began to research his previously unrecorded but remarkable life and, in so doing, was surprised to discover that no comprehensive account of the other Chinese who came to Britain existed. This seemed a further puzzling gap, and one I decided to try to fill.

The primary focus is on the Chinese who travelled to Britain from the area that is now the People's Republic of China, including Hong Kong. Part One covers 1687 to 1900, a period when there were few Chinese visitors, and so is relatively comprehensive. As the number of Chinese arriving in Britain significantly increased after 1900, the individuals included in Part Two, covering 1901 to 1987, have been selected to illustrate broad themes and to highlight a number of individuals whose British visits are especially noteworthy.

As the English translation of Chinese individuals' names can vary significantly, and place names have changed over time, I mainly have chosen the form used at the time. In spite of my enthusiastic research, there may well be some factual errors or oversights and, if so, I apologise for this.

The range of research material employed would have been almost unthinkable before the internet and so my thanks go to all those who digitise archival material and make it freely available. The British Newspaper Archive, Ancestry, and similar sites have also been invaluable. As I did not set out to create an academic book there are no footnotes or links to sources. My researches ranged far and wide, and for those wishing to find out more about the individuals and events contained here, an internet search is more than likely to lead to the same, or other, sources. I have endeavoured to ensure that I have avoided any breach of copyright and to gain permissions where I felt these to be required, but in drawing on such a range of material over such a long timeframe it is possible I may have inadvertently erred. If so, I apologise, and I hope that any such breach will be excused by the wider aim of bringing to light the rich lives of Chinese travellers to Britain. Any omitted acknowledgement will of course be added in any future printing.

A number of works are mentioned in the text, and others of particular use in my research were the aforementioned *The Chinese in Britain, 1800–Present* by Gregor Benton and Edmund Terence Gomez, published in 2008 by Palgrave Macmillan; 'Limehouse Blues: Looking for Chinatown in the London Docks, 1900–40' by John Seed, published in the *History Workshop Journal*, Volume 62, Issue 1, 2006; and 'Chinese Impressions in the West', *Renditions Magazine*, Numbers 53 and 54, published by the Chinese

University of Hong Kong. A few of the books by Chinese writers that were written in English or were translated at the time have been republished, including the *Silent Traveller* books by Chiang Yee and *Mr Ma and Son* by Lao She. Others can be found as second-hand copies or in downloadable form on the internet, such as *London Through Chinese Eyes* by Min-ch'ien T. Z. Tyau.

My thanks to the staff at the Bank of Scotland Archive; the relations of John Hochee, who allowed me to draw on the excellent, unpublished book by Guy Duncan on the lives of Elphinstone and Hochee; the Chinese in Wales Association for permission to draw on the video account by Mrs Fung Siu Chin of her life; Karen Soo and Nasreen Akhtar for permission to use material drawn from her interview with Frank Soo for the BBC Gloucestershire project 'Voices: Our Untold Stories'; Lucy Sheen for material from her website; and Katriona Holmes and her family for material about Cheng Su and the BBC's Far East Services section. Thanks also to the various sources for images as listed.

Barclay Price
thechineseinbritain@gmail.com

PART ONE
1687–1900

1
The Most Beautiful Kingdom

But I suddenly dream of riding a boat, sailing for the sun.
Journeying is hard,
Journeying is hard
There are many turnings –
Which am I to follow?
I will mount a long wind some day and break the heavy waves
And set my cloudy sail straight and bridge the deep, deep sea.

            Li Po (701–762), translated by Harold Witter Bynner

Music transcribed from that played by Kiqua, in London. *The Gentleman's Magazine*, 1756. (Public domain)

The Most Beautiful Kingdom

Although contacts and trade between Europe and China had existed for about 2,000 years, it was not until the sixteenth century that European ships were able to reach China. The Portuguese were the first to reach Chinese waters and in 1557 established the port of Macau (known originally as Macao) in southern China. This provided Portugal with a base for trading with China and Japan. As well as traders, Jesuit missionaries travelled to China and by the end of the sixteenth century Jesuit missions had been established in Macau, with many of the priests becoming valued advisors to the Emperor and the imperial government.

It was not until 1637 that a British ship under the command of Captain Weddell of the East India Company (EIC) managed to reach China, but the British attempt to establish a trading relationship with the locals was rebuffed. The EIC finally secured a trading post in Taiwan in 1672, ten years after the Chinese had expelled the Dutch East India Company from the island. This base enabled the EIC to commence regular trade with the Chinese, and by 1700 the company's base had moved to Canton.

Despite Britain having no direct trading route to China until the 1670s, British interest in China had developed long before, mainly due to Marco Polo's published adventures in the thirteenth century, and other travellers' accounts. Also, Chinese artworks, porcelain in particular, had reached Britain well before the 1670s and were much admired by the royal court and the aristocracy, although both Chinese and Japanese articles were defined as 'Oriental', and few had any understanding of which country had produced the objects they adored and proudly displayed.

Tea from China was increasingly popular in many European countries, but it was not until the mid-seventeenth century that it appeared in Britain. The first reference was in an advertisement by a London coffee house in 1658 that advertised for sale a 'China Drink, called by the Chinese, Tcha, by other Nations Tay, alias Tee'. The rise in its popularity stemmed from the marriage of Charles II to Catherine of Braganza. She was a Portuguese princess and a tea addict, and her passion established tea as a fashionable beverage, first at court and then among the wealthy classes as a whole. The EIC's tea imports rapidly expanded, but the beverage remained expensive as a result of the Chinese monopoly on tea growing and it being heavily taxed in Britain.

Although many in Britain were curious about China, the Chinese rulers believed their country to be morally and culturally superior, and few Chinese had any curiosity about foreign countries or desire to travel to distant lands. Throughout the centuries China had asked nothing of the outside world but to be left alone and, until late in the nineteenth century, anyone who suggested China would benefit from Western ideas was heavily criticised for being unpatriotic. Thus, when in 1687 the first Chinese visited Britain, his arrival was a momentous event. He was Michael Alphonsus Shen FuTsung, who had travelled to Europe with the Belgian Jesuit Father Philippe Couplet.

Shen FuTsung was born around 1658 to a Chinese physician from Nanking who had been converted by the Roman Catholic Church. Shen was taught Latin by the Jesuits. Couplet had come to Europe to update the Vatican on Catholic affairs in China and to seek permission from the Pope to allow Chinese clergy to participate in services, develop a Chinese-language liturgy and incorporate certain Chinese rites into the Jesuit's work in China. Couplet's original plan had been to spend a year in Europe before returning to China, but Pope Innocent XI rejected these proposals and Couplet, together with Shen, decided to stay on in the hope time might see the Pope change his mind. Their extended stay stretched to eight years.

In May 1687 Shen, and a few months later Couplet, travelled to Britain. The arrival of the first Chinese in Britain created immense interest and Shen was given an audience by James II. The king was so captivated by Shen's appearance he commissioned Sir Godfrey Kneller to paint Shen's portrait, which he had hung in the room adjacent to his bedchamber. As he was able to converse in Latin, while in Britain Shen spoke with many key members of society, including Robert Hooke, the natural philosopher and architect who had experimented with acupuncture and built an abacus, which he used in his lectures. Shen also travelled to Oxford to meet Thomas Hyde at the Bodleian Library. The Bodleian had built up a collection of about 100 books in Chinese over the previous seventy years, but no one knew what they contained. Hyde was delighted when Shen arrived and agreed to help. When Shen left after a few months Hyde gave him a letter in which he wrote, 'Sir, the bearer hereof, the Chinese, hath been with us at Oxford, to make a Catalogue of our Chinese books, and to inform us about the subjects of them. We have some of Confucius's books; but most of what we have is physick. His Latin is a little imperfect; but it is well he hath any Latin.' In the following months Hyde and Shen corresponded. In reply to one question from Hyde seeking information about specific Chinese characters, Shen replied in Latin: 'Most distinguished and learned master, I received your honour's letter and the adjoined (Chinese) characters, of which the explication is *che* – chariot, *ma* – horse.' In April 1688, just before James II was overthrown, Shen and Couplet left London for Lisbon. There Shen completed his training to become a Jesuit priest and, in 1691, set off to return to China. Unfortunately, he died en route, as did Couplet on his voyage back to China two years later.

The eighteenth century saw the EIC's trade in Chinese porcelain, silk and lacquerware grow; in 1730 the EIC imported more than half a million pieces of Chinese porcelain. This stimulated interest in the Chinoiserie style – from *chinois*, the French for Chinese – and the fashion swept the British court and the aristocracy. China was seen as exotic and its images of fantastic landscapes, fabulous birds and dragons inspired British designers and craftsmen to create their own imaginary versions of the East. By the 1730s most country houses had a Chinese room, and numerous mock Confucian temples and Chinese bridges adorned estate gardens throughout England.

Yet any real knowledge of China was limited until 1738, when an English translation by Robert Brookes of a French history of China was published, grandly entitled *The General History of China Containing a Geographical, Historical, Chronological, Political and Physical Description of the Empire of China, Chinese-Tartary, Corea, and Thibet; Including an Exact and Particular Account of Their Customs, Manners, Ceremonies, Religion, Arts, and Sciences: The Whole Adorn'd with Curious Maps, and Variety of Copper-Plates*. The original had been written by Jean-Baptiste Du Halde, a French Jesuit historian. Although Du Halde never travelled to China, he drew on Jesuit missionaries' reports and collected Chinese materials to create this first detailed account of the country's geography and many aspects of Chinese civilization. Brookes' introduction stated:

> China is the most remarkable of all Countries yet known, the English Reader must be greatly pleased to find the exactest Account of it that has ever yet appeared in our Language. P. du Halde from whom this Work is done, has not only taken greater Pains, but has had infinitely better Helps than any other Author who has wrote on this Subject. For, besides the printed Relations, he has had the Advantage of a prodigious number of Manuscripts, written by the most skilful of the Missionaries, and where these have seemed not sufficiently clear, he has had the Opportunity of satisfying his Doubts from the Conversation of those who were best able to give him the truest Informations.

Dr Samuel Johnson wrote to Brookes: 'I, therefore, return you my thanks for having undertaken, at so great an expense, to convey to English readers the most copious and accurate account yet published, of that remote and celebrated people, whose antiquity, magnificence, power, wisdom, peculiar customs, and excellent constitution, undoubtedly deserve the attention of the publick.'

It was not until 1756 that a second Chinese visited Britain. Loum Kiqua was a Chinese merchant and he too became an object of intense curiosity. Although he had an audience with George II, as Kiqua's only foreign language was imperfect Portuguese, a language few in London spoke, he found it difficult to converse and so appears to have had few other meetings with members of London society. The little that is known about Kiqua mainly comes from the details that the artist Thomas Burford affixed to his portrait of him:

> The Chinese came to Lisbon in 1755, was there at the Time of the Earthquake, and providentially escap'd with Life; after many hardships & ill treatments from the Portuguese, he came over to England, in 1756, where he met with different usage, having had the Honour to be seen by his Majesty, and the rest of the Royal Family, most of the Nobility &c.

by whom he was much caress'd. Having made application to the Honble. the East India Company for his passage home, he was kindly receiv'd and generously accomodated on Board one of their Ships to carry him to Canton, his Native Country.

One of the only other accounts of Kiqua is contained in a letter, printed in *The Gentleman's Magazine*, from a writer who simply signs himself A.B. 'A few days ago I accidentally fell in company with the Chinese merchant latterly arrived from Canton; I was glad of that opportunity of being informed of some of the customs and manners of his native country, but as he understands little of our language, I was disappointed; however, to make up the want of conversation, he played several Chinese tunes upon a musical instrument something resembling a guitar. I own, I could not help being surprised to find that the airs he played, though very simple with respect to composition, yet contained the life and spirit that are wanting in most of our country dances.' The writer, having musical ability, wrote down one of the airs. 'I have not attempted to make a dance of this air, being convinced it will be much better executed by others; And if this proves an entertainment to the gentlemen and ladies, who are fond of that exercise, it will be a great pleasure to your humble servant.' This is the first recorded mention of Chinese music being played in Britain. A few weeks later, Kiqua, frustrated at his inability to communicate in Britain, left to return to China.

The lack of Chinese visitors to Britain was not surprising. Travelling abroad required permission as the law deemed all Chinese to be the property of the Emperor, and few of China's educated classes had sufficient curiosity about Europe to undertake the long and hazardous sea journey. At best, the journey took seven months, though mishaps could extend the travel time a great deal, and many ships travelling the route were lost at sea.

One who was curious to see Britain was Tan Chitqua. He was a well-established artist based in Canton who crafted lifelike clay portraits, about 30 to 40 centimetres in height. His main clientele in Canton was visiting Europeans and through his contact with them, he had learnt a little English and heard about Britain. Although the Chinese authorities were disinclined to give permission for distant travel, journeys within eastern Asia were allowed so Chitqua successfully applied for permission to travel to Batavia (now Jakarta, Indonesia), although his intended destination was always Britain.

Chitqua arrived in London in 1769 and took lodgings 'at the hatter's on the corner of Norfolk Street'. A contemporary report described him: 'He is a middle-aged man, of a proper stature; his face and hands of a copperish colour, is elegantly clothed in silk robes, after the fashion of his country; speaks the Lingua Franca, mixt with Broken English; is very sensible, and a great observer.' Once settled, Chitqua set up a workshop and resumed making clay portraits to commission. The sculptures were made by forming clay around a bamboo frame. The clay remained unfired and once dry was painted. Many had detachable wigs made of the subject's own hair. Due to their fragility only a few survive, including one of the London druggist and tea merchant Thomas Todd that is in the Museum of London today. The sculptures were sold at 10 guineas for a bust and 15 for a full-length figure.

James Boswell visited Chitqua at Mr Marr's Hat Shop and described him as 'not a man of fashion but an ingenious artist in making likenesses in terracotta, which he works very neatly... I got him to read a little to me from a fan with Chinese characters. It was just what Mr Johnson told me of another Chinese: a sound like the ringing of a small bell.' Another to recount his meeting with Chitqua was the antiquarian Richard Gough, who wrote:

> He has been long enough among us to have done with an interpreter, though his English is broken, and his speech thick ... On his head no hair except the long lock braided into a tail almost a yard long. He wears the dress of his own country. He complained much of cold, but had no fire; and preferred the country to London only for quietness from noise, for he meets no insults on the street. ... I always understood that it was a capital offence to quit the country, but am since told it can be compounded for £10.

Again there was royal interest in the Chinese visitor and Chitqua was invited to meet George III and Queen Charlotte. He also was invited to exhibit one of his sculptures at the Royal Academy's exhibition in April 1770, and he is included in the group portrait of the Royal Academicians painted by Johann Zoffany. Although Chitqua's English was far from fluent he helped identify the content of a number of Chinese books at the British Library.

In 1772, Chitqua set off to return to China but, as *The Gentleman's Magazine* recounted, things did not go as planned:

> Having embarked on board the East Indiaman *Grenville* at Gravesend, he discovered that the common sailors were unaccountably prejudiced against him; owing, probably to his strange dress and appearance. Added to this, he had one day the misfortune accidentally to fall overboard, and being saved from drowning by being buoyed up by his loose habit, after floating with the tide near half a mile, he was taken up half dead. This, with the superstitious fear of the mariners and their brutish imprecations against the 'Chinese dog', whom they deemed a madman, so alarmed him, that he begged the carpenter to make him a coffin, and carry his corpse ashore, as it was not lawful in his country to be buried in the water.

To protect Chitqua the captain decided it would be prudent to land him at Deal and arranged for the ship's pilot to escort Chitqua back to London. However, this was not an end to the unfortunate situation. 'When he arrived there, another distress befell him; he could not recollect or express intelligibly where he lodged; and a mob gathering round the hackney coach, began to abuse and beat the pilot, for having, as they supposed, kidnapped a foreigner.' Fortunately, a passer-by recognised Chitqua and calmed the situation. Chitqua was forced to wait another year before he was able to set off again and in the interim took to wearing English dress so as 'not to be deemed a Jonah'. Chitqua died in China in the mid-1790s, possibly having committed suicide.

The fourth Chinese visitor was brought to Britain by the twenty-four-year-old John Bradby Blake when he returned from China in 1770. Four years before, Blake had gone to Canton as an employee of the EIC and while there became fascinated by the potential of growing useful Chinese vegetables in Britain. On his return, he arrived with seeds and plants which he had collected, and also the seventeen-year-old Wang-y-Tong, as he had an understanding of the medicinal properties of Chinese plants. Again, the exotic appearance of a Chinese visitor entranced many and he too became a minor celebrity in English intellectual circles. Initially, he lived with Blake and there met many luminaries including Josiah Wedgwood, with whom he shared information about the production of Chinese porcelain, and the physician Andrew Duncan, to whom he explained the principles of acupuncture.

When Blake returned to Canton, where he died in 1773, Blake's friend the Duke of Dorset arranged for Wang to live at Knole House in Kent and work as a page for the Duke's mistress, Giovanna Bacelli, probably to add ornamental and oriental flavour to her entertaining. While at Knole, Wang is thought to have attended the nearby Queen Elizabeth's Grammar School (now Sevenoaks School). In 1776, Reynolds painted Wang's portrait for the Duke and recounted that the young man's journey was

> ... partly due to curiosity and a desire of improving himself in science, and partly with a view of procuring some advantages in trade, in which he and his elder brother are engaged. He arrived here in August, and already pronounces and understands our language very tolerably, but he writes it in a very excellent hand ... he has a great thirst after knowledge, and seems to communicate readily what is communicated to him.

It is not known exactly when Wang returned to China, but he is recorded as being back in Canton by the 1780s.

While these four early Chinese visitors were acclaimed by English society, the arrival of the fifth Chinese in Britain went unnoticed.

2

Britain's First Chinese Gentleman

Who understands any place he reaches in life?
Man is like the flying geese tramping on melting snow.
By chance they leave some claw-mark there,
But the geese fly without caring whether they go East or West.

Su Tung-Po (1037–1101), translated by Chiang Yee

Gravestone of William and Helen Macao in St Cuthbert's Churchyard, Edinburgh. William Macao was Britain's first Chinese resident. (Author's collection)

The fifth Chinese to arrive in Britain neither gained an audience with royalty, nor met with fashionable members of London society, nor had his portrait painted. Even more surprisingly, although he was the first Chinese to marry and settle in Britain, his place in British Chinese history has been obscured until now. Nothing is known about his life before he came to Britain. His Chinese name is not recorded but his given English name was William Macao. Although it is not known where he came from in China, his English name may indicate that he came from Macau (then spelt Macao), although as he was brought to Britain by a Scot, perhaps there also was a droll nod to the most common Scottish surname prefix. Given that later in life William Macao was fluent in English and successful in a career that required skill in calculation and figures, later becoming part of Edinburgh's professional class, it seems probable that he came from an educated Chinese family.

Although the first recorded mention of Macao dates from 1778, from other information it seems probable Macao arrived in Britain by at least 1775, so in his early twenties. The only account by Macao of his early years in Britain was given to the Reverend Donald Sage, Minister of Resolis in Ross-shire, and the account of their meeting in 1824 is contained in *Memorabilia domestica; or, Parish life in the North of Scotland 1780–1869*. Sage wrote:

> When at the Assembly I had a note from Mr. William Macao, a native of China, asking me concerning Miss Urquhart who resided at Resolis. Mr. Macao left his native country as the body servant of the family of Braelangwell in the parish of Resolis, and had, under Christian training, been reclaimed from heathenism to a saving knowledge of the truth as it is in Jesus. ... In his note he expressed his desire to see me either at my lodgings or at his house at No. 1 Dundas Street. I called, and had a short but very interesting conversation with him. In his becoming acquainted with divine truth, he had been indebted to Miss Betty Urquhart, as to one among others who had been instrumental in leading his mind to right views on that all-important subject. Miss Betty Urquhart was the daughter of Mr. (Charles) Urquhart of Braelangwell, and the sister of the late Dr (David) Urquhart, his son and successor. Dr David Urquhart studied for the medical profession, and went abroad, whether to China or India I cannot say. On his return to his native country he resided on his paternal estate.

There is also a description of Macao in the memoir of James Laurie, Edinburgh's Town Clerk, written in 1858: 'Forty or fifty years ago, there was a Chinese gentleman in the Excise Office in Edinburgh by the name of William Macao. In his latter days, he was a slightly made, little, old man, with a glazed yellow face, and the regular Chinese eyes.'

From Macao's account to Sage it would appear that he was brought to Scotland by Dr David Urquhart, who was born about 1745 and had worked as a surgeon for the EIC in Bengal. It is likely Urquhart returned to Scotland sometime around his father's death in 1776 to take up his inheritance of Braelangwell Estate. The estate of Braelangwell, consisting of 4,200 acres, lay in the parish of Resolis, on the Black Isle, the northern part of the rich farming lands on the south side of the Cromarty Firth. In the eighteenth century the area consisted of arable land, meadow and pasture, woodland and plantations, and areas of moor. Almost all the farms were occupied by tenants, holding small areas of land. The fact that there is no record of Macao arriving in Britain is thus easily explained. His status as a servant was radically different from that of the previous Chinese visitors; a servant, even a Chinese one, would not have been someone to be feted by society. More significantly, he went to work and live in a remote part of Scotland, far from London society. Also it is unlikely that Macao would have worn the colourful Chinese dress that made the previous Chinese visitors stand out, as such flowing robes would hardly have been appropriate for life in northern Scotland.

Sage's account implies that Macao became a Christian and was baptised into the Protestant religion while living at Braelangwell. If so, this would have been by at least 1778 and thus the earliest recorded instance of a Chinese being baptised in Britain. Given that Protestant missionaries did not arrive in China until the early nineteenth century (although the Roman Catholic church had been converting Chinese since the sixteenth century) Macao would appear to be the first Chinese to be baptised into the Protestant church. His baptism would have taken place at Resolis Parish Church on the Black Isle.

The neighbouring estate to Braelangwell was Newhall, consisting of some 3,500 acres. It was owned by the Gordon family and in 1761 was inherited by William Gordon, an advocate. His sister, Henrietta, was married to Thomas Lockhart, a Commissioner of Excise in Scotland, and they lived in Edinburgh. The first surviving document mentioning Macao is the Male Servant Tax Roll for Edinburgh dated 19 September 1778, in which he is listed as a footman working for Thomas Lockhart. Thus it would appear that Macao moved into the service of Urquhart's neighbours. Thomas Lockhart had married Henrietta Gordon in 1766, two years after having been appointed one of Scotland's Excise Commissioners. The Commissioners were not government officials but gentry who were nominated by Parliament. Thus the posts, which carried a substantial salary, were gained through political patronage, although those appointed were required to be efficient and so such posts were not a sinecure. As one newly appointed Commissioner commented in 1736: 'We meet every day of the year Sundays and holidays excepted at nine in the morn, and have full employment at the Board till twelve, so that I am always obliged to go from home at eight ... and never return before two. To a person of a lazy disposition, this would not be a very agreeable life ... there's no £1000 a year in the King's gift so dearly earned.' By the time Lockhart was appointed the salary had been reduced to £500, but whether the work was halved is not known. The Commissioners took decisions on staffing matters, including establishment numbers, promotions, transfers and disciplinary actions, and exercising summary jurisdiction on charges brought against anyone evading custom duties. The minutes of the day show that much of the work of the Scottish Commissioners was controlled by the Treasury in London. Bids for extra staffing or small increases in levels of pay required permission from London and replies to requests could take months. One long-standing dispute over how the Scottish Board accounted for its work dragged on for a year, with the minutes recounting each side's position growing longer and longer. Although there was a separate Board of Customs responsible for overseeing the on-going campaign to tackle the smuggling and other forms of custom duty avoidance that was rife, the Board of Excise also had a concern as it adversely affected their revenue income, and they had overall responsibility for the costs of policing the coasts.

Around 1775 Lockhart purchased a newly built house in Edinburgh's fashionable George Square. Between the Lockhart's house at Number 23 and their neighbour's at Number 22 was a lane and, in 1779, exasperated by the chill wind that blew through the gap in winter, Lockhart had a small house, now number 23a, built to block the wind. It was at their house in George Square between 1775 and 1778 that he and Henrietta had their first three children, and there that Macao would have lived while working as Lockhart's footman. Only the wealthiest people could afford a footman and the position was of significant status in the hierarchy of servants. As footman Macao would have run alongside Lockhart's carriage, for which Lockhart employed a male driver, and performed livery duties such as attending to visitors arriving at the house and running errands. Given the relatively modest scale of Edinburgh's new Georgian townhouses, few employed butlers, and as Lockhart does not appear to have had one it is likely that Macao would have waited at table, including when there were guests. The diarist James Boswell was friends with the Lockharts, as indicated by his diary entry for 31 January 1776: 'Lockhart has been very obliging to me in granting solicitations for offices in the Excise, yet by the most unaccountable negligence I had never once waited on him. My wife had been latterly introduced to Mrs Lockhart, and we sent them a card to sup, after my wife had called and my lameness had been mentioned. It was very kind in them to come. I was in excellent spirits.' He also dined at their house but unfortunately makes no mention of Macao in his entry for 19 April 1780: 'Dined with Commissioner Cochrane at Commissioner Lockhart's, a hearty good dinner. No other company there but a Miss Christie and Mr Ross, Secretary of the Post Office. I drank porter and port and Madeira and a bottle of Claret, and wished for more.' Yet Macao clearly was a valued servant for in 1779 Thomas Lockhart assigned repayment of a debt of £100 (equivalent to around £10,000 in today's value) to his footman.

When Henrietta's brother, William, died in 1778, she, as the only surviving child, inherited the Newhall estate although she and Thomas continued to live in Edinburgh. In December 1780, when Henrietta was pregnant for the fourth time, Thomas Lockhart died. It is not known if the death was expected or sudden, but either way the shock to Henrietta would have been severe as it was only two years since the death of her brother, and she had three infant children and was pregnant with a fourth. Fortunately, the distress did not adversely affect the pregnancy and a son, Charles, was born some months later. The death of Lockhart would have been a major concern for Macao as it put his future in doubt for, soon after, Henrietta decided to live permanently at Newhall. She sold the George Square house and thus had no need of a footman. While Macao moved back to Newhall where he is recorded as receiving payment from the Tenant and Overseer of Newhall Estate on behalf of Mrs Lockhart, it would have been clear to both Henrietta and Macao that his future did not lie in the Black Isle. So Henrietta arranged an alternative future for the family's valued footman. Firstly, she made a bond in Macao's favour for the substantial sum of £300 (equivalent to £30,000 today) to be paid at some point during her lifetime or from her estate, and, secondly, through her deceased husband's contacts, procured for him the post of Assistant for Male Servants in Edinburgh. An appointment to even such a relatively minor government post was conditional on patronage, as at this time family networks were crucial. Without Henrietta's assistance, it is impossible that Macao's eventual future path would have been open to a Chinese.

Thus, in 1782, Macao returned to Edinburgh to begin work at the Board of Excise's offices in Chessels Court, probably assisting the clerks working for the accountants who managed the Board's financial affairs. The Board provided accommodation for their new employee in St Leonard's Hill, an area of a few houses that stood among fields and market gardens to the south east of the city, below the crags of Arthur's Seat. This was a time when the Board of Excise was expanding and the Commissioners had submitted a request to the Treasury for two more clerks:

> We humbly conceive it would be unnecessary to communicate to your Lordships the new duties which have been imposed since the year 1750, and which have proved another fruitful source of additional labour. Those (tax duties) on Carriages, Malt, Glass, Auctions, Tea Licences and Male Servants must be fresh in your Lordships recollection. We shall only in general observe that the additional trouble in collecting and accounting for these duties is not so great when diffused over some hundreds of offices in the Country. Yet it is severely felt when all those vouchers come to the centre... (to cope) the Comptroller has brought in and pays out of his own pocket, an extraordinary Clerk more than was ever known in this office.

Macao clearly proved a willing and effective employee for in 1786 the Board of Excise promoted him to Assistant Clerk. It is not known how much he was paid but it was sufficient for him to employ a servant at his lodgings by 1787.

In 1788 the Board of Excise moved to Dundas House in St Andrew Square in Edinburgh's New Town. The mansion, modelled on Marble Hill House in Twickenham, was commissioned by Lord Dundas, at the time probably Scotland's most influential person, and when completed in 1774 was one of the first buildings in Edinburgh's new development. Although St Andrew Square was complete, the other streets of the New Town were still being built, and construction work would take another twenty years. While Macao may have seen impressive Chinese and Portuguese buildings in Macau, he, like the other inhabitants of Edinburgh, must have been fascinated to watch the completely new Georgian town evolve. Macao clearly settled quickly into his new life and his financial skills led to further promotion, becoming one of eleven Accountant Generals, at an annual salary of £45. The work involved 'receiving from a great number and variety of Officers around Scotland, accounts of the Quantities of the respective Commodities for which the Merchant, Manufacturer or Trader is chargeable; in computing the Duties to be paid, entering the same, and taking account of all the monies received at the Chief Office and in bringing to a total in every week, all receipts and remittances into His Majesty's Exchequer'. Another of Macao's roles can be seen from a newspaper advert in 1799 seeking information on an army deserter: 'Whoever will lodge the said deserter in any of his Majesty's jails shall receive two guineas of reward, over and above the allowance of twenty shillings for apprehending deserters by applying to the Provost of Inverness or Mr Macao, Excise, Edinburgh.'

In 1786, the widowed Henrietta Lockhart had married her neighbour, David Urquhart of Braelangwell. Given both had employed Macao in his younger days it is likely that they kept in touch with his progress in Edinburgh and doubtless helped when, in 1792, with the approach of his fortieth birthday and now earning a good salary, Macao looked to marry. This was far from straightforward. Not only was Macao the only Chinese man in Scotland, he was an alien, being 'one born in a foreign country, out of allegiance to the British Crown'. This was an issue at the time for as the impact of the 1789 French Revolution expanded and anti-royalist fervour increased, more and more aristocrats fled France, many moving to Britain. In 1793 the British Government introduced the Aliens Act in response to alarm at the uncontrolled influx of foreigners from Europe and anxiety that some might bring radical ideas to Britain. Although the Act did not restrict entry by foreigners, it required them to record their origins, occupation, length of time in the country, and the intended duration of their stay. Interestingly, Macao's name does not appear in the Edinburgh Aliens Register, perhaps because he had lived in Scotland for many years and was employed by the Government. Yet his legal status was as an alien and one important restriction on aliens was that they could not own property. It seems certain that Henrietta and David Urquhart must have helped to arrange a wife for Macao as the woman selected was Helen Ross, a daughter of William Ross, and the Ross family were connected to the Urquharts; a branch of the Ross clan were known as Ross of Braelangwell. Such a match would only have been agreed if the Ross family had an assurance from people they knew that Macao was suitable. While Helen's father may have had some concern about Macao's alien status, he would have been reassured by the fact that any children born to William and Helen would be legally British subjects. So permission was given and William and Helen married in 1793.

The fact that Macao was not a British citizen had no effect on his career and in 1794 he moved up another rung, to Excise Accountant. In 1795, Helen gave birth and the baby was christened Ann. Another daughter was born the following year and named Henrietta, no doubt in honour of Henrietta Lockhart/Urquhart, who had been of such help. Needing more space, the family took an apartment in a lodging house at 16 South Frederick Street in the New Town. A third child, William Ross, was born in 1801 but, unfortunately, Helen's next birth a year later ended in tragedy. The baby boy was stillborn and, as a result of the problematic birth, Helen died a week later. She and the baby were buried in the graveyard at St Cuthbert's Church, Princes Street, Edinburgh. The emotional shock for William Macao and his infant children must have been immense. As well as coping with the arrangements for the burial of both his wife and stillborn son, he now was left a widower, with a five- and a four-year-old daughter and a one-year-old baby son to care for. At this time the majority of men and women whose partners died, particularly those with young children, remarried, but Macao did not. This may have been because by 1801 Henrietta Urquhart was dead and David Urquhart had remarried, so the required patronage to find a suitable wife was perhaps no longer available. Whatever the reason, Macao cared for his three young children on his own, though he would have employed at least one servant to help.

As with almost all people living in Scotland in this period, Macao's Christianity was central to his life and hopefully his religion gave him solace at what must have been a very difficult time. Sundays were for God, when the New Town would have been especially quiet. Apart from their solemn walk to and from church, often accompanied by their servants, the residents stayed indoors during the Sabbath. All deliveries, cleaning, building, etc. were banned and even the communal gardens would have been off-limits. In addition to attending church, all middle-class families at the time also worshipped in their own house, and the servants joined in these family services. William would have read a passage of scripture and led a prayer, and then all those present would have sung a psalm. He was a member of the congregation at Rose Street Burgher Church (known as the Burgher Meeting House). The minister, Dr Hall, was a popular preacher and attracted such a large congregation that the church was too small to accommodate all those who came to worship. 'Every ingenious expedient seems to have been employed to crowd more occupants into the pews, and to increase the number of these by fitting up waste corners, and even by encroachment on the passages. Still, after all, members could not be put in possession of sittings.' Church services at this time did not include any instrumental music, although the congregation would sing psalms. Until reversed later in the century, the congregation sat to sing and stood to pray. Often members of the congregation attended both a morning and an early evening service. In 1807, Macao was apppointed as one of the elders of Rose Street Burgher Church and participated in the Session Meetings, at which church business was conducted. The business mainly consisted of applications to join the congregation, requests for financial support from members of the congregation who had fallen on hard times and judgement on members accused of immorality or crime. At a meeting in October 1816 Macao was one of the nine elders in attendance at the Kirk Session to consider a charge brought against one of the congregation, John Philp, a shoemaker. The minutes report that Philp 'who being charged with the crime of Adultery acknowledged his transgression. The Moderator spoke to him at length upon the heinousness of the crime, after which he was suspended from all the Ordinance.' Often those found guilty would be required to confess their sins in front of the congregation and the public shame that brought was acute.

During Macao's time as a church elder there were on-going discussions about how to alleviate the church's lack of space. Negotiations with nearby owners to buy adjoining property and extend the Rose Street site came to nothing. Finally, in 1819, it was decided to move to a new church, to be built in Broughton Place. However, this was not a decision welcomed by all. There was discord between those who thought a new church the best option, and those who believed it a waste of money and did not wish to leave Rose Street. The published history of the church rather skates over what was a bitter debate: 'It would neither be interesting nor edifying to detail the controversy which took place in reference to this matter.' By the time of the move to the new Edinburgh Broughton Place United Presbyterian Church in October 1819, the rancorous dispute had come to a head. Three hundred and fifty members of the congregation refused to move and remained at the Rose Street church for their worship. A number of members were so upset by the unchristian acrimony that they resigned. Macao was one. His letter of 7 October addressed to The Session set out his reasons: 'Gentlemen – From the late very unpleasant misunderstanding and division in the congregation together with other cogent private considerations, I have been induced after mature deliberation to declare myself publicly no longer a constituent member of your congregation, consequently am no longer competent to hold any office in it. Therefore I do hereby resign my office in it as an Elder accordingly. Signed Wm Macao'.

Macao's career continued to advance, with his appointment to be Cashier of Yachts in 1805. In this role he had responsibility for financial matters relating to the Excise's fleet of 'Cutter Yachts', powerful, fast ships used by the authorities for controlling smuggling and other illegal avoidance of customs duties. By now he was earning £327 a year, a relatively high salary for the period. When the war against the French came to an end, the Royal Navy became responsible for tackling smuggling and so took over command of the Revenue cruisers. This meant the post of Cashier of Yachts became redundant and Macao was appointed Junior Accountant General.

While Henrietta and Ann would have attended one of the small private schools that existed around the city which focused on developing young women's social skills, William Ross would have attended a small private preparatory school until the age of eight and then attended one of the three Edinburgh boys' schools. There boys were taught Latin grammar and a few other subjects until they were fourteen or fifteen, at which point they would enter university or take up a career. William Ross chose to study to work in the law and began an apprenticeship with a Writer to the Signet (solicitor).

Another illustration of how Macao had become assimilated into the professional world of Edinburgh was his appointment as a committee member of the Edinburgh Subscription Library in 1811. He may well have been invited to join by Dr Hall, the minister of the Burgher Meeting House, as soon after the Library had been founded in 1794 Hall was elected its first President and continued to serve on its committee. The Library was one of a number in Scotland opened to provide access to books, as these were expensive. The stated aim of the library was to collect 'the most valuable books in miscellaneous literature' as well as 'the most eminent publications of the season'. Members paid an entrance fee and an annual subscription. On paying the entrance fee individuals received a share, which they could sell if the member no longer wished to use the library, or pass on to a descendant. By the time Macao was on the committee, the library had premises on South Bridge and a paid librarian.

On 28 May 1818, Macao bought Bank of Scotland stock to the value of £83 6s 8d (equivalent to £6,000 today) little knowing that this purchase would lead to him challenging the Government over a major constitutional issue. It had been the Government's original intention that the 1793 Aliens Act would end in 1818. However, late in 1817, due to continued concern about foreigners entering Britain, the Government decided to update, rather than end, the Act, and the legislative process began its process through Parliament in early 1818. On 30 April of that year, three individuals bought Bank of Scotland stock. Today this would not seem unusual, but in the previous ten years only three purchases of bank stock had taken place. So George Sandys, the bank's secretary, was surprised to see three purchases made in one day and puzzled by the fact that the three buyers were London-based merchants with foreign-sounding names: Herman Sillem, Frederick Grautoff and John Barandon. When the next day two Frenchmen and a Prussian Count also bought shares Sandy's surprise turned to alarm. He urgently contacted the bank's directors. After some investigation the director's discovered that an ingenious person, prompted by the news that the Aliens Act was to be extended, had come across a clause in the Scottish Parliament Act of 1695 establishing the Bank of Scotland. This clause stated that all foreigners (aliens) who became partners in the bank by purchasing stock of at least £1,000 Scots would 'thereby become a naturalised Scotsman ... and as such, a naturalised British subject to all intents and purposes whatsoever'. The clause had been inserted as in 1695 Scotland had been keen to attract foreign finance and skills. The minimum stock purchase of 1,000 Scots pounds equated to £83 6s 8d sterling in 1818. Thus a number of aliens, including Macao, had purchased the required minimum amount of stock presuming that by the clause they would gain British citizenship. This was an extraordinary opportunity as the only existing means by which foreigners could become naturalised British subjects was through an individual Act of Parliament, a complicated and hugely expensive process, and available to few.

As the number of aliens purchasing stock rose to more than 100, there was Government outrage: 'Can it be right that an owner of such stock might sell it the next day, and the stock travel across the Continent, and make every man a British subject who bought that share?' the Foreign Secretary queried. 'All the provision of the law would in that manner be evaded, and natives of foreign countries would in that way obtain rights which they could do in no other. Could it be supposed that the Bank of Scotland have the right, by a simple transfer of a certain quantity of their stock, to render all acts upon the subject of aliens inoperative?' In response the Government decided to insert an additional clause into the 1818 Act stating that 'all persons who had purchased Bank of Scotland shares since 28 April should be deemed aliens'. There was strong hostility to this draconian retrospective clause by the parliamentary opposition. Sir Samuel Romilly voiced the opposition of the Whig MPs, 'Parliament had, by solemn statute, recognised by five several acts of the British Parliament, encouraged foreigners to take shares in the bank by bonus of naturalisation: they trust to the word of Parliament: they purchase the stock: and the Government brings forward a proposition which, by its retrospective operation, is to tear from them, by the hand of law, those very rights which the law had bribed them to purchase, and had undertaken to secure.' The bank was now in a difficult position. Many of the purchasers had not confined themselves to the minimum purchase and the new investment had resulted in a 15% increase in its market value. The directors feared that the Government's retrospective clause would lead to a sell-off of stock and a fall in the bank's capital value. The directors also regarded the original Act establishing the bank, and the special clause, as an expression of the bank's glorious past.

As neither the Government nor the Bank of Scotland were comfortable with the position, it was agreed that an individual who had bought stock should be supported by the bank to bring a case to the Scottish courts so that the legality of the clause could be tested. The stockholder selected was William Macao, though why he was chosen is unknown. Perhaps he was one of the few alien investors to live in Edinburgh and was known to be a respected member of Edinburgh's middle class. In early December 1818 a Summons in the Court of Session was raised on behalf of William Macao against the Officers of State (the Government). Although the summons was in Macao's name alone, the Bank of Scotland was fully engaged in the process, instructing Macao's lawyers and paying the legal costs. As all parties understood the need for speed, Macao's case was heard in the First Division Court by the judge Lord Alloway on 2 January 1819. Both sides brought a range of arguments and case law in support of their opposing stances. Macao's advocate, George Cranstoun, contended that as there had been no changes made in the intervening years to the original Bank of Scotland Act, the clause was still in force, and that as the Act of Union had transferred the right to British citizenship to all Scots, the court should rule that Macao had acquired British citizenship. Acting for the Officers of State was The Lord Advocate, Alexander Maconochie, who argued that the clause in the original Act referred only to those buying stock at the time and did not extend to those purchasing stock at a later date and, more importantly, claimed that only Parliament had the right to bestow naturalisation to any individual.

Lord Alloway gave his judgment the following day: 'Having heard the parties procurate at great length, and having considered the same, finds, that as provided by the Act of 1695, for erecting a bank in Scotland, the clause cannot be limited and restricted to original partners ... not only are all the privileges at present conferred by the Bank by the statute, but it has been five times renewed by British Acts of Parliament since that period. Thus, the pursuer having joined as a partner of the bank is, while he remains a partner thereof, a naturalised Scotsman, to all intents and purposes, whatsoever.' While on the face of it this judgement appeared to be a victory for Macao, as Alloway had legally deemed Macao a Scot, the judge had avoided taking a view on whether this bestowed British citizenship. Given this key point remained unresolved, it was decided that the matter should be considered on appeal by all the judges of the Court of Session.

Eighteen months later the twelve Law Lords of the Scottish Court of Session convened to consider the appeal. Macao's advocate began, 'The respondent is concerned at his status as a subject in this country in which he has lived since his earliest years as this is a matter of no slight importance to him. The respondent is far from presuming to call into question the justice or expediency of the various successive Aliens Acts that have been passed from 1793 downwards. Being ardently attached to the constitution of this country, in which he has passed the greatest part of his life, he is far from maintaining that an extraordinary influx of foreigners may not, on some occasion, be attended with danger or detriment to the state. But in former times, in England, both before and after the Union, the general policy of Government has always been to encourage foreigners to settle in the country, so that it might reap the advantage of their skill and capital. On many occasions were the arts and manufactures of England thus benefitted.' He then gave a number of examples where the right to nationalisation had been bestowed without individual Acts, and when mentioning one precedent quipped, 'This at a time when the Throne was filled by a Prince, himself a foreigner.' The key opposing argument from the Government's advocate was that it was inconceivable that a foreigner could become naturalised without ever having set foot in this country through simply purchasing bank stock, or that an enemy of the State could equally gain British citizenship. He insisted that only Parliament had the right to bestow British citizenship. In November 1820 the twelve judges published their opinions and although there was no consensus on all the points, the court ruled that it was for Parliament alone to bestow naturalisation and that it was not tenable that 'a purchaser of the bank's stock could hold a higher situation that the most illustrious foreigner naturalised under a special act'. This reversal of Lord Alloway's judgement brought Macao's twenty-month Scottish citizenship to an end. The Bank of Scotland agreed to support Macao in an appeal to the House of Lords and this was heard in May 1822 but was rejected.

Macao's lengthy legal battle with the Government does not appear to have been of a concern to the Board of Excise, as in 1823 Macao was given what would be his final promotion, becoming Accountant of the Superannuation Fund, although his salary remained unchanged at £327 per annum. On 30 March 1826 Macao, now aged seventy-three, retired. The Board of Excise minutes simply record, 'James Dundas, General Accountant has agreed that William Macao be allowed to relinquish his position.' As the Government had introduced the first unfunded non-contributory scheme for all its civil servants in 1810, Macao, having served the Board of Excise for forty-five years, received a superannuated lump sum pension of one year's final salary.

On 31 October 1831, William Macao died at Henderson Row, aged seventy-eight. He was buried alongside his wife in St Cuthbert's Cemetery. In spite of William Macao having been born and grown up in the totally different environment and culture of China, he assimilated seamlessly into Edinburgh life. This must have required considerable self-reliance and significant ability. Although Macao's Scottish citizenship conferred on him by Lord Alloway lasted less than two years, he holds a unique place in the history of British citizenship, being the only individual since the Act of Union to have been legally designated a Scottish citizen; a deserving accolade for this 'alien' who made Scotland his home.

Ann Macao remained unmarried and lived in Musselburgh until her death in 1873. In 1829 Henrietta married John McConnell, a thirty-five-year-old advocate, and the couple emigrated to Canandaigua, a small village in New York County, and became farmers. Before her death in 1833, Henrietta gave birth to a daughter, Jane, who died unmarried, aged twenty-one. William Ross, who had become a Writer to the Signet (solicitor) in Edinburgh, married Caroline Anderson in 1832 and they too emigrated to Canandaigua. They had no children. William Ross became an American citizen in 1838.

3
Manning British Ships

> I climb up high and look on the four seas,
> Heaven and earth spreading out so far.
> Frost blankets all the stuff of autumn,
> The wind blows with the great desert's cold.
> The eastward-flowing water is immense,
> All the ten thousand things billow.
> The white sun's passing brightness fades,
> Floating clouds seem to have no end.
> Swallows and sparrows nest in the wutong tree,
> Yuan and luan birds perch among jujube thorns.
> Now it's time to head on back again,
> I flick my sword and sing Taking the Hard Road.
>
> Li Po, translated by Liu Wu-Chi

Crew of the warship *Zhiyuan*, built by Charles Mitchell and Company, 1895. (Public domain)

The Chinese in Britain

The British East India Company (EIC) was established in 1600 to develop trade with South-East Asia (the East Indies) through a Royal Charter from Elizabeth I. By the eighteenth century, as the Mughal Empire in India declined in power, the Company began to build trading centres – known as 'factories' – all along the west and east coasts of India. The company gradually increased its territorial control in India, ruling either directly or indirectly via local puppet rulers and, to protect its monopoly, the company established its own army, which, by 1803, had about 250,000 soldiers comprising both Indian and British men. To sustain its increased trade with India the EIC expanded its fleet and enlisted Indians as crew. The Indian seamen were commonly called Lascars, a word coined by the Portuguese from the Arabic word for a guard or soldier. With the establishment of Canton, the company expanded its trade into China and towards the end of the eighteenth century had begun to employ Chinese seamen.

The products purchased in China by the EIC were silk, porcelain and, increasingly, tea. Initially, much of the cost was offset by the export to China of British woollens and metals, but as Chinese demand for British goods waned and the British thirst for tea increased, the company was forced to find more and more silver to foot the bill. It became more difficult for the EIC to find the required silver and it decided to sell in China the opium grown in India, as this was a highly lucrative commodity and much in demand. However, the sale of opium had been banned in China by Imperial edict of 1729 and the EIC could not directly sell it in China without risking being expelled from Canton and thus having its supply of tea cut off. To get round the ban the EIC established an illegal system whereby the actual business of selling the opium was managed by private traders. Yet it was the company that oversaw almost all of its production in India and took the bulk of the huge profits. From 1730 to 1800, the amount of opium being sold by the EIC to China quadrupled, resulting in a considerable increase in the number of Chinese opium addicts. Although EIC's trade monopoly was abolished in 1834, private British merchants and ships continued to sell opium illegally in China and the trade grew.

It also was forbidden for any Chinese to leave the country without permission or take a job on a foreign ship, but many took the risk of making their way to Canton or Macau where they were smuggled aboard EIC ships. At this time the British Navigations Act decreed that foreign seamen could not crew EIC ships leaving Britain, and so the Chinese seamen who worked on the ships from China were dependent on the company to arrange for them to return to China as passengers. As ships sailing between Britain and Asia had to time their journeys to fit in with the trade winds, the Chinese sailors had to spend months in London waiting to return to China and were not allowed to work while in Britain. By 1800 it is thought that about 200 Asian seamen were employed by the EIC and that this rose to around 1,500 by 1815, although when the Anglo-Asian routes were opened to other British merchants operating from London, the number of Chinese being employed by the EIC quickly reduced.

Manning British Ships

At any one time many of the Indian and Chinese seamen would have been at sea, and some lived on board the ships when in port, but the number temporarily lodging in London was still significant. One estimate for 1812 puts the number at around 500. When the EIC ship, *Herefordshire*, arrived in London in 1814 the crew contained twenty-five Chinese seamen. That number as part of the crew of one ship was not uncommon. Many of the sailors who arrived in London after their four-month journey from Canton were in poor health and deaths were a regular occurrence. And even those Chinese who arrived in reasonable health often suffered from the British winters. There are almost no direct accounts by any Chinese sailors of their lives while temporarily in Britain. One, purporting to be based on an oral account by Xie Qinggao, a crew member on a British or Portuguese ship in the 1780s or 1790s, relates that he was impressed by London's wealth and the imposing buildings and, perhaps unsurprisingly for a sailor, by the number of prostitutes. Those Chinese who were temporarily in Britain awaiting return to China and who ran out of money could not obtain charitable relief, so many were forced to beg.

By the 1790s there was a growing outcry at the plight of begging sailors, both from those who had little sympathy with the foreign sailors' predicament and just wanted the beggars cleared off the streets, and those who more charitably insisted that the men should be properly looked after. In response the EIC contracted several London individuals to provide lodgings and necessities to these foreign seamen. However, this arrangement did not work as well as the company hoped so it took over an old barracks, Kings' David Fort, in Shadwell, near Sun Tavern Fields, and converted it to house the Asian seamen. The seamen staying in the barracks were provided with a blue jacket and trousers lined with flannel, a Guernsey knitted woollen sweater, shoes, stockings and a cap, and given regular meals. The barracks had no furniture so the sailors used their own hammocks and bedding, although some slept on the bare floorboards. They seem to have been cared for reasonably well, as confirmed by a visit from members of a parliamentary enquiry that had been established to report on the conditions of Asian seamen at the barracks. The different national, ethnic and religious groups were accommodated in separate parts to reduce conflict and the visiting members commented on how much better the Chinese maintained their quarters compared with the Indian seamen. Many press reports claimed the Chinese seamen were ragged and dirty, but if so, these were a minority and probably only those forced to beg on the streets owing to having lost their money or been robbed.

In 1799 the company brought one of its English-speaking Chinese employees, John Anthony, from Canton to London to oversee the management of the barracks and ensure the occupants were properly cared for. As the role also included overseeing the Indian sailors, Anthony took on a partner, Abraham Gole, who, having previously worked in India, could speak some Hindustani. A few months after arriving in Britain, Anthony decided to marry Gole's daughter and make Britain his home. After being baptised, mandatory for anyone marrying at the time, Anthony wed Esther and they set up home in Angel Gardens, next to the barracks. In 1800 two British men broke into his house and stole clothing and money. The thieves were arrested and put on trial. Anthony and one of his employees, Awing, appeared as witnesses at the Old Bailey. Awing was allowed to affirm the truthfulness of his testimony by the Chinese oath-taking that involved breaking a plate, rather than swearing an oath on the Bible; the first time this had been allowed in Britain. An account of a later trial in 1852 described the process.

> This witness being a Chinese, was examined through an interpreter, who explained that the form of examining a witness in China was not exactly on oath, but upon a declaration to the effect that he would speak the truth, the whole truth, and nothing but the truth; and if he said anything contrary to the truth, it would draw down an imprecation upon him: after using this form, the witness broke a saucer in pieces. This related to the oath 'If I lie may my soul be smashed to pieces as this plate.'

Any foreign seaman temporarily lodging in London was at risk of being cheated, robbed or assaulted. In 1804 Erpune, a Chinese sailor lodging at the EIC's barracks, had his money stolen. At the trial of the two accused, Thomas Gunn and Ann Alsey, Erpune, with Anthony acting as interpreter, told the court he had been taken to Gunn's house where he had met Alsey: 'I gave into Mr. Gunn's hand one dollar for the girl. I undressed, and only kept my waistcoat on. My thirteen dollars were in my waistcoat. When I awoke, my dollars were gone, and the girl was gone.' The Chinese were paid in Spanish dollars, nicknamed 'Pieces of Eight', which were worth just less than five shillings sterling. Alsey confessed that she had stolen the money, but only because Gunn had encouraged her to do so, and asked the court to be lenient; which it was, for she was sentenced to only one year in 'the House of Correction', whereas Gunn was transported for fourteen years.

There were sporadic assaults against Chinese seamen. In 1855 a group of Chinese sailors were attacked by a number of drunk English sailors who, 'for a lark', decided to cut off the pigtail of one of the Chinese. As a result a knife fight ensued in which one English sailor was wounded and one of the Chinese killed. Yet it appears that there were as many instances of violence between the Indians and the Chinese, and between different Chinese factions. This was not surprising given the number of men from different backgrounds cooped up together in the barracks. In 1806 there was a full-scale riot between several hundred Indian and Chinese. Although it began inside the barracks, the fighting quickly spilled out into the neighbouring streets. No one died but there were many injuries, including fifteen serious enough to be hospitalised, and eighteen of the rioters were arrested. In a later incident between two opposing Chinese sects a gambling disagreement escalated into a pitched battle with knives and one Chinese man was killed. Such crimes and disputes were infrequent and the lives of the great majority of the Chinese seamen lodging in London would have been relatively untroubled, if tedious.

Anthony and Gole were effective managers who ensured life in the barracks was tolerable, and both were well respected by the sailors they looked after. Their contract from the EIC was immensely lucrative and both became wealthy men within a few years. Anthony decided to buy property and as non-British nationals were disbarred from so doing, he began the hugely expensive process of instigating an individual Act of Parliament to naturalise him as a subject of the King. This did not provide citizenship, but made the individual a British subject with some of the rights of citizenship, including owning property. In his application Anthony stated that he had become a Christian 'of great piety' and of good character. Having taken the requisite oath, the Act was passed in 1805, making him the first Chinese to become a naturalised British subject. While the Act was working its way through the parliamentary system, Anthony bought a country house at Hallowell Down in Leyton where he employed a Chinese steward, Wing. Sadly, he did not survive to enjoy his new status, as he died a few months after the Act was passed into law. His obituary stated that, 'he was carried to the grave in a hearse drawn by six horses, preceded by four natives of China dressed in white, being the mourning of their country, with four lighted wax tapers in their hands. Two mourning coaches followed, with the friends of the deceased, and above 2,000 of the neighbouring poor and other persons.' After Anthony's death, Gole continued to oversee the Asian seamen's welfare and following his death in 1819 his son, also Abraham, took over, managing the barracks until its closure in the 1830s.

The impact of the Napoleonic War brought an economic recession and, in 1813, Irish stevedores attacked Chinese seamen who were unloading ships as the Irish men saw this as threatening their livelihood. However, as the Chinese seldom managed to gain employment on shore while in London, there were few repeat occurrences. In 1814, as a result of a parliamentary enquiry, the Government introduced legislation to improve the sailors' conditions. The Act, *Better maintenance and care for Lascars and other Asiatic seamen arriving in the United Kingdom*, ruled that if any foreign seaman had 'want of Food, Clothing or other Necessities' and they were assisted, such costs would be recoverable from the owners of their ships.

Many young Chinese took jobs working on British ships and, for the majority, what became of them depended on their treatment at the hands of those they encountered. In 1864 eight seamen of various nationalities on board the English ship *The Flowery Land* mutinied and killed the captain and all the crew except for three Chinese, a cook, a steward and a young boy who was the ship's lamp-trimmer. The three Chinese were trapped below decks and when the mutineers rowed off with plundered cargo they scuttled the ship and all drowned. Luckier was a Chinese boy named John Sidney. In 1861 he appeared in a London court as a witness and the newspaper report described him as 'very well dressed in the English fashion, with an overcoat and silk handkerchief across his arm, and whose general appearance except his face was quite English'. Mr Yardley, the magistrate, was surprised when, before giving his evidence, Sidney said he wanted to thank the magistrate. When asked why, Sidney explained that three years before he had been taken on as a steward by Captain Morley of the ship *Resolute*. It had been Morley who had named him John Sydney and had treated him well. However, having been paid off from the ship after it docked in London, Sidney had fallen into the hands of a man who robbed him of everything. Sydney explained that it had been Mr Yardley who had sentenced his robber to twelve months' imprisonment and hard labour, thus releasing Sydney from the criminal's clutches. Following the sentencing, Sydney had been assisted by the landlord of the Blue Anchor, near to London Dock, who had provided clothes and accommodation, and money to live on. After thanking the magistrate for helping give him this new start, Sydney told Mr Yardley he planned to go to sea again. A few years before, the same Mr Yardley presided over the trial of a Chinese seaman charged with wounding a fellow countryman. The accused's Shanghai dialect defeated the interpreter who had been brought to the court, so Lieutenant-Colonel Marsh Hughes, an officer in the Bombay army, and one of those who had established the Home for Lascars and Chinese Seamen, brought a teenage Chinese girl who spoke English fluently to interpret. In court she said her name was Amoy, that she was a Christian and a native of Canton, but no more is known. Mr Yardley arranged for her to act as interpreter throughout the trial.

During the Opium Wars many Chinese children lost their parents in the fighting. One such boy was found by the Cameronian Highlanders and passed into the care of the Master of Arms of the Royal Navy ship, *Conway*. The boy, who was about ten years old, was given the English name Henry. He sailed to Britain with the ship and on the way was taught to read and write English. When the *Conway* docked in Portsmouth in 1842 the boy's story was reported:

> The poor boy appears to be truly grateful for the kindness evinced towards him, and he is a great favourite with all the Officers. He is very strict in his religious duties, never omitting grace before and after meals. His father was struck on the skull and his mother in the body by a cannonball, and fell immediately. His narrative is very interesting, depicting the horrors of war and a siege. Numerous persons daily visit and converse with him. He is at present dressed in the English costume, and attracts great notice amongst all classes.

Henry was then taken under the wing of Commander Hall, the captain in charge of the Royal Yacht *Victoria and Albert*. In October 1844, when the yacht brought the queen to Dundee, the city gave a grand ball and Henry attended, 'dressed in the costume of his country'. He no doubt enjoyed the grand occasion with the soldiers in 'their gay and gorgeous uniforms'. It is not known if he was allowed to join in the dancing to Stewart's Edinburgh

Quadrille Band or stay up till midnight when 'the refreshment rooms were thrown open where all the delicacies of the season, together with abundance of the dance-inspiring champagne, awaited the pleasure of the gay throng'. Nor is it known what became of Henry, though given his adoption by Royal Navy officers it seems possible he would have become a sailor.

In spite of better regulation there always were unscrupulous captains and shipowners ready to take advantage of the Chinese seamen. A letter to *The Times* in 1853 complained about the recurring problem of non-payment of wages and the abandonment of Chinese sailors by devious ship captains. 'I have had to apply to the Foreign Office to send home six Chinese who were wandering about our streets penniless, and who had been deserted by their captain,' wrote one correspondent. The following year, three Chinese sailors were arrested for begging in the public streets and through an interpreter explained that they neither knew the name of the vessel in which they had come nor the name of the captain under whose orders they had worked. Unable to find employment on another ship bound for China they had been 'forced to throw themselves upon the compassion of the public.' In 1857 a number of missionary societies working in London's East End opened 'The Strangers Home' to provide support. The building in Limehouse could accommodate 220 foreign seamen and alongside Christian instruction offered a library of Christian books in Asian and African languages, laundry rooms, bathrooms and sanitation, a dining hall and a safe depository for valuables.

Following the ending of the EIC's monopoly on trade in Asia in 1834, British ships had begun to trade with China and Chinese seamen began to lodge in other ports, primarily Liverpool and Cardiff. In Liverpool the numbers increased from 1866 as the Blue Funnel Shipping Line, part of the Holt Ocean Steamship Company, ran steamers directly from Liverpool to China and began to employ many Chinese as crew. This led to more boarding houses for Chinese seamen opening in the area around the docks. In London, the increasing numbers of Chinese in the East End began to be reflected in newly built streets being called Ming Street and Canton Street. As the nineteenth century advanced fewer Chinese were employed on British merchant ships, but the Royal Navy began hiring Chinese seamen. The 1871 England census records about 180 Chinese sailors employed on Royal Navy ships, most working as cooks or firemen (stokers) in the boiler rooms of the steamships. Many of the Chinese who worked on British ships perished at sea. When the steamship *Glencoe* sank off Beachy Head in 1889, among the fifty-two crewmen who perished were three Chinese cooks and twenty Chinese firemen.

Chinese naval officers came to Britain to train on steamships and in 1877 ten Chinese naval students were attached to British ships. Although they were allowed to serve as sub-lieutenants on board the Navy's ironclads, the cadets were not allowed to learn gunnery or torpedo warfare: 'China are (sic) fast becoming naval powers, and, while permitting our manufacturers to provide them with ironclads and ordnance, the Admiralty probably think that it carrying generosity to the extent of folly to teach them how to use their tools.' In addition to training its naval officers, China looked to improve its fleet and between 1875 and 1888 commissioned twelve cruiser gunboats from Charles Mitchell and Company. These were built on the Tyne and the first six were sailed to China by British crews. China decided that the next four should be crewed by their sailors and be 'the first to bear the Dragon flag from British shores to the Far East'. Thus, in 1881, about 200 Chinese sailors arrived in Newcastle under the command of Admiral Ting Ju-chang. The admiral arrived in Portsmouth and while there visited the Royal Naval Hospital Haslar, a massive building built in 1754 and, at the time, the largest brick building in Europe. As there was delay to the completion of the gunboats, he spent four months in Britain before sailing them to China. Ting visited various cities and spent time in London. He also went to a session of Parliament: 'Every seat available for strangers was occupied, and the black coats in the diplomatic gallery were lightened up a little by the conspicuous blue costume of the Chinese Admiral Ting.' Accompanied by his naval secretary, Captain Lin Tai Tean, and other officers, he visited Cambois Colliery, near Newcastle: 'The party were escorted to the colliery office, and after donning suits of pit clothes, including leather caps – they having tied their pigtails up in a bunch on their heads – followed Mr Forster the conductor of the party. He having got into to cage, the Chinese visitors – some of whom seemed very reluctant – followed, and were lowered into the workings, and were shown all the different processes employed in the winning of coal.' With the Chinese Minister, the admiral attended a State Ball at Buckingham Palace given by Queen Victoria and also was a guest of the queen at her review of the Volunteer Armies that took place at Windsor Castle.

The delay meant a large number of Chinese sailors also stayed in Newcastle for the four months, much to the delight and interest of the locals: 'On Saturday the Chinese vessel was thrown open for inspection from one o'clock in the afternoon until about eight at night, and the throng of persons who took advantage of "visitors' day" to inspect the ship, who scaled the ladder by the tide of the *Haa Shin*, and penetrated every nook of the vessel, was on an exceedingly large scale. The Chinese sailors regarded the influx of sightseers with their characteristic good humour, and the courtesy shown to all – and the fair sex in particular – was most marked.' A number of the officers took the opportunity to sightsee further afield: 'One of the officers arrived in Berwick on Saturday night and took up his residence at the King's Arms Hotel. He was dressed in an ordinary naval uniform, and wore no cap, his pig-tail being coiled upon his head in the shape of a turban. His general appearance attracted notice.'

Two of the young sailors died while in Newcastle and the local newspaper described the funeral of one, Yuan PeiFu:

> The coffin was conveyed by boat from the steamer to the quay, then placed on a four-wheeled gun-carriage, and the Chinese ensign thrown over it.

About 160 of the ship's crew accompanied the remains of their late comrade. Twenty of these dragged the carriage by means of ropes, and the remainder of them filed into marching order, four deep ... The procession was withal a solemn one. The demeanour of the sailors was quiet and respectful. There was no music of any kind, and the noise created by the dragging of the carriage and the light tramp of feet were the only sounds emitted. At intervals the procession halted for a few moments while Joss paper was burnt in front of the cortege. This paper is believed 'to be convertible in the next stage of existence into the means of providing the necessaries of that new life.' ... From a utensil somewhat in the shape of a teapot, was poured a consecrated liquid around the edge of the grave and the coffin. One of the company uttered a few words in the Chinese language. A number of tapers were lighted and stuck into the ground at the foot of the grave. The company then abased themselves, going to their knees and almost touching the ground with their foreheads. While in this position another short address in the native tongue was given in low tones. The admiral of the *Shin* wished the grave to remain open till next day, but owing to the number of people who visited the cemetery during the morning when it became known where the deceased Chinaman had been laid, the grave had to be closed. The funeral of the second Chinese sailor Gu Shizhong took place on Friday morning, his remains being placed in a grave immediately alongside that in which his late comrade was laid the previous morning.

With so many sailors in Newcastle waiting to crew the gunships to China, it was hardly surprising that there were occasional accounts of disorderly behaviour. One Chinese sailor appeared in court charged with being drunk and disorderly, and having assaulted a local policeman. However, the police told the court they wished the charges to be withdrawn 'on account of his being a foreigner... We have often seen the Chinese sailors led into public houses by Englishmen in mistaken acts of kindness.' Another, Chi Zhongyou, fell in love with a local girl, Annie Fenwick, and wrote to tell her of his feelings. Whether she reciprocated his sentiment is not known, although when she came to say farewell on the day Chi left for China aboard one of the gunboats, she brought a frosted cake, with the ship's name, *Chaoyong*, and Chi's name written on the top in honey. She also gave Chi a jar of biscuits as a gift for his mother. 'When shall we meet after this hasty departure? Who can relieve me of this lingering love?' Chi wrote as he sailed for China. Chi and Annie never met again, but hopefully a Chinese sweetheart eventually cured Chi of his lingering love. On the day before his departure Chi Zhongyou visited the graves of his two dead comrades, and realising he had forgotten to take flowers, rushed to the Fenwick's home. He asked Annie and her sister Margaret to plant some flowers for the sailors the following Sunday. In 2012, Deng Xinli, a Chinese reporter, visited the cemetery and discovered several yellow flowers growing next to one of the graves.

4
Domestic Service

My servant wakes me: 'Master, it is broad day.
Rise from bed; I bring you bowl and comb.
Winter comes and the morning air is chill;
To-day your Honour must not venture abroad.'

      Wang Wei (699–759), translated by Arthur Waley

The Commercial Traveller (Lord Charles Beresford) by Cloister (Charles Garden Duff) for *Vanity Fair*, 1899. (*Vanity Fair*)

Economic pressures have always driven migration and for centuries the search for a better life had led many Chinese to settle in other South Asian countries. However, it was not until the nineteenth century that more than a handful of Chinese travelled further afield for work. The Ambassador to Britain in the 1870s, Zeng Jize, explained: 'Chinese people who wish to go abroad to make a living are not legally prohibited from going. However, Chinese people have a fierce bond to the land and unless they are in desperate circumstances are unwilling to leave the land of their family and ancestors. Those prepared to travel thousands of miles from home are poor people with barely the means to provide for themselves. How would they have the means to take their loved ones with them?' Similarly, in his account of his time in Britain, Wang Tao writes of a successful Chinese businessman living and working in Scotland as being a 'guest' in Britain, as Wang could not conceive of any Chinese choosing Britain as their home. It was the growing demand for labour in America, Australia and other emerging countries that led to large numbers of Chinese travelling beyond Asia, and a percentage of those making permanent homes there. However, with no similar demand for foreign labour in Britain, apart from as crew on ships, few Chinese came to the country to work or to settle before the twentieth century.

In 1793, Sir George Staunton accompanied by his son Thomas, travelled to China as Britain's first emissary. On the journey the young Thomas learnt Chinese and impressed the Qianlong Emperor with his grasp of the language. Sir George Staunton brought back a Chinese servant, although what became of him is not known. Later in life Thomas worked as an interpreter for the EIC and assembled a library of 3,000 Chinese books, and a collection of Chinese works of art and artefacts. He also planted Chinese plants interspersed with chinoiserie pavilions at the family's Leigh Park estate. Doubtless some Chinese who worked as servants in Britain before 1900 have gone unrecorded, although the ten-year census returns from 1841 record the place of birth for all individuals and details of those born in China can be examined. Also newspaper articles and official records often contain references, such as an account of a House of Lords Appeal case in 1846 that is the earliest reference in Britain to a Chinese female servant. The woman, named Kowhan, worked for Mrs Matthysson, the wife of a British merchant in Macau, but it may be that Kowhan was only brought to Britain to appear as a witness in the appeal by Mr Matthysson relating to his divorce. Although Kowhan took the oath by breaking a plate in the Chinese way, she refused to give evidence. The Lord Chancellor, Lord Brougham, instructed the interpreter to ask her who her God was and, on being informed it was Buddha, directed the interpreter to tell the woman that 'Buddha will punish her most severely if she does not speak the truth and that she will also be punished in this world if she does not speak the truth.' This convinced Kowhan to give evidence that confirmed Mrs Matthysson had committed adultery.

The Chinese in Britain

The Chinese who worked as servants were mostly young men like William Macao, who had been brought back to Britain by men working for the EIC or other companies in China. In 1851 No Power is listed as a servant in the house of Alexander Matheson in Hanover Square, London. Matheson had been the senior partner of Jardine Matheson, the leading trading firm in the Far East, until retiring in 1847 to become the Member of Parliament for Ross and Cromarty. Another Chinese servant, Monkey Hadjee, aged twelve, is recorded in 1861 as working for John Cole, a Master Mariner and at the time captain of the ship, *Velocity*, and living at 52 Tooley Street in Southwark.

A rare detailed account of a Chinese working as a servant is contained in the memoirs of Charles William de la Poer Beresford, styled Lord Charles Beresford. In 1867 Beresford, who had been one of the sub-lieutenants on *The Royal Yacht Victoria and Albert*, was promoted to lieutenant to serve on the steam frigate HMS *Galatea*, commanded by Queen Victoria's son, the Duke of Edinburgh. Over the next two years, the ship toured the world. While in Kowloon in 1868 Beresford took on a young Chinese boy as his servant, whom he named Tom Fat. In his memoirs Beresford describes Tom as 'an invaluable servant, clever, orderly, indefatigable and devoted. I attired him in gorgeous silks, and he bore my crest with perfect unassuming dignity. He kept my purse, and expended my money with prudence, even with generosity.' When HMS *Galatea* returned to Britain and anchored at Plymouth, it was reported: 'The young Chinaman in blue blouse and pigtail, and the elephant the Duke brought home for the Prince of Wales, were the chief objects of attraction on deck, as they were later in the procession of the ship's company through the streets.' In 1874, Beresford was one of thirty-two aides chosen to accompany the Prince of Wales on a tour of India and Tom, who now 'spoke English like a sailor', went with him as his valet. The prince insisted on dressing for dinner, even in the jungle, but permitted the men to cut off the tails of their evening coats, thus creating what would become known as the dinner jacket. When Beresford returned to Britain, acting as the aide-de-camp to the Prince of Wales from 1875 until 1876, and also taking his place as a Member of Parliament, Tom continued to work as his valet. Beresford recounts that 'Tom was universally popular. I took him everywhere with me. In his way, he was a sportsman. One day, hunting with the Duke of Beaufort's hounds, I mounted him on a skewbald pony. We came to a nasty slippery place, a bad take-off, a wall to jump, and the road beyond. Tom's pony took it safely. A big, hard-riding guardsman who was coming up behind us, not liking the look of the place, shouted to me, "Is it all right?" "That hideous Chinaman has just done it," I shouted back. Not to be outdone by a Chinaman, the guardsman rode at the fence, his horse went down, and he got a dreadful toss. When he got up, he was furiously angry with me.'

Tom often would provide Beresford with ready cash, and while Beresford occasionally wondered how his Chinese valet always seemed to have plenty of money, he was, in his own words, 'careless in those days, and kept no accounts'. It was not until 1878 that Beresford discovered the secret of Tom's wealth. Tom, who was in Scotland with Beresford, asked if he could return to London early and his employer agreed. When Beresford returned to London, his servant was missing and after a few days Beresford advertised for his whereabouts, offering a reward. Beresford later recounted: 'Tom was arrested the next day at the Criterion Restaurant, being one of a party of thirteen (of whom twelve were ladies) to whom Tom was about to play the host. It turned out that during his week in town, my faithful servant had spent £70.' It transpired that needing ready cash, Tom had gone to Beresford's club and said he needed money for his master. When asked for Beresford's IOU, Tom forged the document and this brought to light the fact that over many years Tom had, with 'remarkably expert penmanship', forged his master's signature on cheques totalling nearly £1,200. As Beresford knew the bulk of the cash had been spent on him, he was puzzled why Tom had not just asked for a cheque instead of forging one. 'The Oriental mind is inscrutable; but whether or no Tom considered that he was robbing me; he believed he was justified in so doing.' Tom was sentenced to five years' penal servitude. However, Beresford was sympathetic and secured his wayward servant's release after a short time and found him a position in China. In 1898, when Beresford was in China representing the Associated Chambers of Commerce, he tried to trace Tom, but without success. Beresford's last words on his valet and forger were: 'China took him and swallowed him up. And that was the end of Tom Fat.'

Fortunately no other Chinese servants appear to have found their way into court as a result of misguided services to their employers. Joseph Le Ching appears in two censuses. In 1881 he was employed as a footman by the widow, Caroline Houghton, in Addison Road, London, and ten years later happened to be visiting William and Clara Smith on the night of the census and is listed as an 'Old servant on visit', though the relationship between Mrs Houghton and the Smiths remains unknown. The 1881 census also records two teenage boys who were employed as servants; one working for Mrs Virginia Donaldson, the widow of an iron merchant in Glasgow, and the other working in Sunderland for William Byers, owner of a company making ships' anchors.

An infamous court case in the 1890s partly revolved around a young Chinese boy who briefly came to Britain in 1885 as a servant to the twenty-year-old Earl Russell, the brother of the philosopher Bertrand Russell. Earl Russell was travelling in America with his private tutor and in San Francisco took a fancy to two boys, one Black and one Chinese. He was intent on taking both back to Britain as servants but his tutor eventually limited Russell to just taking the Chinese boy. The court heard that a few months after Russell and the Chinese boy had been living in Britain, one of Russell's guardians, a barrister, removed the Chinese boy from Russell's house and had him shipped back to China. Russell told the judge that he had no idea why the young boy had been peremptorily removed. Some years later Russell wedded Mabel Scott but after just a year of marriage she filed for divorce on grounds of cruelty. Scott's attempt to obtain a divorce failed and a few months later her mother printed and circulated a leaflet claiming that the Earl had been guilty of homosexual conduct. One of the examples she gave was Russell's relationship with the Chinese boy. Russell successfully sued for libel and Lady Scott was jailed for eight months. Earl married twice more and his last wife left him alleging 'behaviour of a secret nature that made it impossible for a decent woman to stay'.

Although there may have been a very small number of instances of Chinese of both sexes having sexual relations with their British employers, before 1900 there is no record of any Chinese woman being brought to Britain to work as a prostitute. While there was widespread prostitution in all British dock areas, and Chinese seamen among the clients, the services were provided by poor British women. However, in other parts of the world female Chinese, and probably boys too, were imported as sex workers. For example, in San Francisco it was estimated that between 1850 and 1870 around 6,000 Chinese women were brought by gangs from China to be forced into prostitution.

Lillie Langtry's page boy was another instance of a Chinese boy being admired in San Francisco in 1885 and brought back to Britain, although in this case there was no suggestion of impropriety. Langtry, a famous actress and, for many years, the mistress of The Prince of Wales, (later Edward VII), had been touring in America when she came across the boy, Wang-Fo. A magazine article described him:

> The door of Mrs. Langtry's house in Eaton Square is opened by a young Celestial named Wang-Fo, endowed with a pigtail of exceeding length and a surcoat of pale purple silk. There are colossal footmen in attendance, but the picturesque substitute for a boy in buttons is Wang-Fo, a Chinaman in whom there is apparently no guile, and who was picked-up in 'Frisco by Mrs Langtry, who, with the beautifully confiding nature of woman, believes him to be the son of a sometime wealthy merchant in that lively city – in short, the son of better days. Wang-Fo politely inducts the visitor into a morning room, furnished with a capacious couch of black satin... Presently appears Mrs Langtry, robed in an elegant costume which would prove very trying to a less beautiful complexion... Under one splendidly moulded arm the actress carries a purely white English terrier with a suspicion of the bulldog in his head and forelegs, a dog who came into his mistress's possession by accident, and has since been her constant companion.

A few years later, when Langtry returned from another American tour, a London newspaper printed an interview under the heading 'The Lily and her Pets'. On being asked what had become of her little Chinese boy Langtry replied:

> Oh, like all his race, he got tired of too much civilization and made up his mind he would return to the land of his fathers. He was a delightful little fellow. Did you ever hear of his historic fight with a boy of Lord Charles Beresford's in Eaton Square? The battle was a long and furious one, but my small Celestial came off victor in the end. Once in a fit of temper he cut off the greater part of his own pigtail, thus inflicting on himself the deadliest possible insult. However, I punished the boy by having a false tail made and spliced on to the stump of the real one. He objected to that proceeding very much. I have not filled up his place, and I have no pets at all now. I fear my mode of life is too migratory to suit any of the animal world; so I haven't even got a dog with me.

Perhaps the inference that her Chinese page had simply been a pet was merely the journalist's spin, although perhaps not.

In 1891 Lock Kie Yipsing was working as a butler for John Henry Leech, an explorer, collector and entomologist. Leech had spent many years travelling to a number of countries collecting butterfly specimens but gave up travelling in 1887 and settled at Hurdcott House, near Salisbury. There he wrote a three-volume book on the butterflies of China, Japan and Korea. It seems likely that Yipsing became Leech's servant in China and returned with him. Leech provided Yipsing with a cottage on his estate and Yipsing married an English woman, Ellen. They had at least one son, Leonard. Also around this time, Chang Hon Shon was employed as valet by John Peverell Rogers, another retired army officer, at Rogers' house in Cornwall. Rogers was a captain in the Royal Artillery and he married Maria Miloro in New Zealand in 1880 and retired from the army in 1883.

In 1893, Ah Kwan, a twenty-two-year-old who probably had recently arrived in England, placed an advert in the *Portsmouth Evening News*: 'Chinese Boy, from his excellency the Hon. C.V. Creagh, Governor of Borneo, wants a situation as Footman or Under Cook. Speaks English.' Charles Vandeleur Creagh for whom Kwan had previously worked had been a Deputy Superintendent of Police in Hong Kong before being appointed as Governor of Borneo and it may have been at that point he employed Kwan. Creagh returned to Britain on leave in 1889 and possibly Kwan travelled with him and decided to stay in Britain. The advert resulted in Kwan landing a job as a footman to a retired soldier, Major Ardwick Burgess, at Hendon Hall. The Major and his wife were prominent citizens of Hendon and on a number of occasions opened their grounds for fund-raising events. One of the events they mounted was a fundraiser for Hendon Football Club and this included a staging of Mrs Jarley's Waxworks, which included an effigy of 'Chang the Chinese Giant', of whom more later.

The Chinese in Britain

A few other Chinese appear in the census returns working in other jobs but information about almost all of them is limited to the brief census records. In 1861 Gin Longfoo was employed making shoes for John Lynch, a bootmaker of Little Bolton, Lancashire; John Akew worked as a barman in the Elephant & Castle Tavern in Southwark, London; and Joseph Geesking was a tea dealer in Stockport. Later census returns list Chinese working as tea merchants, a waiter, a cotton goods merchant, an interpreter and tobacconist shop owners. Two females appear, one working as a nurse and the other as an apprentice dressmaker in a Scottish Roman Catholic convent. The small number running their own businesses are described later.

As the nineteenth century came to a close there were many newspaper articles discussing the difficulty of procuring servants and in 1899 it was reported that householders in London had formed a syndicate to employ Chinese servants. *The Aberdeen Press and Journal* commented:

The experiment has been tried, and has proved a success. Near Clapham Common there is a house where three Celestials have for four years discharged the duties of cook, housemaid, and scullery maid. Their employer reports most favourably on their conduct. They are industrious, contented, and in every way competent. Those who have travelled in the East, and have had the good fortune to secure a Chinese servant, will readily endorse this verdict. The Celestial has one great advantage over his European competitor in domestic service He makes the interests of his master his own and cannot be surpassed for fidelity and honesty.

5

The Origins of Chinatown

As long as I was living in the village
They said I was the finest man around,
But yesterday I went to the city
And even the dogs eyed me askance.
Some people jeered at my skimpy trousers,
Others said my jacket was too long.
If someone would poke out the eyes of the hawks
We sparrows could dance wherever we please!

>   Han-shan (*c.* 800), translated by Burton Watson

Pennyfields Road, London, 1929. Photograph by Langier (from *Wonderful London*).

Although a few lodging houses and shops run by Chinese clearly existed in London, Liverpool and Cardiff from earlier in the nineteenth century, none appear in census returns before 1871. Thus the first officially recorded shop, in 1871, was that of John Acca who was living with his family over his General Store at 98 Great Peter Street, London. Seven years earlier he had married Sarah Ann Biven, the daughter of a hatter from Melksham in Wiltshire. In 1882 Acca successfully applied for naturalisation and by 1891 is listed in the census as a rag merchant. He died in 1896, aged fifty-seven and his wife a few years later. They had three daughters, two of whom lived on in the house; Sara, with her husband Leon Goodman, a Polish marine dealer, and her unmarried sister, Louisa. There were four sons. Arthur died in his teens; Albert married in 1915 but was killed in Flanders in June 1917 while fighting with the 9th Battalion of the East Surrey Regiment; John became a metal merchant, married and had at least three children; and Walter, who married in 1896 at the age of eighteen and had at least one child, ended up in prison in 1899. He had been working for Leo Sunderland, an electrical engineer, but left after three years to work for a wire manufacturer. A few months later Walter returned to work for Sunderland and while there stole forms with the company's letterhead on them, which he forged as orders to purchase cable from the India-rubber Gutta-percha Telegraph Company. He then sold the cable at a knockdown price to his former employer and pocketed the cash. Walter was sentenced to ten months' hard labour at the Old Bailey. After serving his sentence he worked as a stationer in 1901 in Croydon, but nothing further is known.

It is not until 1891 that a small number of lodgings run by Chinese appear in the census records. One in Liverpool's Frederick Street was managed by Gee Swo, and Choy Cum Hang and his British wife, although at the 1891 census only one seaman is shown as boarding. Wang Shing, who described himself as 'a dealer in Chinese Goods', also offered lodgings and at the 1901 census had seven seamen lodging in his house. Few other Chinese businesses appear in official records before 1900, apart from a few laundries that are discussed in Chapter 17. Of course there may have been small enterprises that went unrecorded. The 'opium smokes' that existed in London's East End certainly would have avoided any official notice, though perhaps the entry for Lum-For-Sow in Limehouse as a 'tobacconist, etc.' indicates that more than tobacco was available!

The census returns up to 1901 contain only a few instances of marriages between Chinese men and English women, although a number would have gone unrecorded and there would have been other informal liaisons. Suspicion about anyone asking personal questions would have caused some to refuse to provide the necessary information while others would have been unable to communicate sufficiently, owing to a lack of English. For either reasons, or both, it is no surprise that there is no census entry for the couple written about by Richard Rowe in the late 1870s, and published posthumously in *Life in the London Streets; or, Struggles for Daily Bread*.

Across the court and up another dark little staircase into 'Johnson's' dirty bedroom. Johnson is a Chinaman, but he has an English 'wife', who sits before the fire grumbling – because they have to pay 4s a week for a house that lets in the rain. There are a few dirty prints on the walls, and a little oblong chimney-glass, with the backing almost worn off. On the dirty bed reclines Johnson, a corpse-complexioned, sapless-looking man, whose face twitches until he succeeds in lighting his charge of opium. When asked why he smokes opium, he answers that he could not 'go to sillip' (sleep) if he did not smoke it, and when an inquiry is made as to the number of pipes he could smoke in a day, he says five hundred dozen, if he could get them. A Chinese lodger in Chinese costume (a slender, taper-fingered, black-moustached, almost obsequiously polite young fellow, who is sitting at a little table reading a Chinese history of the Taiping Rebellion), bares his white, gleaming teeth in a broad smile when he hears his landlord give this hyperbolical estimate of his powers. The two Chinamen cannot talk to each other in Chinese, as they come from different provinces. From what they say to each other and ourselves in 'pigeon English', we gather that the lodger came over to England as a ship's cook, and is now staying to see a little of the country, supporting himself by selling penny packets of scent in the streets. At Johnson's hint he brings out the box in which he keeps his stock, and soon disposes of sundry little white and pink parcels of some atrociously sickly-scented stuff. Johnson next shows us the modicums of opium, which he sells his customers for 6d, 8d, 1s 6d, and so on, and then taking a stickless gas-candle, he shambles off the bed and down his narrow staircase, to light us out. As he stands at his doorway and looks out into the fog, he holds the candle above his head. When the light falls on his filmy-eyed, twitching; sickly-yellow face, it looks not unlike that of a galvanised corpse.

Even though a small number of Chinese would have gone unrecorded, it is clear that at the end of the nineteenth century Liverpool's Chinatown area was barely developed and London's was tiny, as an article about Limehouse by J. Pratt in an 1895 issue of *The Gentleman's Magazine* indicates.

A single street with Chinese boarding houses and shops on both sides of the way. It exists by and for the Chinese firemen, seamen, stewards, cooks, and carpenters who serve on board the steamers plying between China and the port of London. All the while their vessels are in port these almond-eyed birds of passage lodge on shore in these boarding houses, and deal at these shops, which also enjoy the custom of the Chinese Ambassador at the other end of London. These Chinese shops are the quaintest places imaginable. Their walls are decorated with red and orange papers, covered with Chinese writing indicating the 'chop', or style of the firm, or some such announcement. There is also sure to be a map of China, and a hanging Chinese almanac. There is another kind of Chinese almanac in book form, published in Pekin, which, among other useful information, tells which days are lucky and which unlucky. It is a pity this is no longer done in the almanacs of Europe. It is obviously of the utmost importance to anyone who contemplates getting born, or dying, or being married, to know the luckiest days for doing it. The atmosphere of the Chinese shop is indescribable. The smell of tobacco I like, and the smell of opium I like, and the smell of joss sticks I like, but there are others such as the smell of Chinese cooking. The visitor to Chinatown finds cooking going on at all hours. This quite contradicts the common notion that the opium smoker never eats. Besides the actual cooking all the knife and fork work is done in the kitchen. The viands, whether the meat or vegetables, are served at table cut up ready for transferring to the mouth. The pair of chopsticks used in eating are of wood or ivory, and both are held in the right hand. As shopkeepers here supply the Chinese Ambassador, there is an opportunity for the inquiring stranger to sample not only the more homely fare, but also the most aristocratic. I have also partaken of Chinese tea. Tea is, so to speak, always on tap in this locality, and is offered to every customer at every shop. In fact, the Chinese are very hospitable in every way, and generally refused to charge even for the opium we consumed. They would also, after they came to know us, give us a present at parting, such as a cigar each, or some other token of goodwill. Ladies may be interested to know that the tea cosy is not used here. In place of it they keep the teapot warm in a wadded basket. The tea, served without sugar or milk, is in appearance as clear as sherry. Of course the tea the Chinese drink themselves and the tea they sell to us are two very different things. There is a legend, I hope without foundation, that the tea sent to Europe has already been used in China for cleaning carpets. But this cannot be true, because carpets in China are never cleaned. Tea shares with the opium pipe the proud characteristic of being one of the most popular medicines of the Chinese. But for ailments of an obstinate nature there are a few Chinese remedies to be had in these shops. It is noteworthy that practically no minerals are in use for this purpose, but only vegetable substances.

Platt continues:

None of the handbooks to London invite the tourist to do "China before breakfast." Chinatown is marked upon no map. The Lady Guide Office never personally conducts there. The popular novelist, it is true, is aware of its value as furnishing local colour for his shilling shockers. But judging from what I have read of these works the writers never take the trouble to inspect the opium dens themselves. They rely upon their imagination for the thrilling pictures they draw of them. Occasionally in the silly season, a journalist, badly off for copy, sandwiches a paragraph about the Chinese

The Origins of Chinatown

between the Great Sea Serpent and the Gigantic Gooseberry. But as the reporter appears to consider it necessary to be escorted in his tour of inspection by either a policeman or the Chinese missionary, I need hardly say that he sees little of the genuine article. Chinatown is, above all things, suspicious of the official that goes among its inhabitants taking notes. Even Charles Dickens attained a very slight degree of its confidence, judging by the confused account of the process of opium smoking which he gave to the world in the last chapter of his last work, *Edwin Drood*. A long apprenticeship is needed before the European learns to smoke opium as it should be smoked.

Platt then provided a detailed explanation of how opium was smoked and a Chinese man and an English woman who managed one opium den, quite likely the same pair described by Richard Rowe.

So sincerely attached to one another were the old couple who kept it they might without impropriety have been called Darby and Joan. I once took a lady artist to see this interesting pair. She was delighted with them, and they with her. The Chinaman even went the length of allowing her to sketch him in the act of smoking. Those who know the dread this people have of anything that suggests publicity will appreciate this concession at its full value. The lady never revisited them, but they often spoke of her, and always wished to be kindly remembered to her when they saw me. Another former visitor whom they were never tired of recalling was no less a person than the Prince of Wales. Upon his departure, it appears His Royal Highness gave the old man a sovereign. He had never forgotten that coin, although, in the lapse of time, it had acquired something of a mythological halo. Johnny was an epicure, eating very little, but requiring everything to be of the best. He was a literary man, and had quite a small library of Chinese books. He had a taste for art, and displayed conspicuously upon his wall for twenty years an amateur effort (the work of a Chinese sailor), being curiously enough the picture of an English church. It is now in the possession of a friend of mine. It was sold, with other effects, upon his eviction from his old quarters, including his scales for weighing opium, his opium lamp, his gambling-cards, his dominoes, two photographs, and reading books. I never lost sight of him till the day of his decease, which took place in Cornwall Street, in his sixty-fourth year, and after that I traced his widow from one address to another, until she was taken in charge by some charitable ladies. Since then I have heard nothing further of her, and know not whether she is living or dead.

Our London friends have often brought out for our benefit their Chinese stringed instruments, and made Chinese music for us. Some of these instruments are played with and some without a bow. And there is a two-stringed instrument in playing which the bow passes between the strings. These same strings, by the way, are never of catgut, but always of wire or silk. A Chinese virtuoso wrote down for me the nine characters which represent the Chinese scale of nine notes, the last being the octave of the second, while the last but one is the octave of the first. When he played to us the pretty children of the boarding house keeper, who already learn to prattle Chinese as well as English, joined their voices in the words of a Chinese song. One day, while the talk ran on songs and music, the shopkeeper took us out into his backyard to see his pet singing bird. It was a Mongolian bird valued at £2 or £5, even in China, and of course worth more here. It did not sing until made to do so by a curious process of decoying, consisting of the owner making motions with one hand to imitate the presence of another bird in the air outside the cage. This excited the poor shanma, which, after running up and down its limited dwelling several times, burst into melody. The Chinaman informed me, so tame was the bird, that he was accustomed to take the cage into Victoria Park and there give its inmate liberty for a time, and he could call it back to its cage whenever he pleased.

The Chinese religion may be said to be a Chinese puzzle. There are three religions in China, and everybody seems to belong to all of them, and, in fact, the worship of ancestors underlies them all. Here in London a room is set apart in every tenement for the family altar. We take off our hats on entering it as we should on entering a Christian church. At the back of the altar is a picture representing the deity to whom it is consecrated, or else a sheet of red or orange paper bearing his name. To the front of this stand a row of vases filled with sand. In some of these vases artificial flowers are stuck. In others joss sticks are burning. Besides the offering of flowers and of incense, an offering of food is never absent from the shrine. In Chinese London the food offered to the joss house consists of a cup of tea and plate of grapes, apples, mixed biscuits and sweets. Upon funerals and other exceptional occasions mock money is burnt. The Chinese are too thrifty to make burnt offerings of real coin. This same room which contains the objects of worship is also used because of the luck brought to it by the presence of the deity, for purposes of a different kind. This is the gambling saloon with its gaming table surrounded by a dense crowd.

6

Astonishing Acts

There lived years ago the beautiful Gongsun,
Who, dancing with her dagger, drew from all four quarters
An audience like mountains lost among themselves.
Heaven and earth moved back and forth, following her motions,
Which were bright as when the Archer shot the nine suns down the sky
And rapid as angels before the wings of dragons.

Du Fu (712–770), translated by Harold Witter Bynner

In 1816, the first advertisements began to appear for performances by Chinese jugglers. The troupe was advertised as having come 'from the Court of Pekin' but that may have been simply promotional invention. Like all Chinese jugglers their act combined juggling, acrobatics and magic. 'The Chinese jugglers continue to exhibit their wonderful performances, and to attract numerous spectators; many of whom do not tire of repeatedly witnessing

Tuck-Guy performing at Drury Lane *c.* 1850s. (Public domain)

the astonishing feats of these foreigners.' In 1818, the Chinese jugglers had a more unusual booking in London as they performed in the nude at a Royal Academy lecture on the naked figure.

> Some have been so illiberal as to censure such exhibitions at the Royal Academy, but this extraordinary display of the muscles in forms and uses never before beheld, was a circumstance of the utmost service to Artists; it was a display that might never again appear in Europe; the actions of an African, at the Academy, had surprised them, those of the Indian Jugglers had astonished them, but the present ones surpassed all belief or power of description. The Chinese Jugglers then, performed their positions, and the distortions of their extremities surpassed everything that could have been conceived of them. The room was immensely crowded; the applause at the conclusion was general.

These jugglers toured Britain for about five years, and may have left for Europe or America.

In May 1824 the arrival of two Chinese men and a woman in London sparked intense newspaper coverage as this was claimed to be the first ever visit by a 'distinguished woman from the Celestial Empire'. The newspapers explained that one of the men was her husband and the other her brother, the latter being reported as having visited Britain before.

> Lady Yhou Fang Queon is about twenty years of age, rather fair, but with long glossy black hair. Her features are cast in the Tartarian mould, but are regular, and far from unpleasant. Indeed, she might be said to be beautiful, setting aside local prejudices; at least the expression of her countenance is pleasing and bespokes gentleness and courtesy, mixed with a modest reserve. Her nails (which is an indubitable mark of gentility in China) are suffered to grow to a most inconvenient length; and her foot is almost incredibly small. Considerable mystery hangs over the circumstances of her departure from the Celestial Empire and this is not surprising, when we consider the strictness of the Chinese laws against expatriation.

By early June the reason for their trip to Britain was clear as it was reported that the Waterloo Rooms in Pall Mall had been fitted out in Chinese style and Yhou Fang Queon was to be exhibited there dressed in her Chinese costume, with her husband and brother in attendance.

> The rooms are furnished near possible after the manner in China. In the centre of the room there is oval platform, raised about 18 inches from the ground, covered with scarlet cloth, and yellow at the sides, with a railing two feet high to prevent intrusion. A canopy, after the Chinese

order, is suspended over the platform, with points on which there is a winged dragon, a bell hanging from his mouth suspended by short chain. Several very curious lamps are suspended from the dome of the temple, the walls of the room are entirely covered with drawings by the artists of Pekin, representing the battles of the Chinese on land and sea, hunting and fishing matches.

A week or so later came the news that the opening of the exhibition had been delayed as 'our beloved Monarch should first be gratified with sight of this celestial beauty'. Regrettably, King George IV never got to view the Chinese lady for in July the newspapers were agog with news of a most tragic nature.

Unfortunately Lady Yhou Fang Queon and her husband had not sufficiently calculated on the effect which might he produced by difference of climate, food, and habits of life, particularly by the different pressure of the atmosphere. This last cause appears to have operated very powerfully on the pulmonary system of both husband and wife. The husband was first affected with a spitting of blood, which was equally sudden and violent, and which no medicine could arrest, and put an end to the Chinese Gentleman in a very few days. The Lady became more gradually sensible of the pernicious effects of the climate. She, however, at length began to spit blood, and Dr Webster, of Grosvenor Street, was called in, but he found her lungs very much affected, and the disease advanced with such rapidity as to baffle all medical art. One morning she awoke with a cheerful air, saying she had seen her husband, who had ordered her to come to him, and, therefore, she knew she must die, an event which accordingly took place not many hours afterwards.

Three years later Mr Ayong Chonotie arrived in London with two Chinese women who were displayed in an exhibition entitled 'The Chinese Ladies, the only Female Natives of the Celestial Empire ever seen in Europe'. As this was staged at the Waterloo Rooms, and the room again 'splendidly decorated in Chinese style', it seems likely that Mr Chonotie was Yhou's brother and had found more robust ladies to bring to Britain. The public flocked to see the two young Chinese ladies.

Their names are Attoi Whoatty and Powynen Guattoa; the former is 24 years of age, and the latter 18. In stature they are under the middle size, speaking with reference to our women, which is the general standard of their countrywomen. The skin of these females is inclined to a pink colour, and their features closely resemble those which we have been accustomed to see in Chinese paintings, except being somewhat harsher in expression, owing to the prominency of their cheekbones. There is no exaggeration in the extreme smallness of the Chinese women's feet. The shoe of Attoi Whoatty, which we had in our hands, does not exceed four inches. We saw them pass through the room and go upstairs to their chamber, and it was evidently as difficult a task to them as it would be to a child just beginning to walk. Both these women appear to be in a very delicate state of health. Their long finger nails and small feet indicate that they are persona of some consideration in their own country, which render their appearance here, and under such circumstances, the more extraordinary.

The Chinese ladies toured the country and it is likely that the clothes of one of the young women had to be carefully draped to disguise her very pregnant shape, for she gave birth to a daughter while in Manchester. She was described as the wife of Chonotie, and one can only wonder who was responsible for the other Chinese woman also having a baby just six months later. The first baby to be born was included in the public showing but soon after the second birth the Chinese ladies, Chonotie and the two infants disappeared from British view.

In 1853 another family troupe of Chinese magicians and jugglers arrived at Liverpool on a ship from America. This troupe claimed to have been the chief performers at the Chinese Emperor's court until forced to flee having become Christians and thus come under threat from anti-Christian violence. Of course, as there was great concern in Britain at the persecution of Christians within China, this may just have been clever PR. One of the main performers was Tuck-Guy, whose knife-throwing trick was a standout of the show:

Placing his daughter, a prepossessing girl of about thirteen years of age, at one end of the stage, and causing her to stand with her back against some soft wood, her hands expanded and her fingers separated, he retires to distance. A parcel of very large knives are produced, he picks them up one after another, and, apparently without taking aim, or occupying any time in preparation, slings them recklessly at the child. With wonder amounting to amazement the spectator perceives that every knife has been aimed in the most accurate manner, and that they have been planted one between each of the girl's fingers, one on each side of her cheek, and others close around her neck, but that not one has grazed her skin, though all have entered deeply into the wall behind her. The laughter of the child and the humour of the parent convince the beholder that neither has any fear, while on no occasion has the girl sustained injury, though the feat has been performed by them many thousand times. This unique and unrivalled specimen of sharp practice – if it may be so termed – was viewed with great interest all present. There were several other feats, and the entertainment was upon the whole well deserving of the applause which was elicited.

Astonishing Acts

In 1855 Tuck-Guy was lodging in Blue Anchor yard in London with his wife and children when he was attacked by eight Chinese. Four were arrested and at the trial, Tuck's ten-year-old son, Shee, gave his evidence in English: 'I remember the night my father was cut with knives – Apoi came first, and asked my father to lend him money – my father said he could not – Apoi ran away and came again with seven other persons – there were eight together – three of the prisoners cut my father with their knives – my father did not have any knife, or cut anybody – I called for help – I called, "Policeman, policeman!" – there were no other persons near.' The four accused were found guilty and sentenced to four year's penal servitude.

Chinese jugglers continued to be popular and one well-known juggler who performed in music halls across Britain was Tien (Albert) Arr-Hee. Around 1860 he became a Christian and married a British woman, Francis, and they lived in Rose Court in London. In 1861 one of his juggling props was stolen and in the report of the ensuing court case he was described as 'a most intelligent Chinese, speaks English very well'. John Ahsam, who performed as Arr Ahsam, was a magician and his act at the Exchange Hall in Stamford in 1862 was well-received:

> On Friday and Saturday Arr Ahsam, gave an exhibition which certainly merits a few words of special commendation. Natives of the East have always been remarkable as professors of the art of legerdemain: the Chinese in particular seem to possess a natural aptitude for these mysteries, and if we may judge from the skill of Arr Ahsam this distinction it not ill deserved. The way in which he produces almost interminable yards of ribbon from his throat almost surpasses belief.

He married Emma Sage and they lived in Liverpool. They had one son, John, who became a ship's cook. When Ahsam retired from the stage around 1870, he opened a small tea store.

Another regular performer on British stages from the late 1870s was Ali Ling Look, billed as *The Great Chinese Salamander – the Lord of Fire, Cannon and Sword*, whose act involved a number of seemingly dangerous stunts including swallowing a long walking stick, rubbing a red-hot iron bar along his bare arm, eating pieces of metal and drinking boiling oil. The climax of his act was to swallow a sword up to the hilt and then fire a cannon loaded with a tightly packed ball of paper that was balanced on the sword's handle. Look balanced the small cannon so that it was pointing directly at the audience, who would elicit shrieks of concern as it was fired, but at the moment of firing, Look tipped the cannon upwards so the pellet flew above the spectators' heads. In 1881 he was performing at Brighton's Oxford Music Hall and up in the sixpenny seats of the theatre's gallery a young boy, George Smythe, lent over the gallery rail to get a better view. After his wife applied the red-hot iron to the touch hole to explode the charge, Look tipped the cannon upwards as usual but not high enough, for the pellet was propelled towards the upper circle and struck Smythe in the head, killing him instantly. Mr and Mrs Look, and Mrs Botham, the proprietor of the Oxford Hall, were charged with manslaughter but the jury found them not guilty. In spite of this setback The Great Salamander continued to perform for a number of years afterwards.

Chinese music was sometimes played as part of jugglers' acts or as a speciality item in variety shows. At Southampton's Theatre Royal in 1851 following a performance of the play, *The Black Doctor*, 'some Chinese performers gave a grand concert, both vocal and instrumental. The instruments were of different shapes, but the sounds produced from each were the same, resembling the screeching cat-squeal of the hurdy-gurdy. Their singing was also, to European tastes at least, of the same unharmonious character.' It is likely that it was the same musicians who performed later that year: After Mademoiselle Rousseau had completed her 'dazzling acrobatic performance on horseback the audience was treated to a musical finale by some Chinese performers upon a series of well-toned and harmoniously-tuned bells that completely took the audience by storm, and drew down a unanimous encore'.

In late 1864 James 'Marquis' Chisholm, a Scottish pianist and composer, was touring China and in Shanghai noticed Chang Yu Sing, a young man from Foochow. Chang was not a man easily missed as he was at least 7 foot 8 inches in height. Chisholm later wrote an account of his meeting Chang but it is unlikely to be close to the truth for he was a man prone to exaggeration and colouring the facts to make a great story. What is clear is that as soon as Chisholm saw Chang he recognised that this exceptionally tall man offered a chance to make money. Exhibitions of live human curiosities had been a part of travelling fairs in Britain since the 1600s and these 'freak shows' that displayed bearded women, dwarves, the extremely fat and the very thin, and conjoined twins, had grown in popularity during the Victorian period. 'Giants' were much in demand and Chang was the tallest Chisholm had ever seen. How Chisholm convinced Chang to leave China is not known although Chisholm recounts that it took extensive negotiation with Chang's parents. One of their stipulations being that, in case of Chang's death in a foreign country, Chisholm had to ensure that the body was embalmed and returned to Foochow. To ensure this a coffin long enough to contain Chang's great height was made in China and became Chang's travelling companion wherever he travelled. It is possible that this is true, in part, although as Chisholm created many fake stories around Chang's life to promote the act, the travelling coffin may have been yet another PR prop.

Chisholm brought three others from China as part of the act: a dwarf, Chung-Mow, who was just under 3 feet in height, to give even greater prominence to Chang's stature; a Chinese who spoke some English to act as an interpreter; and Chang's 'wife' who was a Chinese hired to act the part as Chang later married a British woman. In early 1865 Chisholm and his four Chinese companions arrived in Britain with Chang now renamed Chang Woo Gow. Chisholm hid Chang away and forbade him from going out as he was concerned that a public sighting of the giant would lessen the demand for the exclusive shows and harm ticket sales. The Egyptian Hall in Piccadilly was booked for Chang's first appearance, a significant investment by Chisholm as this was one of the main London venues for popular entertainments and lectures. To ensure his investment paid off, Chisholm took out a number of fake adverts in newspapers to arouse interest. One such sought lodgings with a bed at least 9 feet in length. He also crafted an imaginative account that purported to be Chang's autobiography and which was widely disseminated in newspapers.

> Chang's touching autobiography states with Oriental simplicity, which has all the charm of poetry, the reasons which have induced him to come to this far western country. His father and grandfather were both so tall as make him appear small and insignificant by their sides... It was the grief caused by the death of Chang's favourite sister, ten inches taller than himself, that first induced him to think of acting upon the deathbed advice of his father – 'Go, let your mission be, when I am gone, to travel up and down throughout the world, and when you come to your old home again the spirit of your father will be glad.'

Many accounts claim that Chang spoke between six and ten languages, but again this considerable linguistic aptitude may have been an invention by Chisholm, rather than reality, though Chang certainly came to speak English later in his life.

Chisholm sought to create a presentation that was more of a stylish exhibition than a freak show. He had Chang dress in opulent clothes, created a special ambience for the presentation and even composed a special tune, *The Great Chang Polka*, which he played as part of the show. The first display of Chang and Chung took place in April and, to Chisholm's relief, the public flocked to see the show, paying one shilling for entrance. When the public entered the room, they found Chang sitting on a throne-like chair on a raised platform, 'gorgeously attired in a brocaded robe of white and particoloured silk, with a massive string of beads round his neck, a handsome cap upon his head, and the orthodox thick white soles to his Chinese boots. Chang sat motionless, save for light fluttering to and fro of the fan he held in his left hand.' To one side stood his Chinese interpreter, on the other sat his 'wife' and at his feet, Chung-Mow. A tinkle of bells announced the show's commencement and then, to a crescendo of larger bells, Chang slowly rose. Chisholm then launched into his rousing polka as Chang descended into the audience, allowing them to take in his great height.

> This Chinaman of gigantic proportions, who has travelled from the land of the Celestials to these western regions of barbarism for the purpose of

exhibiting his manly proportions to the gaze the British public, held the first of his levies on Monday evening. Also on show is a grotesque dwarf. Chang looked like nothing so much as a gigantic heathen idol which had been suddenly endowed with life. He is well worth seeing. He is incomparably the best-looking and most intelligent giant ever exhibited in our time, and one almost embarrassingly gentle and polite.

Chang's supposed wife, the 'Golden Lily', would exhibit her tiny delicate bound foot, to gasps of amazement. Her main role, however, was to sell to the audience 'cartes de visite' – small photos of Chang – and fans and tiny carvings in scented wood or ivory. Chang immediately gained star status. He was invited to meet the Prince and Princess of Wales and other royal personages at Marlborough House and, at the request of the royal highnesses, wrote his name in Chinese characters on the wall of the room at a height of 10 feet from the ground. The act toured throughout Britain and Ireland and in 1869 Chang was taken to America by the great showman, P. T. Barnum. He then travelled to Australia and there met and married Catherine (Kitty) Santley who had been born in Liverpool. Chang was well known for his philanthropy, often giving up to 50% of the money from ticket sales to needy charities. When performing in Bendigo in Australia, he donated money to the local Benevolent Asylum and in gratitude, members of the public fashioned a wax effigy of Chang that was displayed at the Bendigo Easter Fair until 1895.

At what point Chisholm ceased to be involved is not known, but Chang appears to have become managed by Edward Parlett as his career developed. In 1875 Chang and Kitty went to live in Shanghai and there had their first child, Edwin. In 1879 they travelled back to Europe and their second child, Ernest, was born in Paris, Both children were of normal stature and so saved from being exhibited on stage later in life. Chang and his family, now called Gow, settled in Britain and Chang returned to his extensive touring schedule. By this time few of his appearances were on his own, but usually as a part of various 'freak shows', and for a time he appeared in tandem with a 'Norwegian Giant'. While performing in London they both attended a session of Parliament.

The Chinese giant, and the Norwegian giant, all of whom are on view at the Aquarium, with his dwarf companion, both radiant in Celestial costume, entered the Speaker's Gallery, taking up places in the back row, to the extreme discomfiture of those who had secured places in the front of the Strangers' Gallery. Chang sat himself down, and, taking the dwarf on his knee in much the same way as a lady would pick up a favourite lap dog, settled himself down to take what appeared to be a great interest in the parliamentary debate. The interesting visitors did not remain long, but when they rose to leave, there was something like a general stampede of members into the lobby to get a view of them.

In 1880, Barnum again enticed Chang to tour in America as part of Barnum's *Greatest Show on Earth* by offering him the significant fee of £120 a week, plus travel and living expenses. In addition, Chang was allowed to retain all the profit from his merchandising. Barnum had him appear in a variety of personae, including as a Mongolian warrior and, somewhat bizarrely, a French soldier, in a show that also contained twenty trained elephants, a bearded lady, clowns and a pair of giraffes. During his period in America, Kitty and the two young children lived in Manchester. On his return from his well-paid tour of America Chang bought a house in Southcote Road in Bournemouth, as he had been diagnosed with suspected tuberculosis and living by the sea was recommended as a cure. The house, which Chang named 'Moyeun', had high doors constructed to accommodate Chang's height. Although Chang continued to tour, he and Kitty also ran a tearoom and an 'Oriental Bazaar' selling Chinese curios, bronzes and silks and Chinese tea from their Bournemouth house.

Chang continued to appear on stage until the death of Kitty in the summer of 1893. He died four months after his wife's death. The warm regard he was held in by the British public was shown by the widespread reporting of his death and the many generous obituaries. 'In part his success was due to his amiability; he never sulked or disappointed the public, but acted like a man of refinement and culture, as indeed he was.' More than 100 mourners attended his funeral. On the day of his death, Chang made a will in favour of his two sons, signing it in Chinese characters. As they were minors, the orphaned boys were put into the care of William Day, a friend of the Gows. Day was a photographer and when Ernest finished school he became Day's assistant for a time. He later went to Nyasaland (now Malawi) to work in a bank but, unfortunately, soon after arriving died from Blackwater Fever. His brother, Edwin, became an assistant in an ironmonger's shop, married, had two children and died in Liverpool in 1947.

7

Wealth and Poverty

> I shut the doors and barred the windows
> And left the motherless children.
>
> Song-Yu (319–298 BC)

The first two children of mixed British Chinese parentage to be brought to Britain from China were cousins, yet their lives could not have been more different. Their fathers were sons of Francis Magniac, a French Huguenot goldsmith and a highly skilled maker of complicated clocks and automata, who had married Frances Attwood in London in 1776. They had eight sons and three daughters. Magniac exported many of his clocks and watches to China and, around 1801, sent his eldest son, Charles, to Canton to manage

View of the Canton Factories by William Daniell, *c.* 1805. (Yale Center for British Art)

Wealth and Poverty

his Chinese business. Once in Canton, Charles expanded the firm and in 1811 his brother, Hollingworth, joined him and Magniac & Co. became one of the foremost British businesses in China, providing merchants in Britain and India with services in marketing, banking, shipping, and insurance.

In India, the East India Company (EIC) and other ventures were comfortable with inter-racial relationships. It was there that the term Eurasian was coined to identify a person born to a British father and an Indian mother. Some Eurasian children, including orphans, were sent to Britain to be educated, and there were many examples of British men marrying Indian women, although in very few cases did they take their wives back to Britain. Eurasians were employed by the British in India as translators and soldiers – and some were mistresses – although by the 1780s there was a growing ambivalence about inter-racial relationships, partly from a concern that people of mixed race might be uncertain which side they supported in any conflict, and so certain restrictions began to be introduced.

The situation in China was completely different. The Chinese had a fierce aversion to inter-racial relationships and the British men working in China recognised that an affair with a Chinese woman might be detrimental to their business dealings. Yet a number were willing to take the risk as there were no foreign women allowed in Canton, one of the complaints contained in a Petition sent in 1830 to the British Government by the British merchants: 'Even the sacred ties of domestic life are disregarded, in the separation of husband and wife, parent and child, regarded unavoidable by a capricious prohibition of foreign ladies residing in Canton.' For those who did take a Chinese mistress there was an unwritten rule that the liaison should be kept strictly private. Thus, in 1807, the small British trading community in China, and no doubt relations and friends in Britain, were shocked when Charles Magniac publicly acknowledged an illegitimate son that he had conceived with his Chinese mistress by naming the child Charles, a normal custom for the first-born son, but a scandalous choice for an illicit mixed-race baby. This was such a challenge to the social conventions of the time it implies that Charles regarded his relationship with the Chinese woman as affectionate and bonded, rather than merely sexual. However, Charles accepted that his illegitimate son could not be a Magniac and so the boy was given a different surname. Again the choice seems to confirm Charles' affection for the mother of his child, for the surname he chose was her Chinese name character, 'Hope'.

As Magniac & Co. was the leading trading company in Canton, Charles probably judged his action would not harm the firm and his assessment proved correct, it continued to flourish. By 1819 the company was almost wholly trading in opium and when prices began to escalate as a result of Chinese officials endeavouring to stop sales of the drug, the Magniacs bought all the opium they could secure, and the speculation made them a fortune. Around 1815 Charles Magniac dispatched his mixed-race son, Charles Hope, to Britain to be educated. Whether Magniac planned to have his son return to him in China later is unknown for Charles Magniac fell seriously ill and was advised to return to Britain. He set sail in January 1824 but died in Paris. In his will Charles left his son a substantial sum of money. The fate of his Chinese mistress is not known. After completing his education, Charles Hope lived in London and began to work as a tea broker. This involved bidding for the chests of tea brought into London at the half-yearly auctions and selling the tea on in smaller lots at a profit. A tea broker's success was based on his proven ability to distinguish the best quality teas by smell, taste and experience, as many adverts of the day emphasised: 'We have employed a Tea Broker to purchase for us, whose great experience, and peculiar manner of selecting fine flavoured and strong Teas ensures that we can offer teas of such qualities as to merit approbation.' Tea auctions were held in The London Commercial Salerooms on Mincing Lane – nicknamed the 'Street of Tea' – and so Charles had an office in nearby Fenchurch Street.

In April 1837 Charles Hope submitted a Denization Petition to the Government. This process, dating back to the thirteenth century and discontinued since the late 1900s, was one by which an alien could obtain certain rights otherwise only normally enjoyed by the country's subjects, including the right to own land. Charles explained that his father had been a British subject and his mother 'a native Chinese' and that he had been left £8,600 (in the region of £1 million today) by his father and wished to buy property: 'but taking the natural character of my mother, an alien, I am prevented by law from holding property. I have been brought up in and have resided in this country and I intend to make this country my place of residence.' His petition was supported by the partners of Smith, Payne & Smiths, a reputable London Banking House, who confirmed that Hope had lived in Britain from childhood. The decision to apply for residence may have been triggered by his having entered into a relationship with Caroline Southern, the daughter of a London innkeeper, and it may be that the decision on his petition took much longer than they thought, for in November 1837 Charles, like his father, had an illegitimate son whom he also named Charles. However, fifteen months after the birth he and Caroline married. The delay in marrying following the birth may well have been due to the fact that any woman marrying an alien became one too, and they needed to wait for the successful outcome to the petition. With his petition successful Charles bought a house in Montague Street in stylish Bloomsbury.

The year before Charles Magniac had been taken ill, the youngest Magniac sibling, Daniel, had joined his two brothers in Canton to work in the company. Following Charles's death, it was agreed that Daniel would take control of the firm as Hollingsworth wished to retire to Britain. However, later in 1824, this plan was swiftly derailed by the arrival of another mixed-race son. Soon after arriving in China, Daniel had also taken a Chinese mistress and when she gave birth to his child, Daniel, like his eldest brother, defied convention by acknowledging his son, naming him Daniel Francis Magniac. Again, this act alone might not have threatened the Magniacs' business, but the impetuous Daniel caused worse

Wealth and Poverty

outrage among both the British and the Chinese communities by marrying his Chinese mistress, thus ensuring his son had the Magniac surname. Confronted with the damaging impact on the firm's business by his decision, Daniel swiftly disavowed the marriage, but it was too late. Hollingworth was not prepared to see the company's standing undermined and so forced his younger brother Daniel to resign and leave China. Soon after arriving back in Britain, Daniel splurged part of his pay-off on buying a yacht that he entered in the first Cowes Regatta held in 1826. He also married Elizabeth Frances Sansom, a sister-in-law, and in the marriage record describes himself as a bachelor. What became of the marriage in China, and his unfortunate Chinese wife, remain a mystery. He and his new wife moved to Paris, and there they had two children. In 1876, a year after the death of his first wife, Daniel re-married a Frenchwoman, Celine Delamarre and died two years later.

As Hollingworth still wished to return to Britain he placed the firm in the hands of two reputable Scottish traders, William Jardine and James Matheson. The firm retained the name of Magniac until 1832, as time was required for the new partners to buy out the interests of the Magniac family and remit Hollingworth's capital to England. Then the name changed to Jardine, Matheson & Co., becoming the largest trading company in Asia. Daniel's illegitimate baby son remained in China and Hollingworth returned to Britain in 1828, leaving the boy in the care of Matheson and Jardine. Hollingworth decided to send his young nephew to India to be educated, perhaps on the basis that this would put the unfortunate boy well out of the family's way. However his partners in China expressed concern. They explained that the child suffered from poor health and did not believe India's climate would suit him. Instead, Matheson offered to send the boy to stay with his mother in Inverness and Hollingworth agreed. In a letter of 1831 written to Matheson in Canton, Hollingworth mentions the boy and his younger brother's selfishness: 'I could rather have him to have gone to Calcutta, because unwilling to take up your relation's kindness in the way that has now been done. His unfortunate father is in the same wretched position that I have described, nor, judging from his want of conduct and want of thought and consideration for anyone, do I see any possibility of improvement. He is a continual drain on me, both in pecuniary and in a sense of mental suffering, which cost is the most heavy to be borne.'

Daniel Francis arrived in London on board the EIC ship *Canning* on 9 March 1833 and travelled to Inverness to the care of Mrs Matheson. He attended Inverness Royal Academy, but nothing further is known about his life until the late 1850s. There is an indication that he had contact with his half-sisters in France so it may be that he also had contact with his father, although from Hollingworth's description of his brother's conduct and subsequent events, it seems more likely his father wished to have nothing to do with his illegitimate son. What is clear is that Daniel's life in Britain was far from happy. In 1858 he attempted suicide by cutting his throat and it was his Eurasian cousin, Charles

Hope, who was the principal person to come to his aid. Following the suicide attempt, Charles, possibly in conjunction with Hollingworth, arranged for Daniel to be placed in the care of Dr Forbes Winslow, a doctor who was ahead of his time in the treatment of mental health. The doctor was clearly chosen with care, for in 1840 he had published *The Anatomy of Suicide* that argued suicide came from mental disease. He also opposed the contemporary view that suicide was a criminal act. Winslow managed two private lunatic asylums in Hammersmith, where he pioneered the humane treatment of the mentally ill and it was to one of these, Essex House, that Daniel was admitted on 29 June 1858. The advert for Essex House stated:

> This private Asylum for the nervous and insane is for the reception of a limited number of patients, and is admirably adapted for the cure, and not the confinement merely, of the insane. The house is large, commodious, and replete with every comfort, and well enclosed, pleasantly situated and perfectly secluded from observation and being bounded by all sides by meadows, shrubberies and orchards. The arrangement combines the domestic comforts of a quiet and cheerful residence, with all the necessary regulations of a well-conducted private establishment for invalids requiring a temporary separation from home. It is in Hammersmith, on the Fulham Road, about half-an-hour's drive from Hyde Park.

While Daniel was being cared for at Essex House Dr Benjamin Travers was asked to examine him. Travers was a well-respected London surgeon and was known to the Magniac family as his deceased father had been the senior surgeon to the EIC. His later description of his visit appears to indicate that he had treated Daniel prior to this time.

> I attended Magniac while he was in Dr Winslow's asylum on behalf of his friends, having attended him previously and as I was known to his family they asked that I should see him. I did so. The wound upon his throat was a mere scratch. He had been the subject of great mental depression, was unable to see his way, and being in a feeble susceptible state of mind did the act, as I believe, without design or purpose. And a very few hours served to convince him of the folly of the attempt. However, at that time I judged that he should be very closely watched. I saw him on subsequent occasions, and formed the opinion that his case was one of slow but progressive improvement. I brought him to Mr. Tomkin's and in my opinion he was perfectly sane. I thought it necessary that he should be under the care of a clergyman or a medical man.

Mr Tomkin was a well-regarded surgeon and operated a small private asylum in Witham, a rural village in Essex that had been established by his father. However, instead of being housed in the asylum, Daniel lived with Tomkin and his wife in their house in Newlands Street near the asylum. Although

Wealth and Poverty

living with them in their house, Daniel was treated as a patient in that when he went for walks Tomkin had a member of his staff accompany him and there were a few instances when he was locked in his room. Throughout this period Charles paid Tomkin for Daniel's board and lodgings, and care. When he was out and about, Daniel's behaviour was considered by some residents in the area to be odd and someone complained to the authorities that Tomkin was keeping an insane person in his house, rather than in the safety of his asylum. Regulations introduced in 1840 in response to instances of unscrupulous people placing sane relatives into dubious private metal asylums to defraud them of their inheritances and other abuses required all insane people to be housed in registered asylums and a list of patients recorded. So the Lunacy Commissioners charged Tomkin with the misdemeanour of receiving a gentleman of unsound mind into his dwelling house for profit, the house not being duly licensed, and a hearing was heard by the local magistrates to decide whether Tomkin should be sent for trial. The question for the magistrates was whether Daniel Magniac was insane, as if not he could lodge anywhere, and Tomkin would not have broken the law. Tomkin explained that he had lodged Daniel in his own house from motives of kindness as he thought this would be more beneficial to Daniel's state of mind. In response to the Commissioners' allegation that he had unlawfully received payment to board and lodge Daniel in his dwelling house, Tomkin responded that the bills that were being paid by Charles Hope would have been required whether Daniel was housed in the asylum or his house.

Various people were called to give a view on Daniel's state of mind, but the evidence hardly seemed to indicate that Daniel was insane: 'I have seen him walking about in a state of melancholy, apparently without noticing anything that was going on ... looking in at people's windows – private houses as well as shops.' Another said he had observed Daniel 'smiling at little children in the street and sometimes making faces'. Tomkin's defence lawyer responded to these points: 'Unquestionably Mr Magniac is of weak intellect: his mind is certainly not at 100, or perhaps even at 50; but if that was sufficient to sanction a presumption of Lunacy, fifty men out of every hundred might be consigned to a Lunatic Asylum.' Tomkin stated that Daniel was often 'in a state of profound melancholia and very taciturn' and although he had made no recent attempt on his own life Tomkin maintained that his experience convinced him that Daniel still had a suicidal tendency, and so required constant watching. Charles Hope gave evidence:

> I know Mr. Magniac, and have been in the habit of making remittances on his account to Mr. Tomkin. I presume for board, lodging, and attendance. I remember coming to Witham on one occasion, in 1861, to see Mr. Magniac and at that time I did not make any suggestion as to his being removed to the Asylum, nor did Mr. Tomkin to me. I have known Mr. Magniac about 19 years. I never saw him make an attempt upon his life and when I had opportunities of seeing him in company, he always conducted himself in

a very gentlemanly manner. I never observed any signs of lunacy during my intercourse with him. When I saw him in 1861 he was not treated as a lunatic; he dined and tea'd with me at Mr. Tomkin's table, and was not lighted up to bed; in fact he was treated as any sane visitor would have been.

Throughout all of the hearing Daniel was in court and he was called to give evidence. In response to the prosecutor's question as to how he had been treated he responded that he had 'generally been treated kindly but I have been locked in my room for two or three days, perhaps'. When asked if he had been treated violently at any time Daniel replied: '(with hesitation) Mr Tomkin has laid hold of my coat and forced me upstairs; I call that violence, which I never was subjected to before I came to his place; that was done two or three times ... A year or two ago I tried to get away by the railway, but I did not succeed.' He also explained that he was not allowed any pocket money. 'I think at one time I had some money of my own; since that was gone I have been kept without any money to spend.' Tomkin disputed this. He said he had given Daniel money on a number of occasions, an example being when he wished to buy a dress to send to his half-sister in France.

Tomkin's lawyer argued that there was no case to answer: 'The Commissioners have no proof that this gentleman, who has been treated as a friend and companion by Mr and Mrs Tomkin, and who, as has been shown, had daily sat down at their table and been treated as a guest, was any other than a man of weak intellect, certainly not of unsound mind.' However, the magistrates reluctantly came to the view that in spite of Tomkin being a respected surgeon there was a case to answer. At the trial a few weeks later Tomkin decided not to pursue the question of whether or not Daniel was insane and pleaded guilty. In response the Lunacy Commissioners' lawyer told the court that having made further investigation, the Commissioners were of the opinion

> ... that there is no ground whatever for any imputation upon Mr. Tomkin, who, although he has committed a breach of the strict letter of the law, yet has in all other respects acted with kindness and humanity to the unfortunate gentleman in question. The Commissioners had instituted the prosecution upon public grounds entirely, and having discharged their duty in that respect, they are quite content with Mr. Tomkin's admission that he has been guilty of a technical legal offence.

Although no conclusion had been reached as to whether or not Daniel was of unsound mind, Tomkin must have decided he could no longer accommodate him in his house, and Daniel was moved into the asylum in Maldon Road. Most small private asylums, such as that run by Tomkin, were far from the grim Victorian asylums that often featured in novels. It is likely that Tomkin's asylum, which only had around twenty inmates, would have been relatively comfortable and those living there would have been allowed many freedoms if their mental health allowed it. When the poet John Clare was admitted to a different Essex

Wealth and Poverty

asylum in the 1830s he was given his own key to the house. It is hoped it was a pleasant institution for Daniel lived there for the following thirty years, and throughout those thirty years it was Charles Hope who paid Tomkin's fees.

Unlike his cousin, Charles had a successful and prosperous life. He had two sons, one of whom died in infancy, and a daughter. His surviving son, Charles Samuel, remained unmarried and worked in his father's tea broking firm, and Charles Hope & Co. continued well into the twentieth century. His daughter Frances (Fanny) married Henry Gore, a civil servant in the War Office, and at the wedding in 1875 the Magniac family was represented by two of Hollingworth's sons, their father having died eight years earlier. When Charles senior retired, he and Caroline moved to live at Wanstead, a fashionable vicinity of small mansions on the edge of London, but after Caroline died in 1872 Charles moved back to London, living just off the Strand in London with his son, daughter and son-in-law.

The death of Charles in 1892 brought further misfortune for his poor cousin. The sad conclusion to Daniel Magniac's forlorn life was reported in *The Chelmsford Chronicle* in July 1902:

On Wednesday Dr Harrison, coroner, held an inquest at the Braintree Workhouse touching on the death of Daniel Magniac, 73, a certified pauper lunatic, who died in the institution July 8th. The evidence went to show that the deceased was quite an imbecile, and never spoke. Some days before he died bruises were found on his arms and body, and on shins of each leg there were large contusions. Dr Scott the medical officer, said the man, like all the other inmates of the Workhouse, was extremely well looked after by Nurse Crossley, and ward men watched the patients at night. The doctor added that the bruises on the deceased were in no way responsible for death, which was due to heart failure and congestion of the lungs. The bruises were no doubt caused by the deceased getting in and out bed. The jury returned a verdict of 'Death from natural causes,' adding that no blame attached to anyone. In answer to inquiries from the jury to the deceased's identity, Mr. Smoothy said he was admitted to the Braintree Workhouse about ten years ago, but nothing was known of him except that for some years previous to that he had been a patient in Dr Tomkin's private asylum in Witham. It appeared that the deceased had been supported by a man who had died worth half a million pounds, but on his death the executors declined to support him, and in leaving the Institution be was brought to Braintree as a wandering lunatic. Efforts to further identify the man proved fruitless as he would never speak. Mr. Smoothy tried him once with a present of tobacco, but all he would say was 'Thank you.' Mr. Hills, the deputy clerk to the Guardians, said that since the deceased had been detained in Braintree some person used to come periodically from London to visit him, driving up to the Workhouse in a cab. The visitor, who was since dead, used always to bring the deceased a plum pudding and a half sovereign.

8

Missionary Connections

I started thinking of Jiangnan when I became a guest in Yue.
My tears not yet dry after six years of homesickness.
Now, cast away far over the vast oceans,
Even eastern Yue feels like home.

>Wang Tao (1828–1897), written in 1869 while
in Scotland, translated by Wai Tsui

Ching Wing, Wong Ock and an unidentified person at the Salvation Army Exhibition in London, photographed by Arthur Eason, 1894. (The Eason Collection, Hackney Museum, courtesy of Bridgit Anderson and Jim Four)

Missionary Connections

It was not until 1806 that the first Protestant missionary, the Reverend Robert Morrison, travelled to China under the auspices of the London Missionary Society. Unfortunately, by the time Morrison arrived the Chinese, who had become increasingly concerned about the spread of Christianity, had banned public preaching of the Gospel. With preaching outlawed, Morrison saw it as all the more necessary for there to be a Chinese translation of the Bible. The year before he went to China, it was reported that: 'Rev Morrison is diligently engaged in learning the Chinese language, under the direction of a native of China, now in London: and, with him, is constantly employed in making a correct copy of a Chinese manuscript in the British Museum, containing a harmony of the Gospels, the Acts of The Apostles, etc. These missionaries are intended to go to China, and there to perfect their knowledge of the language; after which, it is hoped they will be enabled to make a correct translation of the sacred Scriptures into the Chinese tongue.'

The 'native of China' helping Morrison learn Chinese was Yong-Sam-Tak, a young Chinese who had come to Britain to improve his English. He was introduced to Morrison and they agreed that in exchange for English language lessons from Morrison, Yong, who spoke both Cantonese and Mandarin, would teach Morrison to read and write Chinese. Morrison's diary entry for 8 October 1805 records: 'Yong-Sam-Tak came to live with me, to teach me the Chinese language, in which I am daily making progress. I expect Mr William Brown, from Scotland, in a few days to assist me. I pray that the Lord may make his coming a means of doing much good. I greatly fear that I am expecting too much from him, and not enough from God.' Yong was described as 'bright, educated with strong opinions and a fiery temper' and as his temperament was quite different from Morrison they did not get on well. Their relationship came to an end when Yong became upset at Morrison's attempts to convert him.

In 1814, the Chinese prohibition against Christianity became stricter with the religion specifically listed under the Chinese law prohibiting 'Wizards, Witches, and all Superstitions'. The law stated that, 'He who propagates the (Christian) religion, inflaming and deceiving the people... shall be sentenced to strangulation after a period of imprisonment. Those who are merely hearers or followers of the doctrine, if they will not repent and recant, shall be transported and given to be slaves.' In 1819 it was reported that:

A Chinese priest had just been strangled, and two others were also under sentence of death. Throughout the whole empire, there are but ten missionaries, five of whom, at Peking, have no communication with the inhabitants unless it be in secret. The only way left to the missionaries to penetrate into the country, is by gaining the messengers or couriers that pass from Macau to Peking, but if discovered, both the missionary and the courier suffer death on the spot.

Yet, the draconian law did not deter Morrison, or others who believed the Chinese should have the chance to find God. In 1823 Morrison completed his task of translating the Bible and a complete Chinese Bible was printed from wood blocks and published in twenty-one volumes in 1823. Assisting him with the printing was Kueh A-gong, who had become a Chinese Protestant convert and was possibly the first Chinese lithographer. It is said that Kueh visited England several times before 1816 but no record of such visits has been found.

The defeat of China in the Opium Wars in the 1840s brought to an end the restrictions on Protestant activity and within two decades British Protestant missionaries were present in nearly every major city and province of China. Missionaries working in China often returned to Britain, sometimes for health reasons, but more often to further the work in China by travelling the country drumming up interest in, and support for, their work, and a number were accompanied by Chinese colleagues. In 1845 the Reverend William Milne toured the north of England delivering well-attended lectures providing 'knowledge of the celestial empire', and was accompanied by Woo Sien Sang. Milne was the second Protestant missionary sent by the London Missionary Society to China and he served as pastor of Christ Church, Malacca. He was the first Principal of the Anglo-Chinese College and chief editor of two missionary magazines. His British lectures were very well attended, unlike those in the past, as Milne recounted: 'In 1834, a course of lectures were delivered, in London, by Professor Keting; at the first lecture, there were present besides the lecturer, only three individuals; at the second, two; and at the last lecture, only the lecturer himself!' *The Manchester Guardian* reported that Woo Sien Sang 'wore the Chinese costume and his features were decidedly Mongolian, of very pleasing, intelligent character. His whole deportment was full of gentlemanly suavity and courtesy ... and (as the lecturer informed his audience) he wore no less than sixteen strata of clothes, to protect him from the cold – a mode of increasing the animal warmth, which it seems the Chinese prefer to our plan of making large fires.' The textile manufacturers in the North of England saw China as a potentially lucrative market and Woo Sien Sang was invited to go to a Bradford textile mill and give his opinion on which cloths might have a ready market in China. Woo advised that the Chinese had a strong objection to all kinds of checks but that plain textiles in fine bright colours would find a ready sale in China: 'Mr. Woo ridiculed the idea that the Chinese had any superstitious prejudices against mixed fabrics.' Woo was reported as teaching Chinese for a time at the recently opened day school for boys, the Collegiate Institute in Liverpool.

In 1867, James Legge, a Scottish missionary, invited Wang Tao (formerly Wang Libing) to travel with him to Scotland and assist him in translating a number of Chinese classic books. Many years earlier, Wang had worked for the London Missionary Society Press in Shanghai assisting Legge with his translation of the New Testament and other books into Chinese. Wang had become a supporter of the Taiping Heavenly Kingdom, a revolutionary movement, and when threatened by arrest by the Qing government managed to evade capture by taking refuge in the British Consulate. He then escaped to Hong Kong and there met Legge, who invited him to stay at the London Mission Society hostel and assist him in translation.

At Legge's home in Dollar, he and Wang Tao worked on the translation into English of a number of Chinese texts, including *The Book of Songs*, *I Ching*, and *The Book of Rites*. Wang Tao travelled extensively within Britain and Europe, writing poems and a journal related to his travels. In 1890 some were published in China as *Jottings from Carefree Travel*. This was the first travel book about Europe by a Chinese scholar. For the publication, illustrations were commissioned from local Chinese artists but as the artists had no knowledge of the actual view, they used their imaginations. Thus the illustration of Holyrood, titled *The Old Palace of Edinburgh*, shows a Chinese palace and Edinburgh's Nelson Monument on Calton Hill is transformed into a pagoda. As Wang was invited to a wide range of places and events, his book offers a diverse account of British life; including street and country scenes; visits to a school, a circus and dances; and accounts of railways and factories. He even describes the interior of a Dundee sweet shop: 'Sweets are stored in different containers and when people come into the shop, they can immediately smell the fragrance.' While Wang provides many accurate descriptions of what he saw, some of his facts are perhaps influenced by local old wives' tales. In Huntly in Scotland he recounted that: 'one person has already reached 150, but is as sprightly as a sixty- to seventy-year old. Scholars have concluded that there have been approximately seven thousand centenarians in history, and no less than a tenth of them have lived in Scotland.'

Wang Tao found the British friendly towards foreigners and commented that they seldom discriminated against people of a different race. If anything, he found most British people only too keen to help, often resulting in those he asked for directions insisting on accompanying him to his destination. 'Immigrants from other countries living in Britain are never cheated. Because they have a harmonious relationship with the inhabitants, they seldom feel anxious. ... People are so gracious and kind that they compete with one another to welcome travellers from afar. There is no need to check in at the customs and visitors are not pestered by the questioning by the officials. People are never suspected to be villains simply because of their exotic clothes and languages.' As before 1900 almost all Chinese visitors wore their native costume, they stood out and were regarded as novel because of their Chinese appearance and attire. Wang comments that this often resulted in children laughing at him and making comments, but on most occasions the police drove the children away. When Wang visited his Chinese friends in Aberdeen, Zhan Wu had taken to wearing Western clothes whereas his wife, Jin Fu, continued to dress in traditional Chinese clothing. The next day when Wang was walking in the street a group of children pointed at him, one shouting, 'It's a Chinese lady!' and another crying out, 'No, it's Zhan Wu's wife!' It appears that, rather than seeing this as amusing, Wang was disturbed by being mistaken for a woman. 'Here I am, a male in my prime, being taken for a woman. Instead of the proud crowing cock, I am like a roosting hen.'

Yet Wang clearly enjoyed some of the attention he received, especially from young ladies, and seldom minded the numerous requests for examples of his calligraphy and poetry, entreaties to have his photograph taken and invites to grand occasions. Wang particularly enjoyed the dances and banquets: 'The ladies were dressed up and their upper breasts were bare. Under the bright light, their skin looked like snow and their faces like flowers, and their jewellery dazzled in the light. After the meal, some ladies played the piano while others danced. When I was asked to sing a song I instead recited a poem so melodiously that everyone clapped their hands.' Other Chinese may have been less keen on often being the centre of attention. One journalist thought so:

> I fear Chinese visitors will not return home with much idea of Western politeness. Wherever they appear in the streets they are followed in the street by a crowd of gamins (urchins), and they are not much better off in polite society. For instance, it is the fashion to invite them to evening parties, and then to ask them to sing. They are a singularly amiable and obliging people, and always comply with the request. There is a good deal of feeling in their singing, but some of it is decidedly new to Western ears, and the result is that Western mouths are on the giggle, and the Chinese find themselves the centre of a group of laughing listeners. Now laughter is not quite the emotion which singers, not being the great (Arthur) Vance or Jolly Nash (music hall celebrities), is likely to excite, and it may be easily imagined that when Orientals' tenderest love songs set Occidentals on the giggle, the Chinese are scarcely flattered. Nevertheless, they bear the rudeness with such perfect politeness that they always respond to an encore.

Wang was impressed by the British women he met and the way they mixed freely with men. He was close friends with two women: Jessie Gillespie and Ellie Spencer.

> Ellie had a beauty to shame a flower and a face to dim the moon; not only that, but she had exceptional wit and intelligence. After each night's delicious dinner, she would play and sing a song at the piano. She taught me the fingering and when I managed to get the tune she always insisted I play it a few times before she'd let me stop. I, in return, recited Bai Juyi's song, *Song of the Pipa*, teasing out the beauty of its pensive tones. Ellie was entranced and had me repeat it word by word. After listening for a time she said, 'I've got it' and the next day she sang a song that had incorporated the sound of my poetry recitation. I can hear her singing it even now.

Like other Chinese who visited Britain, Wang tended to overestimate the status of British women in society, perhaps as a result of the women he met, or simply because their lives were far less constrained that those of women in China. Another Chinese, Zhang Deyi, was equally struck by the difference: 'Foreign girls learn to read, then study astronomy and mathematics. They are less interested in embroidery, sewing, and other female work. They are more drawn to travelling, singing, playing the piano, painting, dancing, and the like.' Wang recounted that unmarried daughters and young wives 'sat with us at the same table, travelled by coach with us, joined in the drinking and gaiety and otherwise mixed freely, totally unconstrained by divisions between men and women. The beauty of their countenance was matched by the purity of their heart, their goodness and conduct ensured that no one showed them any disrespect.'

On his return to Hong Kong in 1870 Wang became an independent journalist, founding and editing one of the first modern newspapers in China. In his later writing, Wang argued that the democratic, technological and scientific ideas developed in the West should not be regarded as something foreign to China, but rather an extension of Confucian ideals. Wang's contention that China needed to reform its military, educational, administrative and legal systems influenced many Chinese leaders of the next generation, including the famous scholar-reformer Kang Youwei and the great Chinese revolutionary Sun Yat-sen.

As Chinese visitors were uncommon, British newspapers keenly reported on the activities of those who came. In 1856, it was reported that the Chinese poet and musician, Cheuk-seen-lan, who was visiting with the American missionary, Reverend Heffer, had been taken to see the large collection of Chinese books at the British Museum. While in 1859, the newspapers were delighted to report that Dong Sien-Sang, who was accompanying another American missionary, Dr Macgowan, had experienced quite a different cultural experience; trying his hand at the sport of curling on an icy pond in Scotland. As few of the visiting Chinese were proficient in English, having someone to accompany them when they were out and about was essential. A newspaper report in the 1860s underlined the problems if this arrangement went awry:

> A very handsome young Chinese woman, in Chinese costume, with a little boy very well dressed, were seen yesterday in Rathbone place, wandering about in a state of bewilderment, evidently having lost their way and unable to make anybody understand what they required. Under these circumstances a lad brought them to a Mr Beadon who took them into his private room, but could get nothing but Chinese out of either lady or child. In this dilemma it was thought best to send the Chinese to a hotel, and if it should turn out that the police were unable to find out their friends request inquirers to call at Mr Beadon's for information.

No follow-up report appeared so presumably the mother and child were safely delivered.

One day in 1860 the residents of Westbourne Grove in London would have been intrigued by the sight of an Englishman dressed in Chinese clothes, his English wife and a Chinese man carrying the couple's small child, arriving at Number 63, the house of Benjamin and Amelia Broomhall. The Englishman dressed in Chinese clothes was Hudson Taylor, Amelia's brother, who had just returned from China with his wife, Maria, and their young daughter, Grace. Seven years before, Taylor had given up his medical studies to travel to China as a missionary. At great danger to himself, he travelled extensively around the country endeavouring to convert Chinese to Christianity. For a time he worked with a Scottish evangelist William Burns and both adopted Chinese dress, in spite of this making them the laughing stock of both foreign and Chinese onlookers. Taylor later said, 'Let us in everything not sinful become like the Chinese, that by all means we may save some.' Then for a time Taylor travelled alone, frequently with little food and often in danger. At one point he was robbed of his travelling bed, spare clothes, two watches, surgical instruments, a concertina, Amelia's photo and a Bible given to him by his mother. Eventually he decided to settle in Ningpo and there married Maria Dyer and they had their first child, Grace. The Chinese man accompanying the Taylors was Wang Laiquan. Wang had been a painter and interior decorator by trade before deciding to convert, becoming an active and effective preacher. When Taylor decided to return to Britain because of poor health, Wang agreed to travel with the family and while in Britain to assist Taylor to translate the New Testament into Ningbo dialect.

Broomhall was a draper and also a Wesleyan Preacher, and was delighted to welcome his Christian brother-in-law and his family, and Chinese friend, to stay until they found their own accommodation. When they did, Wang, as well as assisting Taylor with translating the Bible, helped Maria with the cooking and household chores, and caring for Grace and the further children that were born while Hudson and Maria lived in England. For the next four years, Taylor travelled extensively within the British Isles speaking at churches and promoting the needs of China. Wang often accompanied him and, as Taylor recognised Wang's abilities as a preacher, also often spoke. Taylor gave Wang medical instruction, as well as training in Christian ministry and exposure to the cultural riches of London. Wang returned to Ningbo in 1864 where he married and became pastor of a new church in Hangzhou. In 1870 Wang opened a country chapel at his own expense and helped establish a network of churches led by Chinese and financially supported by the converts.

In 1865 Taylor founded the China Inland Mission and in 1866 returned to China with his family and the largest party of missionaries ever to travel to China from Britain. All the British who worked for the Mission in

China wore Chinese clothing, including the women missionaries, something deemed semi-scandalous at the time. By 1895 Taylor's substantial grassroots missionary effort had resulted in the placing of more than 600 missionaries in almost every Chinese province. In Britain, Broomhall became the British Secretary of the China Inland Mission and editor of the mission's magazine, *China's Millions*. As well as raising funding and fresh missionaries by speaking at meetings throughout Britain, Broomhall became a vociferous critic of the trade in opium, writing two books on its scourge and lobbying the British Parliament to end the trade. When Broomhall was dying in 1911, his son read to him *The Times* newspaper report that the Government had agreed to end the opium trade within two years. Of the ten children he and Amelia bore, five went to China as missionaries.

By the 1870s, there were many people protesting against the trade in opium and at a number of events held to publicise the issue, Chinese individuals were invited to speak. In 1874, 'a Chinese gentleman named Achoi, who spoke English with great animation and fluency' attended one conference at which it was reported that opium smoking was increasing among the Chinese seamen in London. In 1885, Chook Hong Cheong, Superintendent of the Church Missions to the Chinese in Victoria in Australia, spoke on the subject while visiting Britain:

> Mr. Cheong, our lecturer, is not only an earnest Evangelist, but a warm patriot, and has headed a great movement in Victoria against the opium traffic, where four-fifths of the Legislature have just voted for the abolition of the traffic in that colony. Mr. Cheong is now in this country pleading for the cessation of the opium traffic with the country of his birth.

In 1865 the Methodist Reform Church minister William Booth and his wife Catherine formed The Salvation Army in London's East End. The movement was modelled after the military, with its own flag and uniform, and Booth became the 'General' and his other ministers were given appropriate ranks as 'officers' and other members became 'soldiers'. From the outset, the Army worked to help alcoholics, addicts, prostitutes and other 'undesirables' unwelcome in polite Christian society. Its members were forbidden from drinking alcohol, smoking, taking illegal drugs and gambling. The Salvation Army soon had ambitions to be an international force and by the 1880s had a small number of cadets from many nations training to return to their home countries to develop the Army's work.

In 1885 Wong Ock, a Chinese from America who had converted to Christianity and later joined the Salvation Army, arrived in London to train. He lived and trained at the army's 'National Barracks' in Clapton. Formerly the former London Orphan Asylum, the building had been converted as the Army's centre and contained training barracks for 300 male and female cadets with classrooms on the ground floor, workrooms below, and bedrooms above.

The building also included a massive hall that could seat more than 4,500 people. The cadets required stamina as well as faith throughout their six months at the barracks. They rose at 6.30 a.m. when a whistle shrilled reveille and during their second three months, they were brigaded under training-home officers and sent off to launch campaigns in towns and villages. Days could begin with a 3 a.m. call to pray with a dying man, expound against the evils of drink outside a local pub unsure if the publican might turn violent, and end with escorting a runaway girl back to anxious parents. Booth once quipped at a passing-out parade: 'I sentence you all to hard labour for the rest of your natural lives.'

While Ock was in London, the Salvation Army led a major campaign to expose trafficking of young girls for prostitution and called for the age of consent for sexual relations to be raised to sixteen. To highlight the issue, the editor of *The Pall Mall Gazette* published a series of articles describing how he had arranged for the purchase of thirteen-year-old Eliza Armstrong for £5 from her alcoholic mother, with the mother's full consent that the girl would be put in a brothel. The purchased young girl had been taken for safety to Paris and although the investigative journalism was controversial, the articles created a wide public outcry. Over seventeen days a petition received 393,000 signatures contained in a scroll, which, unfolded, measured more than 2½ miles. In July a legion of Salvation soldiers marched from Clapton's Congress Hall to Parliament with the petition. Officers on horseback, a brass band, fifty strong, and a newly formed Army contingent in red jerseys and white helmets – among them Wong Ock – marched in front of a canopied car drawn by four white horses in which the mammoth petition, swathed in Army banners, reposed. At Trafalgar Square, a mile from the Palace of Westminster, where all processions had to halt, the petition was borne on the shoulders of eight officers to the House of Commons. Within days Parliament had passed an Act that raised the age of consent.

Also in Britain as a member of the Salvation Army was Ching Wing who, it was reported, had left China to seek his fortune in California, and while there converted to Christianity and subsequently joined the Salvation Army. Both Chinese appear to have been in the country for a few years as in 1887 and 1888 they took part in a fundraising tour around England entitled *General Booth's Salvation Army Jaunting Car.*

A genuine sensation was created on Sunday in Colchester when as part of the Salvation Army's event two Chinamen, Ching Wing and Wong Ock, genuine and unmitigated Celestials, appeared. Ching was clad in a light blue princess robe, with wide sleeves, over which he wore a dark blue chemise with the Salvation 'S' on the collar and an 'Army' shield fastened on the breast. From the back of his closely-cropped head descended a jet-black pigtail very neatly and elaborately plaited. Wong Ock, a bigger and older man, began to sing and his odd melody was just beginning to cause some amusement when he

Missionary Connections

suddenly turned half-round and gesticulated to the others of the Army who were in the secret and burst out with the well-known refrain of *Rock of Ages* completely overwhelming a titter that had begun to run in an undercurrent through the assembly. While they sang Ching Wing accompanied by waving his large sleeves and clapping his hands vigorously ... In fairly good English, made picturesque by the Celestial accent and intonation, Ching Wing told the story of his conversion. 'Until I give my heart I did not be happy; but I want faith, and He give it to me. I want understanding, and He give it too. Then He give me courage to fight for Him,' adding reverently, 'so He save my soul.' Then Wong Ock spoke: 'My friends, perhaps you never see this Chinese again. Going over water in big ship.' And in conclusion urged his hearers to 'Come to the Lord. No matter whether white man or black man or blue man, I tell you to come.' At the close of the service Ching Wing went nimbly towards the door with the collection box, which he shook scientifically, whilst his pigtail was being examined by a group of curious females. He submitted to the ordeal calmly.

In 1888 Wong Ock went to Hong Kong where he preached in gospel halls, although it appears he was not working under the auspices of the Salvation Army as it did not establish any China base until around 1916. Ching Wing may have returned to America as someone of the same name was a prominent member of Los Angeles' Chinatown in 1906 and worked to obtain compensation for the Chinese in Santa Ana where their houses had been deliberately burned down to drive them out. Santa Ana's city attorney, while questioning the constitutionality of demolishing the enclave, had eventually shrugged and said, 'Do it, burn these buildings up and take the consequences.' Firemen arrived on the scene to protect City Hall from damage but ignored the burning Chinese buildings and city officials clubbed to death the cats, dogs and chickens belonging to the Chinese. When Ching arrived he found his countrymen hungry and shivering in makeshift shelters, and helped move them to Salvation Army barracks where they were sheltered and fed.

Arthur Ephraim Eason's father, a photographer, was a close friend of William and Catherine Booth, founders of the Salvation Army, and Arthur spent a number of years as a Methodist Church Missionary in China. In 1882 he married Minnie Southall in Shanghai and two years later, they had their first child, Ethel. In that same year Arthur rescued a Chinese baby that had been abandoned by its mother and left to drown, and the Easons adopted the Chinese girl, naming her Mae. The Easons had seven more children. Arthur gave an account of his time in China:

With an immense mass of heathenism to confront and with the fewness of evangelistic labourers, as well as with the fact that numbers of Chinese impressed with the truth returning to their former creeds through fear of persecution and other causes, the work of the Christian missionary is necessarily one of great difficulty; and is a severe testing time for faith. But if asked as to results, I should say that things were better in China than I could have expected. Thousands of Chinamen have heard the Gospel who had previously been utterly ignorant of it; and missionaries long to see many more thousands converted from the error of their ways.

Arthur Eason returned with his family, including Mae, to Britain in 1892. He took over his father's photography studio and worked as a Chinese translator for William Clowes, one of the largest printers. In 1914 the Eason family emigrated to Canada but Mae, who is recorded in the 1911 census as attending school in London with her sisters, did not travel with them and what became of her is not known. In 2000, Jim Four and Bridgit Anderson purchased a large collection of glass photographic plates that had been produced by Arthur Eason in his studio in Dalston Lane, Hackney. The images include family portraits, street scenes, promotional photographs for music hall acts and images thought to be of foreign delegates attending the first Salvation Army Exhibition in London in August 1894 at the Islington Agricultural Hall. One photo includes Ock Wong and Ching Wing, and it is likely both of them returned to Britain for the event as Booth was keen for as many nations to be represented as possible:

The Salvation Army Exhibition is a remarkable success. There is no doubt that the army conductors have a genius for self-advertisement, and the Tamil, Japanese, Sinhalese, Chinese, Zulu and other foreign Salvationists, in native costumes, are drawing London. An Indian village, farm colony, a bonnet factory, rescue homes, and a representation of slum life in London are some of the leading features.

In 1890 at a meeting of the Zenana Missionary Society in London, one of the speakers was Mrs A-Hok who was introduced as the first Chinese Christian lady to have visited Britain. Mrs A-Hok, who herself had bound feet, spoke about what she saw as an unchristian practice:

The lives of the Chinese women are made miserable by the horrible practice of binding their feet, and, by the custom of not being allowed to go out, they can never hear the Gospel, unless ladies go into their homes and to them. The rule is so strict that even if there is a missionary preaching in church, or in the street, or even in their own houses, they are not permitted to go and listen.

There was a growing interest in Chinese literature and philosophy, and lectures on Confucianism, Taoism and Buddhism were common towards the end of the nineteenth century. Yet the presentations mostly continued to reflect the commonly held view within both the Roman Catholic and

Protestant churches at this time that the Chinese view of the spiritual world was clouded by superstition and ignorance, and the 'only remedy was the spread throughout China of the Christian religion'. Xue Fucheng, the Chinese Ambassador to Britain in the 1890s brought a different perspective. He argued that the moral underpinnings of Confucianism and Christianity were similar.

> In their moral actions, in their self-discipline and love of others, Christians in the West do not differ markedly from Confucians, yet the Old and New Testaments and other books the church publishes are full of fabrications and incredible assertions that even Chinese popular novels would avoid. Any child could see that their claims are nonsense. When I have discussed Christian doctrine with Western sages, they seem to agree, yet are reluctant to acknowledge the fact. And some think that given the march of science in the West, the church's scriptures will be dismissed in one or two hundred years' time. Yet all these wise men commend the teachings of Confucius. Though I recognise that Westerners are very good at saying the diplomatic things, I am convinced that that their words are utterly sincere.

9

A Chinese Gentleman Farmer

> And many ways he had, not this alone,
> In which his character distinguished shone,
> To duty bound, assiduous in his cares; –
> And blessings came, – three thousand steeds and mares.
>
> *The Book of Odes* (11th to 7th centuries BC),
> translated by James Legge

John Fullerton Elphinstone was the eldest son of William Elphinstone and Elizabeth Fullerton, and was born at the family estate near Airth in Stirlingshire, Scotland, in 1778. Two years after he was born, his father, who

John Hochee and his son in the 1850s. (Collection of the Lowdell family)

had been a captain of an East India Company ship, was appointed a Director of the East India Company (EIC), a lucrative and eminent position. Thus a career in the EIC was a natural choice for John and in 1794, at the age of fifteen, he travelled to Canton to become a company writer; in essence a clerk who kept accounts and records. In Canton he was one of six writers who worked under eight Supercargoes, the name for the principal staff who had responsibility for overseeing all the trading. Two company surgeons and a tea expert completed the British presence at that time, although by 1812 the number of EIC staff had increased to about twenty. Canton was governed by a Chinese Viceroy, appointed by the Chinese Government in Peking, who had full control over all trading and other official matters. The Chinese Viceroy also controlled communication as none of the EIC staff spoke Chinese and it was he who appointed Chinese with English to act as interpreters. The British and the other foreign nations were housed in buildings on the waterfront known as 'Foreign Factories' that sat outside the Chinese city's walls. The warehouse buildings contained living quarters for the staff and visitors, and local Chinese servants were employed to look after their needs. The foreign officials were only permitted to trade with specified Chinese merchants.

Under the agreement with the Chinese, all foreigners were required to leave Canton for about half of each year. During this off-season, some took leave in Britain or travelled to India or elsewhere, while the majority moved to Macau. In Canton they were cooped up in their small areas, so being free to move at will around Portuguese Macau came as a welcome relief. Elphinstone suffered from ill health and spent two long periods recuperating in Britain, although assorted ailments plagued him throughout his life. By 1814 he had been promoted to be one of the Supercargoes and, by 1816, was the President of the Supercargoes Committee. In that year he again took home leave and, as was usual, his Chinese servant, Ahung, travelled with him to Britain, presuming that he would return to China with Elphinstone after his period of leave. However, soon after arriving in Britain Elphinstone decided not to return to China and resigned from the EIC, perhaps assuming that life in China was partly to blame for his recurring illnesses. He asked Ahung to stay in Britain in his employ and the servant agreed. It is not known if Ahung was a competent servant, but one doubts it, for his conduct brought Elphinstone much grief. Elphinstone mentioned in a letter to his mother that his Chinese servant was often drunk and, sometime in 1817, Ahung made a young Scottish woman pregnant. The young woman, Jane MacBean, sued Elphinstone for maintenance of the baby, claiming he was responsible, being Ahung's employer. After much legal toing and froing Elphinstone agreed to pay, although as the child died at the age of one year, payments ended. This was the final straw and Elphinstone sent Ahung back to China in early 1819.

In spite of this bad experience Elphinstone decided to employ another Chinese servant, although this was problematic as there were few Chinese living in Britain at that time. It would have been more convenient to have employed a local man but for some reason Elphinstone was determined and perhaps he contacted his former EIC colleagues and asked them to help in his search, although it is not known if that was how Elphinstone came across John Hochee, a thirty-year-old Chinese. Hochee later recounted that he had arrived in Britain in 1819 and on his arrival went to live in the small village of Braughing, in Hertfordshire; on the face of it, an unexpected place for a Chinese to end up. The explanation may be that Braughing was only a short coach ride away from the EIC training college at Haileybury, and thus it is possible that Hochee travelled to Britain with an EIC employee who lodged in Braughing while working at the college. It is not until 1823 that Hochee first appears in the documented record with his marriage to Charlotte Mole, the seventeen-year-old daughter of Chamberlain Mole, a local Braughing farmer. Although the first mention of Hochee working for Elphinstone is not until 1826, it seems likely that Hochee entered his employment around 1822. It is possible that Elphinstone wished to have his new Chinese servant married and thus avoid any illegitimate pregnancies, and resultant claims on his purse, and arranged Hochee's marriage through local contacts. What is certain is that Charlotte's parents would have been unlikely to agree to their daughter marrying a Chinese who had recently come to the country without the assurance from someone of note that Hochee was reputable and had appropriate employment that would ensure he could support a wife and family. Elphinstone had already decided to buy a property in England and he may have promised Hochee and Charlotte, and Charlotte's parents, that he would provide a house for them.

Unlike many men who worked for the EIC, Elphinstone did not return to Britain a very rich man. A number of loans he made to Chinese merchants in the expectation of significant profit were either not repaid, or the instalments were paid over a number of years. Yet he was relatively wealthy and, having decided against living at any of his family properties in Scotland, in 1825 he bought two properties – a house in London and a farm in Lingfield, Surrey. His London house was at 23 York Terrace, overlooking Regents Park. It was described in a later sale document as containing 'five bedrooms and bathroom, two drawing rooms, entrance hall, dining room and library, and ample domestic offices'. His Lingfield property, Ford Farm, consisted of at least 500 acres with a large farmhouse, although his mother described it as 'small but a great deal of accommodation. In it a number of small good bed chambers. Good stables with new rooms attached to them.'

In 1826, very soon after Charlotte had given birth to their first child in Braughing, the Hochees moved to Lingfield and took possession of Norton's Cottage, which Elphinstone had bought as part of Ford Farm. At some point in the next fifteen years the small cottage was completely rebuilt at Elphinstone's expense and Norton's was transformed into an imposing three-storey small mansion and continued to be the home of the Hochee family. At Norton's, John and Charlotte had a further five daughters and two sons.

A Chinese Gentleman Farmer

When their first son was born in 1828, he was named John Elphinstone Hochee, and Elphinstone agreed to be his godfather.

Although Hochee was often referred to as Elphinstone's secretary, he does not appear to have carried out secretarial duties. Rather he seems to have acted as the foreman of Ford Farm and his English must have been well developed by then, for on the farm he was in charge of nineteen farm labourers and had to communicate effectively with merchants and other locals. He also had a role in managing the letting of other small farms that Elphinstone later bought. These included Milkhouse Farm and Hoopers Farm. A friend of Elphinstone who stayed at Ford Farm in 1827 remarked: 'I really think he (Hochee) will prove superior to any of the common cast of English Bailiffs. And at all events you are sure of an honest account of labour done.' Hochee also had a role as Elphinstone's personal servant, though over the years this transformed into a role more akin to a personal companion. When Elphinstone spent time at his London house, or was at one of the resorts he began to winter at, Hochee usually left the farm in the hands of his assistant manager, Thomas Head, and stayed with him.

Around 1830, no doubt because Hochee had taken on other responsibilities, Elphinstone employed a second Chinese servant, later termed his butler. His name was Johnsue Achow. Again, nothing is known about Achow's past or how Elphinstone found him. By the 1841 census, a third Chinese member of staff had been employed; the twenty-year-old Sam Ford. Elphinstone wrote about his days at Ford Farm in a letter to a friend: 'You may ask what I do there, a confirmed invalid. I preserve a tolerable state of health, at least hitherto, without actual suffering, only by great attention, much physic, but above all by keeping in the open air.' Although Elphinstone's two houses were large, he lived alone, apart from his servants, and remained a bachelor. Family members and male friends, many from his EIC days, occasionally came to stay but Elphinstone mainly avoided socialising. This was no doubt partly to do with his illnesses but he also deemed himself as 'unfit for female company'. In 1847 his cousin, Mountstuart Elphinstone, also a bachelor, retired after a distinguished career in India, including having been the Governor of Bombay. Mountstuart had regularly corresponded with Elphinstone while abroad and on his return to live in Britain he bought a house 10 miles from Ford Farm and the two often met.

At some point in the late 1830s, Elphinstone informed Hochee that he planned to leave Norton's to him after his death. As an alien could not inherit property in Britain, in 1839 Hochee successfully submitted a Denization Petition. This, as mentioned earlier, dating back to the thirteenth century and discontinued since the late 1900s, was a legal process by which an alien could obtain certain rights otherwise only normally enjoyed by the country's subjects, including the right to own land. By the 1840s, Elphinstone began to winter away from Ford Farm; staying in resorts on England's south coast in vain attempts to improve his health. His servants travelled with him wherever he went and as well as his three Chinese servants he employed Annie and Susan Claridge, the wife and daughter of Ford Farm's gardener, Thomas Claridge. Hochee occasionally had to return to the farm on business as the one surviving letter from Mrs Hochee to Elphinstone recounts: 'As Mr Hochee is in haste to get his breakfast, to be in the field, he requests me to answer your letter of Sunday, which he has just received. He is sorry you cannot come to Ford as soon as you expected. But he will endeavour to join you in Brighton tomorrow by the last train.' In 1841, when Elphinstone was in Bognor Regis, he wrote to a friend: 'I think he (Hochee) requires a change more than I do ... we both suffer from a facility to catch cold & weak disordered stomachs.' By the end of the 1840s Elphinstone was living almost all the time in Brighton and after 1853 never returned to Ford Farm. At that point Hochee passed all the management of the farm to Thomas Head so he could be with Elphinstone most of the time.

Hochee was by now a recognised and respected local landowner in Lingfield. At Norton's Hochee employed a governess, two servants and an errand boy. In 1851, 780 people from Lingfield and neighbouring areas visited The Great Exhibition in Hyde Park. Local landowners and employers, including Elphinstone and Hochee, contributed to the costs of the travel and it is possible Hochee joined his family for the outing in London to view the Chinese exhibits. In Brighton too, Hochee and his family were well known. His wife and daughters often joined Hochee when he was there and in 1852, the *Brighton Gazette*'s 'Fashionable Chronicle' section reported that Mrs Hochee and her daughters had 'just removed from the Queen's Hotel after a fortnight's stay'.

In spite of seaside air, Elphinstone's health continued to deteriorate and in March 1854 he died with Hochee at his bedside. Elphinstone was as generous in death as he had been in life, and family members, close friends, servants and other employees benefitted from his will. Achow was assured of the tenancy of his house at Cottage Crosses for as long he resided in Lingfield, and given £1,200 and an annuity of £100 per annum for life. Elphinstone added that should Achow wish to return to China at any time in the future the costs of his travel were to be paid by the estate. Sam Ford received £400. However, it was Hochee who was the primary beneficiary. While the Scottish properties in which Elphinstone still had a share were left to his family, Ford Farm, the Hochees house and several other smaller properties in Lingfield were left to Hochee, together with £19,000 (in total, equivalent to about £1.5 million today). Elphinstone wrote that Hochee's inheritance was 'in consideration of the long and continued attachment and of the services I have received and for the attention he has given to the management and improvement of my landed property in Lingfield'. A few months after Elphinstone's death Hochee finalised his Denization process. This required four referees and Hochee's supporters were all Brighton men, Paul Foskett, Chairman of the

A Chinese Gentleman Farmer

Central Protestant Association; George Lowdell and James William Wilson, both doctors who had attended on Elphinstone; and George Henry Aston, a stockbroker. They wrote:

> We well know and have been personally acquainted with John Hochee of Ford Farm Lingfield Surry for many years who is a Chinese subject about sixty five years of age and is engaged in farming his own land as an amusement, is married to an Englishwoman and has a family of six children ... we have implicit faith in his veracity and much pleasure in vouching for his thorough respectability and loyalty.

Lord Palmerston, then the Home Secretary, was content to authorise it and wrote on the bottom, 'It seems quite a proper case. To be done.'

In the same month that Hochee's denization was finalised, Achow, now in his late forties, married. His wife was Elizabeth Head, the sister of Thomas Head who helped manage Ford Farm and the daughter of the local blacksmith. She was almost half Achow's age but he was now a well-off suitor. More significantly, she was already a few months pregnant when they married. Their son was born in 1855 and christened with his father's name, although he appears to have died in infancy. Two years later Elizabeth died, probably in childbirth, and nine months later Achow married Louisa Ebdon, the daughter of a farmer near Lingfield. Achow and Louisa lived together until her death in 1867. In 1869 Achow married for a third time, to Mary Jane Hastie, the widow of a stationer with a seven-year-old daughter, Amelia. Mary's marriage to Achow took place just two months after the death of her husband, perhaps a necessary rush as she was four months pregnant. The baby was born in September 1869 and named Janet Mary Louisa Achow. It is not known whether the child was Achow's but it seems likely. Achow died in 1871. His widow lived on at Crosses Farm until 1876 when she married again and moved away. Achow's young daughter, Janet, was left in Lingfield, in the care of Annie Savage who had worked with Achow for Elphinstone, and she married in 1894. Of Sam Ford's life afterwards nothing is known.

Hochee, now a very wealthy man in his mid-sixties, gave up farming and concentrated on his large garden at Norton's. In 1856 and 1857 he let the three farms and sold off 'valuable Live Farming Stock, and Agricultural Implements' as he was 'relinquishing agricultural pursuits'. Already well-established as a local land-owner, Hochee settled into the life of a landed gentleman. Unlike Elphinstone, he appears to have enjoyed local social occasions. In 1856, he was one of several 'highly influential gentlemen and farmers of the neighbourhood' who attended The East Grinstead Annual Market Dinner at the Crown Inn. The toast to the Chairman was proposed 'in a very interesting manner by Mr Hochee, a native of China, who has located himself in the neighbourhood for many years as farmer; and we need scarcely state that the toast was responded to in a manner highly flattering to the worthy Chairman.' Entertainment was provided by two professional singers who had 'trolled forth the old standard English songs with a fervour of expression and a quality of tone... We have scarcely ever attended a market dinner at which such a great a spirit of conviviality prevailed.' In March 1861, Hochee was again at the Crown Inn as a member of the East Grinstead Rifle Volunteers. 'In the afternoon the members were put through the manual and platoon drill, afterwards going through various movements in company drill, marched a short distance out of town, and after depositing their arms at the armoury, returned to the Crown Inn, where a sumptuous dinner was awaiting them... Lord West made some very flattering remarks about their appearance, and in justice to that corps he must say the members had displayed much energy and zeal, with it that obedience which was characteristic of a true English soldier.'

Hochee employed ten men to tend his large garden at Norton's, and it would appear that the flowers, plants and fruit produced were of the highest class as many were entered into local shows. 'All the flowering plants shown at the East Grinstead Flower Show were contributed by the gardener gentlemen in the neighbourhood, by far the greater portion being from the gardens of a wealthy Chinese, long resident there, and who preserves that love of flowers for which the Celestials are said to distinguished – Mr Hochee.' In 1857, Hochee displayed an exotic bamboo plant at the Brighton and Sussex Horticultural Society's annual exhibition. Like all men in his position Hochee subscribed to a range of good causes, including a testimonial to Paul Foskett 'in gratitude for his past services in furthering the Interests of Protestantism'. As a keen chess player, Hochee also contributed to a fund to assist the widow of an eminent chess player. Her husband had died of cholera. The prizes at the 1866 East Grinstead and Lingfield Cottage Garden Society's annual summer exhibition were donated by him and included 'prizes awarded to the cottagers of Lingfield for the cleanest and best ordered cottages'. In his final years Hochee also spent much of his time in Brighton and he died there in 1869, aged around eighty. Five years after her husband's death Charlotte built a double cottage that she gave to Lingfield Church, with an endowment of £50 on condition the buildings be known as the Hochee Almshouses, in memory of her late husband. A bust of Hochee was created and displayed at the Almshouses.

Charlotte died in 1882. One Hochee daughter, Jane, died in her teens. The other five all married. Sarah's husband was Thorold Lowdell, the son of the surgeon who had acted as a reference for Hochee. They farmed land nearby and had nine children. Henrietta married Thorold's brother, Sidney, who had followed his father into medicine and practised in Brighton. They had no children. Letitia married Anthony Knight, a solicitor, and after spending a number of years in New Zealand returned to live in Britain. They had four children. Ann married Crawford Pocock, a surgeon, and had one daughter.

A Chinese Gentleman Farmer

Emily wed Frank Abraham, a merchant, though not a wholly successfully one as he ran up a number of debts.

The eldest son, John Elphinstone Fatqua Hochee, attended the EIC's Military College in Addiscombe under the name John Elphinstone Milton. This seems to indicate that a Chinese name was thought likely to hamper his career. Although he joined the EIC army in Madras in 1847, he, like his godfather, suffered from bouts of illness and retired in 1855 with the rank of Lieutenant. He returned to live with his parents at Norton's. In 1856, he went into business with William Gilpin and George Griffin, investing £1000 to establish the London Anti-Oxyde Paint Company. Unfortunately, he quickly discovered that his two partners were not the honest businessmen he had thought, but were using the company's cash for their own ends. Within a year John had to declare the company bankrupt, losing half his investment and having to pay all the company's debts. *The London Evening Standard* reported the sorry affair under the headline, 'Fleecing a celestial'. Later, both Gilpin and Griffin ended up in prison for debt. John never married and died in 1883. The other son, James Hochee, decided to become a doctor and with the support of Elphinstone was sent to Epsom College, a private boarding school with a reputation for producing medical men. He then studied medicine in London and joined the EIC as an army surgeon. In 1858, he was the surgeon on the EIC troopship *Seringapatam* that was bringing 150 injured troops and civilians back from India. The ship spent 114 days at sea and during the voyage smallpox broke out on board, resulting in the deaths of ten soldiers and four children. James became the Police Surgeon for the Metropolitan Police's Finchley Division, based in Fenny Stratford. As police surgeon he was involved in a wide range of criminal cases, from major accidents to murder enquiries. In 1861 he married Emma Fry, the daughter of the curate of Lingfield. They had six children. In his later years James became Medical Officer for the Convalescent outpost of the British National Hospital for the Paralysed and Epileptic in Finchley. He died in 1896.

There is a remarkable postscript to this account of John Fullerton Elphinstone and John Hochee. After Hochee's death, his wife arranged for him to be interred in the grave next to Elphinstone. Although Elphinstone's close friends asked after Hochee in their letters, in all the years Hochee worked for Elphinstone, his family avoided any mention of his servant companion and destroyed all letters and papers that referred to Hochee after Elphinstone's death. What then must the family have thought when they discovered that Hochee was to be buried next to his employer? For two unrelated men to be buried alongside one another was extremely unusual and for many in Victorian Britain would have been thought scandalous; all the more so when one was a member of a distinguished Scottish family and the other a Chinese servant. To ensure this extraordinary burial, Elphinstone and Hochee must have agreed well in advance this was what they both wished, as a double plot would have had to be purchased before Elphinstone's death.

Also, Hochee's wife must have agreed that instead of her husband being buried near her in Lingfield, where the family lived and she eventually was laid to rest, she, in accordance with his agreement with Elphinstone, would arrange for her husband to be interred next to Elphinstone in the Brighton cemetery. While Elphinstone's generosity to Hochee in his will simply could have been a mark of his gratitude for, and appreciation of, Hochee's long service, and a way of ensuring Hochee's family would continue to be well taken care of, their shared grave indicates a more profound regard. Whether their relationship was simply deep friendship or involved some form of sexual liaison will never be known, nor does it matter. What is astonishing is that these two men from different cultures had a relationship so central to their lives that they determined to lie together for eternity, indifferent to what the world might think.

10

Celestial Displays

> In the hall a portrait of a divine woman;
> From the palace emerges a fair lady.
> So lovely, both are painted;
> Who could distinguish real from unreal?
>
> Xiao Gang, Emperor Jianwen of Liang (503–551)

A number of those who traded with China accused the Chinese of being arrogant, corrupt and resistant to progress and these disparaging opinions were often reflected in press coverage. Unsurprisingly, the Opium Wars of the 1840s led to even more xenophobic newspaper articles. Yet in spite of such

Queen Victoria meeting the Chinese 'family' at Osborne House, 1851. (*Illustrated London News*)

anti-Chinese propaganda, the great majority of the British public continued to admire Chinese art and exhibitions of Chinese objects were popular. In 1842, the exhibition 'Ten Thousand Chinese Things' opened in London's Hyde Park to huge acclaim. The collection was gathered together by an American, Nathan Dunn, with assistance from a number of Hong Kong-based Chinese merchants. The exhibition was displayed in a temporary structure resembling a Chinese residence in Hyde Park and visitors entered through a replica of a Chinese Summer House, where they encountered three immense gilt Buddhist sculptures. The introduction to the catalogue for the exhibition stated, 'Here, we have not one object, but thousands; not a single production, but the empire with all its variety of light and shade, its experience, its mind, and the results of both, for four thousand years.' *The Illustrated London News* reported:

> The display allows one to appreciate their pagodas, their bridges, their arts, their sciences, their manufactures, their trades, their fancies, their parlours, their drawing rooms, their clothes, their finery, their ornaments, their weapons of war, their vessels, their dwellings, and the thousand et ceteras which make up their moving and living world. The beauty, rarity, novelty, and extreme singularity of these curiosities are very striking.

The public flocked to see the exhibition in London and in Liverpool and Dumfries where it was later shown. The exhibition catalogue was equally popular, selling approximately 50,000 copies.

In 1848, a Chinese junk, the *Keying*, arrived in London. It had been purchased by a group of enterprising British investors in Hong Kong to send to London to promote the colony. The junk was 160 feet long, had a teak mainmast that towered 85 feet above the deck, and was painted with a large eagle on her stern and two eyes on her bow. Captain Kellet was commissioned to pilot the junk to Britain and he hired a crew of thirty Chinese and ten British sailors. On the *Keying's* long journey it was blown off course and ended up in Boston in America. Later it spent some time in New York and in both cities attracted large admiring crowds, but on board all was not well. The Chinese crew went to court in New York claiming unpaid back wages and money to pay their passages back to China as it transpired that they had been deceived into believing that they were sailing the boat only as far as Singapore or Batavia (now Jakarta). Although the court found in their favour, it is unclear what then transpired, for the junk eventually set sail again to cross the Atlantic and a number of the crew certainly were Chinese. To ward off disaster the Chinese sailors adorned the junk's masts with strips of red cloth to bring good fortune. Unfortunately, this was not sufficient to weather an Atlantic storm, which damaged the boat and disabled the rudder, and resulted in the death of the second mate. The junk, assisted by British ships, finally limped into London in 1848, thus becoming the first Chinese vessel to make the journey from China to Britain, albeit by a circuitous route.

The *Keying* became as popular a visitor attraction in London as it had been in America: 'There is not a more interesting exhibition in the vicinity of London than the Chinese Junk: one step across the entrance and you are in the Chinese world; you have quitted the Thames for the vicinity of Canton.' Apart from viewing the 'remarkable curiosities', visitors could hear traditional Chinese music and see displays of spear fighting. In spite of enthusiasm among the public, the press contained many derogatory or mocking articles about the junk and the Chinese in general. One example was Charles Dickens' description of the *Keying* as a 'ridiculous abortion', more like 'a China pen-tray (than) a ship of any kind'. 'The *Keying* is nothing but a floating toyshop, the risible invention of a stagnant country where the best that seamanship can do for a ship is to paint two immense eyes on her bows, in order that she may see her way ... and to hang out bits of red rag in stormy weather to mollify the wrath of the ocean.' However, when Queen Victoria visited the *Keying* with the Prince of Prussia and others, she was very impressed and wrote at length in her diary about the visit. She described the junk in some detail and mentions the Mandarin of third rank who she thought was an important Mandarin but was in fact one of the sailors employed to greet the public. The newspapers reported:

> Her Majesty requested the gallant captain to precede her through the ship, and to explain the peculiarities of its construction, the subject of which she was desirous to be informed. Her Majesty first visited the state cabin which is full of very remarkable curiosities, the most striking of which is the joss house, or domestic shrine, containing the peculiar idol to which the ship is dedicated – a block of carved wood, richly gilt, rejoicing in the style and title of Chin Tee. After asking a great many questions the royal party left the cabin, and proceeded to the poop. From this elevated part of the vessel the royal party were visible to the thousands of spectators on the shipping and dock walls, and their appearance was greeted with cheering from every quarter.

On a later visit by other members of the royal family, the queen's Highland piper, Angus McKay, accompanied the party and his 'costume caused great astonishment to the Chinese sailors, who chased him about the ship, examining and touching every part of his dress. But far greater was their wonder when he took out his pipes and played a reel. Their astonishment then knew no bounds, and their expression of serious and fixed awe caused great amusement to the spectators.' One suspects their description of the bagpipe music might have echoed British descriptions of Chinese music; a 'screeching cat-squeal'. Gradually, interest in the junk waned and in the spring of 1853 the *Keying* was towed to Liverpool where she lay for two years before being broken up and her timbers used in the building of ferry boats for the River Mersey.

When Dunn died in 1844, *Ten Thousand Chinese Things* was purchased by the American showman, P. T. Barnum, and taken to New York. In 1849, the collection, or at least part of it, was repackaged by Barnum as The Chinese Exhibition and returned to Britain, being first shown in Edinburgh. It was reported that the train taking the exhibition to Edinburgh 'was of great length, consisting of an engine and tender and sixteen exhibition vans. From the breadth of the vans, the platforms at almost every station had to be removed, but scarcely any delay was occasioned to the ordinary trains on the line.' The exhibition was displayed in a large wooden structure erected in East Princes' Street Gardens and again was hugely popular. 'It is unquestionably one of the most remarkable and interesting exhibitions that has ever visited Edinburgh. Every child amongst us hears something of this wonderful eastern land from which has come the well-known Tea – the beverage esteemed by every class. The religion, laws, trade, and amusements of that remarkable people are illustrated in a great variety of ways, and of those minor articles of ornament and taste in the shape of cups, vases, metal work, and fine carvings, the connoisseur in such things will find ample stores.'

When Britain mounted The Great Exhibition in 1851, the first international exhibition of manufactured products, it was planned to include displays from a range of countries, including China. The exhibition was organised by Henry Cole and Prince Albert, and held in the purpose-built Crystal Palace in Hyde Park. As there was no official input by the Chinese Government, the Chinese section consisted of an ad hoc display of artefacts, mainly provided by import companies, as highlighted by a large sign above the exhibits: 'Furnishings exhibited by Hewett's Chinese Warehouse, Fenchurch St.' As Japan was still a closed society at this time the few Japanese objects on display were included in the Chinese section. As host, Britain occupied half the display space inside, with exhibits from the home country and the Empire. India contributed an elaborate throne of carved ivory and magnificent trappings for a Rajah's elephant, while France exhibited sumptuous tapestries and Sèvres porcelain. With such competition it was hardly surprising that the ad hoc Chinese display section was a disappointment to the majority of visitors. At the exhibition's royal opening, as Queen Victoria progressed towards the seating area, a Chinese man in colourful traditional dress stepped forward and performed a kow-tow to the Queen. Given the lack of knowledge of Chinese society in Britain, any Chinese man or woman dressed in colourful Chinese robes was automatically presumed to be someone of high status, so the on-lookers presumed him to be an important visiting dignitary. 'The Queen acknowledged the obeisance and saluted the Mandarin in return; and at her request he was placed between the Archbishop of Canterbury and the Comptroller of the Household.' What is not known is whether the Queen believed the man to be an important Chinese VIP or recognised him to be, in fact, the lowly Mandarin whom she had met when visiting the *Keying*.

There were a number of satirical books that purported to be reports by Chinese visitors casting a jaundiced eye on Britain. One published to coincide with the 1851 exhibition was Henry Sutherland Edwards' *An authentic account of the Chinese commission which was sent to report on the Great Exhibition, wherein the opinion of China is shown as not corresponding at all with our own*. It was written in verse that drew on the standard prejudices about Chinese and illustrated with outlandish cartoons.

> In short, on the eve of the Great Exhibition,
> The Emperor of China sent out, on a mission,
> A man who'd committed so heinous a crime,
> He was sentenced to stop in Great Britain some time.

Although the Chinese display in The Great Exhibition was somewhat limited, The Chinese Exhibition that was brought from Edinburgh to London to coincide with The Great Exhibition proved popular as an additional crowd-puller. *The London Illustrated News* announced this new attraction:

> A pleasing addition has been made to the Chinese Collection, consisting of a Chinese lady, named Pwan-ye-Koo, with small lotus-feet only 2½ inches in length, a Chinese professor of music, his two children (a boy and a girl), the femme de chambre of the lady, and an interpreter. The children are gay, lively, and intelligent, the lady herself agreeable and interesting, and the gentlemen civil and obliging. Chinese concerts form part of the entertainment; the lady Pwan-ye-Koo singing a Chinese air or two, accompanies the professor, who likewise treats the public with an exhibition of his vocal powers. The group is one that has much to commend it: it is picturesque and peculiar, and presents an image in high relief of the native manners of a Chinese family. The conduct of the domestic blended the humble and the familiar in significant manner; and there was air of freedom, and a sense of mutual obligation manifested in the whole party, calculated to make a favourable impression on the spectator.

The tiny bound feet of Chinese women always provoked comment, although one article did not simply point the finger at the Chinese:

> One cannot look at their feet without lamenting the cruelty of barbarous fashion which mistakes deformity for beauty; but it questionable whether it is not the strangeness rather than the cruelty of the fashion that excites our astonishment, for it is not a whit more irrational or cruel, or as destructive of human life, the barbarous custom of tight lacing amongst our own countrywomen.

The Chinese in Britain

While most newspaper reports were enthusiastic, *The Morning Chronicle* ridiculed the Chinese family: 'Fancy his lordship, or any other nobleman taking out a quantity of upholstery and with his wife and children sitting in the midst of it all, week after week, like the "family of rank" that are honouring us with long visit – in return for our shillings – at the Chinese Exhibition. It is rarely that any members of our aristocracy condescend to make shows of themselves, the way we are called upon to believe that the mandarins and persons of rank in China are accustomed to do on their travels.' The article continued by mocking the exhibition of the *Keying*: 'We cannot suppose that so many mandarins can be spared from their official duties in China, to speculate in Exhibitions of Junks, or other specimens of their national industry. Fancy Lord John Russell going out to China with a coal barge, and remaining away for three or four years at a stretch to exhibit it.'

Such derision of 'Chinese of rank' was, of course, unwarranted. It was British entrepreneurs who had arranged for the junk to be exhibited and the 'mandarin' on board was the Chinese crewman employed to welcome visitors. Also, although kept secret, the Chinese family were a fabrication by the American showman, P. T. Barnum. Krystyn R. Moon recounts in her book, *Yellowface: Creating the Chinese in American Popular Music and Performance*, that it was Barnum who decided to add a Chinese family and he set about manufacturing one. He hired one of the guides at Dunn's original exhibition and as the man played music, elevated him to 'a musical professor of the highest rank'. This man's three children were commandeered and a local Boston Chinese woman hired to act the part of his wife and mother of the children. This perfect 'Chinese family' were accompanied by another man, formerly an employee at Redding's Tea Store in Boston, and a Chinese American woman who played the servant's part. To Barnum's delight, his Chinese 'family' were invited to meet Queen Victoria at Osborne House on the Isle of Wight. The press reported:

The party consisted of a Chinese gentleman, named Chung-Atai, his two wives, his sister-in-law, and a Chinese female attendant. The junior wife of Mr. Chung-Atai had the honour of singing to the Queen, whose well-known proficiency as a musician naturally rendered her Majesty desirous of hearing the unique performance of the celestial lady. The elder consort of Chung-Atai presented her Majesty with a beautiful executed Daguerreotype of the interesting Chinese group; and the younger lady left with the Princess Royal a pair of very handsome lady's shoes, embroidered in gold by herself, and the exact size worn her, viz. 2½ inches long by 1 inch broad, both of which offerings were most graciously accepted. Prince Albert, thinking the family would be interested in the numerous plants and flowers of Chinese origin abounding in the garden adjoining the drawing room, conducted his visitors round the terrace and parterres, her Majesty

Celestial Displays

and the royal children meanwhile being much amused at the helpless, and certainly inelegant, mode of walking of the ladies, the contortion of their feet effectually preventing any pedestrian exercises beyond a very short walk. They afterwards returned to Cowes in two carriages, gratified in the highest degree at their reception.

In her diary the Queen describes the family's visit in some detail, including the women's bound feet – 'poor little feet, painful to see'. She also drew a sketch of the women which she pinned into her diary. The Queen thought their dresses pretty and their manners dignified, but was less enamoured when one of the women sang describing it as sound between 'a crying child & a cat!' A different version of the origins of the Chinese family that the Queen met was given later in a contemporary letter written by a Hong Kong resident who stated that, in reality, Chung-Atai was 'a dismissed Police Constable', 'the ladies of rank rather girls from a village near Macau of no rank whatever, who were bought under pretence of being married to well to do people and been gulled into travelling to England' and 'the wife that plays and sings was employed in that capacity in the taverns here'. Whichever version is true it seems certain the Chinese family the Queen met were not quite what they seemed.

When The Chinese Exhibition closed, Barnum auctioned the collection. A third of the objects were bought by one London dealer, formerly a tea importer, and through his shop many of the Chinese objects passed into British homes and continued to influence British design into the twentieth century. A number of the objects bought in the auction were brought together for an exhibition in Brighton in 1854. 'The grand collection of Chinese figures, dresses, and articles of art, from the Celestial Empire, with which many of our readers, probably, became familiar during its exhibition at Hyde Park Corner, has been attracting spectators from among our residents and visitors during the past three weeks.' Although the Chinese 'family' had disappeared, the exhibition included 'a living Chinese boy, about ten years of age, who runs about the saloon chattering to the spectators in very tolerable English'.

In 1862 there was a follow-up to the 1851 Great Exhibition, named the Great London Exposition, or International 1862. It ran from May to November in a building created on a site in South Kensington, London, now occupied by the Natural History Museum. Displays from a large number of countries were included but again the Chinese section was an ad hoc collection of objects loaned by Britons, including pharmaceutical articles, a human skull set in gold, specimens of Chinese type, Chinese screens, a backgammon board, and an ancient bronze incense burner. Three years later a more impressive exhibition was mounted in a room at the Crystal Palace although that 'collection of jewellery, precious stones, enamel, jade, robes, watches, and other articles of taste' consisted of objects pillaged from the Summer Palace in Peking by the British army. Another object pillaged from the Summer Palace was presented to Queen Victoria in 1861. This was the first Pekinese dog to have been brought to Britain. Known as the lion dogs of China, Pekinese were the exclusive property of the Chinese emperors and normally never left the precincts of the imperial palaces, but this poor creature had been seized by British soldiers during their pillaging. Victoria named the dog Looty. As during the Opium Wars, the Hindi word for plunder, 'lut', had entered regular English usage it seems certain the Queen was making a droll reference to his origins. It is reputed that Looty's life at Buckingham Palace was lonely as the Queen's many other dogs took exception to his Oriental appearance, though one assumes this was merely extending anthropomorphically to the dogs British views about the Chinese. A little later Looty was purloined again, this time by the Princess of Wales, and taken to live at Sandringham where he died in 1872.

None of these earlier British exhibitions had any Chinese input and Robert Hart, China's Inspector-General of China's Imperial Maritime Custom Service, thought it important that in future China should take control of major exhibitions and so ensure that the diversity of Chinese culture and ideas was properly represented. Before being employed in 1859 by the Chinese Government to oversee the country's trading, Hart had worked for the British Government in China. When working for the Chinese Government, Hart introduced a series of reforms and also tried to influence those in power to consider other forms of modernisation. He believed that China needed to project its view of the country abroad, rather than allowing foreign perceptions to hold sway, and he saw participating in cultural events as one method. So, when Britain invited foreign countries to participate in the first 'International Sea Fishing Exhibition' in 1883, Hart arranged for China to take part. As the British had not given the Chinese sufficient advance notice, the Chinese section was not quite as extensive as Hart might have wished. Yet the Chinese display proved a success. *The Spectator* wrote:

> There's fascination for a week in the China section alone; in the beautiful fishing fleet, with grass-mat sails, that seems to be coming to shore with a fair wind; in the slender and fragile-looking, but almost indestructibly strong fishing apparatus, all made of bamboo; in the wonderful silk nets; in the curious oyster-culture processes, and seine fishing with rafts. Then there is the tetraodon, a knobbly, bladder-shaped creature, used by the Chinese as a lantern, when he has been scooped; a collection of beautiful shells, and a hammer-headed shark from Formosa; models of boats with luminous edges for fishing by moonlight ... the innumerable inventions that tell of the patient toil of the Yellow People, and their wonderful faculty for utilising everything, render this division supremely interesting.

Hart also arranged for China to publish its own catalogue of its exhibits and this new approach to China's international relations was clearly spelled out

Celestial Displays

in the introduction: 'After the thousands of years that China has spent apart, the gulf of separation has now been fairly bridged over.'

With more time to plan, the Chinese input into the following year's International Health Exhibition in London was far more coherent. This British exhibition was designed to promote good health in the populace through displays and an official education programme, and to show off to the rest of the world the great technological strides made by the Victorians in improving disease control, especially through better sanitation and water purification. In addition to the many Chinese exhibits, a team of about thirty Chinese men travelled to London to participate, including shopkeepers, artisans, musicians, and cooks. When it was discovered on arrival that twenty-four bore the marks of having had smallpox, all were vaccinated during their stay. The Chinese section included various rooms and two shops, costumes, musical instruments, toys, soapstone objects and books. Possibly the most significant inclusion was the first-ever Chinese restaurant that offered the British public the opportunity to sample Chinese food. The Chinese restaurant was staffed by nine cooks, under the command of the chef-de-cuisine of Government House in Hong Kong. While the menu mixed Chinese flavours with classic British dishes, it introduced many dishes and flavours to Britain for the first time. 'Bird's-nest soup – a peculiarity special to China which will be found even more delicious and more nutritious than the far-famed real turtle soup itself.' Other Chinese delicacies available were Dried Bean Curd, Preserved Ducks' Eggs, Chrysanthemum Shoots, Sharks' fins a la Pekinoise, and 'the famous Shaohsing wine served hot in tiny china cups'. There also was a Chinese teahouse serving

> ... the Imperial tea, which costs eight shillings a pound in Pekin, and is really delicious. It is quite true that such delicate flavouring could not stand the addition of sugar or milk, and probably it is on account of the English method of drinking tea, that it is never imported into Europe. Each portion of this tea is separately brewed in a little cup, covered with a saucer, no such thing as a tea pot being known. It stands for about two or three minutes, and is then poured out with the saucer, so held as to prevent the escape of any tea leaves, into dainty china drinking cups.

The Chinese cooks were invited to cook lunch for Queen Victoria at Windsor Castle and the queen wrote that she enjoyed the Bird's Nest Soup and some salmon, but thought the other dishes less appetising. Of the tea she was served she wrote, 'Its fragrance is quite extraordinary & most delicious.' Chinese musicians played in both the restaurant and tea house, and during their stay, were invited to perform at a Royal Garden Party at Marlborough House alongside the bands of the 2nd Life Guards and the 10th Hussars. At the exhibition extracts from Chinese Opera were performed for the first time in Britain, but it is unlikely that many took the music seriously. The writer of

Our Ladies Column, a feature carried in a number of newspapers, certainly did not. 'We were treated to a scene from Chinese opera, the peculiarity of which is that the singers, howlers, groaners, or whatever they may be called, are unseen, and utter their sounds from behind the principal figures who gesticulate and flourish before the audience, suiting their actions to the words which are intoned by the hidden performers. All (events are) acted in dumb show, whilst love song, war chants, and triumphal marches are intermingled with unutterable dialogues from behind. It was the funniest performance I ever saw.'

Mrs Campbell, the wife of the Secretary to the Chinese Customs, taught the Chinese musicians the tune of *God Save the Queen* to conclude their entertainment. One report kindly pointed out that in spite the Chinese instruments only having five notes instead of the Western octave 'their proficiency in the one English tune with which they are acquainted was very creditable to their industry, and to the ability of their instructress.'

11

Studious Endeavours

I sought the honours of the school and literati,
I worked at morn, and midday too,
I strove when other students shirked,
Or wasted time at games.
My heart did burst with learning's longing,
Nothing else could give me joy.
I memorised and worked the harder
To realise my fond desire.

Li Hongzhang (1823–1901)

Statue of Dr Huang Kuan in the Edinburgh Confucius Institute's garden, University of Edinburgh. (Author's collection)

One of the earliest Chinese to study in Britain was Chan Tai Kwong, who came to England in the 1840s. While studying at a Church of England college he took a temporary job as an interpreter at an exhibition of Chinese objects and there met the first Bishop of Victoria, who encouraged him to return to China and become a priest. Although Chan did return to China and commenced a religious career, he left the Church after a short time and, following an ill-fated business career trading in opium, became the Chinese Clerk to the Hong Kong Court.

During fighting at Ningpo in 1841 a nine-year-old Chinese boy called Chow Kwang Tseay was adopted by British marines and taken to India aboard the frigate, the *Blonde*. He then was transferred to the East Indiaman ship, *The Blundell*, and taken to Britain. En route he was given the English name John Dennis Blonde. The East Indiaman ship captain took the boy to his village, Wentworth in Yorkshire, and there the local landowner, Charles Wentworth Fitzwilliam, arranged for John to be placed under the care of Mr Beardshall, who ran the Ashcroft Academy. In 1848 John was baptised in Wentworth Church and later expressed a desire to return to China as a Christian missionary. Fitzwilliam was not against that idea but proposed that first he should learn a trade and arranged for him to be apprenticed to a printer and stationer. Sadly, before John could begin his apprenticeship, he fell ill and died in February 1850. The Earl commissioned a local sculptor to make a headstone for John's grave.

In 1843 James Legge, a Scottish missionary, established the Anglo-Chinese College in Hong Kong and it provided many Chinese with the opportunity to learn English. In 1846 Legge and his family returned to Scotland and with him came three young students from the college – Song Hootkiam, Ng Asow and Li Kimlin. They arrived in May, as reported by *The Aberdeen Herald*:

> On Saturday last our citizens were electrified by the appearance, on their way from the London steamer to their temporary abode, of three live natives of the 'flowery land'. Arrayed in their singular costume, they soon collected a very numerous and miscellaneous escort, by whom, they were most diligently accompanied to their lodgings, the marvel on both sides seeming to be equal. The strangers were strapping lads, apparently about 18 years of age, of very dark complexion, and Tarter (sic) features, but, on the whole, not uncomely in their aspect. They were dressed in blue tunics, silk shoes with wooden soles of very durable thickness, and silk caps closely fitting to the cranium. Each rejoiced in a plaited queue reaching even unto his heels. We understand that these young gentlemen have come all the way from Hongkong, in charge of the Rev. Dr Legge.

The three had been brought by Legge to study at the Duchess of Gordon's school in Huntly to improve their English and strengthen their belief in Christian values, with the plan that on their return to China they would

Studious Endeavours

work as Christian evangelists. Also travelling with the Legge family was a young Chinese woman, Chang Ache, who was the amah (nanny) to the Legge's young daughter. Sadly, not long after arriving in Scotland, Ache was injured saving the Legge's daughter from being run over by a runaway coach. Ache's leg was so damaged she could not walk for many months and returned to China a cripple. The three young Chinese settled into their school and learnt English. Later they joined Legge on his British lecture tours and enchanted audiences with their Scottish accents. Legge and the students returned to China in 1849. None became the Christian evangelicals that Legge had hoped. Ng fell into bad company and was suspended by his congregation, while Li married badly and left the church. Although Song did not pursue a religious career, he became Chief Cashier of the P & O shipping line in Singapore.

Mary Gutzlaff, a missionary teacher in Macau, arranged for four young blind Chinese girls aged between five and eight to travel to Britain to study at the London Blind School. Mary and Lucy arrived in July 1839 and Laura and Agnes in 1842. This was soon after Thomas Lucas had invented an embossed writing system and, within a year of arriving, Laura and Agnes, although just six and eight years old, were able read out a chapter from the Gospel at a Missionary Society meeting. In 1844 two of the girls were sent to stay at the Exeter Institution for the Instruction and Employment of the Blind for a change of air and, while there, attended the institution's fifth annual meeting:

> On the platform in front of the Chairman were placed two young Chinese children in the costume of their country, whose presence naturally excited great curiosity... The Chinese children read, with great distinctness and pathos, the 30th Psalm in English, a performance which was rendered intensely affecting from the expressions of the sublime faith of the Psalmist amidst his mingled afflictions and rejoicings, enunciated in the plaintive tones of their soft voices, associated with their own lowly and singular condition, being intended to be sent back again to their own country, in order to be instrumental in the dissemination of the truths of Christianity there.

Sadly, Mary and Lucy died in their early teens, and Laura in her early twenties, but Agnes became a teacher at the London school. In 1856, now with the surname Gutzlaff after the teacher who had arranged for her to study in London, Agnes travelled to Amoy in China with missionaries from the Chinese Evangelisation Society. She became a teacher in the mission's school and two years later moved to Ningbo to work in a girls' school run by Mary Aldersley, the first female missionary to serve in China. There Agnes taught blind Chinese children and adults to read using the embossed script method. She later moved to Shanghai and on her death in 1869, left money to found the Gutzlaff Hospital.

In the 1840s, Dr William Moon, a blind Englishman living in Brighton, developed a different system of embossed writing for the blind and as it met with success, began experimenting with adapting the system for other languages. He successfully developed an Irish Gaelic version and wondered if a Chinese version might work. By chance he was introduced to John Hochee who was in Brighton with Elphinstone. John Rutherford, Moon's biographer, recounted the meeting;

> Dr Moon met the foreigner the following evening. Soon the conversation grew interesting, and the Chinese gentleman, Mr. Hochee, gratified his visitor by repeating the Lord's Prayer several times in the Ningpo colloquial. The ear of the listener had long been trained in the accurate distinguishing of sounds; and he dictated to his amanuensis the Chinese syllables as his ear had caught them. When he parted from his Oriental friend, he gave himself up for the rest of the night to the task of adapting his alphabet to the Chinese language. On the evening of the following day he was ready to pay a second visit to his new acquaintance. After unrolling his embossed page, he read aloud the words, 'Woo Ting Foo'; but he was allowed to go no further for the Chinaman sprang from his seat and, putting one hand on Dr Moon's chest and the other on his back, patted him before and behind, exclaiming, 'Oh, you got it! Our Father, you got, Our Father! You shall have some tea!' And it was not until he had been refreshed with a cup of fragrant Chinese tea that he was allowed to proceed with the rest of the Prayer, which proved to be substantially correct. Such was the commencement of embossed reading for the Chinese blind, which has since been greatly developed and adapted to several others of the dialects besides that of Ningpo.

In 1860, when the American missionary Dr Macgowan toured Britain giving illustrated lectures he was accompanied by a young blind Chinese girl who had been taught by Agnes Gutzlaff. At each venue the girl, dressed in native costume, 'read with her fingers a portion of scripture from the Ningpo Testament embossed in Moon's Type for the Blind, and her sweet voice and pleasing manner, won for her the affectionate sympathy of the meeting'.

Macgowan also brought to Britain Chee Yui Tang, the twenty-three-year-old son of the Governor of How Chou, to teach Mandarin to missionaries bound for China. In 1861 Chee was appointed the University of London's first Head of the Faculty of Chinese. 'The professor's Chinese title is Chou Yier, signifying Young Mandarin. He speaks fourteen dialects and is thoroughly acquainted with two Mandarin languages. He has come to this country for the purpose of learning English language, manners, and customs, and gaining information necessary for promoting the most friendly relations between the governments of China and Great Britain.' For whatever reason, Chee's time at the university only lasted a year or two and he returned to China.

Studious Endeavours

Although more universities began to create Departments of Chinese, none appointed a Chinese to any of the teaching posts before 1900. All the Chairs or Professors appointed were British men with Chinese language expertise.

By the mid-1860s Legge was living in Dollar in Scotland and in 1868 arranged places at Dollar Academy for three boys from Hong Kong: Boshan Wei Yuk, whose father worked for the Chartered Mercantile Bank of India, London and China; Wong Tongching, whose father was a printer at the London Missionary Society; and Woo Asee, whose father was an opium merchant. The boys first attended Stoneygate School in Leicester before moving to Dollar. A year or so later another boy, John Chew, joined them. Throughout their time at the Academy all four wore traditional Chinese dress and it was recounted that they 'were never annoyed by rude and idle curiosity, as was the case when they ventured to pay a visit to some of our large towns'. As well as the traditional subjects the boys learnt the Highland Fling. Wei's father was so impressed with the school that he presented two silver cups to be awarded to the two duxes of that year. The Chinese boys returned to Hong Kong in 1872. Like his father, Boshan Wei Yuk worked for the Chartered Mercantile Bank of India, London and China, and became a prominent Hong Kong figure, including a member of the Legislative Council. He was knighted in 1919. He named his Hong Kong mansion Braeside in memory of his years in Dollar and wrote, 'I have called my house Braeside from old associations, and after all, in spite of any one's sneers and cynicisms, one's old school and old associations are the best. There one picks up friends whom one always, in after-life, regards with affection ... I have on one or two occasions, entertained six or seven Dollar boys at my house.'

At this time few Chinese studied abroad and almost all of those that came to be educated in Britain had links to the British and American missions in Hong Kong. Elsewhere in China the tendency to insularity discouraged the concept of overseas study and this did not change until the early 1870s when Anson Burlingame negotiated the Seward Burlingame Treaty, which gave Chinese citizens the right to reside in America and specifically included the clause: 'Chinese subjects shall enjoy all the privileges of the public educational institutions under the control of the government of the United States.' This gave power to voices within China who saw the need for a more progressive approach to education and soon a programme was initiated whereby about thirty 'bright young boys from China's coastal provinces' were sent each year to Hartford, Connecticut, to attend American preparatory schools before continuing to colleges in the Northeast. However, there was no similar programme encouraging Chinese to attend British educational institutions. In 1874, the *Morning Post* announced that 'a Chinese official of high rank, dressed in full costume' was visiting England on behalf of the Chinese Educational Mission to visit a number of England's public schools as 'the Imperial Court intend to forward a large number of intelligent Chinese youths to this country to acquire sound educational attainments in physics and the English language. We should not be surprised if this gentleman's inquiries should result in a considerable influx of Chinese into England.' But nothing came of this visit as by then conservative opinion within the Chinese Government denounced study overseas as fostering undesirable Christian and Westernised attitudes. This conservative view was strengthened when the growing anti-Chinese sentiment in America led to restrictions limiting which educational institutions Chinese students could attend.

An exception was made for the Chinese Navy as in the mid-1870s the Chinese Government sought to develop the skills of its officers. Britain was asked if it would provide training for naval students from Fuzhou Naval Academy. The Royal Naval College in Greenwich agreed on condition that Chinese students should 'possess an adequate knowledge of English and sufficient proficiency in the subjects of instruction as to prevent them being a hindrance to the other students'. In 1877 the first twelve naval students arrived in the UK. They included Yan Fu, who, while a student in London, translated philosophical works by Adam Smith and John Stuart Mill and became one of the greatest enlightenment thinkers in modern Chinese history. Another was Sa Zhenbing whose father was so delighted at the honour shown to his son that he wrote this celebratory couplet: 'Our house has a brave who's gone to sea; our nation needs backbone to repulse the barbarians.' Sa later became an Admiral and the Minister in charge of the Chinese navy. Nine of the Chinese cadets attended the college for the nine-month study of engineering and naval architecture, while the other three were placed as apprentices on Royal Navy ships. The students at the college in Greenwich rented houses nearby and 'visited with their tutor many places of interest in London, and were entertained at luncheon at the Wanderers' Club, Pall Mall'. The Chinese students occasionally attended their British classmates' social activities, and perhaps attended one or more of the annual balls given by the sub-lieutenants studying at the Naval College to which the local great and the good were invited. Six of the Chinese students passed their exams and the three who did not were transferred to work as apprentices on Royal Navy ships. Over the next ten years more naval students attended the college, with the last group in 1886 numbering nineteen.

In 1879 Chih-chen Lo-Feng-Luh came to London in advance of joining the staff working for the first Chinese Minister in Britain, Guo Songtau. For about a year he attended lectures by Professor Bloxam on political economy, chemistry and natural philosophy at King's College, London. This period of study may have been to improve his English, which later was much admired, especially when he returned to Britain in the 1890s as China's British Minister. In 1896 when he was Minister in London his two sons attended school in Norwood. For school the two boys were dressed in Western clothes, while at home and when on visits with their father they wore Chinese dress. It was said that when at school they wore their pigtails under a wig which ensured the other boys could not pull them.

Studious Endeavours

Among the first Chinese who came to study at British higher education institutions were four related to Fuk-Tong, a church minister in Hong Kong. Fuk-Tong was educated at the Anglo-Chinese College in Hong Kong when James Legge was the headmaster and, in 1846, was ordained. Unfortunately, just six years later, he was injured in an anti-Christian riot and as a result of the beating, died a year later. His son-in-law, Huang Kuan (also known as Wong Fun), was the first Chinese student to graduate from a British University. He was born in 1829 and raised by his grandmother as his parents had died when he was young. In 1841 he was sent to the Morrison Education Society School in Macau, but after a year moved with the school to Hong Kong following the island becoming a British colony. The headmaster, the Reverend Samuel Brown, was an American minister and in 1847 decided to return to the United States. It is possible that he was not sorry to give up his headmastership of the school for an acquaintance, Charles Taylor, later wrote: 'The original object of the Morrison School was to teach Chinese boys the English language in connection with Christianity; but after an experiment of several years, it was found that the boys had so universally perverted their knowledge of English, by becoming, for the sake of gain, interpreters for opium traders, sailors, and others – generally for wicked purposes – making, to say the least, but very poor use of their English, and none at all of their Christianity, that the benevolent supporters of the school became discouraged. ... Full experience has therefore shown that it is a pernicious labour to teach English to the Chinese, and that the only safe method is to teach them Christianity through the medium of their own native tongue.' Possibly concerned that if his most promising students continued at the school without his support, they too might succumb to misusing their English language skills, Brown raised money from a number of local businessmen to enable three students to accompany him to America, one being Huang Kuan. In America the three were admitted to Morrison Academy in Massachusetts, the first Chinese students to enter an American college. There Huang studied literature.

In 1850, having decided to study to become a doctor, Huang travelled to Scotland to train at Edinburgh University Medical School as it was renowned as a leader in its field and employed many notable teachers. Huang excelled in his studies, particularly under Professor John Balfour, in whose botany class Huang won a number of prizes. In spite of his academic achievements, Huang was running short of funds and faced having to terminate his university studies. Fortunately, help came from a Students' Aid Scheme introduced by the Edinburgh Medical Missionary Society. Founded ten years previously by a group of doctors, its aim was to 'circulate information on medical mission and assist as many Missionary stations as their funds would permit'. As Huang's application for assistance stated that he 'resolved to study medicine, with view to evangelistic labours among his fellow-countrymen' the Society agreed to pay his university fee of £18 10s. In 1855 Huang graduated from Edinburgh University, having presented a dissertation on the functional disorders of the stomach, and was also awarded a Diploma of the Royal College of Surgeons of Edinburgh. The news of him becoming the first Chinese university graduate in Britain was widely reported in the British press. The Edinburgh Medical Missionary Society was impressed by their new doctor: 'Your committee cannot but rejoice in the assurance that thoroughness, soundness, and accuracy in professional knowledge, dexterity and skill in practice, with amenity of manners and kindness of heart, are in the person of their brother, Dr Huang' and arranged for him to become the colleague of Dr Hobson, their medical missionary in Canton. However, the two doctors did not see eye to eye and Huang left to open his own dispensary where he 'exerted himself to discountenance the sale and consumption of opium'. In Canton Huang performed types of surgery never seen before in China, placing him at the forefront of medicine in Asia at the time. He is credited with educating a new generation of Chinese to the wealth of knowledge in Western medicine.

Another son-in-law of Fuk-Tong, Ng Choy, studied law in Britain. Due to the missionaries' influence, Fuk-Tong had included his daughters in his will, something not normally done by Chinese, and thus his daughter, Rose Ho Mui-ling, had money of her own. When she married Ng Choy, who was working as an interpreter at the Hong Kong Magistrate's Court, she provided the necessary support for him to fulfil his ambition to travel to London to study. Ng and Rose lived in London while he attended his law course. In 1877 Ng successfully passed the examinations of the Inns of Court in London, becoming the first Chinese to qualify as a barrister. They then returned to Hong Kong where Ng became the colony's first Chinese barrister. In 1880 he was appointed the first Chinese unofficial member of the Legislative Council and was the first Chinese to hold the post of magistrate. In 1896 he was appointed Chinese Minister in America. Ng's later participation in China's Self-Strengthening Movement and the Chinese Revolution of 1911 brought him the post of Minister of Justice in Sun Yat-sen's first cabinet.

Two of Fuk-tong's sons also studied in Britain. Ho Wyson was the second Chinese to study law in Britain, completing his studies in 1887. On his return to Hong Kong he became the colony's first Chinese solicitor, though it was said that his career was somewhat handicapped by his extraordinarily short business hours. It was joked that his working hours were from twelve to three, with one hour for drinks. Sadly, this relaxed approach to work did not save him from an early death in 1891. His brother Kai Ho Kai attended school in Margate in 1872 and then went on to study medicine at Aberdeen University. After graduating in surgery and completing his clinical studies at St Thomas's Hospital, he also studied law and became a barrister in 1882. While in London he met and married Alice Walkden, the daughter of John Walkden who owned a warehousing business in Cheapside. Kai and Alice moved to Hong Kong,

Studious Endeavours

but Alice died of typhoid two years later. In Hong Kong, Kai, reputed to be the first Chinese to wear Western clothes, strove to encourage an acceptance of Western medicine and was instrumental in establishing the Hong Kong College of Medicine for Chinese that later became the University of Hong Kong. He also continued to use his legal training, becoming a Justice of the Peace and a member of the Hong Kong Legislative Council. Kai is reputed to have influenced Sun Yat-sen's ideas while Sun was studying medicine and, throughout his lifetime, Kai was a vocal supporter for Sun Yat-sen and the idea of a Chinese Republic. The Colonial Office awarded him with a knighthood in 1912, the first Chinese resident in Hong Kong to be so honoured and the Kai Tak Cruise Terminal in Hong Kong is named after him.

Other Chinese who came to Britain before 1900 to study include Hok Tang Chain, who studied Natural Philosophy and Chemistry at Glasgow University, and Ts'o Seen Wan, the son of a merchant, who studied law at Cheltenham College and set up his own law practice in Hong Kong. In 1896, Wu Lien-the, the son of a Chinese father and a Malayan mother, came to Britain to study medicine at Emmanuel College, Cambridge, and proved a remarkable student, winning many prizes. Following his graduation he trained at St Mary's Hospital, London. Wu returned to the Straits Settlement and joined the Institute for Medical Research in Kuala Lumpur as the first research student. In spite of his expertise he was never promoted to a senior post as at this time only British nationals could become medical officers or specialists. Dr Wu later became Vice-Director of the Chinese Government's Imperial Army Medical College. In 1910, he travelled to Harbin to investigate an unknown disease that killed 99.9% of its victims. This was the beginning of the large pneumonic plague pandemic of Manchuria and Mongolia, which ultimately claimed 60,000 lives. Dr Wu managed to obtain imperial permission to cremate the plague victims, something previously prohibited in China, thus suppressing the plague. His decision was a significant point in the modernisation of China's medical services and medical education.

Another early medical student was Cornelius Suvoong who came from Shanghai to study medicine at Aberdeen University. After graduating in 1903 he then undertook further study in Tropical Medicine and Hygiene at Cambridge and in 1908 published a treatise on floaters in the eye. In 1899, while studying at Aberdeen, he applied for British naturalisation but his application was refused and so in 1909 went back to China. On his return he was raised to the rank of mandarin and placed in command of the Hankow Arsenal, but in 1911 he was forced to flee on one of the Government's gunboats when rebel forces attacked the city.

Vivian Ernest Chang's application to become a British citizen was successful, no doubt in part to his being the son of the Secretary of the Chinese Legation in London. In the early 1880s, Chang had attended Allesley Park College in Warwickshire, a boarding school that unusually gave prominence to scientific subjects and prepared students for university entrance examinations. The school's education approach was particularly appropriate for the young Chang, who planned to become a doctor, as the headmaster Thomas Wyles explained: 'My experience as a schoolmaster has revealed to me many cases where the talent for language or mathematics has been so low that the education effected by these has been of the meanest kind; or where the incessant failure has produced a stolid ignorance, a kind of mental paralysis, most disheartening to all concerned. Such cases have come into my hands, and I have seen intelligence rekindled, and mental power aroused, by simple science-teaching, and the power even for other subjects enhanced thereby.' In 1886 Chang began studying medicine at Glasgow University, and there met his wife, Louise. After he graduated as a doctor, they went to Shanghai where Chang set up in practice and 'was greatly esteemed for his amiable geniality combined with an uprightness of character'.

When their first daughter was born the Changs were required under Chinese law to have her feet bound. Louise refused and so the family travelled back to Britain and settled in Leeds, where Chang worked as a family doctor. It was at this point that Chang became a naturalised British subject. The Changs had four daughters, although one died in infancy. Two of the Chang daughters studied at The Leeds College of Dramatic Art and it was reported: 'In *The Backward Child* Miss Vivian and Miss Beatrice Chang, two clever young sisters, brought out the humour of the laughable little farce in quite delightful fashion, and Miss Vivian Chang found scope again for her buoyant sense of fun in *The Wooden Soldier*. Altogether the evening was one to score as a complete success for the talents of the rising generation.' Whether the sisters made a career in the theatre is not known.

Beatrice married Rev'd Hubert Sparling, Vicar of Duckininster, in 1922. The other two daughters remained unmarried and all three lived into their eighties. In 1930 Vivian Chang was killed in a motor accident when his car 'ran backwards down a steep and icy slope'.

12

Delicate Diplomacy

> Vigilant and careful,
> As if coming to an abyss.
> Fearful and wary,
> As if treading on thin ice.
>
> *The Book of Odes*

Bin Chun, 1866.
(*Illustrated London News*)

The Chinese in Britain

China was rightly proud of its rich history. Over thousands of years the country had evolved into the largest, most populous, technologically most advanced, and best-governed society in the world. From this evolved the view that China was strongest through consolidating its rule internally and defending its borders. Unlike Europe, its rulers had no desire to explore the world or expand the empire as they believed their culture and society to be superior to any other. Thus up until the nineteenth century few educated Chinese had any interest in exploring foreign cultures and ideas, and China remained indifferent to establishing formal diplomatic relations with foreign countries.

By 1790, the East India Company (EIC) was keen to see the trade restrictions that China imposed in Canton eased and to have new ports for British trade established in China. There also were some in Government who were unhappy about the EIC's secretive and illegal trade in opium to finance tea purchases and they believed that if Britain could establish a permanent embassy in Peking, the Chinese Government could be persuaded to buy new British products and so reduce the trade in opium. One of the leading voices arguing for this approach was Earl Macartney who had served in India as Governor of Madras. Thus, in 1793, it was agreed that Macartney should lead a diplomatic mission to China that became known as The Macartney Embassy. Unfortunately, no one who spoke Chinese could be found in Britain to travel as interpreter. Even though the EIC's trade with China had grown significantly, the Company had made no attempt to develop any proper understanding of the language. While the EIC colleges began to teach Persian, Hindu and Sanskrit in the first decades of the nineteenth century to better enable trade in India, no attempt was made to teach Chinese. Thus the embassy recruited four Chinese Catholic priests from Naples to act as interpreters. It was then discovered that although all four priests spoke Latin and Chinese, none knew any English.

One of the four recruited was Li Zibiao. He was born into a Catholic Chinese family and, at the age of twelve, taken to a Roman Catholic seminary in Naples where Chinese boys were trained as priests, before returning to China to preach and convert the population. He had been at the seminary for twenty years and this would be the first time he returned to China. During the voyage, Thomas Staunton, the twelve-year-old son of Macartney's secretary, George Staunton, learnt Chinese from the priests and, when three of the priests abandoned the mission at Macau, it was left to Li Zibiao and the young Thomas to act as interpreters. Thomas was later employed as an interpreter for the EIC and became a Member of Parliament.

A major issue of contention was the relative status of the two sovereigns, George III and the Qianlong Emperor. Macartney believed that Britain was now the most powerful nation on Earth, and the Chinese believed their emperor, known as the Son of Heaven, to have no equal. Anyone meeting the emperor was required to undertake the ritual of the kowtow, in which

Delicate Diplomacy

the individual kneels with both knees on the ground and bows so as to touch their forehead to the ground, but the British deemed this ritual demeaning. Macartney demanded that the ceremony must present the two monarchs as equals. Eventually a compromise was reached. At the meeting with the emperor, Macartney genuflected as he would have before his own sovereign, touching one knee to the ground, but avoiding the usual hand kissing, as it was not customary for anyone to kiss the emperor's hand. He then exchanged gifts with Qianlong and presented George III's letter. Young Thomas Staunton was beckoned by the emperor to speak a few words. In spite of the gifts the Macartney Embassy was unsuccessful as the emperor rejected the setting up of a permanent British consulate in China.

Nor did it do anything to alleviate the mutual lack of knowledge and understanding on both sides. Relations between the EIC and the Chinese Government grew more fraught and there were regular misunderstandings and clashes. In 1815 one journal reported:

> We have obtained several documents elucidatory of the causes and nature of some recent discussions between the Viceroy of Canton and the Committee of Supercargoes (merchants), which at one time threatened, not only to end in the suspension of all amicable intercourse, but in a declaration of open war. They disclose determined spirit of encroachment and aggression on the part of the Chinese, the evident tendency which, if not timely checked, was to annihilate the privileges of the factory, and reduce its members to be the unresisting dependents of a government, notoriously tyrannical and oppressive.

To attempt to introduce better relations between the two countries the British Government decided to send another embassy to China and in 1815 Lord Amherst was appointed Minister Extraordinary and Plenipotentiary to the Emperor of China. Unlike the Macartney Embassy, the Amherst Embassy was better equipped in regard to interpreters as in addition to the now grown-up Thomas Staunton, the party included the Chinese-speaking missionary Robert Morrison. The third interpreter was Thomas Manning who, intrigued by China, had learnt the language in France. He then travelled to Canton with the EIC and after some time became determined to explore the Chinese interior, in spite of it being forbidden for foreigners to leave the confines of Canton. He ignored the prohibition and after various failed attempts managed to make his way to Lhasa, the holy city of Tibet, assisted by a Chinese servant. Unable to travel further he had returned to Britain.

Amherst's Embassy sailed to China in 1816 but the mission was a complete fiasco. This time the Chinese were not prepared to compromise over the required kowtow to the emperor. What was a wasted journey became even more of a debacle as the embassy's vessel was shipwrecked on the return journey. Amherst survived and when the second ship taking him back to Britain called in at St Helena he met the exiled Napoleon who is reputed to have said to the diplomat, 'China is a sleeping giant. Let her sleep. For when she wakes, she will shake the world.' Thomas Manning brought two Chinese back with him as he hoped to convince the EIC to employ them to prepare its employees for service in China by teaching the recruits Chinese and explaining the cultural context. However, the EIC was uninterested and both men returned to China.

By the 1830s China was growing increasingly troubled by the illegal opium trade as it was depleting China's reserves of silver and increasing the number of opium addicts. The lack of diplomatic channels between Britain and China meant that there was no mechanism to explore possible measures to alleviate the problem and in 1838 the Chinese emperor decided to act. With no advance warning the Chinese raided the foreign factories in Canton and confiscated about 20,000 chests of opium, blockaded trade, and confined foreign merchants to their quarters. In response the British Government sent an expeditionary force to China and over the next two years Britain and China fought the First Opium War, the first large-scale military conflict between the Qing Empire and a Western imperial power. Some in Britain objected to the war. Thomas Arnold wrote:

> This war with China ... really seems to me so wicked as to be a national sin of the greatest possible magnitude, and it distresses me very deeply ... Ordinary wars of conquest are to me far less wicked, than to go to war in order to maintain smuggling, and that smuggling consisting in the introduction of a demoralising drug, which the Government of China wishes to keep out.

However, Britain's commercial interests demanded that the war continue to a conclusion and eventually the Chinese forces were defeated, with the Qing Dynasty forced to sign a series of agreements that became known as 'The Unequal Treaties'. These included transferring Hong Kong to the British and from 1843 it became a British colony. The war also revealed the military weakness of the Qing Government, which encouraged Britain and other European countries to pressure the Chinese into opening up trade channels. China's attempts to resist these demands resulted in defeat in the Second Opium War and China was compelled to agree further concessions, including allowing Christian missionaries to proselytise within China. By 1860 China was humiliated. The country had been partitioned by the Western powers, the corrupting influences of opium continued unchecked, the traditional values of an entire culture were threatened by Christian missionaries, and internal strife and famine were widespread. Not only was the Qing Dynasty's power gravely weakened but by 1865 China was forced to borrow £1.5 million from Britain, the country's first international debt.

Another outcome of its defeat was that China was forced to accept the posting of foreign diplomats in Peking, although it continued to resist appointing Chinese ministers abroad. In 1866, Robert Hart, the head of China's Imperial Maritime Customs, and Thomas Wade, British Minister at Peking, suggested to the Qing authorities that they send an exploratory diplomatic mission to a number of European countries, including Britain. In spite of widespread hostility within China to the plan, the Qing Government agreed but made clear that the envoy would have no official status. They chose an elderly retired official, Bin Chun. He was accompanied by his son, several Chinese students and Hart's English secretary, Edward Bowra, as interpreter. The group travelled for more than 100 days through Europe and in France. Bin became indisposed due to the exhausting round of visits and events. So when the group travelled on to Britain, Bin initially was too poorly to take part in the arranged appointments but the others participated in a busy and diverse schedule, which included visits to St. Paul's Cathedral, Pentonville Model Prison and Woolwich Arsenal; attending a Horse Show, an opera, a Flower Show and a burlesque. They even viewed a surgical operation. One of the students, the nineteen-year-old Zhang Deyi, kept a diary and one entry records a visit to The Polytechnic Institution in London, established to provide the public with 'a practical knowledge of the various arts and branches of science connected with Manufactures, Mining Operations, and Rural Economy'. One of the exhibits was a diving bell into which members of the public sat and were lowered into the water. Zhang wrote:

> It seems that the compressed air repels the water; the two elements being unable to share the same space. I and a British colleague entered the bell and descended to a depth of ten feet or more, but had no fear of drowning as the force of the compressed air was so powerful. It filled our ears as though we had stuffed earplugs into them and so we could not talk nor hear. When we emerged from the bell the bottom three inches of my Chinese gown were wet. My ears hurt too.

Unusually, the arrival of these Chinese visitors received little publicity and in their first week there were few invitations to society events. However, after it was announced that they were to meet Queen Victoria, they were showered with invitations, including to Lady Waldegrave's assembly and dinner with Lords Milton and Houghton at the Garrick Club. Queen Victoria recorded the meeting in her diary and wrote that the Chinese envoys 'looked just like the wooden & painted figures one sees'. There was criticism of the queen meeting what some regarded as a low-level mission, such as this letter to the *Pall Mall Gazette*:

> Sir, It is to be feared that in a very proper desire to show courtesy to the Chinese Mission, and to give them every opportunity of seeing things in this

country we are falling into an error which may be productive of serious evil consequences. When it comes to their being received in private audience by her Majesty ... it will be subject to misinterpretation in China, and lamentably certain to foster the old barbarian ideas of absolute celestial superiority. ... their rank is scarcely such as to entitle them. They had no audience of the French Emperor. There is no objection to their being made one of the adjuncts to the present brilliant London season, but the thing has now gone a little too far. If a reception of this kind he conferred upon them, what can we do more when a high mandarin of the Chinese empire is sent here?

On the first day of their royal visit the group were taken to Windsor and shown round the gardens and its collection of antiques and art. In the evening of the next day they attended a state ball at Buckingham Palace, given by the Prince of Wales. Bin was delighted: 'I almost fancied I had been transported bodily to the Lake of Gems in heaven, that the crowd around me were the golden-armoured Gods, or the Immortals of fairy-land and that I had bidden farewell to the world below!' During the evening, Bin had a private audience with the Prince who asked him how London compared to China. The envoy carefully replied, 'China has never before sent any envoy to foreign countries and it is only with this imperial commission that we have first learned that there are such beautiful places overseas.' Bin was similarly diplomatic when he met Queen Victoria the next day, who also quizzed him about the differences between Britain and China. Bin replied that British buildings and equipment were much more elaborate in their manufacture, and that Britain's political system also had many merits. The queen expressed the hope that Bin would pass his positive views of Britain on to the Government in China so that the two countries could become even closer.

The excitement of the ball and meeting the Queen may have been dampened to an extent by the group's tour of the industrial North, which included visits to a blind asylum, a school for the deaf and dumb, a coal mine, and various factories. At one stop on their tour, at Aston's, a firm of button makers, Bin's energy flagged as *The Birmingham Post's* extensive coverage highlighted:

> The variety of buttons that were made seemed to amuse the Commissioner very much; but the interminable succession of narrow passages and flights of steps appeared to give him some uneasiness. At length he betook himself to a small room where only a few young women were at work and there he remained. It happened to be teatime when His Excellency dropped in here and a blushing damsel offered him a cup of tea which he accepted and drank with evident relish.

Fortunately, the evening provided the Chinese delegation with some light relief from their factory visits as they were taken to see Hengler's Circus with its many equestrian acts, a pride of real lions and a 'Grotesque Pantomime'. The *Birmingham Journal* reported: 'The Chinese gentlemen were very much amused, and forgot the reputed soberness of their race so far as to laugh most hilariously, and clap their hands like their English friends.' One result of Bin's visit to Birmingham was that Ralph Heaton & Co., better known as the Birmingham Mint, developed trade contacts with China that led in 1887 to the company receiving an order for ninety coin presses and all the necessary machinery for setting up a mint in China. The Birmingham firm supplied workmen to oversee the mint's establishment and trained the Chinese officials in its operation. The Chinese mint could strike almost three million coins a day.

Towards the end of the group's stay in Britain, Edward Bowra's parents invited all the Chinese to their suburban house at Biggin Hill, and their neighbours must have been amazed when the Chinese party in their colourful clothes arrived in their street. Zhang Deyi's diary records the event: 'A bright sunny day and to Mr. Bowra's residence. After dinner our party went into his charming and beautiful garden, where we enjoyed ourselves immensely in playing croquet, dancing and singing songs; and continued suchlike amusements for the whole day.' Bin was both fatigued and jaded after his five weeks in Britain, and may well have been happy to have stayed in the Bowra's garden, or better still boarded a ship for China, but he and his companions had seven more European countries to visit.

In 1867 a second Chinese mission arrived in Britain after visiting America. This was led by Ansom Burlingame, an American politician who had visited China and was seen by the Chinese as sympathetic to their desire to resolve a number of issues with foreign countries, in particular the controls on Chinese immigration to America. The Chinese decided that he, being an American politician with diplomatic skills, would be better equipped to negotiate on China's behalf than any Chinese diplomat and so Burlingame was appointed 'Envoy Extraordinary and Minister Plenipotentiary from the Chinese Government to the Treaty Powers'. Burlingame was accompanied by two Chinese ministers, Zhigang and Sun Jiagu, two clerks, seventeen servants and two English-speaking interpreters, one of whom was Zhang Deyi. Perhaps because the British felt slighted by an American having been asked to lead the mission, or because the mission had first gone to America where it was well received, the British Government was lukewarm about the arrival of Burlingame. He was informed that that the queen was away in Sweden and as Parliament was not sitting, no senior officials were available to meet them.

Zhang again took the opportunity to visit a range of places while in Britain. He recounts a dinner party at which the diners 'amused themselves cracking walnuts. Somebody cracked one with his forehead whereupon they all began to bang them with their foreheads. Some succeeded while some failed, but all made a great noise in doing so. The onlookers put their tongues out in astonishment.' At a mechanised textile mill he was impressed by the Jacquard looms and made the prophetic comment that if China could apply Western methods, Westerners themselves would be in trouble. A number of his accounts highlight the tension between what he was seeing and his Confucian world view. When he visited London Zoo he was much taken by the many animals that he had never seen before, but noted that the zoo had not managed to collect a single dragon or phoenix, though he postulated that as these divine animals were mysterious creatures, they could not be captured. Following his visit to the Cambridge observatory, he acknowledged that the use of telescopes was more precise and far-reaching than the Chinese way of simply staring at the sky, but was disturbed by the Western idea that stars and planets were fixed entities independent of human affairs. 'If celestial objects do not change,' he wondered, 'how do they carry warnings from Heaven?'

In spite of deep-seated resistance within China to Western technologies, by the early 1870s the Chinese began to look to the West for ways to improve the country's equipment and expertise in certain areas. In 1872 the China Steam Navigation Company was established, the country's first non-military modern industry, and it commissioned a number of ships from British shipyards. In 1880, The Steam Navigation Company's general manager, Tong Ting Sing, visited Scotland to survey the construction of two steamboats, the *Fu Shun* and the *Kwang Lee*. Three years later a number of Chinese sailors arrived in Glasgow to crew the *Fu Shun* on her trial run:

> The vessel is intended for passenger and cargo trade, and is admirably adapted for both. The chief cabin is tastefully furnished, and will accommodate 36 passengers, and 560 can be comfortably berthed forward. The steamer was surveyed while constructing by Mr Tong Ting Sing, a Chinese gentleman, whose business capacity and high lingual accomplishments have made him not only the confidential agent of the China Merchants' Company, but also valued adviser of the Pekin Government in all that concerns trade with European nations. The *Fu Shun* and her sister ship the *Kwang Lee* have given this gentleman the highest satisfaction. The *Fu Shun* proceeded down the river shortly after eleven, and in run of precisely two hours reached the Red Head. Captain Andrews is aided in commanding the vessel by four English officers and three engineers, but the crew are wholly Chinese. The smart appearance of these was pleasingly commented on. The maid in attendance on Mrs Andrews and the captain's valet are also Chinese, and the pretty dress of the maid and the flowing pigtail of the man gave an agreeable Chinese local colour to the service in the cabin. The *Fu Shun* leaves our port for Glasgow on Saturday to load for the East.

In July of that year Tong Ting Sing attended the launch of the *Kwang Lee* in Glasgow and at 'the cake and wine luncheon' replied to a toast in his honour:

Delicate Diplomacy

> The Merchants' Steam Navigation Company is young in years, but it might be old in progress. (Hear, hear, and applause.) It began ten years ago, and since that time has had steamers built for the China coastal trade, and most of these are now doing excellent business. We are thoroughly satisfied with the vessels built by Mr Thompson and I am delighted to propose the toast; Success to the Builders. (Applause).

This move towards opening up China to new technology was encouraged by the new Chinese Emperor who, in 1875, sought proposals for further improvements to the Government and the country's development. Among the submissions was one by thirty-five-year-old Xue Fucheng, who argued that China should give greater focus to diplomacy and extend its knowledge of the Western world through research and study abroad. Although this had been what others had been arguing with minimal success, the Emperor was impressed by Xue's ideas and insisted on them being implemented. As a result, in 1877, in spite of conservative voices opposing the idea of an Ambassador to Britain, the Chinese Government appointed its first Minister to Britain.

13
Ambassadorial Engagements

A traveller could be compared to a floating swan beyond seas;
His tracks cover four quarters of the globe wherever he has been.
Among ten thousand evergreens there are two leading roads he sees.
The wheels of his carriage like the flash of lightning roll on.

> Li Hongzhang (1823–1901), composed in 1896
> on the way to meet Queen Victoria

The first Chinese Minister to Britain, Guo Songtau, arrived in 1877. He was an experienced sixty-year-old diplomat, but the conservative faction in China considered him to have liberal tendencies and so arranged for Liu Xihong, someone regarded as free of reformist sympathies, to be his vice-Minister. Liu was

Li Hongzhang and his delegation in Europe, 1896. (Collection of Tong Bingxue)

Ambassadorial Engagements

secretly briefed to keep an eye on Guo and report back on his conduct. Guo and Liu were accompanied by Halliday Macartney who had been appointed as the legation's secretary. Macartney had trained as a doctor at Edinburgh University and then served as a surgeon in the Crimean War, before going to China with his regiment. There he resigned his commission to join the Chinese army, which was subduing the Taiping rebels. He married the daughter of a Taiping Rebellion army general and they lived in Nanking, but when Macartney left for London his wife stayed in China and died there two years later.

Like most of the British press, *The Illustrated London News* welcomed Guo's appointment: 'China has at last awakened to a sense of her position amongst nations. Hitherto she has held herself aloof from the rest of the world, indulging in dreams of her former greatness, but now a gleam of light has broken in upon her. The halo of antiquity and her pride, and which still hangs around her institutions, she now sees has mystified and obscured her vision. She is now aware that, while she has been laboriously toiling the ascent of centuries, other nations, of which she never dreamt, or thought of only in her scorn, have come round the hill and, somehow or other, got between her and the summit.'

Queen Victoria mentioned the 'dignified bearing' of both Guo and Liu when she received their credentials and commented on their fur-lined clothes and fur hats. There was widespread public and media interest in the first Chinese Minister. On their way to the opening of Parliament, the new Minister and his deputy were cheered by on-lookers and at the opening ceremony they stood out. 'Clad in shiny black silk tunics, with but scant embroidery on the breast, and wearing as headgear peculiarly shaped caps apparently of brown plush (or some material closely resembling it), decked with a long scarlet feather, and further diversified by a bright red patch in the middle of the cap the representatives of China offered a striking contrast to their diplomatic colleagues, who, as usual wore uniforms plentifully embroidered in rich gold braid.'

Not long after arriving in Britain, Guo and his wife held a reception at the Chinese Legation. 'This is the first time a Chinese entertainment of the kind has ever been given in Europe by a representative of the Celestial Empire, and also the first occasion on which a Chinese lady had appeared in general society where gentlemen as well as ladies were assembled.' Guo's concubine also travelled with him to London and he encouraged her to learn English. In his confidential reports back to China, Liu specifically criticised the fact that Guo had taken her to the opera. Liu also sent a disapproving report stating that Guo had worn an English coat in cold weather. However, it did not need Liu's critical reports about Guo to convince the reactionary faction in China that the Minister needed to be replaced. Guo met key British technologists and in his dispatches back to China commended the benefits of railways, telegraph facilities, and modern mining methods, and bemoaned the widespread superstition in China that he believed held the country back.

Such thinking was anathema to the majority of those in power who clung to the notion that China could learn nothing useful from other countries. There were accusations that Guo was intent on making China subservient to Britain, and demand grew for him to be recalled and reprimanded. Although the Empress Dowager Cixi decided against removing Guo from his post, she agreed to the banning of the diary of his journey from Shanghai to London that he had sent back to China to be published, and the printing blocks that had been prepared were destroyed.

In spite of the critical response to Guo's views among the conservatives, he continued to argue that China would benefit from change. He actively visited Western institutions including universities, factories, prisons and government departments, and enjoyed a number of state occasions. Also, in spite of the banning of his previous travel diary, Guo continued to keep a journal. In it he described a dance party he attended in May 1878:

The room was filled with men and women, all dressed in strange costumes representing nations from around the world. Some wore the clothes of untamed barbarians and the North American wild men. One woman had on a pointed hat over a foot tall. When asked about it, she said that it was an antique hat made in England over a hundred years before. Another wore a hat that seemed to reach up to the sky with many layers of brilliant colours. She explained it was a design dating from the time of Louis XIV. Such tea parties are indeed quite a spectacle.

Guo also attended a ball given by the Scottish Association where he noted 'the dance music was noisier than ever.'

Eventually, the conservative clamour for his recall became impossible to resist and Guo was ordered back to China. Fearful of what might happen to him if he returned to the capital as a result of the criticism of his views, Guo chose instead to retire to his native village. Liu was appointed in his place but after less than a year as Minister, he too was recalled. In spite of his criticism of Guo's positive views about the West, Liu at times acknowledged that some Western technology was exceptional. He was especially taken by Britain's railways: 'Though the carriage moves at headlong speed, to the accompaniment of a continuous roar, the occupant experiences the same repose as he would sitting in his own library. The sanitation facilities at the end of the train are exceedingly satisfactory. Truly this is speed more miraculous even that what could be accomplished by shrinking the earth.' In spite of his enthusiasm for train travel, in his report back he carefully listed the many reasons why railways would be impracticable in China. Liu also was impressed by his visit to the British Museum:

Here one finds every type of zoological specimen – feathered, footed and finned – and botanical life, and all the rarities of mountain, river, forest, and jungle; in short, there are marvels not recorded in *Accounts of Diverse Things*, and treasures not listed in the pages of *Probing Antiquity* or *Examination of Rare Curios*. These objects greet the eye like a constellation of stars stretched out across the skies, each revealing its essential characteristics ... Through collecting material from far and wide, and even from the most obscure places, the British Museum displays a diversity of objects from a myriad of sources – all housed under one roof. Such is the Englishman's eagerness for learning and refinement.

A few months after Guo had been recalled, Liu himself was replaced by Marquis Zeng Jize who was appointed Minister to Britain, France and Russia in 1878. Unusually, he held the posts for seven years. Although Zeng had received a traditional Chinese education, he was one of the few Chinese officials who had learnt English and took an interest in European affairs. Before going to Britain, Zeng advised the British on the protocol relating to the wives of diplomats: 'They may only occasionally socialise with Western women guests; they will not be required to greet male guests and, in particular, will not attend banquets where male guests are present. If a guest happens to be a very good friend of the diplomat, the wife and daughters may be presented, but they will simply bow from a distance, and will not shake hands.' Yet by 1883 this protocol appears to have been relaxed. In that year Zeng rented a house in Folkestone for six months as this location allowed him access to both London and Paris. At a welcome ceremony held in the town Marchioness Zeng attended with two of the ladies of her suite, one of the first occasions when Chinese ladies participated in a public ceremony in Britain. In Folkestone, the Marquess Zeng introduced friends to the delights of Chinese food as *The Western Times* related: 'To two or three householders his Chinese cook unfolded some of the mysteries of his craft, and dishes were tasted at one house on the Lees which were not to be found in the English cookery book. The terrible secrecy was afterward allowed to be relaxed; and one dish certainly unknown till the Marquess settled in Langhorne Gardens may occasionally be met with among the best sets of dinner-givers in town.'

While in Britain, Zeng came to the view that there was a need for a Chinese 'national anthem' that could be played at state occasions as traditional Chinese music was difficult to perform on Western instruments. So he and his wife composed two anthems suitable to be played. One was *Hua Zhu Ge* which was played at The International Health Exhibition in 1884 in London by the visiting Chinese musicians. However, it was the other anthem, *Pu Tian Le*, that the British Foreign Affairs Office decided to use at official events. It was arranged for the piano by Sir Julius Benedict, a London-based German composer, with whom Zeng often discussed music. *The Musical Times and Singing Class Circular* described the work: 'This national air, supplied by his Excellency the Marquis Tseng, Minister of China to the court of St. James's, is built upon what is known as the "pentatonic scale" and certainly possesses very decided character. How far the harmonies written by so excellent a musician as Sir Julius Benedict might satisfy Chinese ears it is impossible to say, but it is evident that the arrangement of it has been a labour of love; and as, from the source whence it is derived, we may feel certain of the accuracy of the melody, we welcome the little piece as an interesting contribution from a country which has up the present time contributed but little towards the "World's delight" in music.'

In 1885, Liu Ruifen became Minister. This was a period when there was a rise in anti-Chinese attitudes and serious assaults against Chinese settlers in British colonies. As a result of Australia's gold rush, there was a large influx of Chinese to the colony and alarm among politicians and the miners in Victoria led the State Parliament to pass an Immigration Restriction Act. In Canada, many of the Chinese who had been taken from China and California to help build the railways were now unemployed and there, too, controls to limit Chinese immigration were introduced. This 'Yellow Peril' racism was also prevalent in the US and led to anti-Chinese immigration laws. Liu strove to convince the British Government to challenge this rise in Sinophobia but the British Government had little appetite to challenge the policies of its colonies in this regard.

After four years as Minister, Liu was replaced by Xue Fucheng whose ideas had helped establish the position of Chinese Minister to Britain in the first place. Since making his proposal to the emperor, Xue had proved himself an astute diplomat. During his tenure Xue visited many European countries in order to understand the impact of industrial development and explore how the different European political systems affected military power, education, law and finance. He published an account of his thoughts and experiences in Europe in his *Diplomatic Journal of Four Countries*. While in Britain, he wrote a letter home to his son in which he stipulated: 'All my descendants, whether male or female, should begin their education no later than the age of seven and study Western technology and the English language.' Equal education for women was an uncommon stance in China at that time. In a piece about the contrast between Western and Chinese medicine, he argued that there was a greater diversity to Chinese medicines: '(Western) drugs have only heating properties; they lack the functions of cooling, restoring and purging.' Yet he recognised that unlike Chinese medicine where the skills of great doctors died with them, Western medicine benefited from cures being documented, and thus disseminated and further advances made. In the areas of cooking and fashion, he certainly thought China far advanced: 'Where Chinese cuisine includes delicacies from the mountains and oceans, and employs all manners of seasoning and methods of cooking; Westerners know only to fry or stew their food, and they do not even know how good seaweed could be! The Chinese make their summer clothes from delicate, brilliant silk and in the winter from a variety of skins. Westerners all use black felt for their clothes, making them short and tight, quite unpleasant to look at.'

Ambassadorial Engagements

The sixth Chinese Minister, Kung Chao-Yuan, arrived towards the end of 1893. Robert Hart believed that as Kung had worked with Robert Macartney in Nanking thirty years earlier, they would work well together in London. Kung was reluctant to leave China to take up the position but eventually agreed, a decision he must have regretted as his time in Europe was fraught with political and personal difficulties. Like his predecessors, he was also Minister to France and his arrival at a time of heightened tension and fighting between France and China in Vietnam involved him in extensive negotiations. On 7 February 1894 Kung celebrated Chinese New Year at the Chinese Legation and the *London Evening Standard* described the scene: 'In the great drawing room, a kind of altar had been erected, symbolical of the Imperial Presence, covered with gorgeous yellow silk and satin, and ornamented with tapers and incense burners. In the forenoon, the Chinese Minister came to kowtow before the altar, making three deep obeisances, and his secretaries and attaches followed and did the same in the order of their rank, all being in full dress, and wearing their Orders and Decorations.' Kung must have hoped that the Year of the Horse would bring better days but it was even more inauspicious. By the middle of 1894 China was at war with both France and Japan, and Kung had to deal with tense negotiations with France, Britain and other European countries. Then, late in the year, Kung heard that his younger brother had been charged with cowardice in China and was under threat of execution.

China's wars with France and Japan fuelled internal turbulence and hostility to foreigners and in August 1895 ten British missionaries were massacred, leading to British warships threatening reprisals if China did not adequately deal with the matter. In London, Kung was under intense pressure and in the autumn fell seriously ill. For the next year he was almost wholly incapacitated. Thus in August 1896, when the distinguished Chinese politician, general and diplomat, Li Hongzhang, arrived in Britain for a three-week tour following similar visits to Russia, Germany, and France, Kung was not well enough to greet him at Southampton or host the customary welcoming reception at the Chinese Legation. Although Li Hongzhang had no formal ministerial role, his high status in the Qing imperial court meant that he was treated as a VIP by the British Government. The press, too, recognised his high status:

In every stage of his long official career Li Hongzhang has conferred great obligations on the Government he served by his skill in extricating China from perilous positions, and by the judgment and promptitude he showed in making inevitable concessions. ... In his capacity of peacemaker he was almost invariably successful, and to select but one instance, there is no doubt that he alone averted war between England and China after the murder of the missionary, Mr Margary, in Yunnan. Among his achievements in the way of material reform may be named the working of coal mines, the establishment of a navy – practically destroyed during the late war – and the introduction of a railway which seems destined to open up a great part of Northern China, and eventually to connect it with the European system. The merit of these achievements is enhanced by the fact that he accomplished them not merely single-handed but in the teeth of formidable opposition.

Li's party included his wife and two sons. One son was his adopted nephew, an arrangement made when Li had given up hope of his wife giving birth to a male heir, although later she bore him a son. Li was in his mid-seventies and two special chairs were built for his use. One was an adjustable reclining chair couch that was carried by assistants. The other was a wheel chair for when he was out and about on visits. Both had 'upholstery which is richly figured and richly coloured red velvet, the exact tint of which was chosen at the Embassy with a view to what in the Chinese Empire, where so much attention is paid to colour, would be considered as becoming to one of Li's high rank'. In spite of his age Li undertook a demanding series of engagements during his three-week stay. These included royal events, an inspection of the British fleet at Spithead, a visit to the House of Commons, a tour of the Crystal Palace and an evening at the opera. He also travelled to the North of England and Scotland. As well as undertaking a series of visits to industrial factories and shipyards, he found time for sightseeing, cruising on Lake Windermere and viewing the Forth Railway Bridge in Scotland. While in Scotland he heard the bagpipes for the first time and said how much he had enjoyed the sound as it was so like Chinese music. One newspaper wryly commented: 'By those who are familiar with Chinese music this is regarded as the greatest compliment ever paid to the bagpipe.'

Lady Southwark described a visit to her house by Li in her book, *Social & Political Reminiscences:*

He was the grandfather of a little girl of about five years of age, named Nua, whom he brought round with him one evening at Christmas time to a children's party at our house. Poor little mite! How well I remember her! Monsieur Hongzhang upon entering our hall divested himself of a magnificent fur coat, but Nua had to sit throughout a long evening in our warm rooms, muffled up in a thickly wadded silk jacket, exactly like the Japanese dressing-jackets which ladies now wear in their bedrooms, and out of which her little face peered with a strange, uncanny solemnity. She neither smiled nor opened her lips to speak throughout the hours she sat in our drawing rooms; but she showed no disinclination to eat, for she went down to supper with her grandfather and enjoyed a hearty meal, which included champagne. Her hair was quite hidden under a close-fitting cap, and her small fingers were loaded with rings, some of them very strange looking ones, and the little boys of my party every now and then took hold of her hands with awe and examined them with wondering eyes. One ring, I remember, had a chain attached to it, which must have made it very uncomfortable to wear. We invited Nua to dance, but of course, as her grandfather explained, this was impossible. On account of her poor little cramped feet Nua had to remain sitting in one place throughout the entire evening, gazing with most unchildlike gravity at the gay groups of noisy, happy-faced English children. I often wonder what the fate of poor little Nua has been.

Although Queen Victoria was in semi-mourning, and Li not an official Chinese visitor, he was of sufficient importance for a royal audience to be arranged. In August 1896 he travelled to the Queen's summer residence on the Isle of Wight: 'His Excellency will be conveyed from Carlton House terrace to the Victoria Station of the London, Brighton and South Coast Railway in the Royal carriage. On arrival at Portsmouth a royal yacht in waiting is to transport the Minister and his suite to Trinity Pier at East Cowes, which is used by her Majesty and her guests as a private landing stage. They will then be conveyed by Royal carriages to Osborne House, a distance of about a mile and a half.' The newspapers reported:

> The Queen received Li in the large drawing room, which also looks over the terrace, and is splendidly furnished, and filled with pictures, china, statuettes, and valuable cabinets. Luncheon was served in the Indian Room, it being the first time that it had been used since Christmas. The decorations of this apartment (which has cost the Queen about £20,000 altogether) are very elaborate, and it is magnificently furnished; but the Indian Room is rather a white elephant at a place like Osborne. Li was greatly impressed by the beauty of the Osborne grounds.

Victoria recorded his visit in some length in her diary, including the fact that Li's speech was translated by his son into 'badly pronounced English'. At their meeting Queen Victoria used a form of words that one suspects has been used by all later British monarchs when greeting Chinese dignitaries: 'It will always be my earnest desire to maintain the most friendly relations with China and to promote commercial interests between our two countries.'

Li was particularly keen to meet the illustrious politician William Gladstone, who was now in his eighties. The British civil servant in charge of his itinerary suggested there were many who might be offended if he went to see Gladstone while neglecting to accept the many other urgent invitations to prominent houses. Li replied,

> What have these other people to offer me? Bread and wine and musical entertainments? I have never heard of them, any of them, and what should I be spending my time with them for? The Queen, Her Majesty Victoria, of England and Ireland and India, her son, who will be King if

he lives, Mr. Gladstone, Mr. Morley, Lord Tennyson, and the Houses of Parliament, those were what interested me in England, and the ships.

So Li was invited to stay at Gladstone's house, Hawarden Castle, in Wales and he wrote of the visit:

Mr. Gladstone met me at the handsome, green-covered station upon my arrival. A great crowd of his country people were there, and hats were raised and handkerchiefs fluttered while our party descended from the train. Then there was long and hearty applause as we shook hands, both of us bare-headed. I do not know when before, in public, I have been seen anyone without a head covering. Mr Gladstone – for he is only 'mister' for he has refused the highest titles the British Queen could bestow — was much stronger in appearance than I had expected to find him; yet, when we were close together and sat face to face, I could see that he was an old man; much older in his face than I, although there is but nine years' difference, I believe, in our ages. ... Only here, in the home of the greatest living Englishman, have I found real rest since leaving the boat at Dover. Here I have enjoyed for a day such a rest as I have not known since bidding good-bye to China; for it is a pleasurable rest to see and know this 'Grand Old Man'. It is delightful to learn his thoughts and to see things of this world as he sees them. It is the highest prize of public service to be able to retire to such a home life as is his, amid the respect of the world and the love and admiration of his countrymen. If I could be any other person than Li Hongzhang I should want to be William Ewart Gladstone, the Grand Old Man of England.

As he left Britain Li wrote in his journal:

And it is so with London and England. I dined as the guest of Her Majesty at the castle, and great officers of state took me to the Parliament and to the forts and arsenals. I saw the fine parks of London and some of the great thoroughfares; yet I could see in the vast crowds so many people who were poor. Even in the short time of my journey I have learned to distinguish between the different classes of people by the clothes they wear. I cannot tell now of all I saw, nor of my fullest impressions; but I know that I have come to the conclusion that under a grand show many of the countries with great armies and fleets of ships have much misery hidden from the eyes of the world. China is not the only country where there are rags and hunger.

Although Minister Kung managed to rise from his sick bed long enough to see Li off at Southampton for the final leg of his tour in America, Kung had to take to his bed again immediately after. Eventually he was conveyed by ambulance to London Docks where he was assisted onto the P & O steamer,

Ambassadorial Engagements

Australia, to travel back to China. It was later said of Kung that 'he was very popular with foreigners, being a very genial old gentleman, with some knowledge of English, and an excellent appreciation of foreign cuisine.'

A significant figure among the officials who had accompanied Li to Britain was Sir Chih-Chen Lo Feng-Luh. He previously had spent time in Britain working for the first Minister Guo Songtau and had been appointed as Li's private secretary and interpreter. His skilled interpreting had been praised by the British press 'for his tact and perfect command of the English language have saved the dignity of more than one distinguished personage during Li's visit'. Chih-Chen Lo Feng-Luh was appointed as the next Minister to Britain and *The St James Gazette* was effusive:

> Sir Chih-Chen is at once able diplomatist, a scholar, and a thorough man of the world. He can converse on the light topics of the day as readily as anybody, while the scientist or politician will find in him a delightful companion. Your surprise at his mastery of English is soon merged in your astonishment at his varied and extensive knowledge. He will, therefore, be welcome: and all the more because, perhaps, when he knows our language better, he may tell us what those excruciatingly funny jokes that Li made really were. For they might just as well have been made in Scotch as Chinese, so far as our present comprehension of them goes.

As Queen Victoria was on holiday, the new Minister's formal presentation of his credentials was delayed until early May. It was almost embarrassingly further delayed as he and his entourage nearly missed the train to Windsor:

> The staff of His Excellency Lo Feng Lu, the Chinese Minister, were under a slight misunderstanding about the time which the train was to leave, and they arrived at Paddington station about ten minutes late. The signal was just being given for departure when Lo Feng Lu entered the station, gorgeously apparelled, and accompanied by an official carrying his credentials enclosed in yellow silk. Even under these circumstances, the dignity of the representative of the Lord of the Sun and Moon was not compromised. His Excellency walked to his carriage with imperturbable gravity and deliberation, saluting his fellow-diplomatists with ceremonial courtesy. There was a twinkle in the eye of Lo Feng Lu, whose acquaintance with European habits is sufficiently intimate for him to know that railway trains do not wait even for Ministers.

Although his credentials were wrapped in yellow silk and were beautifully written in Chinese and Manchu on a parchment more than a foot long and was reported 'a veritable work of art', it clearly did not make a sufficient impression on the Queen as her diary mentions the American Minister who also was presenting his credentials that day, but not Sir Chih-Chen.

The Chinese in Britain

Sir Chih-Chen brought his wife and sons with him to Britain but, sadly, within a year of arriving in London, his wife died, although she was only in her early forties. The newspaper article announcing her death said: 'Unlike her husband, who is a popular figure in West End society, Lady Lo was seldom seen in London, but tiny members of her numerous family might often be observed driving with their father to the Foreign Office on reception days, where, during the often tedious period of waiting while their father was discussing China, they would have the free run of one of the large waiting rooms, much to their delight.' Sir Chih-Chen remarried in July 1900 at a house in St. John's Wood, London that was specially decorated in Chinese style for the wedding.

Among the attendants who travelled to London with Sir Chih-Chen was the fifteen-year-old, Ye Jinglu. His mother worked as the family's maid and had arranged the position for her son. Ye worked in London until Chih Chen's term as Minister ended in 1901, and then returned to China where he became the manager of his family's teashop and pawnshop. Just before he left London, Ye had his portrait photo taken. Six years later, having just married, he decided to sit for a second portrait photograph. From that point on Yi arranged to have a portrait photo taken each year until his death in 1968, thus creating a fascinating depiction of one man's changes physically and in dress. The photos also provide a snapshot of the rapid political changes occurring in China. In the photo from 1907, Ye wears an outfit typical for men of that time but five years later his hair is short and he no longer wears a braided pigtail. Ye's 1949 portrait shows him reading the newspaper in a style that alludes to a revolutionary photo of Mao and by 1950 he has donned a 'Lenin cap', a style popularised by its namesake.

In early 1897, invitations were issued to heads of state around the world to attend Queen Victoria's Diamond Jubilee in June. The Empress of China selected Chang Yen Hoon, previously the Chinese Minister in America, and Chang sailed for Britain via Canada with twenty officials and a large group of servants. With him he brought a collection of gifts from the Empress of China to the Queen of the British Empire. Appropriately, he sailed on the *Empress of China* but unfortunately, not long before the ship was due into Vancouver, one of the other Chinese passengers on board was diagnosed with smallpox. As a result, the ship was ordered to halt offshore in quarantine. The Canadian regulations insisted on all passengers undergoing fumigation but Chang flatly refused, saying he would resist by force if necessary. The Canadian authorities warned him that if he refused he would be returned to China, to which the Minister replied that even that course would preferable to fumigation, though he would lose his head when he got there for disobeying orders. Urgent telegrams were dispatched to the British Government and the matter was satisfactorily resolved, allowing Chang to continue his journey by another ship.

In London Chang and his large party stayed at the Hotel Cecil, a recently opened grand hotel in the Strand. Although the programme of royal events

Above: Detail showing Tan Chitqua in *The Academicians of the Royal Academy* by Johan Joseph Zoffany, 1771–72. (Royal Collection Trust / © Her Majesty Queen Elizabeth II 2018)

Right: Michael Alphonsus Shen FuTsung in *The Chinese Convert* by Sir Godfrey Kneller, 1687. (Royal Collection Trust / © Her Majesty Queen Elizabeth II 2018)

Wang Y Tong by Joshua Reynolds, 1776. (Collection of the Knole Estate and National Trust)

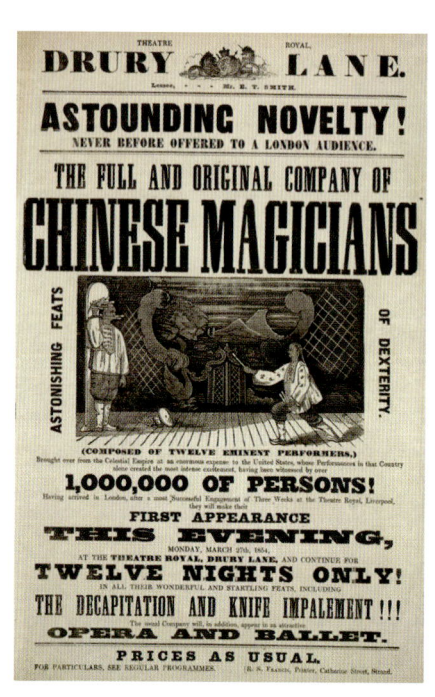

Above: James Legge and the three students who attended Duchess of Gordon's school in Huntly in 1846, engraving by J. Cochran after painting by Henry Room. (Public domain)

Left: The Chinese Magicians, Drury Lane, 1854. (Public domain)

Bottom: *The Chinese Junk, Keying*, engraving by Rock Bros and Payne, 1848. (Collection of the National Maritime Museum, London)

Above left: The Chinese 'family' who visited Osborne House. Hand-coloured albumen print, 1851, presented to Queen Victoria. (Royal Collection Trust / © Her Majesty Queen Elizabeth II 2018)

Above right: *The Great Chang Polka* by George Chisholm, *c.* 1870. (Public domain)

Below: Steamship crew *c.* 1890s. (Public domain)

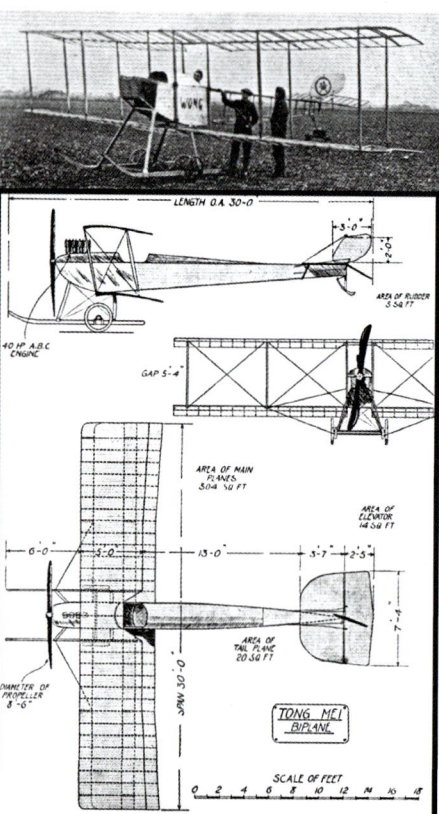

Above left: Ye Jinglu, first portrait in London, in 1901, and last in China, in 1968. (Collection of Tong Bingxue)

Left: Tsoe Wong's Tong-Mei biplane, 1913. (Photo – *Flight* magazine, public domain)

Below: The Mystery of Dr Fu-Manchu by Sax Rohmer. Published 1913. (Public domain)

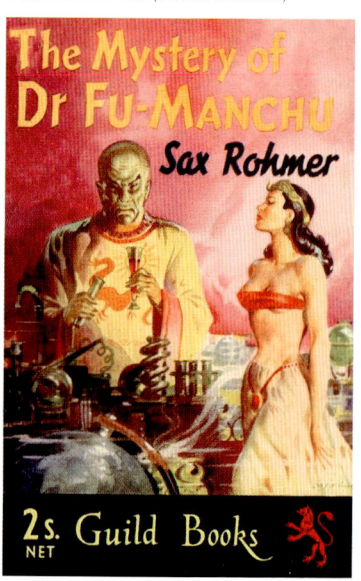

Mr and Mrs Wellington Koo, 1921. (Public domain)

Chinese actors in Somerset Maugham's play *East of Suez*, 1922. (Public domain)

Above: Xu Zhimo. (Public domain)

Left: Pitt Street, Liverpool, 1937. (Public domain)

The Story of Ming by Chiang Yee, published 1945. (Author's collection)

Grave of Kho Sin-Kie, East Finchley Cemetery, London. (Photo by Joseph Ma)

Recording *Miss Wang's Diary* at BBC, *c.* 1960, from left to right: Cheng Yao-Kun, Y. K. Lung, Doris Cheong (Miss Wang), the other three unidentified. (Collection of Lucy Boyle, née Su)

Charles Kao experimenting on optical fibres, 1960s. (© Nortel/Emilio Segre Visual Archives, Hecht Collection)

Kitchen workers watch the London Soho Chinese New Year celebrations through their window in the 1970s. (Courtesy of Alamy; photograph by Homer Sykes)

Chinese and British table tennis teams meet Prime Minister Edward Heath at 10 Downing Street, 1971. (Derek Tremayne Collection, courtesy of the ETTA)

Lucy Sheen and David Yip in the film *Ping Pong*, 1986. (Courtesy of Film4)

did not commence until 20 June, Chang immediately undertook a busy schedule of business meetings, including discussions with Sir Chih-Chen, meetings with British Government officials and the negotiation of a large loan for the Chinese Government. His first fortnight also included a number of social occasions and sightseeing. A few days after arriving, Chang and fourteen of his party visited Knole House as a guest of Lord Sackville, perhaps as Chang was interested to see the house where Wang-y-Tong had worked as a page for Giovanna Bacelli in the 1770s. He attended the annual *conversazione* of the Royal Geographical Society at the Natural History Museum; at the Royal Society, he saw Lord Kelvin demonstrate the electrical effects of uranium; he attended a dinner given by Sir James Blyth, with other dignitaries visiting London for the Queen's Jubilee; was a guest of the Prince of Wales at the opening day of the Ascot horseraces; and visited the Royal Arsenal at Woolwich, where a salute of thirteen guns was fired in his honour. When he attended a session of the House of Commons it was reported: 'Chang looked down rather impassively on a dull hour, when there was nothing more imposing than the tall figure of Mr. Hanbury rising to the table to answer questions. Yet the Ambassador himself who has a ruddy, animated, but Tartar kind of countenance seemed to be enjoying the explanations tendered to him.' On the last evening before the formal royal programme commenced Chang enjoyed a visit to see *The Circus Girl*, a musical comedy, at the Gaiety Theatre.

The formal royal programme began on the morning of Sunday 20 June when the queen, her family, and all the British and foreign dignitaries attended a service of thanksgiving at St George's Chapel, Windsor: 'An arrival who attracted a great deal of attention was His Excellency Chang Yen Hoon, the special Chinese Ambassador, who was attired in a picturesque national costume of rich silk. His Excellency was accommodated with a seat in the choir.' Perhaps the Bishop of London's sermon in honour of the Queen made Chang reflect on his Empress: 'Her Majesty has herself many qualities, and especially spontaneous and genuine sympathy with her people, of whom she had been the mother as the representative. She has pointed the way to higher things.' On Tuesday the Queen's Diamond Jubilee Procession took place. In the morning before setting out Victoria wrote in her diary: 'This eventful day, 1897, has opened & I pray God to help & protect me as He has hitherto done during these sixty long eventful years!' The day had been declared a public holiday and hundreds of thousands of people crowded the London sidewalks to watch. Vendors hawked souvenir jubilee flags, mugs and programmes, and soldiers lined the six-mile procession. The procession started from Buckingham Palace and was led by the queen in an open carriage pulled by eight cream horses. Behind followed carriages containing the guests and Chang was in the fourth carriage in the procession, with Monsignor Sambucetti, the Papal Envoy. As Sambucetti was dressed in the sombre clothes of an Italian ecclesiastic and Chang in brilliantly coloured robes, many in the crowd laughed at the incongruity, before cheering the pair. One reporter commented: 'The Chinese Envoy looked frightfully scared during the first part of the ride. He could not understand this enormous cheering multitude with nothing between him and them but a comparatively thin line of soldiers and police. In Pall Mall he was palpably nervous, but after a while he was reassured, and he sat back regarding these barbarians of the West with a sort of amused pity.' What Chang thought of the day is not known but the queen was delighted: 'A never-to-be-forgotten day. No one ever, I believe, has met with such an ovation as was given to me, passing through those 6 miles of streets, including Constitution Hill. The crowds were quite indescribable & their enthusiasm truly marvellous & deeply touching. The cheering was quite deafening, & every face seemed to be filled with real joy. I was much moved & gratified.'

Over the following five days there was a programme of further events for Chang to attend. These included a lunch hosted by the queen, a royal performance at the opera, a dinner hosted by the Prince of Wales at Marlborough House, a state evening party given by the queen, a luncheon given by The Lord Mayor of London in the Egyptian Hall of the Mansion House, and a garden party in the grounds of Buckingham Palace. On his third last day in Britain, Chang travelled with the other royal guests to Portsmouth where he boarded the Royal Yacht *Victoria and Albert* to watch the naval review: 'A gathering of warships in honour of her Majesty's sixty years of reign, the like of which may never be seen again.' On 2 July, Chang, and his large party, left Britain.

A fortnight later Queen Victoria took time to admire the gifts that Chang had brought from The Dowager Empress of China and recorded in her diary that they included 'marvellous specimens of Jade. China, stuffs, & most valuable'. The gifts also included Tibetan incense sticks for burning on the altar of longevity, a pine tree being the emblem of longevity made entirely of variegated candles moulded into all sorts of shapes and devices and a great embroidered silk hanging inscribed with Chinese characters for 'Glory and Honour'. Before Chang left Britain, Queen Victoria awarded him the Order of St Michael and St George, but his reward for service to China from Empress Cixi was rather different. In 1900 the Empress had him beheaded.

In January 1898 London's Lord Mayor hosted the annual Juvenile Fancy Dress Ball at the Mansion House. More than a thousand guests, including most of the foreign ministers, attended and watched a parade of children in a bewildering variety of costumes, including toreadors, the Mad Hatter from Alice in Wonderland, and three diminutive Napoleons in dark uniform and cocked hat. Sir Chih-Chen was accompanied by his sons, one dressed as Christopher Columbus, in red velvet and satin, and the other as Sir Walter Raleigh. In 1899 and 1900 Sir Chih-Chen travelled extensively round England, meeting businessmen and industrialists, and his two sons accompanied him on all his trips. While in Birmingham he spoke at the city's Chamber of

Ambassadorial Engagements

Commerce. When he told the gathering that it was planned to establish Chambers of Commerce in all the principal cities and towns of China, and that these might be upon the same lines as the Chamber in Birmingham, the local businessmen applauded vigorously. He also commented favourably on proposals to create a Chinese chair at the new Birmingham University, and at other British universities: 'I hope students will not learn Chinese in order to become archaeologists or collectors of old bonds and documents, but so that they may become practical merchants, and sign orders and contracts with the Chinese people and Government.' In many of the towns and cities he visited, banquets were held in his honour and his tour was generally welcomed. Like many newspapers of the day, the *Worcester Journal* commended the Chinese Minister's proficiency in English:

> Something of this success is due his perfect command of English, in a Chinaman unusual, and the mark of great intellectual adaptability. But he adds to this more than an average Englishman's acquaintance with our literature, so that he can make a Shakespearean speech at Stratford, quote Burns in Edinburgh, and in every town of literary associations say the right word; and, more remarkable still, shows a scientific bent and culture and a business capacity which make him quickly master of the essential facts of every manufacturing process which his visits to mills and workshops enable him to see.

The journeys provided Sir Chih-Chen with time to read and on one trip he avidly read all the Sherlock Holmes stories. He also enjoyed perusing London's art galleries. Before visiting, he would study the gallery's catalogue. 'At the National Gallery,' Sir Chih-chen said, 'I have often been amused at the utter ignorance of the people I have found there. They know nothing of the pictures, less of the artists who painted them, and the remarks they make are often decidedly stupid.'

By 1899 there was increasing reports of violence against Christian missionaries and persecution of Christians. This violence, fed by anti-foreign feeling within China, was being fostered by a secret society called Yi Ho Tuan (Righteous Harmony Fists) whose members became known as the Boxers. By 1900, the violence spread and there were repeated instances of the murder of foreigners, European missionaries and Chinese who had converted to Christianity. The Boxers wished to drive foreigners and Christians out of China, and also called for the overthrow of the Dowager Empress. As the rebellion moved towards Peking, the Empress secretly agreed to support the Boxers in their fight against the foreigners in exchange for her being left in power. In June 1900 it became clear that the foreigners living in Peking were in danger and they took refuge in the British Legation. There was a widespread view that Sir Chih-Chen was not responding appropriately to the violence towards Europeans and press coverage turned negative. *The Times* accused the Chinese Minister of duplicity and mendacity over the safety of the foreigners at Peking: 'Denials and excuses still issue from the Chinese Legation in London, and at present there seems to be no intention of intimating to Sir Chih-Chen that we are at war with his country, and that his presence in ours is no longer desirable.' In the face of such disapproval Sir Chih-Chen avoided all social functions. On one occasion when he went to dine at his London club, as he sat down all the other members left the room in protest. Those trapped in the British Legation in Peking were defended by an assortment of 400 European soldiers and sailors who managed to stave off the Boxers until all were rescued by an international force of 20,000 soldiers from Austria-Hungary, France, Germany, Italy, Japan, Russia, the United Kingdom and the United States. Angry at the murders of Europeans, the army ravaged the city and executed those suspected of being Boxers. The Boxer Rebellion was quashed by the international forces and formally ended with the signing of the Boxer Protocol in September 1901. Although the Dowager Empress had supported the Boxers, she was allowed to return to the Forbidden Palace in Peking. However, she was forced to agree to the execution of government officials who had supported the Boxers, the stationing of foreign troops in Peking and payment over the course of the next thirty-nine years to the eight nations that made up the international force of a sum equivalent to £8 billion at today's silver prices; more than the Government's annual tax revenue.

By late 1900, the press coverage of the Chinese Minister had returned to a more positive note:

> Sir Chih-chen Lo-Feng-Luh, is having a special motor car built that he intends to use for his official visits to the Foreign Office. If the representative of the most conservative nation on earth favours a motor car, it seems time for Britishers to rub their eyes, wake up, and not be left behind. The only disappointing thing about this proposed Celestial automobile is that it is to be absolutely plain. The Chinese Minister would certainly add to the picturesqueness of our streets if he had his car decorated with long-fanged dragons. I see immense possibilities in the way of ornamental motor cars.

Other staff in the Legation had to make do with a cheaper form of transport as *The Sketch* recounted in May 1899:

> Quite an interesting sight is to be witnessed on fine afternoons in the Royal Botanic Gardens, at Regent's Park. Several Celestials connected with the Chinese Legation are there cycling, in flapping satin trousers, blue silk jackets, red buttons in their hats, and with their queues swinging loose. And they cycle remarkably well indeed, Chinamen, strange as it may seem, are splendid cyclists.

Ambassadorial Engagements

In 1901 the Chinese Government announced that Sir Chih-chen was to be replaced as Chinese Minister and *The St James Gazette* commented: 'China has not sent into the outer world a more refined and cultured representative than the Minister who is about to leave London. Sir Chih-chen is as intellectual as he is Chinese.' One of Sir Chih-chen's last official acts was to travel by train again to Windsor on royal business, this time to attend the funeral of Queen Victoria in St George's Chapel in Windsor Castle on 2 February. *The London Daily News* reported:

> Sir Chih-Chen Lo-Feng-Luh, the Chinese Minister, in his silk robes chatted with a coal-black dignitary in Court dress. Near them, but walking apart, was the Japanese Minister. For all those personages Royal carriages had been dispatched to the station. But they preferred to walk to Windsor Castle on foot, and the carriages were sent back empty. At two o'clock the slow, solemn tolling of the bell in the Curfew Tower broke the silence which had hitherto reigned, and five minutes later the funeral train steamed mournfully into the station.

The Victorian era was at an end.

14
The Revolutionary

The whole world is one family.

Sun Yat-sen (1866–1925)

Dr Sun Yat-sen.
(Courtesy of the Library of Congress)

The Revolutionary

One of the key figures in bringing an end to China's dynastic rule was Sun Yat-sen and he was one of the last significant Chinese to visit Britain before 1900. Although he never met Queen Victoria, he was among the crowd in London cheering her Diamond Jubilee Procession in June 1897.

Sun was born in 1866 and while attending a school run by Anglican missionaries, converted to Christianity. Sun went on to study medicine and one of his tutors was Dr James Cantlie, a Scottish doctor, who had set up a medical training college for native students in Hong Kong. Soon after qualifying as a doctor Sun became involved with a group of revolutionaries, narrowly escaping arrest by the Qing Government by disguising himself as a woman and fleeing, first to Macau, and then to Hong Kong. There he re-met Dr Cantlie who provided Sun with assistance. Sun then went to America to try to gain support for his Revive China Society and in early October 1896, arrived in Britain. As Dr Cantlie was now living in London, Sun lodged for a few days with him and his wife before Cantlie arranged lodgings for him at 8 Gray's Inn Place. Sun spent his days studying at the British Museum library and on most days visiting the Cantlies.

On 11 October, while walking to the Cantlies' house, Sun happened to be passing through Portland Place when two sturdy Chinese men appeared and forced him into the Chinese Legation. Sun later claimed that he had been followed secretly from America by Imperial Chinese agents who had awaited an opportunity to kidnap him in London. Now a prisoner, Sun was certain that the Chinese authorities would arrange to smuggle him out of the embassy building and force him onto a ship to be taken back to China where, after being tortured to give up the names of fellow conspirators, he would be executed. So over the following days Sun desperately tried to convince the English servants in the legation to smuggle a message out to Cantlie, but without success. During this time no one was aware Sun was captive. Sun's landlady presumed he had gone to stay with Cantlie, while Cantlie assumed Sun was too busy at his London lodgings to come and see him as usual. Having failed to get assistance from any of the English servants, Sun threw notes addressed to Cantlie, weighed down with coins, out of his window but these were intercepted by the Chinese staff. His fate seemed sealed until a new servant, Henry Cole, arrived. Cole agreed to deliver a message to Cantlie and later recounted that Sun convinced him to help by appealing to class solidarity, but perhaps the decisive argument lay in the £20 that Sun handed over to Cole, with the promise of a further £1,000 to follow. When the doctor received Sun's note via Cole he tried to convince Scotland Yard to intervene, but the police refused, saying it was a diplomatic matter. So Cantlie then went to the Chinese Embassy and demanded to see Sun, but the legation staff denied that anyone called Sun was there. He contacted *The Times* with the story but the newspaper was uninterested. In desperation, Cantlie employed a private detective to watch the legation building night and day to prevent Sun being smuggled out. After a few more anxious days and pestering everyone he could think of, Cantlie at last convinced the Foreign Office that Sun had been kidnapped and the building was placed under official surveillance. While this prevented Sun's being smuggled out and on to a waiting ship, Sun was still a prisoner inside the building, which was officially Chinese territory.

Eventually *The Globe* printed the story under the headline: 'Startling Story! Conspirator Kidnapped in London! Imprisonment at the Chinese Embassy!' This forced the Government to act and the Prime Minster, Lord Salisbury, sent a personal note to Halliday Macartney, the ambassador's secretary, demanding that Sun be handed over to the British authorities. Halliday felt he had no choice but to comply and Sun was released. Although Macartney never denied that Sun had been imprisoned in the legation, he claimed that Sun had invented the story of the two sturdy Chinese. He alleged that not only had Sun shown up at the legation of his own free will, he had first come on 10 October and returned the next day. 'Whatever the pundits of international law may think of his detention, they may take it as being absolutely certain that there was no kidnapping and that he entered the Legation without the employment of force or guile.' It is possible Macartney's account was true and Sun went to the embassy and was then detained. If so, Sun may have been seeking to provoke an incident to create publicity about his cause, which he did, by publishing a short account under the title *Kidnapped in London* in early 1897. It is not thought that George Cole ever received the promised additional £1,000 for helping Sun escape but in 1923 Sun sent £100 to Cole's widow.

Sun spent the next fifteen years travelling the world, speaking to expat Chinese communities about his ideas, and encouraging revolutionary change within China. Through his efforts Sun is credited as the founding father of the Republic of China, which brought an end to the Chinese Empire. At the first presidential election in late 1911, Sun was elected President of the new Republic that was formally established on 1 January 1912. Soon after the establishment of the Nationalist Party internal disputes led to Sun being removed as President. In 1920 Sun established the Kuomintang of China (KMT) with headquarters in Canton, but the southern part of China remained in the control of warlords. When Sun Yat-sen died in 1925, Chiang Kai-shek emerged as the KMT leader in all but name and he eventually defeated the warlords in 1927, placing all of China under KMT rule.

PART TWO
1901–1987

15

Below Decks

The ship sailed due east all night,
Pitching, rolling, dragging a tail behind...
The pensive one, his eyes bleary for rest,
Remembers how in his home town
He traced the long course of a night
In the silvery trail of a snail on the windowsill –
'You say we made two hundred miles last night?'

Pien Chih-Lin (1910–2000),
translated by Lloyd Haft

Damage to Chinese laundry in Cardiff, 1911. (Public domain)

During the nineteenth century in countries such as Canada, Australia and the USA that had seen mass Chinese immigration, there was significant violence against Chinese immigrants and, in response, race-based immigration restrictions were introduced. However, in Britain before 1900 there was no equivalent widespread anti-Chinese feeling as the number of Chinese in the country was small, and almost all worked as seamen and resided in specific areas in London's East End, Liverpool and Cardiff. Yet in the early 1900s hostility to foreigners began to increase, encouraged by racist groups such as the British Brothers' League. Although the main concern was at the increased number of Jews coming to Britain to escape the pogroms in continental Europe, the National Sailors' and Firemen's Union (NSFU) used the anti-immigrant mood to launch a campaign against Chinese seamen.

In spite of increased concern about immigrants, opposition to the concept of closing Britain's borders meant that a number of Aliens Bills presented in Parliament during the 1890s and early 1900s were roundly defeated. Liberal British politicians believed untrammelled human movement was a key part of the free trade of goods and argued that Britain should defend its cherished tradition of extending asylum to the politically and religiously persecuted. But in 1905, this opposition was overcome and the Government introduced an Aliens Act, although the Liberals managed to ensure that the Act had an asylum clause that allowed entry to an individual who was religiously or politically persecuted. While the Act was not introduced specifically to control Chinese immigration, it made it difficult for any Chinese who wished to come to Britain. The law required aliens to have a job in the country arranged as a condition for landing, and few potential Chinese immigrants were able to fulfil that condition. Aliens could only land at designated ports, the main ones being London, Cardiff and Liverpool, and immigration officers had the power to exclude any they judged undesirable. The Act also permitted the removal of aliens who were considered unable to support themselves, along with their families, and those who entered the country illegally were deported if discovered. Furthermore, the Act decreed that a British woman marrying an alien automatically lost her British citizenship and became subject to all the restrictions on aliens.

A year after the Act was introduced, thirty-two Chinese seamen travelled from Liverpool to London seeking work without the required 'guarantees of employment'. There was protest by the NSFU at 'the dumping of Chinese labour' and the newspapers added to the outcry with the insinuation that this was an attempt to 'taint' British labour. The unfortunate Chinese were detained in London on their arrival and then sent back to Liverpool.

Last evening the liberated thirty-two stood on the Albert Dock quayside in the cold light of electric arc lamp waiting for four railway buses to come for them, a stolid, silent, unemotional crowd, oblivious of the fact that they had been making history. A queer medley of parcels, reed baskets, and bundles done up in fine canvas lay on the quayside, and each man, from the quantity of packages, must have brought a considerable number of household goods with him. They talked but little, and to the ribald cries of small boys who followed the buses along Commercial Road they were stonily indifferent. At Euston station an official, knowing no Chinese, whistled to them to alight, and a compatriot from Liverpool, taking charge of the party, bundled them with all possible speed through the station to the train, in order to escape the attentions of the fairly numerous sightseers. They sought refuge in the saloon at the front of the ten o'clock train labelled 'Chinese Seamen Party', the blinds were closely drawn, and the door locked. And that was all that London saw of the Thirty-two.

Protests by British merchant seamen against the use of lower paid Chinese crews became common and erupted into violence at a number of ports. In Glasgow, racial violence against both Chinese and black seamen led to local union leaders attempting to promote a segregationist policy in the port, and a call by some that all 'Blacks and Chinese' should be expelled from the industry. In 1908 Havelock Wilton, a trade union leader and Liberal MP, successfully persuaded the Government to introduce a 'language test' for anyone serving on British ships and promised British seamen that he 'would see that no Chinaman is shipped on board a British steamship unless he can pass a language test'. It was argued that seamen who did not understand English or had limited understanding threatened the safety of ships. Yet, in reality, it simply was a barrier to the employment of Chinese and other foreign seamen by shipping companies. However, many Chinese seamen were quick to spot that the law excluded 'British' seamen and large numbers began declaring that they were from the crown colonies of Hong Kong or Singapore and thus exempt. By 1910 it was noted that 80 per cent of London's Chinese seamen were claiming crown colony status compared with 30 per cent the year before. The anti-Chinese stance by the NSFU fed prejudice among white British seamen who believed the use of Chinese labour threatened their jobs. In 1908 violent clashes occurred when British seamen repeatedly stopped Chinese crews from signing on at the Board of Trade offices at East India Dock Road, a few hundred yards from Chinatown. The police had to intervene and after the Chinese had signed on, escort them safely home. The NSFU arranged for the British seamen's concern to be raised in Parliament and Winston Churchill responded that the Government was equally concerned about the use of Chinese labour on British merchant ships.

In 1911 British seamen in a number of ports went on strike and to break the strike, shipping companies employed Chinese to man their ships. This further incensed the British seamen and Chinese sailors were again attacked. In the worst incident British seamen rampaged through Cardiff, attacking and setting fire to all thirty Chinese laundries in the city and to a number of lodging houses.

The NSFU organised protest meetings, claiming the shipowners were employing Chinese because they were cheaper. In response, Glen & Co, shipowners in Glasgow, wrote to the union:

> You are quite mistaken in thinking that it is for motives of economy that we carry Chinese firemen in our steamers. The wages are practically the same as with Europeans. We would, however, be quite prepared to pay considerably higher wages to Chinese than we would to Britishers. They are much more sober, steady and their work much more efficient. We would suggest to you that your Union should turn its attentions to providing a better class of men, as the present standard is deplorably low, and does not compare with the class of foreigners which we are able to get. We quite agree with your remarks that it is a pity that British-owned ships are not manned by British seamen, but the fault does not lie with the owners. We take the best men we can get, and are sorry to say that the foreigner is the better man.

On 4 August 1914 Britain declared war on Germany and large numbers of foreign nationals who came from countries at war with Britain were interned or deported. As many thousands of these 'enemy aliens' had been working on British ships, and about 9,000 British merchant seamen were called up to serve in the Royal Navy, there was a critical shortage of men to crew merchant ships. This forced the Government to change its stance on the employment of Chinese seamen from negative to positive. The NSFU also recognised that the war effort at sea required foreign labour and although its opposition to Chinese seamen remained, the anti-Chinese protests were temporarily halted. In 1915 on *The Wapello*, an oil tanker, of the crew of fifty-three, forty-two were Chinese.

A small number of Chinese had become active in left-wing British parties and in the trade unions, where they strove to represent Chinese interests, gained experience in organising and agitating, and strove to create a Chinese seamen's union. Yet many left-wing British politicians who campaigned for the rights of workers hypocritically attacked Chinese and other immigrants for 'stealing white jobs'. Those who were sympathetic supported the idea of a Chinese union, and the Chinese activists were encouraged by the establishment of the Republic of China and the call by its President, Sun Yat-sen, for his followers to campaign for labour unity. Thus, in 1912 the first union was established but this resulted in violent clashes in Limehouse between those Chinese who supported the idea of a union and the Chinese 'boarding masters' who controlled the seamen while in port, as the union threatened their power over the allocation of jobs. Although this first attempt was unsuccessful, in 1916 the Chinese Seamen's and Firemen's Association was established in Liverpool, with Lee Foo as the local secretary. In the following years the union campaigned to break the Chinese boarding-masters' monopoly on recruiting labour.

The Chinese in Britain

In spite of the bravery of Chinese sailors in Britain's war effort, protests against the employment of Chinese labour resurfaced. At the Trade Union Congress in 1916, a motion calling for the repatriation of all Chinese was proposed. Although the Government did not accede to this trade union demand, when the war ended the authorities introduced an extension to the Aliens Act that specifically introduced restrictions on the employment of aliens in the merchant service, and added penalties for incitement to sedition, or promoting industrial unrest. The Government also encouraged voluntary repatriation of many Chinese seamen and forced a large number to move to France to join fellow Chinese working there as part of the Chinese Labour Corps. Given this government pressure and the continued anti-Chinese attacks, both verbal and physical, large numbers of Chinese seamen were happy to return to China.

Violent protests against Chinese labour and race riots re-emerged after 1918, with Chinese homes and property damaged in London, Cardiff, Glasgow and Liverpool. In response, various Chinese-led organisations, such as The Zhong Shan Mutual Aid Workers Club, were established to unite the overseas Chinese in Britain, to campaign against the racial attacks and fight for improvements to their working conditions. Between the wars more than half the Chinese seamen employed on British merchant ships worked for the Blue Funnel Line in Liverpool. Their treatment on board the ships varied enormously, but many would have echoed the view of one. 'Most of the officers were bone-headed and treated Chinese seamen as if they were mentally retarded.' The anti-Chinese mood among British seamen and the NSFU continued into the 1930s but, again, the outbreak of the Second World War brought a temporary end to demands for fewer Chinese to be employed on British ships. Instead, the main shipping companies in Liverpool recruited about 20,000 Chinese to work on British merchant ships and oil tankers. This significant increase in Chinese seamen resulted in up to 3,000 being based in Liverpool at any one time, and those not boarding on docked ships had to cram into miserable hostels; often with up to sixty men packed into a single room. In addition to the grim living conditions, the Chinese seamen were only paid around one third of the wages of British seamen and were denied the war-risk bonus paid to the British, in spite of many being killed in action.

The sense of injustice among the Chinese seamen led to many refusing to work. Those who had completed their initial contracts refused to sign up again, while others went on strike. In October 1940, twelve Chinese firemen appeared before a Liverpool Magistrate charged with refusing to obey the commands of a ship's officer. They were accused of mutiny and attacking the 3rd and 4th officers with weapons before the ship's master had restored order with a pistol. In spite of the accused men denying the charges, a number were jailed for fourteen days. Similar incidents saw many more imprisoned for simply removing their labour in response to injustices. Those

Chinese seamen protesting against unfair treatment were regarded by the Government, shipowners and ship's officers as constant troublemakers and the most persistent complainants were deported to China. However, in late 1941, Japan's invasion of Hong Kong and Singapore, and the internment of British subjects in Shanghai, made it impossible for the authorities to repatriate striking seamen to China.

In 1942, the Chinese Seamen's Union, a branch of the Kuomintang Government in China, was established and Kenneth Lo, later the celebrated writer of Chinese cookbooks, was employed by the Chinese Ambassador to become the union's organiser. Lo arrived in Liverpool just as another strike began involving 450 Chinese seamen working on a Canadian Pacific Empress liner that was to carry troops to Africa. The shipping companies and port authorities threatened to sack them and withdraw the men's right to land in Britain. Lo and other union representatives tried to convince the British authorities to give in to some of the seamen's demands and so end the strike, but without success. Eventually, news of the stand-off reached Chiang Kai-shek, China's Foreign Minister, and he threatened the complete withdrawal of the total force of Chinese from the Allied fleet unless the British gave way. This threat carried weight and in April 1942, the Government finally was forced to settle. Chinese seamen received a £2 per month flat increase in their pay, received the war-risk payment and improved compensation was provided for relatives of deceased seamen. Yet when, six months later, British seamen were awarded a pay rise, the Chinese were not.

The Communist Party of Great Britain helped a secret Chinese Communist Party branch to form in Liverpool and it became an alternative union, swiftly gaining members. At its wartime peak, the Communist Seamen's Union is said to have had more than 10,000 members in Liverpool.

Although the Chinese seamen were essential to the war effort, the British Government was ambivalent about their employment and the shipowners were unsympathetic to the seamen's struggle for better conditions and pay. Yet in much of the press they were lauded.

> The Chinese seaman of today is very different from his predecessor of a generation ago. He is a child of the revolution and a soldier of China. Often as an engineer, fitter, joiner, repairer, he is doing highly skilled work he never did before and doing it well... New Chinatown is a microcosm of New China and in both, for the first time in the history of their race, all classes are welded into the common pool of emergent nationhood.

The British Council, and other organisations, provided trips for selected groups. A hundred Chinese seamen were taken to Chester by Yen Sang, the Chinese Welfare Officer in Liverpool, and there shown round the town and after lunch at the British Restaurant enjoyed a trip on the river. Chinese seamen working on British ships were active in supporting

China's war against the Japanese and sent large sums to China to support the war effort. 'I was told of seamen who, returning from a long trip, subscribe the whole six months' earnings at one bang,' reported one journalist. 'The Chinese War Victims' Fund receives from Liverpool about £1,000 a month, most of it contributed by seamen.'

When the war ended, the shipping companies swiftly moved to cut costs and the wages for Chinese seamen were halved. Many of the Chinese seamen did not care. They were homesick and fed up of being badly treated, so happy to board the first ship sailing east and return to China. Yet there were many living in Liverpool, and a smaller number in other port cities, who did not wish to leave. Among these were union activists, and others whose justifiable dissent the shipping companies characterised as troublemaking, and the companies wanted them gone. The British authorities also were keen to reduce the overall numbers of Chinese living in the cities, particularly in Liverpool, as housing stock had been depleted due to war damage. Thus, in October 1945, the Home Office took the decision to expel those Chinese seamen who were not British citizens. In spite of no evidence of troublemaking, the 'plucky' Chinese seamen were now branded as 'an undesirable element in Liverpool'. Few of the Chinese seamen could be legally deported, so instead the men's landing conditions were changed so that they were required to leave by a certain specified date. Those who did not leave were rounded up by the police, placed on ships waiting in the harbour and taken away.

Although the Government determined that those who had married British women were to be excluded from repatriation, there was confusion about this point. Many of the husbands, and their wives, were not informed that they had a claim to stay, in part because many in authority found the idea of a Chinese man and British woman living together distasteful. Also the shipping companies avoided hiring many of those Chinese married to British women. Amid such pressure and confusion, many Chinese husbands and partners ended up being forced to leave their British families. In total, about 1,500 Chinese were repatriated by March 1946, of whom around 300 had been rounded up by the authorities.

In 1943, eighteen-year-old Grace was working in the canteen of Liverpool University where she met Nan Young, a Chinese ship engineer. They began to go out together despite her parents' disapproval. Grace was too young to marry without her parent's' consent and they were unwilling to give it. In spite of her family's disapproval, and that of the Roman Catholic Church of which she was a member, she decided to cohabit with Nan, and they set up home in Hull. Other British women also chose to cohabit with their Chinese partners, rather than marrying, as marriage to a Chinese automatically meant the loss of British citizenship, and wives became 'aliens' and subject to legal restrictions. In May 1945 Grace became pregnant and within a few months of the birth, Nan, legally unmarried and therefore subject to deportation, was shipped back to China. Grace considered going with him but was ill at the time so could not. She never saw Nan again and Nan never got to see his daughter. Only a few Chinese seamen managed to return to their Liverpool families. Many, such as Nan, simply vanished, while contact with those who tried to keep in touch withered due to the fluctuating political, social and economic situation. How many British women and children were affected is not known. The figure seems to range from sixty to 120, yet even if at the lowest end, the heartache and hardship that this iniquitous forced repatriation caused was significant. Some of the women ended up having to have their children adopted or placed in children's homes, while others struggled to provide for their families.

After the war ended the Blue Funnel Line continued to employ upwards of 2,500 Chinese seamen and a further 300 or so on shore in the shipyards. The majority of these were Hong Kong Cantonese. By the 1950s the relationship between the company and its Chinese workforce had significantly improved and the company was popular in the city. But by the 1970s, Liverpool had ceased to be a major port and as jobs on merchant ships shrank, Britain's long link with seamen from China came to an end. Those who had been working as seamen left Britain or moved to work in laundries or restaurants.

16

Chinatown

> Say not that East is East and West is West
> For they are whole-blood brothers none the less.
>
> Confucius (551–479 BC)

While many British seaports would have seen a few Chinese seamen passing through, the significant numbers were in London, Liverpool and Cardiff and it was there that resident Chinese communities formed, although by 1901 all were still small. Newspapers had written about American Chinatowns since the 1860s but possibly the first use of the term to describe London's Limehouse was in the *Pall Mall Gazette* of 1900, and a few years later the term was extended to cover Liverpool's Chinese neighbourhood.

In London there were two distinct Chinese communities in Limehouse. Those from Shanghai settled around Pennyfields, Amoy Place and Ming Street, while the Chinese from Canton and Southern China lived around

Design for proposed new Chinatown in Liverpool by Chen Zhanxiang, 1945. (Public domain)

Gill Street and Limehouse Causeway. Although larger numbers of seamen would have been staying in lodgings on a temporary basis, London's permanent Chinese community was little more than 100. Even by 1910 the Chinese businesses in the area consisted of just a few lodging houses, a handful of eateries – called at the time Refreshment Rooms – three or four tobacconists, a ship's chandlers, a tiny Confucian temple, and two or three grocers. One newspaper report described the area thus: 'The centre of Chinatown – its main artery, so to speak – is Limehouse Causeway. Despite its somewhat pretentious name, it is a frowsy, dilapidated, dishevelled district, with fully one-third of its houses in ruins, and quite 50 per cent of the remainder tenantless.' Although the area became known as Chinatown, the neighbourhood was populated by various immigrant groups, as well as native British. When George Orwell stayed there in 1928 he wrote: 'Limehouse was sprinkled with Orientals – Chinamen, Chittagonian Lascars, Dravidians selling silk scarves, even a few Sikhs.'

Liverpool's Chinese community, which was primarily Cantonese, clustered round Cleveland Square and Pitt Street. The Blue Funnel Shipping Line's steamer service direct from Liverpool to China, which had begun in 1866, employed significant numbers of Chinese seamen by the early twentieth century and thus Liverpool's Chinese community grew faster than London's. In 1906 a report identified forty-nine laundries, thirteen boarding houses and seven shops run by members of the Chinese community. The 1911 census records a boarding house run by Fong Jing, aged thirty-three, and his wife, Alice, aged thirty, at 6 Frederick Street, which on the night of the census housed nineteen Chinese seamen. Alice had recently had a baby and there also were four young children from Jing's previous marriage. One servant, Chin Lin Kee, was employed and he also acted as the cook.

In 1907, in response to accusations that gambling and drug-taking were rife in the city's Chinatown and responsible for young British girls being corrupted, Liverpool Corporation set up a commission to investigate. A journalist from the *Daily News*, Myer Jack Landa, visited Pitt Street to see for himself what the area was like and his article, unusually for the time, gave a balanced view:

> Compared with Chinatown in Limehouse in London, the area has very little foreign appearance. Many persons would walk through Pitt Street without noticing much out of the common. A stray coolie, in ordinary English clothes, might be seen shambling along, and a keen observer would notice one or two shops with Chinese notices and packages in the windows. The first impression of the visitor is that it is nine-tenths an ordinary English street, the second, that there is a touch of the Cosmopolitan about it. There is a Scandinavian lodging house, a Japanese Home, one or two shops with the names of the occupants painted in Greek on the signboards, and two or three Chinese establishments. I spoke to a manufacturer who may almost

lay claim to being the oldest inhabitant in the street – an Englishman. 'A lot of nonsense has been written about this street,' he said. 'I have been in it practically every day for forty years, and I have seen none of the murderous fights spoken of; I know of no opium and gambling and I say unhesitatingly that there are English districts not far off that are much worse.' 'A very peaceable lot of people,' was the verdict of another who has worked twenty-five years in the street. 'They don't interfere with the English people, although the latter sometimes interfere with the Chinese.' Pitt Street has been overrun with prying, inquisitive visitors of late, and the inhabitants, native and foreign, are not particularly anxious to give information, or be regarded as an exhibition. I succeeded in entering a couple of Chinese lodging houses. One probably is the most interesting in Liverpool, perhaps in England. It is licensed for twenty-six lodgers, and there were twenty-four Chinamen on the premises at the time of my visit. The proprietor also has a Chinese lodging house in London. His wife is an Englishwoman and she was nineteen when she married nine years ago in Limehouse. She manages the Liverpool establishment in her husband's absence. I could not help regarding it as the most remarkable tribute possible to the Chinamen that she was alone in charge of the establishment. The place was clean, and in this respect in striking contrast to many English lodging houses that I have seen. In the kitchen hung two tooth brushes with pieces of whalebone attached. These belonged to the two cooks. No Chinaman omits the duty of brushing his teeth and of scraping his tongue when he rises. As a rule, he will not say good morning until this is done. On all the walls were notices in Chinese, in the day room were Lodgers playing Chinese dominoes. In the bedrooms a few men hastily put away their opium smoking apparatus as I entered. But the pungent smell was there. There are 'dens', I was assured, but the Liverpool men have neither the time nor the means to smoke to excess. 'Besides,' said one of the residents in the street, 'I'd rather deal with a man under the influence of opium than one under the influence of drink. And the Chinamen don't drink and don't insult women.' 'Do they gamble?' I asked. 'I won't deny it,' was the reply, 'but no more than do the English people on horse racing and football. There are districts not far off where there are no Chinamen, and, believe me, they are less safe for ordinary people to go through.' There are two classes of Chinamen in Liverpool – the seamen, who are but temporary dwellers, and the laundry workers, and there does not appear too much love lost between the two. Each accuse the other of being the undesirables! And Chinamen who hail from different provinces do not regard each other favourably either. The laundries are not to be found in Pitt Street. They are scattered over the city, and some of them have been established many years. There are few Chinese females in Liverpool, and this gives rise to the chief evil. Yet the blame was placed by all of whom I made inquiry on the English girls who run after the Chinamen. The Chief Constable of Liverpool mentioned the same thing in his letter to the Immigration Board, and only on Wednesday two girls brought up in Court were accused of loitering about the laundries. Truth to tell, some of the young Chinamen, in their smart, well-fitting English clothes, are by no means unattractive in appearance. Whether the Commission which the Liverpool Corporation has appointed to investigate Chinatown will bring to light facts which may have hitherto remained concealed is doubtful.

In 1911 Charles King was one of the first Chinese to divorce his British wife. As he was the owner of lodging houses in Limehouse and Liverpool, one wonders if the divorced wife was the woman running the lodging house visited by Landa.

In Cardiff it was reported in 1908 that there were 300–400 Chinese seamen living in the city, mostly lodging around Bute Street, and there were thirty Chinese laundries. The 1911 Census contains entries for three boarding houses in the docks area. Ah Sam, assisted by a bookkeeper, Chang Fook, and two cooks ran one at 218 Bute Street. It had ten rooms and on the night of the census return there were twenty-two seamen lodgers. Along the road at Number 212 was another, called the Chinese Club, managed by Tong Lee and Koo Too Kee, two men in their late fifties. They employed a waiter and a cook and their Chinese lodgers on census night were three clerks, a confectioner, two sailors and a provisions merchant. The third was at 28 Patrick Street and had eight rooms with sixteen Chinese seamen lodgers. It was managed by Ling Same and his British wife, Louisa.

The earliest newspaper account of a Chinese community marking the arrival of the Chinese New Year comes from a newspaper report of Limehouse's celebrations in 1910:

The large Chinese population celebrated the occasion. The day was commenced with ceremonious visits and congratulation, the Orientals going from house to house, each exchanging greeting with their neighbour and leaving visiting cards of immense size, coloured red, bearing the names of the visitors and an appropriate motto printed in Chinese character. The size of the card is regulated in accordance with the importance of the person. All day long the Chinese drank and made merry, their menu including plentiful supply of delicious sweetmeats.

More celebrations greeted the formation of the Republic of China on 1 January 1912, established with Dr Sun Yat-sen as President.

There were high jinks in Chinatown in London on Thursday to celebrate the arrival of a cable announcing the proclamation of the Chinese Republic. The revolutionists' flag – a pretty national emblem of red, with a blue corner and a star of white – flew all day from practically every house in the neighbourhood. Noisy Chinese firecrackers and fireworks of all sorts were going off all day and for the greater part of the evening, whilst groups of Chinese congregated in the shops and talked long and earnestly on the birth of a new era for their country. They produced the new flag with great pride to the English visitor, and gazed long and admiringly at the newspaper pictures of Dr Sun Yat-sen, which can now be found on the walls of every residence. The eating houses there at night were doing a great business. Dozens sat in the house of Lum Yut Wah in Limehouse Causeway eating chop suey.

In the early 1900s many of those living in the Chinatowns would have had their heads partly shaved and the remaining hair worn in a queue (plaited into a long braid). This 'pigtail' style was often caricatured in Britain. In China some began to challenge the insistence on this hairstyle and the new Republic accelerated change and the queue style became a thing of the past, to the regret of one writer describing Limehouse: 'Of late years this quarter has lost in picturesqueness by the disappearance of the pigtail and the adoption of European dress, consequent on the advent of the Chinese Republic.'

There was a significant amount of self-help within the Chinatowns. If a wife ran short of money while her husband was at sea, others would lend her cash until he returned. Many Chinese seamen were generous to children; giving them sweets or, in some cases, buying shoes for children with bare feet. A number of mutual-help organisations were established in London and Liverpool, usually mirroring different Chinese ethnic groups. Those in London included the Chinese Mutual Aid Association, the Chun Yee Association and Sunday School, the Oi Tung Association and the Zhong Shan Mutual Aid Workers Club, while in Liverpool organisations included The See Yep Chinese Association and the Che Gong Tong Chinese Association. These provided support for the visiting seamen and a place for Chinese to meet socially and help organise campaigns for better working conditions. In Liverpool an annual Chinese picnic for children and their families was organised throughout the 1920s and '30s. This event was hugely popular and for a fortnight or so in advance the children would count down to the day by singing 'twelve more days to the Chinese picnic', 'six more days to the Chinese picnic…' The children were taken by ferry across the Mersey to Birkenhead and from there by train to Barnstondale where the picnic was held. The train journey was part of the day's excitement as for many of the children this was their only steam train ride in the year.

From around 1910, the President of the Che Gong Tong society in Liverpool was Lock Ah Tam who had come to Britain as a ship's steward in 1895 and stayed, becoming a shipping agent and later superintendent of the Chinese seamen. He married a Welsh woman, Catherine, and they had a son and two daughters. Lock was a well-respected and active member of the Chinese community. One evening in February 1918 while drinking in the Chinese Republic Progress Club that he had helped found, Lock was attacked

Chinatown

by a group of drunken Russian sailors and hit over the head. The incident was not serious enough to call the police and as Lock's head injury was not bad enough to require hospital treatment, he shrugged off the incident. However, the blow had caused neurological damage that began to manifest itself by a complete change of character. Lock began to drink heavily and experience violent mood swings. By 1924 his life had deteriorated to such an extent that he was made bankrupt. In late 1925 a party was arranged to welcome home the Locks' son, Ling Ah Tam, who had spent the previous seven years studying in China. The party was at the family's house in Birkenhead and in the early hours of the morning of 2 December a neighbour and a servant were aghast when Lock appeared, foaming at the mouth and brandishing a shotgun. As they watched in horror, Lock fired one barrel, killing his wife, and then the other, killing his seventeen-year-old daughter, Cecelia. His eldest daughter Doris was standing next to her mother and sister and said, 'Oh daddy, what did you do that for?' Lock then produced a revolver and shot her, though she did not die until some weeks later. Ling Ah Tam managed to flee and so was unharmed. The witnesses to the shooting reported that after he had shot his wife and daughters, Lock calmly lit a cigarette and turned to a shocked friend and said, 'If I get hung, take my body and bury it by that of my wife and daughters.' He then went to a phone box where he rang the police, telling them to come and arrest him. The whole city, and especially the Chinese community, was in shock at the news. Lock Ah Tam was well-known and no one could understand why he had murdered his family. The funeral procession of Cecilia and Catherine, and later of Doris, drew thousands of mourners to Birkenhead. In spite of his defence pleading that Ah Tam had experienced an epileptic fit caused by his earlier head injury and thus the killing had been an act of temporary insanity, the jury found Ah Tam guilty of murder. He was hanged at Walton Jail on 23 March 1926. On the day of the execution, Catherine's sister handed a bunch of daffodils to the warder and asked that they be dropped into Ah Tam's grave.

Gambling in Britain had been made illegal from the mid-nineteenth century and in 1906 the Street Betting Act further criminalised all gambling, except for betting at racecourses, which, at the time, was the preserve of the wealthy. Yet despite its prohibition, gambling was rife among all communities and there were regular police raids on illegal gambling clubs and arrests of those organising the betting. With limited social activities available, gambling was a common pursuit among the Chinese and they too were targeted by the police and many were arrested. Whether the Chinese communities were targeted more than others is hard to judge, but the press and popular fiction certainly highlighted gambling as a Chinese vice, as this 1920 newspaper article highlighted:

> Scotland Yard's has grown concerned at the alarming increase of gambling in the Chinese quarter, chiefly through the medium of a game known as

Puckapoo (Pai Gow, a game played with Chinese dominoes). To this game is largely attributed the growth of the undesirable relationships between Chinese and white women. Last July the Chinese Consul General visited Poplar, and in consequence of a notice afterwards issued by him there was a noticeable abatement of the gambling. Later, however, it broke out again. The police raided two Limehouse gaming houses and arrested six Chinese principals, three English principals, and 30 frequenters. The Chinese were sentenced to imprisonment and recommended for deportation, and the raids, it is stated, led to the closing of other gaming houses in the district. The evil of puckapoo is that enormously high prizes are possible for very small stakes. Women and even children in the district will stop at nothing to raise the small sums necessary to play.

Gambling in Chinese communities was almost always linked to opium smoking in press reports and much fiction and, more often than not, the claim was made that this combination of gambling and drug-taking was enabling Chinese to ensnare white women. Such claims ignored the reality that almost all the Chinese living in Britain led quiet, routine lives, and were hardworking and well-behaved. Also the British wives of Chinese affirmed them to be good husbands although a newspaper account in 1910 of one contented wife was unable to resist adding a negative spin: 'There lives in Pennyfields a small tobacconist named Tsang Wah with a young white wife, comely of face and sweet of voice. Oddly enough, in such intervals as are afforded her, this lady sings and dances in the West End music halls. Surrounded by her little band of pretty, dark-eyed children and her grey-haired mother, Mrs Tsang Wah spoke of her Celestial husband in the most natural, matter-of-fact way, accepting the situation with simple and very cheerful fatalism.'

Up until 1916, the use of opium and other drugs was legal. Shoppers could buy cocaine from Harrods in special boxes designed to be sent as morale-boosting gifts to loved ones serving in France during the war. What was illegal was for anyone other than a pharmacist to buy or sell the drug, and thus those Chinese who imported and sold opium illegally were the target for police raids. From 1916 its use was restricted to 'authorised persons' prescribed by doctors and thus anyone else using it was open to arrest. In one police raid in Liverpool about sixty Chinese were arrested and charged with being 'unauthorised persons found in possession of prepared smoking opium'. The police reported that opium and smoking utensils were discovered under floors, concealed in chimneys, and other parts of the houses.

In his book, *London Through Chinese Eyes*, Min-ch'ien T. Z. Tyau challenged the misperceptions about Limehouse's Chinatown:

> We may call these places 'dens' for all that they are so clean and orderly and so little withdrawn from public gaze. We may deplore the injurious physical effects which follow over-use of the opium, however small the proportion of

cases of definitely traceable injury may be, either to the number of smokers or to the Chinese population. But we have to recognize first the universal human tendency to some form of indulgence in stimulants, and secondly the fact that all the 'dens' in these two streets together will not furnish from one month's end to another any such spectacle of degradation or rowdyism as may be seen nightly in almost any public house. So, too, with the gambling... More money passes over the little tables in any City coffee room at lunch time than is lost and won here in a day. Neither in its earnestness nor in the size of the stakes does the playing compare with what goes on at 10,000 bridge tables in clubs and drawing rooms in London every night.

Yet the public continued to believe that the Limehouse Chinatown portrayed in the lurid books of Sax Rohmer and Thomas Burke was the reality; so much so that the area became a popular destination for thrill seekers. The travel agent Thomas Cook began charabanc tours through the streets of Limehouse, staging fights between men with fake queues shouting in Mandarin, and waving machetes in the air. But tourists were disappointed to discover that the den of vice and infamous centre of potential world domination described in popular fiction was in fact effectively just two streets, and the vast majority of the Chinese who lived there ordinary families who spent no time in opium dens or engaged in orgies. 'If they have secrets,' wrote one deflated tourist, 'they seem to keep them well.' After visiting the East End Chinatown the novelist Arnold Bennett wrote, 'On the whole a rather flat night. Still we saw the facts. We saw no vice whatever. The Inspector of Police gave the Chinese an exceedingly good character.' The writer Lao She, who lived in London between 1924 and 1929, also commented on the disparity between the reality of Limehouse and the media myths. 'If there were twenty Chinese living in Chinatown, their accounts would say five thousand; moreover every one of these five thousand yellow devils would certainly smoke opium, smuggle arms, murder people then stuff the corpses under beds, and rape women regardless of age.'

Yet, there also were a few Chinese voices critical of the inhabitants of the British Chinatowns. In 1922 Mr Oon, Chairman of the Union of Chinese Students in Britain, spoke at a conference in Edinburgh and after criticising 'the lurid cinema producers whose false artistry clings to the pigtail and the murderer's knife' then expressed concern that people accepted 'the dweller in Limehouse as a type of China... The Chinese people regret the presence of these people. We resent their presence more than you do. We would like them to be shipped back at once. They mitigate against the good name of the Republic.' Given the negative stories and police raids, it is not surprising that many Chinese were ambivalent about official visits to their neighbourhoods. On one occasion representatives of the Liverpool Health Committee visited the Chinatown area to investigate the conditions and took a photographer.

A Chinese man who resented having his photo taken offered to fight the photographer and a crowd assembled to watch the fun. The police suggested the photographer leave the street in order to prevent a disturbance and although he did, three Chinese attacked him, and began kicking him about the head and body. Fortunately, other Chinese rushed to the assistance of the photographer and his assailants ran off. As the photographer had managed to photograph them before they attacked, the three were later arrested.

By the mid-1930s the Chinese populations in Limehouse, Liverpool and Cardiff had declined owing to the repatriation of many Chinese sailors following the end of the First World War and a general reduction in shipping. Chung Chu, who kept a café on Limehouse Causeway, said in 1931 that the loss of shipping entering the London docks meant there were no jobs for the Chinese and Anglo-Chinese children who were living there: 'The boys find work hard to get, and the girls drift about the streets being ostracised by white girls of their own age.' Those who could afford to, began to move out. Some opened the first of the restaurants in the area round Gerrard Street that many decades later would form London's new Chinatown. A survey in 1930 concluded that Liverpool 'had only about 500 adult Chinese males and there had been considerable inter-marriage with white women. Many out of work have been deported, and the present small Chinese community is sprinkled all over the city, chiefly as laundry keepers.' Attempts to stem the decline in the Chinese population were made. In 1928 children in Limehouse began to be given Chinese lessons in one of the restaurants and in 1935 premises were acquired to establish the first Chinese school. *The Nottingham Journal* reported:

> London's astonishing East End showed another facet of its richly varied life at a function I attended in Pennyfields yesterday. It was opening of the Chung Hwa school by the Chinese Ambassador. Here little children, East Enders by birth and half-Chinese by parentage, talk Chinese well as English They are to receive education at the new school which will preserve this double nationality for they will be provided at the Chung Hwa Foundation with lessons in Chinese language and history and literature to supplement the ordinary education of the Londoner. Sir Robert Ho Tung gave a sum of money which has enabled the school to move from rooms over a restaurant in West India Dock Road to a pleasant house in Pennyfields.

In addition to education in Chinese culture and history, boys received instruction in gymnastics and boxing, while girls learned needlework and cookery. Up to 200 children attended. The building also served as a social club for the Chinese community and visiting seamen. Viscount 'Willy' Astor, a wealthy American-born attorney, politician, newspaper publisher and philanthropist also helped with fundraising for the school and arranged for performances to be given by the children from the club at fundraising events

Chinatown

aimed at London society, including one held in his home in St James's Square. Other informal Chinese schools were established and to enable children to attend, these usually were held on Sundays and so became known as the Chinese Sunday Schools. However, many of the British Chinese children were unhappy at another day in school and slipped away to play instead. Some Chinese fathers insisted on sending their sons to China for a period to learn the language and customs, often against the wishes of their wives as, in some cases, the boys were away for many years.

In the 1930s a nucleus of Chinese began to form in Manchester as the Nationalist Kuomintang Government opened a consulate in the city to co-ordinate Manchester's textile trade with China.

In 1935 George V and Queen Mary celebrated their Silver Jubilee and the royal couple made a surprise visit to the East End of London. In the car was their nine-year-old granddaughter Princess Elizabeth, later Elizabeth II. Unfortunately, their foray into the East End was kept so secret that the police were unaware and when the Royal car was held up at traffic lights cheering subjects swarmed round the vehicle. Police cars eventually arrived to escort the royal party but in the narrow streets of Chinatown the car was slowed to walking pace and Chinese streamed out of their houses to see the king and queen and little Princess Elizabeth. It was reported that the royal couple seemed a little overawed by the warmth of the demonstration.

Redevelopment and slum clearance in the dock areas forced others to leave. Although the properties in which the Chinese lived were reported to be clean and well looked after, many of their British neighbours lived in less sanitary conditions and so the local councils saw a need to replace the old properties. In 1934 Limehouse Causeway was widened and a maze of alleys and side streets, including several occupied by Chinese businesses and lodging houses, were demolished. In the mid-1930s a local Liverpool newspaper announced, 'Plans have been provisionally approved for the rebuilding of Chinatown.' This seemed to imply that a new Chinatown was envisaged but that was not the case. In reality there were many who wished to see the Chinese dispersed for they regarded the term 'Chinatown' as giving a negative view of their city. The local paper fed that view: 'Many residents in Pitt Street and Frederick Street are becoming increasingly resentful of that particular area being dubbed "Chinatown". The fact that the Corporation has been responsible for some attractive housing developments in Pitt Street has accentuated still further the inaptness of the term... The much dwindled Chinese colony will have to find a new home.' In 1937 an article in *The Times* commented, 'A special problem will be to provide alternative accommodation within the area for a number of Chinese and coloured persons at present living in Pitt Street.' While the redevelopment was started, the demolition of Liverpool's Chinatown area dragged on for years.

When the Second World War began, the planned demolition in the Chinatowns of Limehouse and Liverpool had only partly progressed and many of the old streets were intact. However, as both areas were close to the docks, German bombing completed much of the flattening that the councils had planned. While the number of Chinese in London's Limehouse continued to dwindle, the Second World War revived the Chinese community in Liverpool as the city became a reserve pool for up to 20,000 Chinese seamen serving on the British merchant ships and oil tankers. This resulted in huge pressure on accommodation. One woman, whose Chinese husband was at sea, was approached to see if she could lodge some seamen. The woman had two small rooms to spare and imagined lodging two men. However, she was informed that nine men could be squeezed in, and they were.

In 1944, Chen Zhanxiang, who had recently finished studying at the Architecture School of the University of Liverpool, where he had been taught by Professor Holford (who would later lead the redesign of London after its damage from wartime bombing), put forward a plan for the rebuilding of the city's Chinatown. He envisaged a new Chinese quarter that he suggested would be a fitting memorial to the Chinese seamen who had died in the war while serving on British ships. Chen's plan was for accommodation for 1,100, thus enabling the Chinese community that had been dispersed throughout the region to be reunited, plus a Chinese theatre, community centre, restaurants and shops. The design featured Chinese elements. Sadly, Chen's plan, while supported by many, did not go ahead. Later Chen would work on a plan for the redevelopment of Peking that would ensure that the city's ancient buildings were retained, but again his plan was not taken up and many of that city's historic buildings were demolished.

In 1945 the Chinese Christian Church centre was opened in Liverpool by the Merseyside Churches' China Committee, an inter-denominational body composed of representatives of the Anglican Church, the Free Churches, the Society of Friends, and the Salvation Army. The centre arranged visits to Chinese patients in Merseyside hospitals and gave English lessons to local Chinese. The centre contained a small chapel, in which church services were conducted in both Mandarin and Cantonese. The Blue Funnel Line re-employment of Chinese seamen, almost all Hong Kong Cantonese, brought a revival, with Chinese shops and clubs opening in the Chinatown area. Although the laundries disappeared, Chinese restaurants and take-aways and a range of other Chinese businesses including travel agencies, and legal and accountancy firms, flourished.

From the 1950s onwards, there was a steady increase in the number of Chinese residing in Britain as a result of further immigration, and second and third generation British Chinese. The 1951 census recorded 12,500 Chinese and this increased to 38,750 by 1961. As the two primary occupations of the time – laundries and then restaurants – required dispersal to be economically viable and almost all the immigrants came to work in the catering industry, the increased number did not lead to significant expansion of the Chinatowns. Compared to other immigrant communities, the Chinese

Chinatown

were the most dispersed; many families running a laundry or a restaurant were the only Chinese in their town. Yet small Chinese communities began to develop in larger cities including Birmingham, Manchester, Aberdeen and Coventry, and there was further expansion in Liverpool. By 1971, Britain's Chinese population was 96,030.

This account is largely focused on the Chinese who travelled to mainland Britain but by the 1960s there also was the beginning of a community of Chinese in Northern Ireland. In the *Belfast Newsletter* of 1955 a writer asked, 'Belfast people appear to be very conservative when it comes to eating out, judging by restaurant menus. I should like to see a little more enterprise in catering. Why not Chinese restaurants, where we can enjoy the delights of noodles, pancakes and chop suey?' The writer's wish was eventually granted for in 1963 The Peacock Chinese restaurant opened in the city and its owners were among the first Chinese to move to live in Northern Ireland. Over the next decade more Chinese moved to the region including Anna Lo, who had been born in Hong Kong in 1950. She decided to move to the UK in 1974 to be with a young Canadian pilot she had met and in order to obtain a visa enrolled as a student in a secretarial school in London's Earls Court. When her relationship with the Canadian pilot ended, she took up with a young Irish journalist working in Belfast. One day Lo received a letter from the Immigration Department informing her that her study visa was at an end and she was required to return to Hong Kong in ten days' time. Not wishing to leave Britain she proposed to the young journalist that they marry so she could remain and he agreed.

Thus, in October 1974, Lo moved to live in Belfast, a city in the grip of sectarian violence. Only three years before, one of the few city-centre Chinese restaurants had been badly damaged by a bomb, and by the time Lo arrived most Belfast restaurants were closed due to people's fear of going into the city centre in the evening. No doubt the threat of bombs was a worry, but Lo had much else to concern her. As she writes in her autobiography, *The Place I Call Home*, 'So many things were alien to me – the culture, the systems, the climate, the geography, the diet and the language.' She also was having to spend time shopping to find clothes to fit her small frame and size 3 feet. Lo progressed to working for the BBC and became a Chinese interpreter for the police, helping Chinese who were reporting car accidents, burglaries and growing numbers of racial incidents. At the time she was also bringing up her two boys. By the 1980s there were about 8,000 Chinese living in Northern Ireland and Lo became a part-time social worker, assisting those in the Chinese community dealing with challenges. In 2007 Lo agreed to stand as a political candidate for the Alliance Party in the South Belfast constituency and was selected, becoming the first Chinese to be elected to any parliament or devolved assembly in Britain. Sectarianism was rife in the politics of Northern Ireland, as well as in society, and, like many politicians, Lo was threatened and a police guard had to be mounted in her street. In 2016 the continual threat of violence and growing racial abuse led Lo to leave politics.

London's Limehouse Chinatown, already small, almost disappeared as a result of the damage to property from German bombing. By the war's end, although small numbers of Chinese continued to live there, it was no longer the Chinatown of popular imagination. In 1951 the *Daily Worker* reported that there were only a few cafés and laundries, a handful of Chinese seamen, and a fairly impoverished population of fifty resident families living in the area. The Chun Yee Society remained, providing a space for the seamen who still lodged in the area and support for those who retired from seafaring. By 1960 this decline was so advanced that it appeared London might no longer have a Chinatown. However, the cluster of Chinese restaurants that had developed in the Soho area from the 1920s began to act as a nucleus for a new Chinatown. In 1947 Samuel Chinque opened an overseas branch of Xinhua, the news agency of the People's Republic of China, in the area. Chinque had worked as a merchant seaman and after settling in Liverpool was employed by the Chinese Seamen's Union, helping fight for equal pay for Chinese sailors. In 1935 he joined the Communist Party of Great Britain. When Japan invaded China he was prominent in campaigning for Britain to support China in its fight against Japan and during the war he worked in Liverpool's fire brigade as an auxiliary firefighter. His support of the Communists in China, who were in opposition to the nationalist Kuomintang Government, made him a focal point for seamen, revolutionaries and students from the Chinese diaspora who shared his espousal of the Communist cause. To help promote their cause, prominent Chinese Communist revolutionaries asked Chinque to establish the first Chinese news agency in Britain in London. As Xinhua was the only British-based organisation to represent, and speak for, the Chinese Communist party, Chinque became the communist's ambassador in all but name. Following the 1949 Chinese revolution, Britain, with other Western countries, instituted a trade embargo on China and during the early 1960s Chinque was a member of the negotiating team that lobbied the post-war Labour Government to re-establish trade. Chinque continued working until his seventies, and remained a formidable and charismatic figure. In his late seventies, he floored, with one blow, a racist skinhead who had assaulted him on a London tube train.

Another man who established an early non-restaurant business in London's new Chinatown was Chen Jun. He had worked as an apprentice hairdresser in Japanese-occupied Shanghai and when the Communist party took control in China moved to Hong Kong. There he worked in an up-market hair salon frequented by Hong Kong's elite, and married and began a family. In 1966 he left to start a new life in Britain, for the first few years leaving his family in Hong Kong. His first job was working in a hairdressing salon on Monmouth Street. 'My monthly wage was £22, even less than what I earned in Hong Kong', Chen recounted. 'I often had bread for three meals a day, sometimes with milk. Seldom could I have rice. I watched every penny, even sleeping on the salon floor to save rent. There were hardly any Chinese and I had few friends. It was two years before I was reunited with my wife and daughters.' In 1968 Chen opened the China Beauty Salon – the first hair salon in Chinatown. At its peak his wife and ten hairdressers worked there. Twelve years later he went into partnership with some friends and opened The Luxuriance Restaurant in Gerrard Street and later a second restaurant, Lux II, in Virginia Water. He continued to operate the hairdressing salon until 2000, when it closed after thirty-two years of business.

By 1965 there were around twenty Chinese restaurants in the area and in January 1970 *The Times* ran an article headlined, 'New Chinatown comes to Soho'. This listed the Chinese-run businesses in Gerrard Street as seven restaurants, two hairdressers, a beauty salon, a Far East travel agency, a supermarket and two car hire firms. An estate agent told the paper, 'The Chinese are falling over themselves trying to rent space here.' Tse Kwe-tao, who had recently arrived from Hong Kong to run the Chamber of Chinese Traders, was asked why this had happened in Gerrard Street. 'It is pure chance. Gerrard Street has become a centre, so Chinese people tend to come here,' he said. In 1978 the London Chinatown Chinese Association was established to support and expand businesses in the area and in 1987 the number of restaurants had grown to 100. By 1981 the Chinese population in Britain had increased to 155,000 and the next three decades would see the number grow to in excess of 400,000, strengthening the UK's existing Chinatowns and sowing the seeds of others.

17

Sweat and Steam

(One piece, two pieces, three pieces,)
Washing must be clean.
(Four pieces, five pieces, six pieces,)
Ironing must be smooth.
I can wash handkerchiefs wet with sad tears;
I can wash shirts soiled in sinful crimes.
The grease of greed, the dirt of desire ...
And all the filthy things at your house,
Give them to me to wash, give them to me.

Wen Yidou (1899–1946), translated by
Chuimei Ho and Bennet Bronson

Hop Lee Laundry, Castor Street, London *c.* 1900. (*Limehouse China Rediscovered*)

Sweat and Steam

Laundering clothes before the advent of washing machines and electric irons was a laborious process and one that servants particularly detested. In the nineteenth century clothes were soaked in a tub of soapy water, often as it was heated over the fire. The clothes then would be agitated by a wooden tool with pegs on the end, called a dolly stick. Any clothes that were stained would require scrubbing on a washboard, and salt, lemon or citrate of potash were used to remove any ink blots or splashes of tea. As the tub could only take a limited amount, it would need to emptied and refilled so that the clothes could be rinsed in clean water, possibly more than once. Then they would go through a mangle turned by hand to get rid of as much water as possible. After this they would be hung out to continue drying. Once dry, they had to be starched and ironed using heavy metal 'flat' irons heated in a fire or on a stove. From the mid-nineteenth century a growing concern for cleanliness and a desire for fashionable white clothing meant clothes had to be washed far more often. As this coincided with a rise in the cost of servants, a market for private laundries developed and these quickly spread throughout the country. Some were large operations using some form of machinery and employing significant numbers of mainly women, but most were small one- or two-person concerns. Many charitable institutions established laundries to earn money with the work being carried out by orphans, young girls and 'fallen women'.

The earliest Chinese laundries opened in the ports where the seamen resided. For the majority of Chinese who had decided to give up seafaring and settle in Britain, racial prejudice among workers and employers meant jobs they might otherwise have filled were unavailable. Thus some form of self-employment was the only answer and providing laundry services was chosen by many. This had the advantage of needing almost no capital as the equipment and materials were relatively inexpensive. As long as a man could afford to rent an appropriate space, usually with living space attached as the hours of work were extremely long, a small business could be launched. Laundries also had the benefit of being work that could be done jointly by a man and wife, and, often, with help from the children. As many Chinese who opened laundries had limited English, marrying a woman who spoke English was invaluable, as well as providing another pair of hands. Thus many were operated by a Chinese man and his British wife, and the first to appear in any British census was such a partnership. In 1871 the census records William Achong and his British wife, Sarah, as working as a laundry man and laundress, possibly from their house at 36 Maxwell Road in London's Fulham. In 1879 Achong had to sue the artist James McNeill Whistler for an unpaid bill of £8 for washing. Although Chinese men who opened laundries were not threatening British men's jobs, they were criticised for stealing women's work. When Yee Chin opened the first Chinese laundry in Liverpool in 1886 this accusation was levelled at him. Although Yee Chin's business does not appear to have been attacked, three years after starting in business his house was broken into, and money and a gold watch stolen. Worried that this might occur again, Yee bought a revolver. When, a few months later, burglars broke in again, Yee shot at the intruders, wounding, but not killing, one of the notorious young thieves. Yee was charged with grievous wounding but the jury decided he had fired in self-defence and found him not guilty.

In the 1890s a report into working conditions for women in laundries uncovered long hours and poor conditions, including excessive heat and constant steam. Calls for legislation to improve conditions resulted in the large partly-mechanised laundries being brought under the Factory Act, but the smaller laundries, which included all those run by Chinese, were excluded. Although working conditions in all of these remained unhealthy, inspections appear to indicate that those operated by Chinese were of as fair a standard as possible, given the activity. Around 1900 the first large laundry to employ Chinese labour opened in London. It employed thirty-eight Chinese men and one Chinese woman and was run by two Jewish businessmen. The two men planned to open more but they ran into resistance: firstly, from their Chinese employees who took them to court to claim unpaid wages and secondly, from protests by the Women's Union.

> This meeting profoundly regrets the attempts now being made to import Chinamen as laundry workers, and while cherishing the English tradition of hospitality to those who seek our shores as the land of liberty, would urge the public and the legislature that this is not a question of spontaneous emigrations, but of exploited labour. Encouragement to irresponsible foreign speculators to import alien workers, who, differing not only in race and language, but in their ideas of life and morals, has proved in other civilised countries a serious menace to the health of the State.

By 1901 there were attacks against laundries. The premises of the first Chinese laundry in Poplar in London was stoned by a hostile xenophobic crowd and ten years later in Cardiff, rioting seafarers wrecked about thirty laundries. Some of the antagonism came from a concern jobs would be lost to British workers, but undoubtedly was also fostered by negative stories in popular writing and newspaper reports that portrayed Chinese laundries as covers for prostitution and gambling. While there is no evidence of the former, there certainly were laundries where gambling took place and when arrests were made, newspaper coverage ensured those arrested were shown in a damaging light. One group of Chinese charged with illegal gambling was described as 'a motley crowd of Oriental figures' while another paper reported that defendants in court on a similar charge were all well-dressed 'despite the fact that they were all laundrymen'.

In spite of such racial stereotyping and violence, the public appreciated the quality of the services provided and the number of Chinese laundries grew significantly. By 1910 there were about 100 Chinese laundries in the

Liverpool area and thirty in Cardiff. Not in Glasgow though, as a Scottish newspaper was pleased to report in 1907: 'Unlike London and Liverpool, the Glasgow immigration authorities have been successful in preventing undesirable aliens making Glasgow their permanent abiding place. So far, all attempts by Chinese to establish laundries have failed.' Yet Glasgow was the exception for most towns and cities had Chinese laundries. In her book, *Profit, Victory and Sharpness*, Vivienne Poy recounts that her father, Richard Lee, who had been sent from Hong Kong to study in Oxford, mentioned a laundry in the town run by two Chinese by the name of Zhou:

> (They) are to be admired. They arrived here, by mistake, eleven years ago. They wanted to go to London, Ontario, Canada, to make a living. However, the tickets that were bought for them were incorrect, and neither knew that there were two Londons in the world. When they arrived in London, England, no relatives came to meet their boat, and they knew something was wrong. Not knowing whether to laugh or to cry, they realised they had arrived in a different part of the world, with no friends and with very little money. A few days later, they made their way to Oxford, and opened a laundry establishment. They worked hard and had become very well known for the best laundry service. Almost all the students in Oxford send their laundry to them. It shows that, for those who are abroad, with hard work, they will succeed.

Although by the 1930s there were upwards of 500 Chinese laundries spread throughout the country, these were a small percentage of the overall number nationally. While increased mechanisation in laundries brought greater competition and led to the demise of many smaller ones, Chinese operations were able to survive due to unstinting commitment. Most were operated by a husband and wife on their own, with older children often assisting. The families lived frugally and the couple who did the bulk of the work coped with fatigue from long periods of standing, endured skin ailments such as blisters and eczema, tolerated inferior living conditions and worked very long hours.

Quan Soo's family were farmers but around 1905 he signed on as a seaman on a British ship. Arriving in Britain at the age of twenty or thereabouts, he decided to stay and opened a laundry in an area of Manchester. In 1908 he married Beatrice Wittham, a twenty-year-old who had had been abandoned as a child and brought up in the Manchester Industrial School for Girls. This was a form of children's home and trained young girls for domestic service until their sixteenth birthday. One of her tasks at the institution would have been laundering. In 1909 they had their first child, a son, and a few years later moved to open a laundry in the village of Fairfield, near Buxton, in the Peak District. There they had a second son in 1914. A few years later the family moved again, this time to Sheffield where they may have worked at a laundry owned by another Chinese. There their only daughter, Beattie, was born. Around 1918, they moved for the last time, taking over a laundry in West Derby that had been opened ten years earlier by Sam See. West Derby was a leafy suburb of Liverpool, and the house and laundry were next to a pub and a dairy. From 1920 to 1931 four more sons were born. Doubtless the eldest boys and their daughter would have been required to assist, especially as Beatrice had four young boys to look after.

Some of the Chinese men who operated laundries arranged to marry women from China, often by post, and many of the young women who came to Britain to marry had little idea of their future life. One was the seventeen-year-old Fung Siu Ng whose mother arranged for her to marry Chi Mau Chin, a man from her village who was working in a laundry in Britain. Fung Siu travelled to Britain believing she would have a comfortable married life but her dreams were shattered as soon as she arrived. She was immediately put to work with her husband in the laundry and as she did not know anything about washing clothes, Fung Siu was given the task of ironing the laundered clothes. The laundry was so basic that she had to iron approximately 100 garments a day with a heated iron bar wrapped in a towel. She constantly suffered from painful blisters on her hands. Working six days a week, for long hours, Mrs Chin was constantly tired and, as she spoke almost no English, was lonely and unhappy. Mr and Mrs Chin were so poor that they could only afford to eat once a day, and that meal was not until 1 a.m. when they finally finished work. She recalled that, on occasions, kind neighbours gave them biscuits to supplement their diet. Even when they bought a sack of rice, which her husband collected by wheelbarrow when it was delivered to the railway station, they cherished the rice so much they barely ate any, living instead on potatoes and bread.

The Chins moved to Swansea to run the KKK laundry, one of just two in the city. 'Every day was the same. More ironing and more ironing.' Later, friends lent them £500 so they could buy part ownership of the Ming Yon restaurant on Castle Street.

> I would work at the launderette every day and then I would help out at the restaurant on Fridays and Saturdays. Working at the restaurant was hard going at the time. We didn't have wages but we hoped to do our best so that we could earn more to keep on living.

Throughout this period, Mrs Fung raised four children, three of whom were born at home as she had could not afford to take time off work to go to hospital. Although she gave birth to their fourth child in hospital, Mrs Fung returned to work the following day. 'A midwife came to bathe the baby and told me I couldn't carry on like that, that I needed to rest.' Life for Mr Fung was as unrelenting. Being on his feet for up to eighteen hours a day eventually damaged his foot, and after an operation he too had to go straight back to work, resulting in it continuing to cause him pain. In spite of the years of hardship, in old age Mrs Fung took pleasure from her achievement in successfully having brought up her children.

> I have been here for 58 years. I wasn't very happy back then. It was very hard going for a long time. But now I'm older. My children, grandchildren, I have a lot of friends, am happy now. I have seven grandchildren, three grandsons and four granddaughters. Some have already graduated from university. I'm very proud. My sons and daughters are all loving, they have good careers and live good lives. No matter that I struggled, I have loving children and feel very lucky.

In 1944 a number of Chinese who had served on British merchants ships during the war arrived in Liverpool and were discharged from their ships. The men were allowed to land in Britain by the immigration authorities on the understanding that they had a fixed period of stay, often as little as a month, and during that time had to report once a week to the police. Many decided to take a chance and disappear into the Chinese community, and usually ended up working illegally in laundries. Like all illegal immigrants, each lived with the continual fear that one day the authorities might detect them and send them packing. By 1949 Chan Heung may have thought he was safe but while working in a laundry in Gloucester he was arrested by the police and charged with being an illegal alien. Heung was sent to prison for three months but the magistrates decided not to recommend to the Home Office that he be deported. The year before, Thoo Chi Phu was also in court charged with having entered the country illegally. When Thoo appeared in court in Hereford, his eventful life was recounted. He and his Chinese wife and child had moved to Singapore and Thoo got a job working for the British merchant navy. In the Japanese bombing of Singapore, his wife and child were killed and Theo became a gunner aboard a British oil tanker. When he arrived in Liverpool in 1944 he had been given a one-year permit to stay and during that year remarried and he and his wife opened a laundry, and began a family. When it was discovered that he had overstayed his permit, he was deported back to China. But Thoo was determined to return to his wife and family in Britain. On his way back, while temporarily in Amsterdam, he received a letter from his wife telling him that their laundry had been burned down and that many of the customers' clothes had been lost. Thoo stowed away on a boat to London and in spite of speaking almost no English managed to make his way back to Hereford. There he and his wife managed to rebuild the business and eventually reimbursed all the customers who had lost their clothes in the fire. In court the police informed the magistrates that Thoo had been most helpful during the investigations and that during his residence in the city had been law-abiding and of good character. Thoo's lawyer pleaded for his client to be allowed to stay:

> Here is a Chinaman who has served England well both in war and peace. During the war he played his part as a ship's gunner in the fight to preserve freedom and since then has behaved as a good citizen and has conducted a laundry business most efficiently and satisfactorily. He has been a good friend of this country and I would appeal to you to exercise your discretion not to grant a deportation order. Allow him to remain with his wife and child, to be a useful citizen and to be near the spot where one of his children is buried.

The magistrates took no time to agree that Thoo should not be deported and after paying a £1 fine for having contravened the Aliens Act he was able to leave the court to return to his family. 'I can be completely happy now I know I can stop in this lovely country,' Thoo said.

Although the Second World War brought an upsurge in work for the small laundries, by the 1950s self-service laundromats and increased ownership of washing machines were making them uneconomic. By the 1960s most Chinese had closed their businesses, and many moved into the restaurant trade.

18
Changing Taste

I often wish to consult my chopsticks,
Which always taste what is bitter and what is sweet before I do.

Chinese saying

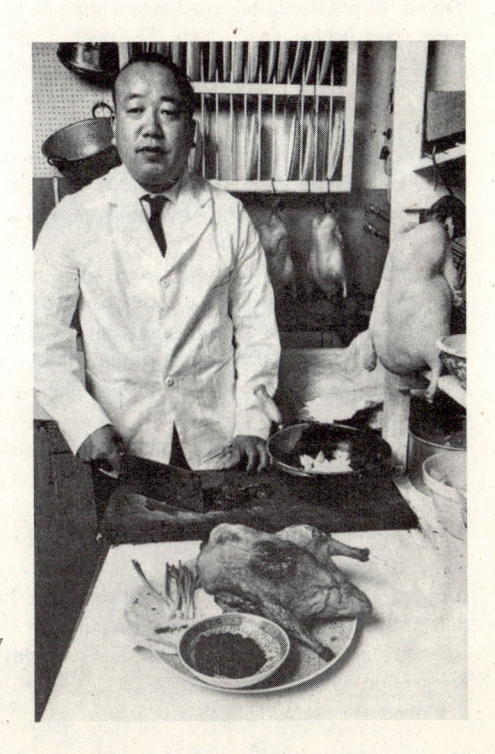

Chef Kuo Teh-lou in the kitchen of his London restaurant Kuo Yuan, 1965. (Photo by David Montgomery for *Tatler* Magazine © Montgomery estate/Mary Evans Picture Library)

The Chinese in Britain

Apart from a handful of eateries that served the local Chinese community in London's Limehouse, Cardiff and Liverpool, there were no Chinese restaurants in Britain before the early 1900s. Thus when a Chinese restaurant formed part of China's contribution to the International Health Exhibition in 1884 there was widespread interest and many rushed to sample Chinese food, although how authentic the dishes were is hard to say. Certainly the fancy French titles *Chaudfroid de cailles à l'Essence* and *Crépinette de Vollaile* à la *Cantonaise au Varech Violet* are unlikely to be seen on a Chinese menu today.

Most accounts state that it was around 1906 that the first Chinese restaurant opened in central London catering for non-Chinese diners. However, there is a newspaper report from 1901 of an attempted burglary at 'the well-known Chinese restaurant in New Oxford Street' but no other details are given. Among the first were The Chinese Restaurant in Glasshouse Street, Piccadilly; the Cathay, off Piccadilly Circus; and Maxim's, in Soho. Some restaurants employed ship's cooks such as Chung Koon who had worked for the Red Funnel Line. Although the clientele of Chu Chong's refreshment rooms at 18 West India Dock Road was primarily Chinese, a few daring non-Chinese occasionally ventured there. One local recalled the cooks sitting in the alley behind the restaurant next to a large chopping block and, with one stroke of the cleaver, beheading chickens. The kitchen was reputed to be scrupulously clean, no doubt as a result of the two mongooses that Mr Chong kept to control the vermin. One of the non-Chinese who dared visit recounted: 'The walls were hung with various notices, one stating that the proprietor is prepared to furnish whole "golden" pigs, properly conserved, and glazed, for ceremonial purposes, of any size, at 1s 4d per lb... On the stairs hangs a diploma setting forth that Mr Chong Chu is a member of good standing of the Ancient Order of Druids!'

Fung Shaw opened The Nanking restaurant in London's Denmark Street after failing to get into politics. He came to Britain around 1900 and by the late 1920s was an organiser of Chinese sailors in London and active in the Labour Party. In 1927 he was adopted by the Holborn Labour Party as its prospective candidate in the forthcoming General Election, although at the time the Holborn group had been expelled from the National Labour Party owing to its refusal to eject Communist members. Fung denied he was a Communist and claimed he supported the policy of the Labour Party, although he admitted his views were left wing. At a conference organised by the London Trades Council in that year, when Fung arrived to speak the audience greeted him by singing *The Internationale*. Fung spoke about the British conflict with China and condemned the British naval bombardments that already had killed thousands of innocent Chinese and destroyed their cities. 'Yet the Government, not satisfied with this aggression, is now sending more bombs, ships and guns.' A 1932 article in an Australian newspaper described The Nanking:

Changing Taste

Mr. Fung Saw is something of a politician, and to his restaurant come many of the more youthful of the budding Parliamentarians. These, together with composers and song writers, their publishers and film artists, comprise the chief of Mr. Fung's clientele. The hall of feasting is reached by long, steep steps, which lead to an exceptionally large, light, and lofty basement. There is another and a more prosaic entrance through a hall door on the ground floor, but somehow no one ever seems to notice it, and so we descend the more picturesque steps. Inside, the decorations are reminiscent of a Chinese junk, and the walls are decorated in vermilion and in greens and yellows, which only a Chinese artist is able to use to Oriental perfection. Mr. Saw explained that he had a large back room, which he reserved for Chinese business men, but as Chinese merchants do not so often come to London the hall at the back is usually thrown open to all.

In 1934 Fung offered the use of the back room to Sajjad Zaheer, a young Indian Marxist, for a meeting of thirty-five young Indians who crowded into the small room. The group was a mix of writers and university students, all with left-wing sympathies and they agreed to form the anti-imperialist Indian Progressive Writers' Association that would become one of South Asia's most influential literary movements. When the restaurant closed it became the Regent Sounds Studios where, in 1964, the Rolling Stones recorded their first album.

Ley On opened his first restaurant in Gerrard Street in 1926. A few years later he saw a pasta-making machine in the window of an Italian shop along the street and asked the owner, Luigi Ugo, if he could make noodles for his restaurant and for his business providing food for Chinese sailors in Limehouse. Luigi agreed to have a try and after Ley showed the Italian how to make the noodles, the shop became a supplier of noodles to many of the Chinese restaurants. Ley's restaurant was one of the stars of London's Chinese restaurant scene. It was reputed to be the one most frequented by non-Chinese, and was particularly popular among celebrities from the entertainment world. By 1932 it had moved to the corner of Wardour Street and Meard Street, and was renamed Chop Suey. It moved again, to 89–91 Wardour Street, as recalled by the Chinese cookery writer, Deh-Ta Hsiung:

> I remember stories from my first wife's father who used to go to Ley-On, one of the very oldest Chinese restaurants on Wardour Street where the China Society would meet every month – that was in the 1930s but I've heard people talk of eating there in the 1920s. Ley-On moved premises three times that I know – and never more than a few hundred yards either way in the same street.

An Australian journalist described a visit:

> The premises consist of two floors with entrances in both thoroughfares. Here may be purchased every kind of Chinese food and even delicacies

like shark's fin, while bowls and other crockery, ivory chopsticks, Chinese pencils, and Chinese gramophone records are on sale, and are exhibited in cases round the walls. The lower room has some very amusing paintings, for when Ley On opened his restaurant he invited his artist friends to roll up and help in the decorating. Strange tales told out of Burmah, Indo-China, Siam, and every corner of the Eastern world may be gathered and conjured from these walls.

In 1929 the German director Richard Eichberg was looking for actors to play Chinese characters in his new film, *The Flame of Love* and, possibly through film contacts who ate at Ley On's, cast Ley in a minor role. This was the start of Ley's film career and in addition to running his successful restaurant, he had a number of minor parts, including in two Powell & Pressburger wartime films, *49th Parallel*, in which Ley played an Eskimo, and *Black Narcissus*. Ley's last film appearance was in 1950 as a Chinese Captain in *The Black Rose*, in which Saxon archers travel to China to fight for a Mongol warlord, played by an embarrassed-looking Orson Welles. Another restaurant owner who appeared in a film was King Ho-Chang, who played Jim, a Chinese musician, in the 1930 film *Piccadilly*. It seems likely that Ley simply enjoyed the glamour of film making and meeting film stars, rather than harbouring any ambition to be a star himself. He had a 230-page leather-bound book, on the cover of which was printed in gold letters, 'Mr Ley-On's Autograph Book', in which he collected the signatures of many of the stars of the films he acted in, and celebrities who visited his restaurant. In 2013 the book was auctioned in London and the autographs included Frank Sinatra, Ava Gardner, Clark Gable, Elizabeth Taylor, Errol Flynn, Johnnie Ray, Denis Compton, and all thirty-one members of the 1948 Chinese Olympic Team who were in London for the Olympic Games. Ley On was more than willing to tolerate the idiosyncrasies of famous diners. In 1941, the actress and comedienne, Kay Kendall, breezed into Ley On's with a friend after having been to see a show and immediately buttonholed the maître d'. 'We want the best table you have,' she said, 'and we've only got one pound to spend.' Unfazed, the maître d' led the pair to one of the restaurant's prime tables where they were given a splendid meal, though it is certain the bill came to more than the one pound Kendall was charged.

In the 1920s, restaurants were opened in Paris by some of the Chinese who had remained in France after being employed in the Chinese Labour Corps in the First World War. The British writer, Harold Acton, who lived there between the wars, thus discovered a taste for Chinese food. On his return to London he hired a personal chef, Chong Sung, who had worked in a Chinese restaurant in Wembley. Acton recounted that his new cook brought 'a lacquered canister of tea, cumquats, a pot of ginger, and myriads of smaller parcels of rice, vermicelli, lychees, mushrooms and other dainties like precious herbal and geological specimens'. Although Acton extolled Chong Song's flavoursome cooking, his friends resisted invitations to dine as their chauvinism led them to associate Chinese food with outlandish ingredients such as snakes and bird's nests. Acton did not care. He said that by eating Chinese food he was 'half in China, and as time went on I wished to be wholly in China'. Acton fulfilled his ambition to be wholly in China by travelling to teach at Peking University in 1932. He lived in China until 1939, studying Chinese language and publishing respected translations of Chinese drama and poetry.

A few Chinese eating places existed in Liverpool before the war. In March 1939, 300 guests enjoyed a Chinese banquet at the Adelphi Hotel, held to raise funds for the Chinese Campaign Committee. The dinner was cooked by Low Hong, chef at the Chinese restaurant of Foo Nam Low in Pitt Street, the first time food prepared outside the hotel's kitchens had ever been served.

Before the 1950s, few Chinese restaurants existed outside of Liverpool and London as dining out was mainly restricted to the wealthier classes when travelling or on holiday, and tastes in food did not extend to Asian food. Two early ones dating from at least the early 1940s were The Chinese Restaurant in Edinburgh, where Chiang Yee ate in 1944 while researching his *Silent Traveller in Edinburgh* book, and The Blue Barn in Cambridge where Kenneth Lo recalled eating while studying in the town. Lo recounted that The Blue Barn was a tiny establishment with just twelve seats ranged along a counter and a menu limited to three dishes; Chop Suey, Chow Mein and Fried Rice. It was destroyed by a German bomb and as the Luftwaffe also destroyed Kwong Shang Lung's Chinese grocery shop in Liverpool's Pitt Street, and no doubt some Chinese eating places in Limehouse, one wonders if this was part of some fiendish German plot against Chinese gastronomy.

Following the end of the Second World War, jobs on British merchant ships swiftly began to decline, laundries were becoming uneconomic and employers were unwilling to hire Chinese. Thus many Chinese looked for alternative employment and by a lucky coincidence many British people who had served in the forces in Asia during the war returned to Britain with a less conservative palate and an interest in Chinese food. Thus many Chinese began to open restaurants and among those that appeared in the late 1940s were The Ping Hong in Manchester, the Marlborough Café in Newcastle and The Wah Yen in Glasgow. However, Chinese ingredients were hard to source. When Deh-Ta Hsiung arrived in Britain in 1949 he recalled:

> There were no Chinese ingredients in the shops – why would there be – no Chinese shops either – so we would rely on goods brought to us by people coming back from Hong Kong. I even remember Soy Sauce packed in tins and at home in Oxford we'd get the occasional sack of rice gifted from Chinese Embassy staff who knew my father.

The lack of authentic ingredients led to fabricated dishes such as Chop Suey, although it was not only the lack of traditional ingredients that resulted in most Chinese restaurants, offering pale imitations of real Chinese food. The restaurants depended on attracting British patrons and British taste was still cautious. When Lily Kwok opened her restaurant in Middleton, Manchester, in 1959 she made sure she would attract locals by adding chips with curry sauce to her kitchen repertoire. The popularity of Chinese restaurants was partly that they offered a substantial meal for less than competing establishments, and their late opening hours appealed to those wanting a meal after the pub.

While the dishes on offer in the early restaurants may not always have been top quality and the décor utilitarian, demand and interest soon led to more Chinese restaurants offering authentic Chinese fare. This trend was assisted by the Communists taking power in China. In 1950 the British Government recognised China's Communist regime and informed the staff of the Nationalist Chinese Embassy, who were now out of a job, that they could stay in Britain if they wished. The Nationalist Government, which had moved to Taiwan, offered staff who wished to stay in Britain compensation in US dollars. By chance, the year before, the Chinese Ambassador had hosted a dinner for Princess Elizabeth and the Duke of Edinburgh at which Chinese food was served. The royal visit was supposed to be secret but the press found out and to the delight of the Legation's Chinese chef, Mr Zee, his name appeared in the newspapers for the first time. Zee recognised that he could use this publicity to open his own restaurant and invested his compensation in opening The Asiatic in London. Zee later explained: 'One might say that we started up in the restaurant business because we wanted to eat! But we also wanted to be able to enjoy good Chinese food.'

The rising popularity of Chinese food led Billy Butlin to open a Chinese restaurant, The Lotus House, at his Clacton-on-Sea Holiday Camp in 1958. It served happy campers chicken chop suey and chips and the majority of those who dared to try this novel dish found it to their liking. It was around this time that the legendary Chinese takeaway was born. Some accounts say it resulted from London's Lotus House in Bayswater being so popular that those who could not get a table asked if they could take the food home, although given Limehouse's importance in the story of the Chinese in Britain, perhaps the claim that the takeaway was invented at Charlie Cheung's Local Friends in Salmon Lane, Limehouse, should be the one recognised. It was also in the late 1950s that shops such as London's Hong Kong Emporium began to open, offering better and authentic ingredients. The growth of Chinese restaurants and take-aways created a demand for more Chinese to work in them and by chance this need coincided with the Labour Government's introduction of the 1948 Nationality Act. This offered individuals living in Britain's remaining colonies the opportunity to claim British nationality, and freely enter and settle in the 'Mother Country'. Many in Hong Kong were experiencing economic hardship as a result of the influx of refugees from Communist China creating competition for jobs, and low-priced rice from

Changing Taste

Southeast Asia putting pressure on the economic viability of rice farms in Hong Kong, so a job working in Britain beckoned for many – especially as limited English was no barrier to working in a Chinese restaurant kitchen. In 1960, of the 1,115 residence permits agreed for Chinese, all but twelve had jobs arranged in advance, whereas only around seven per cent of applicants from India and Jamaica had jobs lined up in Britain. Almost all Chinese who came at this time left their families behind and, although paid less than the average British manual worker, earned far more than they could have in Hong Kong and as they lived cheaply, were able to send money back to support their families.

In 1954 Kenneth Lo chanced to meet a friend who ran a London publishing company and they discussed the rising interest in Chinese food. There were few Chinese cookbooks and Harrison offered Lo an advance of £50 to write one. Lo agreed and delivered it seven weeks later. The book was a risk, as Lo had not had the time to test all the recipes. However, *Cooking the Chinese Way* sold 10,000 copies and launched Lo on a new path as a cookery writer. He later recalled, 'I never dreamt the excursion would turn out to be my personal Long March.' He published more than thirty books on Chinese cooking, selling more than a million copies around the world. Lo's grandfather was Sir Chihchen Lo Feng-Lu, the Chinese ambassador to Britain in the 1890s, and Lo's father, who studied in Britain and was the first Cambridge undergraduate to own a motor car, also worked at the Chinese Legation in 1919. When he came to London he brought his family, including the six-year-old Lo and his brothers. Lo later compared the journey to London as feeling like a trip to the moon. He and his two brothers came down with flu soon after arriving and the doctor who treated them struggled to pronounce and spell their Chinese names, so labelled their medications Charles, Kenneth and Walter. Unfortunately, the translation of Kenneth in the Lo's native language of Fukienese approximated to dog shit, a nickname his classmates were swift to call him when the family returned to China three years later.

In China, Lo studied physics and also became tennis champion of North China, before returning to Britain to study English at Cambridge. During the Second World War, while working as the industrial relations officer for the Chinese Seamen's Union in Liverpool, Lo's belief in the power of food quickly came into play when he invited disputing West Indian and Chinese seamen to settle their disagreements over a lavish Chinese banquet. Before stumbling into fame as a chef and cookery writer, Lo sold Chinese calligraphy brushes, cards and prints of classic Chinese paintings to London shops, and gave tennis lessons. Among his tennis pupils were the children of the chef and restaurant critic, Egon Ronay, and when Ronay discovered Lo knew about Chinese food, he invited him to become an unpaid inspector of Chinese restaurants for *The Good Food Guide*. Lo recounts that in the early 1960s, 'I ate at more Chinese restaurants than anyone in his right mind would want to. The quantity of indifferent food that I had to eat was quite alarming.' He discovered some restaurants were using diluted Marmite as a cheap substitute for Soy sauce. Yet he was no snob about food. He was as happy with a bowl of noodles properly cooked and prepared with care as he was with any gastronomic creation. In 1980 Lo and his wife, Anne, founded the London restaurant, *Memories of China*, offering dishes from various regions of China, including his native Fujian province. It was instantly rated among the best Chinese restaurants in the country. A year later they opened the first Chinese cookery school in Europe. In 1982, Chinese food reached into millions of British homes when the BBC commissioned Ken Hom, an American Chinese, to make a cookery series, *Ken Hom's Chinese Cookery*. The companion cookery books sold more than 1.5 million copies. Chinese food was becoming a standard part of the British diet.

A different political situation led to another head chef from the Chinese Embassy in London setting up his own London restaurant. In 1960 Kuo Teh-lou, who had been in London for some years, received instructions to return to China that he feared would lead him to be detained in a Communist Reform Camp in China. 'I was afraid I would lose my freedom for since 1957 my attitude was not very favourable to the Communists,' Kuo later told the press. 'So after cooking breakfast at the Embassy I made an excuse that I had a headache and could not attend the daily indoctrination meeting. I walked out and took a taxi to stay with friends.' He then successfully applied to the British Government for political asylum. Kuo opened the Loon Fung restaurant in London, serving the first Pekinese dishes in Britain. By chance, a few months later, the King and Queen of Thailand dined there at the invitation of Dr Chen, the ex-first secretary of the former Republic of China Embassy. Perhaps Chen chose Kuo's restaurant with an eye to the publicity generated by the royal couple dining at the restaurant of the recent defector from the Communist cause. However, the Thai Embassy was quick to state that the luncheon had 'no political implications' so Dr Ko may simply have chosen it to enable the King and Queen to sample Kuo's specialty, Peking Duck. A visit by another royal couple, the fashionable Princess Margaret and Lord Snowdon, put both the restaurant and Chinese food on the map and Chinese food became part of the Swinging Sixties, with such stars as Mick Jagger and the Beatles being seen at fashionable London Chinese restaurants.

In 1961 the Association of Chinese Restaurants estimated there were 1,000 Chinese restaurants in Britain and that around 100 more were opening annually. Although in the previous year about 1,000 men had immigrated to Britain from Hong Kong to work in catering, a 50 per cent increase on the previous year, this was still insufficient to meet the demand for workers. In response to this shortage, the British Association of Chinese Restaurants sent a representative to Hong Kong to recruit more and the next year the number of immigrants rose to 2,000.

At the time, the Hong Kong Government estimated that of those who left Hong Kong to work in Britain 99 per cent went to work in a Chinese restaurant. To encourage immigration from Hong Kong the Government introduced a special migrant one-way airfare of £85 from Hong Kong to London; far less than the standard fare of £208. Almost all those who came left behind their wives and children, and few could afford a return flight to visit them until a number of airlines flying from mainland European destinations began offering cheap return airfares to Hong Kong. In response the British airline, BOAC, successfully applied to the Air Transport Licensing Board for permission to introduce a special economy class fare for Chinese immigrants in Britain to travel back to Hong Kong to visit their families.

Although the number of Chinese restaurants continued to expand, by 1963 the shortage of staff had become less acute, except for chefs. Many British hotels and restaurants serving British and French food also were short of chefs and attracted Chinese ones with higher pay. Like many chefs, the majority of Chinese ones trained on the job. For a large percentage of the Chinese immigrants who came to work in restaurants, life in Britain was unsatisfactory. Very few were able to bring their wives and children and so were lonely. Their isolation was compounded by long working hours and minimal, if any, English, both of which were barriers to social life. Unlike other immigrant groups who either came understanding some English or were forced to learn the language if they wanted a job, the Chinese working in Chinese restaurants had little motivation to learn English as they were working with fellow Chinese. Even the waiters had only to learn a minimal amount to be able to communicate with customers. In 1962, when The Commonwealth Immigration Act gave settled status to those who had come to Britain from the Commonwealth, many Hong Kong Chinese working in Britain decided to make their lives in Britain and so their wives and children travelled from Hong Kong to join them. Thus the predominantly male character of the Chinese immigrant community in Britain began to change. As wives and children joined the restaurant workforce, businesses began to be transformed into family enterprises. Previously, most male Chinese restaurant workers lodged together or lived in a room above the restaurant, but the arrival of families required a move to rental or owned accommodation, bringing more Chinese into contact with the wider community. Their children also began to bring contact with non-Chinese families, and parents were driven to learn English as otherwise tackling many tasks was problematic.

William Poon arrived in 1967 and took a job as a dim-sum chef in Birmingham, and a few years later opened his own take-away. However, this did not suit him and instead he became the chef for the Hong Kong House student centre and the VIP chef at the PlayBoy Club. In 1969 he established the Poon's Wind-Dried Products factory and, four years later, opened his first Poon's Restaurant. Like others at the time, the lack of certain authentic ingredients meant he had to improvise and he also adjusted a few dishes to suit the liking of the Western customers. Noting that many customers had difficulty deciding what to choose from the lengthy list of available dishes, Poon came up with the idea of various set menus, an idea swiftly taken up by other Chinese restaurants. Following the success of his first restaurant, Poon invited his brothers to join him and the family opened four more restaurants. Poon's in Covent Garden, London, became a favourite of stars of entertainment and in 1979 the excellence of his cooking won the restaurant a coveted Michelin star. Poon retired from his business in 2003. Throughout his long career as one of Britain's leading Chinese chefs, he declared that he had never cooked chop suey and, one assumes, never for a moment considered serving any dish with chips and curry sauce.

By the early 1970s it was estimated that there were about 12,000 Chinese takeaways and 3,000 Chinese restaurants in the UK, and the diversity and quality of Chinese cooking in Britain continued to improve. By the 1980s there were Chinese restaurants and take-aways in every part of the UK, from Charlie Chan's in Thurso to the New Hong Kong in Penzance, with some 14,000 others in between. This growth brought a demand for wholesale supplies of ingredients. In 1969, Woon Wing Yip, who had arrived in Britain from Hong Kong ten years earlier with only £10 in his pocket, progressed from being a waiter to part-owner of a restaurant in Clacton-on-Sea. He then decided to start a business as a wholesaler and importer of Chinese food ingredients for the restaurant trade. His first Chinese supermarket was opened in Birmingham and over forty years his company has grown to own superstore branches in Manchester and Greater London, and to trade internationally. In 2010, after receiving an OBE from the Queen, Britain's first Chinese tycoon said, 'I was so surprised and feel very honoured, especially after coming here as an immigrant. I knew when I arrived in the UK that I wanted to be more than a waiter.'

When the Peking Opera were booked to perform in Britain in 1986 the British promoters were keen to ensure that their dietary needs were well catered for and so made a point of hunting out the best Chinese restaurants in each city the company were to visit. One dietary need the promoters had not considered was chocolate: they were taken aback when told that the world-famous troupe of singers, dancers and acrobats were confirmed chocoholics and each of the fifty members of the company required two bars of chocolate a day. Not having budgeted for supplying more than 6,000 chocolate bars, the promoters turned to Rowntree Macintosh for support and six weeks' worth of Yorkie bars and Kit-Kats were provided.

19

Unwelcome Action

Chariots rumbling; horses neighing;
Soldiers shouting martial cries;
Drums are sounding; trumpets braying;
Seas of glittering spears arise.
And the old man went on speaking
To the stranger from afar:
"Tis the Emperor, glory seeking,
Drives them 'neath his baleful star.
Guarding river; guarding passes
On the frontier, wild and drear;
Fighting foes in savage masses—
Scant of mercy, void of fear.'

      Du Fu, translated by Charles Budd

Chiu Yiu Nam, wearing his George Medal, 1983. (Public domain)

In 1914, when the First World War broke out in Europe, parts of China were under the control of various foreign countries including Britain, Japan, Russia and Germany, and the country was financially chaotic, highly unstable politically, and militarily very weak. The Government was concerned that the military conflict could spread to Chinese territory and so declared China to be neutral to avoid the warring countries carrying out military operations on Chinese soil. However, China's neutrality was partly ignored when Japan, with British military support, seized the German Treaty Ports.

At the outbreak of the war the British Government introduced the Aliens Restriction Act, requiring all aliens to register with the police. 'Enemy aliens' who came from countries at war with Britain were interned or deported and many thousands of these had been working on British merchant ships. Also about 9,000 British merchant seamen were called up to serve in the Royal Navy and thus there was a critical shortage of merchant ship crews. Thus, in spite of previous strong opposition to the employment of Chinese on British vessels by the Seamen's Union, the Government and the shipowners had no choice but to hire large numbers of Chinese seamen. From being condemned as unfit to serve on British vessels, the Chinese were now regarded worthy to risk their lives in support of the British war effort. Needing work and with travel to China disrupted, few Chinese seamen had any choice but to crew British merchant ships in spite of the risk of attack by German submarines. Many ships were sunk with the loss of Chinese crew members. On one ship alone, *Benlarig*, of the thirty-eight crew members who died at sea, twenty-one were Chinese.

Many were fortunate to survive. In 1915 a German torpedo struck *Strathnairn*, a merchant ship carrying coal from Wales to Russia, and the boat began to sink. One lifeboat containing the captain and Chinese seamen collided with the vessel's side and all the occupants were washed into the sea. Fortunately, they were able to regain the lifeboat and after being at sea all night, the captain and Chinese were rescued by a Royal Navy vessel. The experience of the first engineer and the Chinese carpenter was less happy. They only saved themselves by clinging to a capsized boat together, being rescued after nine hours' physical and mental agony.

Although Chinese seamen were assisting Britain's war effort, opposition to their employment by the unions and British seamen continued and when the war ended, the reward for many of the plucky Chinese seamen was to be compelled to leave Britain. 'The people principally affected by the Government's repatriation of aliens will be first the Chinese, whom there are numbers of in seaport towns, mainly London, Liverpool, and Cardiff. Permission to stay will be accorded only in very exceptional cases to Chinese who have acquired businesses in Great Britain.'

There is no record of any Chinese born in China and living in Britain being called up to serve as a soldier in the First World War; but one son of a Chinese and British couple did serve in the British Army, and there may well have been a few others. William Yipsing, who appeared in Chapter 4

Unwelcome Action

working as a chauffeur in London, married Sarah Weaver in 1913, and the following year joined the Army Service Corps where his driving skills would have been valued, and served throughout the war as a private. This corps was responsible for land transport, and the supply of food, water, fuel, and technical and military equipment. Although William does not appear to have been transferred to action in the trenches, large numbers of those who were employed in non-combat duties were required to become active soldiers due to the large number being killed or wounded. Requiring replacements for these non-combat tasks, Britain and France began to employ foreign workers from their colonies, including China. Around 140,000 Chinese men, about half of the foreign labour units deployed, were recruited and travelled to Europe to serve in the Chinese Labour Corps on the Western Front. Many were killed and wounded, even though they were not serving as part of combat forces. (The next chapter recounts the experience of one Chinese who served in the Chinese Labour Corps.)

At the end of the war none of the Chinese who had worked for the Labour Corps in France and Belgium were allowed to enter Britain. An internal government directive gave the confidential reason: 'The entry of Chinese into Britain may at any moment lead to racial riots which are to be avoided at all costs.' The British Government had employed a large number of Chinese who spoke English to act as interpreters among the Corps, many from establishments established or run by British missionary societies in China and, at the end of the war, a number asked to be allowed to study in Britain. The authorities refused and *The Times* criticised the decision to force the interpreters to return to China. 'A fine opportunity of enlisting some hundreds of missionaries for British ideals and commerce in China was sacrificed on the altar of bureaucratic myopia.' For almost a century the record of the 140,000 Chinese who had been vital to the Allied victory was disregarded. During the war a giant canvas was created in Paris showing a victorious France surrounded by her allies. This originally included portrayals of Chinese Labour Corps workers but, in 1917, when the United States joined the war, the Chinese were overpainted with portrayals of American soldiers.

China ended its neutrality in February 1917 as a result of the sinking of a civilian ship carrying Chinese by a German U-boat. Around 750 of the 1,950 crew and passengers died, including 543 Chinese. This act, a breach of international law, led to China breaking off its diplomatic ties with Germany. In January 1915, Japan secretly issued an ultimatum of Twenty-One Demands to the Chinese Government. These included Japanese control of former German rights and a ninety-nine-year lease in southern Manchuria, an interest in steel mills, and concessions regarding railways. In spite of China having a seat at the Paris Peace Conference in 1919, the former German concessions were not returned to China and the country had to accept the Japanese Twenty-One demands. A major reaction to this humiliation was a surge in Chinese nationalism. In the 1920s, with China weakened by continued internal conflicts, Japan continued its aggression by appropriating Manchuria and the 1930s saw sporadic fighting between Japanese and Chinese forces. In 1937 Chiang Kai-shek, the head of the Nationalist Kuomintang party that ruled China, decided that Japan's imperialism had to be confronted and declared war. This was, in effect, the beginning of the Second World War in Asia, which would result in huge political changes. Eventually, its aftermath would see the nationalists replaced by the Communist party, led by Mao Zedong, and the decline of British influence in Asia, with the eventual loss of the British colony of Hong Kong.

China was the only non-European country to fight fascism and its involvement was crucial in defeating the Japanese-German axis. Yet in so doing, it paid a heavy price. Over the eight years of war 14 million Chinese died, up to 100 million became refugees, and the country's modernised infrastructure was almost wholly destroyed. Following the outbreak of war between China and Japan a diverse range of groups in Britain, including politicians, Church leaders trade unions and peace organisations, came together to establish the China Campaign Committee (CCC). The CCC arranged events to protest against the Japanese, including calling for a boycott of Japanese goods, and to fundraise for aid to China. By 1940 the CCC had organised nearly 3,000 events throughout the country, many involving Chinese in Britain speaking out against Japan's aggression. The war in China affected many Chinese living in Britain. News of the fate of relations in the areas of conflict was patchy, or non-existent, and many of the Chinese studying in Britain found themselves in financial difficulties as their families were unable to send them money. One such was Kenneth Lo, later the famous cookery writer, who was studying at Cambridge. When he explained his plight to the college authorities they agreed to waive his fees and provided him with financial support. After Britain declared war in 1939 Lo managed to obtain a job as Fire Watchman for the university library, which earned him some money, although, as Lo recounts, many other Chinese students at Cambridge were forced to take jobs picking tomatoes.

By early 1939, with the threat of war in Europe looming, the British Government began issuing gas masks to civilians as the *Liverpool Daily Post* reported: 'People of all races and colour from Somalis to Finns, in brief all people ordinarily resident in the city, are being fitted and supplied with gas masks. Last night it was the turn of the Chinese colony, or at least the remains of what once was the picturesque centre of Oriental animation in Liverpool. With the advent of the shipping slump the Chinese population dwindled from 2,000 to scarcely 200, and in Pitt Street, the heart of Liverpool's Chinatown, there are now only fifty established residents.' As a shop owner, Kwok Fong was appointed the area's deputy-senior warden and the gas masks were distributed from his shop in Pitt Street. Most of those trying on the masks for the first time struggled, and the Chinese were no different, except for 'Mr. Kwok's young son, who proved his mastery of the details after the first

Unwelcome Action

attempt'. One suspects that not everyone in the Chinese community was keen on wearing a gas mask for, in 1941, when German bombs created a gas cloud in the Rock Ferry district, Kong Few and his assistant ran out of their laundry shop 'with tears streaming down their cheeks'.

Opposition to Chinese sailors had led to the Chinese communities in both London's Limehouse and Liverpool shrinking, but Liverpool's boomed again as the port saw the establishment of the Chinese Merchant Seamen's Pool with approximately 20,000 men contracted. Many came from east China – often simply called Shanghainese – whereas previously the majority of Chinese employed by the shipping companies had been Cantonese. Many of the Chinese seamen were employed to crew the oil tankers on the dangerous Atlantic run, but all merchant ships were at threat from German submarines. On 12 January 1942 the unescorted *Cyclops*, a merchant ship owned by the Ocean Steam Ship Company of Liverpool, was at sea southeast of Nova Scotia when it was attacked by a German U-boat. *Cyclops* had twice been attacked by German submarines during the First World War and managed to avoid being hit, but this time it was not so fortunate. A torpedo caused extensive damage and those not killed in the first explosion abandoned ship. However, the ship did not sink and some crewmen began to re-board, at which point the submarine fired a second torpedo. Its explosion caused *Cyclops* to break into two and the ship sank in five minutes. On board were about ninety-five crew, of which around one-third were Chinese, plus seventy-eight Chinese seamen being transported to Canada to man other British ships. Many of the Chinese crew and more than half of the Chinese seamen travelling as passengers lost their lives.

One who ended up involved in the war by unfortunate timing was Lin Jintai. He had sailed to Britain as a fireman on a British ship that docked in Liverpool in 1940. Lin was young and had decided that being at sea was too lonely a life, so planned to return to his family immediately on reaching Britain. Unfortunately, during the journey, the Japanese invaded Shanghai and Lin was stuck in Liverpool. 'All contact with Shanghai was lost. I couldn't even find a way to send my money back to my mother. Having no choice, I stayed. During the war I could hear the bombs every night and couldn't go to sleep. There were thousands of Shanghai people in Liverpool, mostly young men.' Lin never did return to China as he met a waitress in a cafe and they married in 1944.

In spite of being lauded by the press as 'plucky Allies', the Chinese seamen were shabbily treated. Chinese seamen were only paid around one third of the wages of British seamen, and were denied the war-risk bonus paid to British merchant seamen. Another source of anger was the lack of compensation for relatives of those killed in action. T. W. Chen, secretary of the Chinese Seamen's Union, complained that, 'Although about a hundred Chinese seamen have been killed in British ships since the war began, we have had no success in attempts to obtain compensation for the relatives of the men killed at sea comparable to that paid to British seamen.' By March 1943, more than 800 Chinese seamen had died, with about 250 reported missing and a similar number notified as Prisoners of War. During the Normandy landings in 1944, up to 700 Chinese are thought to have died.

In response to ill-treatment and the disparity in pay, many Chinese seamen refused to work and as a result a number were fined and some jailed. In the face of growing discontent and a threat from the Chinese Government that it would withdraw all Chinese seamen from British ships, the British Government improved pay and conditions. Negative views about the Chinese were reinforced with accounts that Chinese seamen were more prone to panic than British seamen when ships were under fire. When the Alfred Holt-owned ship *Automedon* was attacked by the Germans, one British engineer reported that 'pandemonium broke loose and the Chinese firemen came stampeding up the ladder'. However, the version of Cheong Wong, one of the Chinese stokers, seems more likely: 'Everybody on the ship was frightened and quite panicky – it didn't matter whether you were Chinese or European.' In reality Chinese seamen were just as likely to panic or be brave as other seamen. D. L. C. Evans, captain of the British merchant ship *Glenartney*, wrote after undertaking a rescue mission in the Atlantic in 1941:

> The Chinese crew were truly excellent, working to the point of exhaustion ... As an illustration of the spirit prevailing, the Chinese boys made it clear that any attempt on the part of the survivors to offer any reward or gratuity would be most offensive to their feelings, and would be met with disdainful refusal. I can only say with all the sincerity that I possess that I am proud to have been in command of such a ship, manned by such excellent officers, midshipmen and crew.

A number of Chinese won medals for bravery in action, including Ho Kan, the quartermaster on *The Empress of Scotland*. Built in Glasgow for the Canadian Pacific Steamship, the passenger liner was originally named *The Empress of Japan* and went into service in 1929, sailing between Vancouver, Yokohama and Hong Kong. The ship could carry almost 1,200 passengers and it created a new speed record for the trans-Pacific route. In 1939 the ship was requisitioned by the British Government and converted into a troopship. After the Japanese attack on Pearl Harbor, Winston Churchill ordered her name be changed. While carrying Australian and New Zealand troops to the battle zone in November 1940, German aircraft attacked and began to dive-bomb the ship. Ho Kan, the quartermaster, nicknamed Silent Ho as he only smiled when satisfied, was steering the vessel at the time and throughout the attack that lasted five hours, Ho managed to steer the ship so that it avoided taking a direct hit. His fearlessness saved the *Empress* and the troops and crew. In recognition of his bravery he was presented with the British Empire

Medal by the king at Buckingham Palace. As the medal was pinned on his brand-new uniform it was reported that Silent Ho smiled.

One of the most remarkable stories of survival at sea during the war involved Poon Lim, a steward on the British merchant ship *Benlomond*. When it was sunk by a German U-boat 750 miles off the South American coast in November 1942, Lim donned his life jacket and managed to jump overboard before the ship's boilers exploded. After about two hours in the sea, Poon Lim found and climbed aboard an 8-foot-square wooden raft. The raft contained several tins of biscuits, a 40-litre jug of water, some chocolate, a bag of sugar lumps, some flares, two smoke pots, and a flashlight. When the water and food on the raft ran out, he made a fishing line out of the flashlight wire and some rope so he could catch fish, and used a canvas life jacket covering to catch rainwater. On one occasion when a storm spoiled his fish and fouled his water, he resorted to catching a bird and drinking its blood to survive. On another occasion he managed to catch a shark, clubbing it to death with his water jug half-filled with seawater. On two occasions Lim thought he was about to be rescued but both times his hopes were crushed. The first was when a freighter sailed close to his raft but, in spite of his shouting for help, the ship sailed on, perhaps thinking him a Japanese sailor. The second was when he was spotted by a United States Navy patrol seaplane that dropped a marker buoy in the water. Unfortunately, a storm arose and the raft was swept away from the marker, and he was lost again. Eventually, after 133 days at sea, Poon Lim's raft drifted near land and three Brazilian fishermen rescued him. As a result of his ordeal, Poon Lim lost 9 kilos but was able to walk unaided upon being rescued. He spent four weeks in a Brazilian hospital before returning to Britain. He was the only one of the 54 crew to survive. When he was told that no one had ever survived longer on a raft at sea, Poon Lim replied, 'I hope no one will ever have to break that record.' George VI presented Lim with a British Empire Medal and the Royal Navy incorporated his tale into manuals of survival techniques. After the war Poon Lim decided to immigrate to the United States but the quota for Chinese immigrants had been reached. However, because of his fame he received a special dispensation and eventually gained citizenship. There is no record of how many of the 35,000 merchant seamen who died while serving on British ships were Chinese, but the number is likely to be in the thousands as around 15 per cent of those serving were Chinese.

A small number of Chinese served in the British armed forces. One was Leong Kwong Chee, a Malayan-Chinese who had been studying aerial surveying in Singapore and came to Britain and joined the RAF as an aerial photographer. Also a number of children born to Chinese men and British women, and thus British nationals, were called up. Four sons of Quan and Beatrice Soo, who ran a laundry in Liverpool, joined the forces and their other son trained as a cadet. Jack served in the Royal Engineers in the Middle East, and Harold and Ronald became Flight Sergeants in the Royal

Air Force and flew as gunners on bombers. Ronald died when the bomber he was flying in crashed during a raid on Germany. He was twenty-three years old. Frank, who by the outbreak of war was the first British Chinese professional footballer, and a first-rate player, spent the war in England helping train pilots in the use of an automatic radar system that assisted pilots to land 'blind'. As the authorities decided it was good for public morale to continue with competitive football, all the top players were assigned posts in Britain so they could continue playing. Frank played for a RAF team and was allowed, when available, to appear as a guest player for any club. Soo was a prominent player and the last-minute appearance of him, often with his brilliant teammate Stanley Matthews, boosted crowds. During and after the war, Soo played for England.

For everyone in Britain, German bombing was a threat but those living near strategic targets were at far greater risk. This included docks where the bulk of Chinese had settled and in the early stages of the war, some British Chinese children were among the large numbers of children evacuated to the safety of the country or suburbs. Many civilians were killed, injured or displaced by the intense German bombing, but there is no record of the total number of Chinese civilian casualties. In 1940, seventy Chinese living in a lodging house in Limehouse were killed in one of the first bombing raids of the war. Chang Sing Keen, a ship's cook, was at sea in 1941 when he received word that he had to return to Liverpool to identify members of his family, including his mother, who had been killed by a bomb in Pitt Street. The properties of many were destroyed or severely damaged. The bomb in Pitt Street destroyed Kwong Shang Lung's Chinese grocery store at Number 12 and the Foo Nam Low restaurant next door, and in July 1942 it was reported that 'Limehouse Causeway is a total wreck, and not much of Pennyfields has survived the Blitz.'

Although negative comments about the Chinese continued, China's fight against Japan was positively recognised. In July 1942, to mark the fifth anniversary of the declaration of war between China and Japan, China Week was organised with events throughout Britain. One was a series of talks on Chinese culture and language given by Diana Wong who had come to Britain as an infant and began an acting career in the mid-1930s, appearing in many plays on the British stage. She had spent some time in Paris and there became engaged to a British broadcaster. The couple managed to flee the city as the Germans invaded and married in England. Her husband was Roy Plomley and in January 1942 he began broadcasting his *Desert Island Discs*, which would become one of the most iconic BBC radio programmes. In 1944, the Ministry of Information commissioned Carl Heck to direct a short documentary, *Chinese in Britain*, to provide a positive portrayal of Chinese living in Britain at the time. It highlighted positive cultural exchange and integration, and promoted the view that those Chinese who returned to China would help to spread British democratic values. It consisted of a series of segments, with overlaid commentary. The film begins with images of the room that Sun Yat-sen was held in at the Chinese Embassy – 'It was British democracy that saved his life,' intones the voice-over. Later sections include shots of bombed areas of London – 'Bombs in London by German planes or bombs in Chungking by Japanese bombers feel very much the same'; injured Chinese sailors disembarking and being taken to convalescent homes; Chinese doctors, scientists and engineers at work; and BBC broadcasts to China. The film ends with the comment, 'The Chinese in Britain provide one of those living links that are forging the unity of the new family of nations.'

In 1942 the United Aid to China Fund ran a series of newspaper advertisements seeking funds for China's war with Japan. One featured a photograph of Yang Hui-min, a Girl Guide: 'She doesn't talk about her bravery, though in the height of the Battle of Shanghai she carried her national flag through the Japanese lines to a surrounded Chinese battalion! She's China. One of China's fighting women.' Four years earlier, Yang had briefly visited Britain on her way to America to represent China at the World Youth Congress and the papers carried accounts of her heroic deed, although most accounts were inaccurate. During the Chinese retreat from Shanghai 300 men, known as the Doomed Battalion, stayed to fight in a house yards from the International Settlement. Yang volunteered to try to take food to the besieged battalion. Cutting her hair short and dressing as a Boy Scout, Yang wriggled her way over 2 miles of ruined buildings until she reached the soldiers. She also took a Chinese flag and inspired by her bravery the defenders flew the flag the next daybreak in front of thousands watching on the far river bank. For another advert that described how children in China were at risk from Japanese bombing just as children in Britain were threatened by German bombs, the Fund required a photograph of a Chinese infant and asked Mrs Cheng Yao-Kun, a recent arrival in Britain, to be photographed with her young son, Ching Chung, who was renamed for the advert, 'Little Wu Lien of Chungking'.

Although the war in Europe ended in May 1945, it was not until August 1945 that Japan surrendered. The Chinese celebrated Japan's defeat across the country. 'As the great concourse of men and girls began to converge on the East India Dock Road and Pennyfields, crackers and Chinese fireworks began to explode all over the streets. The strange International crowd that gathered – with its overpowering Chinese flavour – was suddenly the strangest and almost certainly the most joyous crowd In London.' Yet for large numbers of the Chinese seamen in Liverpool, and some of their families in the city, the end of the war was not a cause for celebration. Within a few months of the peace the British Government and the shipping companies began expelling large numbers, many being forced to leave their British families.

British Royal Fleet Auxiliary (RFA) vessels are civilian-manned ships, owned by the Ministry of Defence, that support the Royal Navy by transporting fuel, ammunition, supplies and Army and Royal Marine personnel. In the past, many of the crews were employed from places where the British Navy had bases, such as Malta, Singapore and Hong Kong, and a significant number of those working on board these ships were Chinese. Although RFA vessels had been employed in conflicts involving Britain after the Second World War, such as Suez, Korea and Vietnam, none were engaged in action and there were no casualties amongst the sailors. This changed in 1982 when Britain responded to the invasion of the Falkland Islands in the Atlantic Ocean by Argentina. About twenty RFA ships sailed to Britain from around the world to prepare to take on soldiers and supplies for the war. While the ships were docked in Portsmouth, Chinese crew members protested that their civilian contracts did not mention participating in a war. Their ships' captains and the Ministry of Defence disagreed, stating that this was covered in their conditions of employment. Cheung San-fan, the cook on board the ship, *Sir Galahad*, approached his captain to voice the crew's concern. Captain Roberts recalls Cheung coming to speak to him.

> The Chinese crew on board put together a declaration stating they did not wish to fight in a war that had nothing to do with them. You can't blame them for that. The Chinese crew, most of whom had been working on the ship for some time, and were very hard working and kept a good ship, knew we were on a ship prepared for war. *Sir Galahad* was painted grey, after all.

Despite the protest, the ships sailed with their Chinese crews. In the Atlantic, all ships became part of the Task Force, as the fleet became known, and all non-military personnel fell under the Navy Discipline Act. Failure to obey any order meant instant court martial.

On 8 June two of the ships, *Sir Tristam* and *Sir Galahad*, arrived in Fitzroy, a settlement on the Falklands, to unload soldiers, ammunition and vehicles. Although all the soldiers had been unloaded from *Sir Tristam*, there were delays in unloading the soldiers of the Welsh Guards from *Sir Galahad* and a large number of soldiers were on deck ready to disembark when both ships were attacked by Argentine planes. Two bombs hit *Sir Tristam*, one exploding in a small compartment killing two Chinese crewmen. Three bombs struck *Sir Galahad*, one passing through a hatch hitting the tank deck, one hitting the engine room and galley, and the last striking the officer's quarters. These were types of bombs that created fireballs, rather than explosions. The bomb that hit the tank deck caused most of the casualties, for that was where most of the troops were concentrated, along with 20 tons of ammunition and a large quantity of petrol. The deck became an inferno. At least forty-five soldiers were killed and many were set on fire, resulting in 150 being injured, many seriously. Chiu Yiu Nam, an Able Seaman, was working on *Sir Galahad's* upper decks helping to load helicopters with equipment when the bombs hit. He was a drilled member of the ship's fire-fighting team so donned an asbestos fire-fighting suit, although it only provided partial protection, and started tackling the ferocious flames. Then, realising that there were soldiers trapped inside the ship, he fought his way through the smoke and flames into the ship's bowels, where he was confronted by scenes of confusion and devastation. After leading out one man, he went back for another. Chiu Yiu Nam continued to return, taking men to safety until he realised that there was no one left alive. Only then did he obey the order to abandon ship. Of those who survived, at least ten owed their survival to Chiu Yiu Nam.

Chiu Yiu Nam was remarkably modest about his bravery. Although Captain Roberts quizzed the survivors in his crew about their role during the bombing of *Sir Galahad*, Chiu did not mention his heroic act. It was only later that a Commanding Officer in the Welsh Guards interviewed his guardsmen and heard about an unknown rescuer whose identity had been hidden behind a protective hood. Further inquiries revealed that this had been Chiu. Initially reluctant to be officially recognised, in 1983 Chiu did agree to fly from Hong Kong to London, where the Queen invested him with the George Medal, one of Britain's highest awards for civilians. As seamen contracted abroad by the British Navy were not eligible for pensions, the medal was all that Chui received from the British Government, yet he was forced to give up work as a result of the effects of the lethal blue asbestos and smoke he breathed saving the British soldiers. Chui died in 2012, aged sixty-two. In 2013 his medal was auctioned for £29,000.

Cheung San-fan was preparing a meal for the soldiers on board *Sir Galahad* because their landing had been delayed when the bombs struck. The one that exploded near the galley instantly killed two of the Chinese crew: Leung Chau, an electrical fitter, and Sung Yuk-fai, a butcher. Cheung was thrown to the ground. 'My legs were trapped under something heavy, I couldn't see anything because the electricity had gone,' Cheung recounted. 'Breathing was difficult. I managed to kick free and get up, feeling my way to the door, where I stepped on a body. I couldn't see who it was. I didn't feel any pain. All I could hear was this ringing in my ear. I managed to get out to the back of the ship where they were lifting people up by cable to rescue helicopters. That's when I saw through the smoke that the skin on my arms was peeling off like tree bark and my hands were charred and misshapen. One of the soldiers helped me get on the helicopter, where I collapsed and couldn't move. I was freezing. I remember someone taking off his coat and putting it around me. I could hear them talking to me, but I couldn't respond.' Cheung had suffered 65 per cent burns to his face, hands, arms and legs and underwent a long series of skin grafts. 'At first, during my recovery, I wanted to die,' Cheung recalled in an interview he gave to *The South China Times* in 2007. 'My nerves were completely exposed and the pain was so excruciating my whole body would shake from the core. I just didn't want to be alive. I would think about my family and the tears would flow.' After his hospital treatment Cheung was flown back to Hong Kong, and for a number of years required further skin-graft surgery, painful physiotherapy and counselling. He was left with unsightly blisters and red-raw scarring that caused people to shy away from him in the street. Cheung was awarded the South Atlantic Medal and, because he could never work again, received two cash pay-outs totalling HK$360,000 from a trust fund collected via public donations from around the world. He also received a small pension from the British Government. In the Falklands War eight Chinese seamen died.

In January 2006, a commemorative plaque was unveiled in Liverpool dedicated to the memory of Chinese seamen who had served in the British merchant fleet during the First and Second World Wars, and to the families of the men who were repatriated unfairly.

> To the Chinese Merchant Seaman who served this country well during both World Wars. For those who gave their lives to this country – thank you. To the many Chinese Merchant Seamen who after both World Wars were required to leave. For their wives and partners who were left in ignorance of what happened to their men.
>
> For the children who never knew their fathers. This is a small reminder of what took place.
>
> We hope nothing like it will ever happen again. For your Memory.

20
One Immigrant's Story

After you came back to my home,
You never complained that we were poor.
Up till midnight every night,
We had our breakfast after noon.
Nine or ten days eating pickles,
Then one day we'd have dried meat.
East and west for eighteen years,
Together we shared both bitter and sweet.

Mei Yaochen (1002–1060),
translated by Kenneth Rexroth

Soo Yow (Yuen Yi) – front, centre – with members of his Chinese Labour Corps squad, *c.* 1916–18. (Courtesy of Karen Soo)

Yuen Yi was born in 1897 in Taishan, Canton, in the Pearl River Delta. The area experienced natural disasters and a full-scale war with its Northern neighbours in the 1850s and '60s. Thus when opportunities arose to leave China to work abroad in Hawaii, Cuba, the United States and elsewhere, lots of men left, many to work on building the Central Pacific half of America's Transcontinental Railroad. Life was still hard in 1916 when the French and British began recruiting for men for work in Europe and again many men from the area signed up. Few knew about the First World War in Europe and the contracts simply mentioned that they would be employed on jobs in industry and agriculture, so what awaited them was a shock. The fighting in France was resulting in large numbers of Allied soldiers being killed or wounded, and men previously employed in non-combat duties, such as digging trenches, moving equipment and repairing roads, were required to become active soldiers. In the face of this critical shortage of manpower, Britain and France decided to employ workers from their overseas colonies. The British and French authorities recognised that asking men to sign up to work in a war zone was unlikely to convince many to travel to Europe so the contracts were left vague.

The journey for all the Chinese that were hired involved three months of gruelling travelling. Many made their way to Shanghai to board a ship to take them across the Pacific to Vancouver, Canada. As the British and French governments wished to avoid paying the normal landing tax for anyone entering Canada, they had agreed that the Chinese would be transported non-stop in sealed carriages to Halifax on the far coast, where they were to be shipped to Britain. This was a four- to five-day train journey and the conditions would have been grim. Accommodation on board the ship to Britain would have been no better. An internal memo of guidance in the British department co-ordinating the transfer of the Chinese stated: 'The Chinese can be packed fairly tight, even for a long voyage.'

It was hardly surprising that many Chinese died on the sea journey to Liverpool and the city's cemeteries contain graves of some. Others arrived ill. On one occasion, 150 Chinese arriving from Halifax had to be taken to Liverpool's Belmont Road Military Hospital as all were suffering from mumps and needed to be isolated. *The Liverpool Courier* reported: 'The fact that none of them could speak English rendered the work somewhat difficult, an interpreter in the person of a Chinese corporal having to remain in the hospital during the whole of the time that any of the Chinese patients remained.'

Yuen's journey may have been less arduous as he travelled by ship all the way to France and being strong, survived the long journey without mishap, although the shock of discovering what the work really entailed must have been immense. Yet there was no alternative. Thousands of miles from home and in a war zone, the 160,000 Chinese workers were dependent on the British and French for food and shelter. The tasks required to support the

One Immigrant's Story

fighting included loading and unloading equipment, ammunition and other materials; building and maintaining trenches, roads, railways and airfields; and clearing away bodies and spent ammunition. There was significant initial resistance from the British troops to the influx of Chinese, although eventually the Chinese Labour Corps became popular for their endurance and strength, and this helped alter misperceptions about the Chinese among many. As one soldier commented, 'As children we were taught to believe that both Cain and coolies were murderers from the beginning; no coolie was trusted; he was a yellow dog, he would stick a knife into you in a dark alley on a dark night. He was treacherous. Today we have outgrown this puerility.' A British labour officer, Captain McCormick noted: 'They were strong, healthy looking men, capable of enduring great physical exertion, and could work at an extraordinarily high pressure if they thought they could reduce the numbers of hours to be worked, to free them so that they could sit on their "hunkers" in little groups gambling.'

Yuen quickly learnt some French and was put in charge of a labour squad. On one occasion the Germans began bombing an airfield while the Allied planes were airborne. To enable the planes to land again Yuen and his squad were ordered to fill in the bomb craters although the airfield was still being bombed. Although Yen survived, some of his squad did not, and during the war many Chinese died from bombing and shelling, and disease. Although he did not become directly involved in the fighting, a few did. *The New York Times* reported:

> Remarkable incidents connected with the prolonged battle are becoming known. One of the most dramatic was the audacious and successful effort of a scratch battalion in closing a gap in the British line. Major General Sandeman Carey, seeing this gap suddenly open, at once improvised a force to close the breach. It was a miscellaneous body, composed of mechanics, aerial artificers, signallers and men of the labour corps. For nearly six days this scratch force gallantly held its position on the left of the fifth army. Although we don't know how many Chinese were involved in this fighting, we are quite certain that at least some Chinese labourers were there.

After the war as many as 80,000 of the Chinese Labour Corps were retained to clear mines or recover bodies. Although the French allowed those who wished to stay in France to do so, and about 3,000 did, Britain refused entry to all the Chinese workers.

Yuen decided he did not want to return to China and as Britain's doors were closed, chose to head for America and boarded a ship that he thought was bound for New York. However, it sailed to Liverpool where he disembarked, almost certainly illegally. But Chinese in the city were happy to assist and he found a job in a laundry within days of arriving. Chinese laundry owners were unconcerned as to whether their employees were legally in Britain or not. They just wanted strong, willing workers. For a number of years Yuen worked in various Chinese laundries and boarding houses across England and Wales, surely having to be itinerant as he lacked the necessary legal papers. During this time he changed his name to Soo Yow to make it easier for non-Chinese to understand.

In 1927 he married Edith, a British woman, and they opened a small laundry in Oxton Road, in Birkenhead. They had three children: Maisie, William, who died in infancy, and Cherry, born in 1934. In 1936, for whatever reason, Soo and his wife divorced and Cherry stayed with her mother and Maisie with Soo.

Needing a mother for his infant daughter, and someone to assist in the laundry, Soo travelled to China and returned with a Chinese wife. They had eight children, two of whom died in infancy and a third, Alan, when just nineteen. Life would not have been easy. The small two-storey house contained the laundry on the ground floor and the living accommodation upstairs. The Birkenhead house only had electricity on the ground floor so upstairs where the family lived the rooms were lit by candles. Soo's son, Frank, who helped out, recalled the laundry in the 1940s:

> I remember the laundry had a great big cauldron, about 5 feet across and heated by a coke fire underneath. All the dirty clothes were piled in and boiled, before being transferred to a large wooden tub for rinsing. The clothes were then spun dry in a hydro and then transferred to the drying room with wires strung across the ceiling. The room was heated by an iron coke stove which was also the heater for the flat irons. The flat irons were more versatile than the electric irons available then. In fact, stiff collars could only be formed or shaped with a flat iron – electric irons were too bulky and couldn't get hot enough. Only Chinese laundries were able to produce the very stiff collars as preferred by the police and armed forces and for formal dress wear.

As well as the long hours and back-breaking work, economic decline in the area would have been a worry. In 1939 the Birkenhead Chamber of Commerce Retail Traders' Association expressed concern 'at the number of empty shops to be found in Birkenhead, and particularly in the Oxton Road district'.

In the run-up to the outbreak of the Second World War everyone in Britain received instructions on where to go in the event of an air raid. For those living in Oxton Road, the cellars of the Birkenhead Brewery just along the road served as their air raid shelter. On the evening of 9 August 1940, the Air Raid warning sounded and the Soo family made their way to the safety of the Brewery's deep cellars. That was the first bombing of their area and it may have been on that night, or a few months later, that their property was severely damaged. Undeterred, Soo, helped by his family and neighbours, moved the laundry to another property in the street. In spite of his busy work life, Soo found time to help the Chinese community and was one of those who re-established the See Yep Association in Liverpool that provided a community focal point. There the Chinese played Mah Jong and, once or twice a year, a group performed live Chinese opera on a Sunday afternoon.

Around 1947, Soo and his wife began looking for a new laundry to run. The only one in Cheltenham was run by Mr Search who was having trouble finding staff and Soo bought it, and he and his large family moved there. To promote the new ownership Soo took out an advert in *The Gloucester Echo*: 'The Chinese Laundry, Winchcombe Street, Cheltenham is now under new management. A three-day service is in operation. New customers can be accepted. Collars and dress shirts a speciality. Soo Yow.' The Cheltenham laundry was larger and more mechanised, with industrial washing machines, spin dryers, an ironing press and tumble dryers. Soo worked an eighteen-hour day for five days of the week, with an hour's rest in the middle of the day, and three to five hours on one other day. The laundry was closed on Sundays. Soo's son described the plentiful food that helped keep everyone working hard over long days.

> My mother did all the cooking. We had a big breakfast between 8 and 9am that included eggs, bacon, sausages, fried bread, fried cheese as well as Chinese breakfast food like congee, a rice dish and dim sum, similar to dumplings. At 11am there would be tea, cakes and sandwiches. Lunch at 1pm would be a Chinese meal with a variety of regional dishes not available even in today's Chinese restaurants. Tea and cakes at 4pm, another full Chinese meal at 7pm and a final fry up at about 10pm. I often had pork chops on a plate of rice at this time of night. My father would carry on working until 1 am.

As the Cheltenham laundry was bigger than some, Soo employed a few young non-Chinese women, although the whole family were required to help. When the children came home from school, they would assist and fit their homework in when they could. However, more staff was required so relatives were employed. At one time there were fourteen people living in three rooms. For the first ten years in Cheltenham they were the only Chinese family in the town. Soo was a large, strong man and although he experienced racial discrimination he faced it down or, on occasion, used his Kung Fu skills to fight back.

In 1958 Soo opened the town's first Chinese restaurant, Ah Chow. It later changed its name to The Mayflower. Few of the Cheltenham public had tasted Chinese food before and, like most provincial Chinese restaurants of the time, Soo's kitchen had to tailor its menus to suit. Sally Prosser, a food writer, recalls eating at Soo's restaurant in 1961:

We are in the Ah Chow in Cheltenham. The waiter brings canned pineapple juice as our starter from the set menu. Then the main dishes appear including sweet and sour king prawn, round balls of batter which are slightly soggy in the middle swimming in a lurid neon orange sauce. My sister and I are thrilled and baffled in equal measure by these new foods. A few years later, it became The Mayflower with flock wallpaper and deep red furnishings and there we had crispy seaweed (actually deep-fried shredded cabbage), Kung Po prawn (sweet and sour with pieces of pineapple) and duck with pancakes and plum sauce.

These delicacies were a hit and the Ah Chow had queues every night. As well as the restaurant, Soo continued to run the laundry, but when the business became uneconomic he and his son turned it into a Chinese gift and fancy goods shop, another first for Cheltenham. Soo and his family also bought a take-away business from an uncle in Gloucester and renamed it the Peking House Takeaway. This they sold after a few years to a couple of cousins.

If Soo Yow did enter Britain illegally, that fact disappeared into the mists of time and he became a British national in the mid-1960s. Like so many immigrants he came to the country with nothing and, through hard work, established thriving businesses and produced a large, happy family. Soo died in 1980.

21

Portraying China

And then he heard accounts of an enchanted isle at sea,
A part of the intangible and incorporeal world,
With pavilions and fine towers in the five-coloured air,
And of exquisite immortals moving to and fro.

Bai Juyi (772–846),
translated by Harold Witter Bynner

Dymia and Hsiung Shih-I and Diana Wong, 1938. (Public domain)

The Chinese in Britain

In 1901, when London's Whitechapel Gallery first opened, its second exhibition was *Chinese Life and Art*, which drew around 130,000 visitors during its six-week run. A second Chinese art exhibition was shown in the gallery in 1913 and proved equally popular. In that same year, the British Museum appointed Laurence Binyon, an English writer and art scholar, as Keeper of a new sub-department of Oriental Prints and Drawings. He was influential in introducing many artists and poets, including Ezra Pound, to East Asian visual art and literature. Yet the general public's perceptions of China were being formed through popular fiction and plays, and almost all of these portrayals of China and the Chinese were entirely bogus.

Earlier writers, such as Dickens and Conan Doyle, had portrayed the opium dens of London's Limehouse as sources of crime and degradation, but it was in the early twentieth century that this fabrication became more pronounced. In 1913 Sax Rohmer published the first of his widely read novels featuring Dr Fu Manchu, the evil Chinese genius bent on destroying white civilization, and thus helped create an enduring myth of the Chinese as sly, inscrutable and unscrupulous. Another writer whose work fed into the anti-Chinese mood was Thomas Burke. His book, *Limehouse Nights: Tales of Chinatown*, published in 1916, included salacious imaginings of illicit affairs between Chinese men and English women, fuelled by opium. There were many in Britain who hoped that the war with Germany would purify the country and rid it of what they perceived to be degenerate foreign influences, and Burke's fiction confirmed the prejudice of those who believed that Chinese decadence was a symptom of Britain's moral decline, although his book was criticised for its immoral acceptance of inter-racial relationships. In the British press the Chinese continued to be the butt of racist jokes. One parody in the magazine *Punch* showed a British officer speaking to a Chinese labourer. The officer's side of the conversation is in perfect English, whereas the Chinese is speaking in lampooned pidgin English.

Archibald Sinclair, a Scottish MP, was one of the few who challenged this tendency for the Chinese supporting Britain to be seen through bigoted eyes. Speaking in Parliament, and recognising that humour might make his point better than a reproach, the MP recounted a purported exchange in France. 'A British officer looked up and saw an aeroplane, and he said to a Chinese; "Look an aeroplane." The Chinese looked up and said, "Yes." The officer said, "Isn't it wonderful? It is flying." To which the Chinese replied, "Yes. Isn't it meant to?"

Chinese themed plays, operas, pantomimes and musicals continued to be popular in the early twentieth century, but almost all simply used a fantasy China as a setting for exotic or comic effect, such as *A Chinese Honeymoon*, a musical comedy in which Chippee Chop was one of the main characters, and *The Chinese Lantern*, described as 'a medley of real drama, musical comedy, the farcical, and the enigmatical'. In 1904 the promotion for the play *Alone in China* promised that:

Lovers of thrilling melodrama will probably see something very much to their liking. It is the story – the first, I fancy to be adapted to the stage – of the Boxers' Rising and the burning of the mission will be a sensational scene. One of the striking pictures of the production promises to be the service in the Temple of the God Kwan Tai, with its complete Chinese ritual, its chants, and sacrificial offerings.

In the variety theatres Chinese jugglers and acrobats still appeared. Life on the road for all variety entertainers involved constant touring and living in less than salubrious digs or lodgings. For most it was a lonely life and flings with local admirers far from uncommon. In 1915, Duo Ding Sing had a two-week booking in Sheffield and whether it was his acrobatic skills or his looks that enticed a young girl to run away with him after his final performance at the Empire Theatre is not known. They had met after his first performance and Duo wrote her various letters pleading with her to abscond with him. Finally she agreed, and the two slipped away after his final performance. As the girl was only sixteen, her father reported her disappearance to the police and eventually the pair were tracked down, living together in lodgings in Glasgow. Duo was charged with abduction and in court made out he could not understand English, to which the judge retorted: 'If you can talk to her you can talk to us!' Duo was acquitted as the court accepted he had believed the girl to be older.

Possibly the first-ever play to be performed in Chinese was *The Dragon of Wrath*, which was staged at London's Little Theatre in 1910. The company was brought from Peking under the leadership of Madame Chung, a leading actress in China. The play was performed by Chung and eight Chinese actors, plus Chung's four children and five British girls who played the parts of slaves to the Princess. In China men and women did not perform together at this time, so Madame Chung sharing a stage with male actors was a new experience. The play generated a lengthy review in *The Bystander* magazine:

> How far it may be considered good art to embellish a native play from the Far East with a very Western magic-lantern display we need not stop to inquire. One of the most-applauded scenes is a sort of serpentine dance performed by a large silk veil as big as the stage itself. The corners of the veil are held by attendants, who contrive by shaking it gently to send it floating into the air, where it undulates gracefully like a mountain cloud while the gentlemen in charge of the lighting arrangements flash upon it rich slabs of colour of sufficient variety to exhaust the resources of any ordinary box of paints. During this spectacular interlude the Chinese actors look on, not, I imagine, without a little mild surprise at the peculiar taste of English people in matters of dramatic art. As long as the play keeps in its native element it has a delightfully fairylike air, which the dainty appearance of Madame Chung does much to sustain. She is a graceful little creature, with tiny feet not unlike those of a Dutch doll.

In 1912, 'The Pageant of China' was mounted in the amphitheatre at London's Crystal Palace. This, however, was only partially authentic. The event, which was performed over a number of evenings, involved 1,000 amateur performers, although whether any were Chinese is not known. However, the event did include sixty Chinese who were brought from Hong Kong to be seen 'at work in a miniature Chinatown, but it may be a matter of some regret to visitors that only one of the Chinese immigrants who safely passed the officials at Newhaven last week still retains his pigtail'. The pretend Chinatown included a Chinese theatre and a Chinese restaurant. In the arena a reproduction of the Great Wall of China, the Terrace of the Imperial Palace, a tea house and other buildings in Chinese style were built and three moments from China's history were enacted; the final one depicting the recent revolution. 'There will be a realistic battle, in which Peking is sacked and the Imperial Palace is stormed and burnt to the ground. As a contrast to the more dramatic side, there are to be a number of ballets and a feast of lanterns. Special care has been taken to ensure the accuracy of the costumes and the correctness of some of them is ensured by the fact that they were obtained during the looting of Peking.'

An American play, *The Yellow Jacket*, was staged in Britain and was performed in the style of Chinese traditional theatre. It was promoted as 'a Chinese play as seen in the old Jackson Theatre in San Francisco'. However, this was of interest to a limited audience and far more successful with the public was *Chu Chin Chow* that opened in August 1916 and ran for more than five years. It was based on the pantomime favourite, *Ali Baba and the Forty Thieves*, with the main character transformed into a Chinese. Its spectacular scenery and parades of exotically costumed young women made it a smash hit. Yet while such shows were popular, and led to a fashion among women for dressing in oriental costume, their light-hearted fantasies of China did nothing to provide an accurate image of the country or counter the negative perceptions of the Chinese. And in case anyone in the audience might be led to think better of the Chinese through seeing a show such as the musical *San Toy*, the theatre critic of *The Illustrated Sporting and Dramatic News* was quick to counter such positive thoughts. 'I should not expect anyone who knows his Far East to be hypnotised by the glamour of Mr Edwardes' *mise en scène* ... The fact is that China is absolutely the most sordid and most sombre country under the sun – the one corner of the earth's face which never catches a smile upon.'

Many of the Chinese characters that appeared on stage were malevolent and evil creatures. In 1913 the producers of a new play, *Mr Wu*, contacted a group of Chinese students and asked if they might look at the script and give their opinion as to whether or not the play might provoke prejudice against the Chinese in Britain as the plot concerned the diabolical revenge of an Oxford-educated Chinese for the seduction of his daughter by the son of an English shipper in Hong Kong. After reading the script the students replied that they thought the ending was particularly anti-Chinese and suggested it be changed. However, the producers ignored their suggestion. At this time all plays required the permission of the Lord Chamberlain before they could be staged and so the students, with support from the Chinese Legation, petitioned the Lord Chamberlain to refuse permission. The Lord Chamberlain's office replied:

> Mr Bendall (the Examiner of Plays who was requested by his Lordship to attend the final rehearsal and make a special note of the points raised in your protests) states that although there is no doubt that Mr. Wu of Hong Kong devises a horrible form of revenge for the seduction of his daughter, the contention could not be upheld that Mr Wu in his brutality is represented as a typical Chinaman any more than his daughter's seducer is represented as a typical Englishman. In Mr Bendall's judgment the protesters are over-sensitive in fancying that the truculence attributed to this fellow-countryman of theirs is likely to prejudice any British audience against their countrymen generally. The picturesquely grim drama may be disliked for its inherent painfulness, but it cannot be justly condemned for any breach of international good feeling.

Frustrated, the students sought the view of a dramatic critic of a prominent Liberal journal. His view was that the play was of little merit and suggested that any campaign to keep it off the stage would only give it publicity. 'I think it a stupid and ugly play, and hope that we shall not see much more of it.' The students took the critic's advice, perhaps erroneously, for the play ran for twelve months. It was also turned into a silent film starring the American actor, Lon Chaney, thus engendering far more booing and hissing in its depiction of an unsavoury Chinese.

When in November 1918 Billie Carleton, a young star of musical theatre, died from a drug overdose supplied by the Scottish wife of a Chinese living in Limehouse, the press had a field day. This was Britain's first celebrity drugs scandal and newspaper coverage fed the moral panic about the threat to women from drugs and the attentions of non-white men with accounts of 'unholy rites of a circle of degenerates' and 'disgusting orgies'. Even the normally staid *Times* reported that both de Veulle and Carleton 'had been at an all-night orgy in a Mayfair flat where the women wore flimsy nighties and the men silk pyjamas while smoking opium'.

Yet some challenged the anti-Chinese mood. In 1922 Somerset Maugham set the action of his new play, *East of Suez*, in China and he and the director, Basil Dean, decided that to create 'local colour' in the bustling opening scene they would hire sixty Chinese performers for non-speaking roles, probably local Chinese living in Limehouse. When the Actors Association heard of their plan it was outraged. Its secretary, Alfred Lugg, said: 'Given there are quite sixty competent English actors available it is preposterous that such a thing is being considered.' Maugham and Dean were unmoved. The sixty Chinese appeared and all received the standard appearance fee. Five years later, five Chinese boys and a Chinese girl from Limehouse acted in another Maugham play, *The Letter*, and toured with the play around Britain. Yet the popularity of Sax Rohmer's Fu Manchu novels meant that many plays continued to feature menacing Chinese, including Rohmer's own play, *The Eye of Siva* with its 'sinister Mandarin'. London's stages were so chock-full of wicked or depraved Chinese characters that in 1928 the Chargé d'Affaires of the Chinese Legation in London complained to the British Foreign Secretary Sir Austen Chamberlain about 'the increasing tendency in Dramas and Plays which are now being produced in London to represent Chinese people in consistently vicious and objectionable form. No other Oriental nation,' he continued, 'is thus singled out for objectionable dramatic treatment, so far as its people are concerned.' The Foreign Office passed on his complaint to the Lord Chamberlain's office, but again the complaint was rebuffed.

In 1924 The British Empire Exhibition was held over 10 acres at Wembley and fifty-six colonies and dominions were represented. The aim of the exhibition was to highlight the importance of the British Empire to the world, and establish economic links and a sense of community among the coloniser and her colonies. As a British colony, Hong Kong was invited to participate. There was initial resistance from the Hong Kong Government as it doubted the expense was justified, but it reluctantly agreed to participate and the organisation was co-ordinated by the Hong Kong General Chamber of Commerce and the Chinese Chamber of Commerce, with support from a number of significant Chinese individuals. Hong Kong's participation was a pavilion in the form of a China street containing buildings in Chinese architectural style. Inside there were examples of Hong Kong industries, model junks, and art objects. The Chinese aspect of Hong Kong was emphasised by displays of Chinese medicine, silk production and other activities. About 175 Chinese were brought from Hong Kong to staff the displays and shops, and to work as cooks, waiters and musicians at the exhibition's Chinese restaurant, used by Hong Kong dignitaries and merchants to entertain British guests and create business links. The British Government decided to run the event again in 1925 and Hong Kong was once more represented. Although an astonishing 27 million visitors attended the two events, the exhibitions did little to create any sense of a Chinese community within Britain. Nor did it do much to alter misperceptions among the British public about Hong Kong, or China generally.

In 1919 *Broken Blossoms*, a silent film by the acclaimed American director D. W. Griffith, was released. Although set in London's Limehouse, albeit the one of popular imagination and thus filled with opium dens and brothels, the film was shot in America. The film was based on one of Thomas Burke's books that did much to reinforce negative views about the Chinese. Griffith altered Burke's main Chinese character from someone who frequented opium dens and whorehouses to a Buddhist missionary, although the missionary still visited opium dens when depressed. Ten years later, *Piccadilly*, a British silent film, directed by the German E. A. Dupont, unusually featured an inter-racial love affair that was portrayed sympathetically. Given the later rise of London Soho's Chinatown, it is interesting that this early film was set in a nightclub and restaurant in Soho. It starred the internationally famous American-born Asian actress Anna May Wong. Her success was unusual for in America at the time, oriental characters were almost always played by white actors – known as 'yellowface' parts as the actors were required to apply yellow make-up. To allay any possible outrage the kiss between her and her English co-star, Jameson Thomas, was cut from the American version. Another film, *The Flame of Love*, again starring Wong, also contained a scene where the lovers kissed and the film company later cut the scene, in spite of the director calling the ban on Chinese and British actors kissing as 'stupid and inconsistent'. In some Asian countries the film was banned altogether. It was in this film that Ley On, the owner of the fashionable restaurant in Soho, received his first minor acting role. The film was one of the first with sound and was recorded in three languages – French, German and English – with the actors having to record voice-overs for the three different versions. However, such more nuanced portrayals of Chinese were overshadowed by the clichés in the hugely popular silent British serials featuring the Sax Rohmer Chinese caricature, Dr Fu Manchu, and versions featuring the evil doctor appeared through to the 1960s.

The first-ever Chinese film shown in Britain appears to have been *The Legend of the Willow-Pattern Plate*, widely shown in Britain in 1927 and enjoyed by the queen at a private showing. A British reviewer commented: 'Except in the wild gesticulations of the angry parent, romantic film acting in China seems to differ very little from our own.' However, this was unique for the time and so-called Chinese films were those such as *West of Shanghai* starring Boris Karloff as a Chinese bandit. There were occasional opportunities for listeners to the BBC to hear Chinese music. In June 1930 the *Radio Times* announced: 'Tonight will be Chinese night on the wireless. A special orchestra has been recruited from among the Chinese colony in London for a Chinese programme, which is to be broadcast at 9.45. The programme will include Chinese dialogue as well as the national music.'

At the end of 1932, a group of British collectors led by Sir Percival David, an aristocratic banker and admirer of Oriental art, decided to mount a comprehensive exhibition of Chinese art in London. Extensive negotiations with the Chinese Government led to agreement and The International Exhibition of Chinese Art opened in November 1935 at the Royal Academy of Arts in London. The Chinese authorities were confident that the exhibition would reveal the grandeur of Chinese culture to a wider public and, perhaps more importantly, help gain sympathy and support for China's resistance against Japan's continuing attempts to occupy Chinese territory. At the press launch for the exhibition, Cheng Futing, the special commissioner appointed to oversee the exhibition by the Chinese Government, made sure that the political impetus for the exhibition was clear to the gathered journalists. 'You will see not mere objects of the art of China but, with your mind's eye, you see the culture and civilisation of China as well; for these things were not created by the bayonet but were produced by the love of beauty, and nothing is, of course, more beautiful than peace, righteousness and affection.'

In advance of the exhibition a number of books on Chinese art were commissioned and, as had been the case in the past, those asked to write about the subject were Western experts. Unusually, the publishers Methuen decided to commission Chiang Yee to write a book on Chinese painting. His book, *The Chinese Eye*, provided an introduction to the fundamental principles of Chinese art and the cultural context within which to appreciate it. Unlike other books which tended to be academic in content, Chiang offered a more accessible approach, based on his personal experience as a practising artist.

> I have only just learned the correct time for taking tea in England; and I understand that one should add milk and sugar, and eat some cakes as well. But our habit is not so: we have no regular time for tea; we drink it when we like, and not merely for refreshment: it is a form of sociability, a unifying element whenever friends meet. Nor do we need any milk or sugar to flavour it; we think the natural flavour and scent of the leaves should reach our palate in their original purity, and so we sip it appreciatively, little by little instead of cup by cup. This habit of ours is not without its application in the work of art. We feel that a painting need call for no elaborate technique; it should speak simply from the power of its basic inspiration. That partly explains the Chinese preference for plain ink; we use few colours to help out the effect, just as we do not add milk or sugar to improve the tea's favour. If we are drawing a single flower or bird, we often leave a black background; as I said, we take no cakes with our tea!

The book received both critical and public acclaim. Art critic Herbert Read wrote: 'Chiang has explained the Chinese conception of art so clearly and thus enabled us to appreciate its qualities with a true aesthetic understanding.' This was one of the first books in English that enabled a Chinese to communicate information and ideas about their culture to Western audiences directly, without mediation by Western writers. In 1938, Chiang published a second book on Chinese calligraphy and it also was met with enthusiasm by reviewers: 'No praise is too high for this book, which is at once instructive and delightful. It is emphatically commended to all lovers of Chinese art.'

The International Exhibition of Chinese Art contained about 800 objects from the Chinese Government collections and 3,100 pieces drawn from some 240 collections from other countries. The magnificent range of bronze and jade, ceramics, paintings, sculptures and other objects, shown in sixteen rooms, included treasures never seen before by Westerners. Although the exhibition only ran for three months, it attracted around 400,000 visitors and 109,000 exhibition catalogues were sold. The exhibition also caught the wider public imagination. The British Colour Council recommended that the 1936 season's fashion colours would be 'Mandarin Blue', 'Chinese Green' and 'Manchu Brown' and 'Canton', a milky jade green shade. Shops promoted wallpaper and textiles with Chinese designs and fashionable people took to wearing Chinese style gowns. 'The Queen orders a Jewel Blue dress' reported one fashion magazine. Associated events were held around the country and the enthusiastic press and public response delighted the Chinese Government.

The exhibition elevated the status of Chinese art through international press coverage, which universally acclaimed the uniqueness and universality of Chinese art and civilization. The exhibition also helped shift the stereotypical British conception of Chinese art as decorative objects to fine art – although as Chinese calligraphy was new to most, it confirmed for many the impression of China as a remote, ancient, and mysterious empire. It also gave further impetus to an interest in Chinese culture among writers, artists and intellectuals. Writers such as Arthur Waley introduced Chinese poetry and other literature to a wider public through sensitive translations. There was great alarm in the press when news broke that the ship carrying the priceless collection – valued at the time at £10 million – back to China had gone aground near Gibraltar. Admiralty Tugs rushed to the rescue and fortunately the ship was refloated without damage to any of the objects.

Coincidentally, the year before this exhibition the first play by a Chinese playwright was staged in Britain. *Lady Precious Stream* was written and co-directed by Hsiung Shih-I, who had come to Britain in 1932 to study English literature at Queen Mary University of London. In China he had worked as a literature professor in the universities of Peking and Nanchang, and had translated several English novels and plays into Chinese, including Bernard Shaw's *Man and Superman* and James Barrie's *Peter Pan*. Hsiung met various British writers and playwrights and it was George Bernard Shaw who suggested that he consider writing a play. 'Try something different. Something really Chinese and traditional,' Shaw suggested. Encouraged, Hsiung set to work to adapt the plot of the traditional Peking Opera's *Red Mane Horse* into a stage play. The result was *Lady Precious Stream*, which was premiered on 27 November 1934 at the Little Theatre in John Street, London, by the People's National Theatre. The play, with its themes of romantic love, fidelity and treachery, featured striking costumes designed by the great Chinese opera performer Mei Lan-fang, and was an instant success. The play ran for 1,000 performances and transferred to Broadway in 1936. It was made into a film in 1938 and adapted for British television in 1950. The play's script was adopted as a classroom text in Britain during the 1930s and the 1940s and, until its themes became less fashionable, was regularly performed by amateur theatre companies. In 1944, at the height of the war, it was performed in Regent's Park Open Air Theatre. Mei Lan-fang who designed the costumes was in Europe to perform Peking Opera in Berlin and Moscow and visited London to try to arrange a British performance. *The Yorkshire Post* reported on a tea party given at the Savoy Hotel hosted by Hsiung in Mei's honour.

> He has been this country only a fortnight, and speaks little English, but in the Autumn he will give London a taste of his quality as there is talk of a play to be performed in Chinese. This afternoon's party was distinctly Oriental. Mr. Mei Lan-Fang appeared in an occidental lounge suit, but diminutive Mr. Hsiung greeted his guests in the blue robe which has made him a familiar figure In London. Miss Anna May Wong was one of a large company of stage people who attended.

Unfortunately, nothing came of Mei Lan-fang's planned London performance.

Hsiung followed up the success of *Lady Precious Stream* with a play based on a thirteenth-century Chinese work, but decided that his third play should be set in twentieth-century China, and recount the country's political struggles and portray realistic characters. The result was *The Professor from Peking*, which explored China's internal political struggles across three time periods – centred on 1919, 1927 and 1937 – with the lead character, Professor Chang, shown conspiring to gain power and mistreating a string of wives and mistresses. Hsiung's attempt to show British audiences something of China's recent political history was not well received. When the play opened in 1939 at the Malvern Festival the reception was lukewarm as few in the audience had sufficient interest in the recent political machinations of China and many thought his immoral main character risked reinforcing racial stereotypes of the Chinese as devious and violent towards women. The writer Edward Plunkett, a friend of Hsiung, thought the playwright's decision to replace 'the land of dragons, peach trees, peonies, and plum blossoms, with its ages and ages of culture, slowly storing its dreams in green jade, porcelain and gold with one complicated by telephones and Communism' was a mistake.

Representations of China on Britain's stages continued almost wholly to be stereotypical mis-portrayals, with such characters as Widow Twankey, the washerwoman in Aladdin, traditionally played by a man in drag, a firm favourite. In 1942, the writer, Hsiao Ch'ien went to see a production of *Aladdin* and afterwards wrote that such portrayals of Chinese 'would be very entertaining if such poetic fantasies remained the monopoly of the amusement world'. He went on, 'As a child I was very fond of standing before those magical mirrors in a fun palace to see myself twisted and transformed... Since I grew up I have long missed this secret pleasure, until I went to a Birmingham pantomime called *Aladdin* in which my country was made out to be a Turkish bath, with my people all in fancy flowery jackets.' Hsiao's uncomfortable viewing of the make-believe Chinese was made all the more unnerving when 'a fair lady sitting next to me screamed out, "Look, here is one!"'

Delly Kin was a Chinese juggler who first appeared in 1937. She was described as 'a petite Chinese lady, skilled with ball, circular ashtray, and plate which she rolls round her parasol, and nimbly swings coloured lights and water-filled cups'. Her off-stage name was Delly Man-cheung and she married the owner of a Chinese restaurant. In 1944 they had a baby and as her husband was working, and Delly about to start a tour, the couple advertised for a nursemaid to look after their ten-month-old son, and appointed a young Belgian woman. One evening the couple returned home after working to find that the nursemaid and their baby son were missing. The police were called and began a search for the missing woman and the abducted baby. By late the next day there was still no word and while her husband stayed at the flat for news, Delly decided that the show had to go on. In spite of her distress she travelled to the theatre and it was while she was in the middle of juggling that a whisper reached her from the wings. 'Your baby is safe.' Being a true professional Delly's eyes never wavered from the objects that she was juggling round her head, and she completed her act before rushing to the wings where she broke down in relief on hearing that her stolen child was safe. It transpired that the presumed kidnapping was in fact the result of the Belgian nursemaid getting lost in London's streets. Delly continued to perform into the mid-1950s.

The first Chinese to study at The Royal Academy of Dramatic Art was Tsai Chin who came to Britain in 1952. In 1958 she was cast as Sui-Lan in the film, *The Inn of the Sixth Happiness*, with a large number of British Chinese children from Liverpool. Then she landed the lead role in the London stage production of *The World of Suzie Wong*. Although the play received poor reviews from the critics it was a commercial hit and Chin received good reviews. Harold Hobson in *The Sunday Times* wrote, 'Tsai Chin has cool clear beauty and considerable talent.' Chin recorded one of the songs from the play, *The Ding Dong Song*, written by Lionel Bart, which became a hit, particularly in Asia. As a result she recorded further songs and developed a cabaret show, which she toured throughout the United Kingdom. London's *Evening News* was impressed by the way she held her audience. 'There wasn't a murmur, not even the clatter of one piece of cutlery.' She continued to act on stage and in films, including playing Fu Manchu's daughter in the 1960s film version and helping to 'assassinate' Sean Connery in *You Only Live Twice*. Chin was one of the few Chinese actors to appear on British television in the 1960s, often playing a nurse as in the series, *Emergency Ward 10*. In 1972, Chin portrayed Wang Guangmei, the wife of Liu Shaoqi, Chairman Mao's chief rival, in *The Subject of Struggle*, a docudrama directed by Leslie Woodhead that focussed on Wang's trial by the Red Guards. The reviews were unanimously positive: 'Tsai Chin leaves *The World of Suzie Wong* a long way behind with this brave, haggard performance.' For a time

Chin acted in America and in 1980 directed China's premiere production of Shakespeare's *The Tempest*. In 1990 she agreed to play the title role in Henry Ong's one-woman drama, *Madame Mao's Memories*, in spite of the fact that both her parents had died in China as a result of Mao's Cultural Revolution, in which Madame Mao had a hand. Chin said of her decision, 'I was determined to be a good deal fairer in my representation of her than she ever was of my father.'

By coincidence the first Chinese to graduate from the Royal Ballet School in London also had her career breakthrough in *The World of Suzie Wong*. Nancy Kwan was the daughter of Kwan Wing Hong, a Cantonese architect who, while studying in Britain, met and married Marquita Scott, a British model. Kwan's childhood began in dramatic circumstances. When the Japanese invaded Hong Kong, her father disguised himself as a coolie and hiding Kwan and her infant brother in a wicker basket on his back, escaped from Hong Kong. Marquita also managed to escape to Britain. She later divorced her husband and when Kwan and her brother were in their early teens, they came to Britain to join their mother. After finishing her studies at the Royal Ballet School, Kwan returned to live in Hong Kong and there successfully auditioned for the lead in the film version of *The World of Suzie Wong*. The film was a box-office smash and critics lavished praise on Kwan for her performance. Although only eighteen years old, Kwan became a Hollywood icon. She moved to live in America and enjoyed a successful film career, including appearing in a number of films shot in Britain. In 1961, the King's Own Yorkshire Light Infantry announced that they were seeking someone to train their soldiers for military involvement in Malaya (now part of Malaysia), including learning some Chinese and how to handle chopsticks. The regiment's advert stated that they sought an attractive instructor so that more soldiers would attend the sessions. Kwan, in Hollywood at the time, sent a cable: 'Please consider me a candidate as Chinese teacher for Yorkshire Light Infantry. I am fluent in Chinese, fabulous with chopsticks, and fond of uniforms.' Sadly her application was turned down by the regiment. 'Miss Kwan is too beautiful. I think she would be too much of a distraction,' the regiment's commander explained.

In spite of the warfare raging throughout China, in 1938 five Chinese chosen to entertain the public in Europe made a long and arduous journey from the interior of China to Hong Kong, and then travelled by cargo ship to London, arriving in December at the height of a raging blizzard. The journey and cold weather were too much for the eldest, Grandma, she caught pneumonia and died two weeks after arriving in the capital. Although relations with Germany were already tense, one of the five was allowed to travel to live there, while the remaining three settled into their new life at London Zoo. The giant pandas were an instant hit with the public, but sadly Sung died within six months of arriving, and Tang the following year. The sole survivor, Ming, still a cub when she arrived, became a much-loved celebrity. Panda dolls, panda sweets, panda cakes, panda neckties, and panda pictures appeared in London shops, and Ming starred in a film, *Pandemonium*, and appeared on early television. Bert Hardy, one of Britain's best-known photographers, captured the playful Ming behind one of his cameras on a tripod, seemingly taking a picture of his son and the photograph was published around the world. Throughout the war Ming was regarded as a symbol of normality and a morale-booster for British children, and when Ming died on Christmas Day in 1944 *The Times* published an obituary, virtually unheard of at the time when only the deaths of the great and the good, and the not so good, graced its obit pages: 'She could die happy in the knowledge that she gladdened the universal heart and even in the stress of war her death should not go unnoticed.' Puffin Picture Books commissioned Chiang Yee to write and illustrate the children's book, *The Story of Ming*, in which he writes: 'Is it not curious that Ming came to England on Christmas Eve, 1938, and went away Christmas Day 1944? We might say that she was just like Father Christmas coming to bring happiness.' During the Cold War from the 1950s to the 1970s Chinese pandas were used by China as a symbol of re-established diplomatic relations. The US received a pair following President Richard Nixon's ground-breaking trip to China in 1972 and two years later, Britain's Prime Minister Edward Heath requested two pandas during a trip to Beijing, and Chia and Ching duly took up residence in London.

Although it was not until 1955 that London audiences had an opportunity to see a Chinese Opera company from China, there were various non-professional performances in earlier years. In 1947 two short Chinese operas, including a section from *The Fisherman's Revenge*, were performed at the Westminster Theatre. The performance was organised by Cheng Bing, a son of the Chinese Ambassador, Cheng Tienxi, and the cast consisted of three members of the Chinese Air Force, two students, the wife of the first secretary to the Chinese Embassy and the Secretary to the Chinese National Relief and Rehabilitation Administration. Queen Mary attended the performance and wore a Chinese robe for the occasion, which she informed the ambassador, Dr Cheng, had been a gift from one of the Ching Emperors to the royal family. Cheng was delighted. 'It was an exquisite piece of embroidery and, of course, appropriate for the occasion.' A number of the diplomatic staff at the Republic of China Embassy in London, who lost their jobs in 1949 as a result of the Communist Party taking power in China, stayed in Britain and one, Wang Jiasong, created an informal Peking Opera Club with fellow ex-embassy staff. They regularly met to sing arias together through to the 1980s.

In the early 1950s performing companies from Communist China began touring continental Europe and the theatre impresario, Peter Daubeny, decided to bring The Peking Opera Company to London. However, there was concern within the British Government that allowing Chinese companies to perform in Britain could promote Communist ideology. The British Ambassador in Switzerland was sent to see the Peking Opera perform and reported to the Foreign Office that the performance was 'as unpolitical as Spartak playing Arsenal at football'. Permission was given and the first cultural visit to Britain by a troupe from the People's Republic of China went ahead. In addition to its successful season the company performed in front of Queen Elizabeth as part of the annual Royal Variety Performance. *The Times* reported: 'When Wang Ming-Chong has to represent the Monkey King invading Heaven, he uses in fifteen minutes as much energy as a hardworking labourer would use in 15 hours.' The British playwright Peter Shaffer attended one of the company's performances at which an extract of *Where Three Roads Meet* was given. He recounted: 'The scene takes place in a lodging house in the dark. Except the scene was performed in brilliant light; light so ferocious that it almost suggested darkness. There was a fight, with real swords I recall. The effect on the audience was extraordinary, because it was wildly funny and wildly dangerous as well.' The playwright admitted it was this that gave him the idea for his successful play, *Black Comedy*. Two years later, Daubeny presented another season of Chinese Classical Theatre with performances by the seventy-strong Operatic Group of the Republic of China. This company had been formed in 1949 by members of the Original Peking Opera Troupe when they fled to Taiwan, along with the National Government of the Republic of China, after the Communist takeover on mainland China. The programme stated that Taiwan was the true inheritor of Chinese theatre, which had not been compromised by Communist ideology; a claim that brought protests from the Chinese Communist Party.

In 1958, The Classical Theatre of China arrived from Communist China to perform in London but, unfortunately, part way through its run, cancelled its performances. Dr Chu Wu, the company's representative, explained: 'We cannot go on performing because of the present political atmosphere with the British Government having sent troops to Jordan to support the intervention of America in Lebanon. This is an aggression against the Arab people and seriously endangers world peace.' Growing political tensions between Britain and China, followed by the clampdown on much artistic activity within China during the Cultural Revolution from the mid-1960s to the mid-70s, meant very few Chinese companies came to Britain until the late '70s. However, by the mid-80s appearances by Chinese companies and artists in Britain were relatively common. At the 1987 Edinburgh International Festival the Chinese soprano, Dilber Yunus, sang the role of Gilda in the Finnish National Opera's production of Verdi's *Rigoletto*; the Shanghai Kunju Theatre staged three plays, including *The Peony Pavilion*; and an eighty-strong dance company performed *The Soul of the Terracotta Army*, a dance drama inspired by the emperor's warriors unearthed near Xian.

Chinese acrobats continued to appear in circuses, variety shows and pantomimes. In 1954 the Chy Bao Guy family were one of the acts in the Plymouth Varieties' production of *Aladdin*, and were still performing into the 1970s. A reviewer wrote:

They are a colourfully dressed and definitely versatile quintet from China. The senior member confines himself to flag waving (which is by no means as easy as it sounds, considering that the flag is about 10 feet across) and streamer throwing, while the youngsters tumble, dive through knife-edged hoops, fight each other with fearsome mediaeval weapons and indulge in mass plate-spinning.

In 1978 John Percival, *The Times* critic, reviewed the Chinese Circus and was particularly impressed by one young acrobat who, while balancing on a high monocycle, kicked up a bowl thrown by an assistant and balanced it on his head. He then kicked up a teapot and balanced it on a stand held in his teeth. Percival's review continued: 'Right my lad, I murmured, determined not to be impressed. Now pour yourself a nice cup of tea. Bang on cue he did so. Collapse of stout-hearted critic.' Percival was equally impressed by the Chinese dancers who performed with the Central Ballet of China that came to London in 1986. One of the ballets performed was *Variations*, created by the English choreographer Anton Dolin in the 1950s. Percival wrote, 'I cannot remember a better account of this bravura showpiece since the exceptional cast for whom it was made thirty years ago.'

In 1973 the Royal Academy in London again hosted a blockbuster Chinese exhibition. 'The Genius of China: An Exhibition of Archaeological Finds of the People's Republic of China' ran from September 1973 to January 1974 and again drew large crowds. It included objects from the Palaeolithic age to the end of the Yuan Dynasty in 1368, with all the treasures on display having been excavated by archaeologists of the People's Republic of China since 1949. The standout exhibit was Princess Tou Wan's jade burial suit that had been found only five years previously. Among the Chinese visitors to the opening of the exhibition was Professor Hsia Nai, one of China's foremost archaeologists. At the opening Professor Nai proudly showed Edward Heath, Britain's Prime Minister, the ticket he had kept from the 1935 exhibition that he had attended when studying Egyptology at University College London. The exhibition again stimulated an appreciation among a wider public of the richness of China's culture and the country's significant history. This was given further impetus by press coverage of the discovery in the 1970s of the Terracotta Army, created in 221 BC, near Xi'an. It would be 2007 before an exhibition of a number of the finds came to Britain but when it arrived, it was deemed the exhibition of the year with more than 850,000 visitors.

By the 1950s a few Chinese films began to be shown in Britain, although not widely, and British and American films with their artificial portrayals of Chinese remained almost all the public saw. An article in *The Times* in 1952 commented, 'One way and another China has provided filmgoers in the West with many a glimpse of things that were strange to them. They were, of course, very much stranger to the Chinese.' In 1958 Bert Kwouk landed a small part in the film, *Inn of the Sixth Happiness*. Kwouk was born in Warrington, Lancashire, but brought up in Shanghai. He returned to Britain with his parents in 1947 and after spending seven years in America returned to Britain. It was then that a girlfriend 'nagged him into acting'. He became Britain's most successful Chinese actor from the 1960s to the 1980s, best known as Cato Fong, the energetic sparring partner of Peter Sellers' comically inept Inspector Clouseau in the hugely successful *Pink Panther* series, although he was also frequently cast in Japanese roles. It was not until 1986 that a truly Chinese-British film appeared. *Ping Pong*, directed by the British born director Po-Chi Leong, is a comedy mystery that touches on the theme of British Chinese struggling to integrate with British culture while retaining their Chinese cultural heritage. The film was a timely riposte to decades of Chinese stereotypes but, although critically acclaimed, it failed to find wide public success. It starred Lucy Sheen, who had been one of the hundred orphaned Chinese babies sent from Hong Kong to Britain for adoption in the early 1960s, and David Yip, who was born in Liverpool to a Chinese seaman and an English mother.

On 9 February 1959 the young Chinese pianist, Fou Ts'ong, made his British debut at London's Albert Hall and 'there was a great turn up of London's Chinese to see him'. The reviews of his performance were unanimously positive. Fou grew up in Shanghai and studied piano with Mario Paci, the Italian founder of the Shanghai Symphony Orchestra. The year after his London debut he decided to leave China and settle in London. In 1960 he married Zamira Menuhin, the daughter of Yehudi Menuhin, but they later divorced. Fou then married the Chinese pianist Patsy Toh who also had been born in Shanghai and studied in Britain in 1948. While Chinese classical music artists were admired, few in Britain had any interest in traditional Chinese music and the reaction by most who heard it was mocking. Liao Zilan, a guzheng (Chinese zither) musician, came to Britain in 1983 at the age of thirteen and recalled her first meeting with a harp teacher in Manchester. The teacher told her that she had been in China and attended a Peking opera, but thought the music sounded like someone dropping crockery in the kitchen. Liao Zilan grew up in Guangzhou (Canton) and began learning the guzheng at the age of three. Her father was a musician and her mother a dancer. By the age of nine she had won many prizes in China, including the prestigious National Youth Music Competition award. The family moved to Liverpool when her father was appointed the Chinese culture officer for the city. She later graduated from the Royal Academy of Music in London and with a rising interest in world music began performing with a wide range of musicians. One was Peter Gabriel, the renowned singer-songwriter and a champion of world music. She admits that she had never heard of Peter Gabriel at the time. 'In China at the time we weren't allowed to listen to rock music. It was banned. I remember at some stage listening to pop music from Hong Kong, which I loved. But rock music from other countries was not widely heard.' She married John Wardle, a bass guitarist, who had made his name as a member of Public Image Limited (PiL), a ground-breaking rock band. Liao explained, 'Chinese music has a very long history and there is so much in it that the west still doesn't know about. China had been closed for such a long time, so, unlike Indian, Jamaican, Caribbean and African music – which have really been explored by the west – Chinese music was a mystery until recently.'

In spite of British television becoming more multi-racial from the 1960s, Chinese roles and presenters remained remarkably absent from British television screens through to the mid-1980s. The only television drama from that period to feature a lead Chinese character was *The Chinese Detective* starring David Yip. British theatres continued to stage versions of *Aladdin* with an assortment of male actors or TV comedians playing Widow Twankey, the Chinese washerwoman.

Yet at the Darlington Hippodrome in 1983 there was a small revolution that pointed the way to a slow change in perceptions. The Hippodrome's Christmas show was J. M. Barrie's *Peter Pan* and not only had the theatre broken with custom by having Peter, the boy who would not grow up, played by a man, rather than by a petite adult woman as was traditional, but it also cast David Yip in the role.

22

Academic Achievements

> Softly I am leaving,
> Just as softly as I came;
> I softly wave goodbye
> To the clouds in the western sky.
>
> Xu Zhimo (1897–1931)

Boxer Indemnity Scholarship students in Cambridge, 1930s, left to right, seated, Kwoh-Ting Li (economics), Tang Peijing (mathematics), Chow Hung-Ching (law); centre, standing: Wu Qiyang (economics), two others standing, unidentified. (Public domain)

Academic Achievements

By 1900 it had become fashionable for the more adventurous and wealthy Chinese parents to send their children abroad to study at overseas universities and Sir John Jordan, Britain's Ambassador in Peking, thought more could be done to attract such students to Britain. So, in 1908, Jordan proposed that British educational establishments respond positively to 'the growing desire evinced by the literary and commercial classes in China to send their sons abroad for education in foreign schools, universities and technical institutions'. He argued that those who came to study in Britain would establish friendships with British students that could prove of future value and would return to China with positive views about Britain. In response, a committee that included the Professors of Chinese at Oxford and Cambridge, the Principal of King's College, London, and the Secretary to the Chinese Legation, was established to consider how best to move forward. The committee drew up a list of institutions prepared to accept Chinese students, and reputable boarding houses and families willing to host students.

The promotion of Britain as a place for Chinese to study was supported by the Chinese Ambassador, Li Ching Fong, who had taken up the post in 1907. His son was already in England preparing to attend Cambridge University. The ambassador said that he planned to take a greater interest than his predecessors in Chinese students being educated in Britain and announced that the Chinese Government had decided to send no fewer than 150 students each year to Britain. One of the few Chinese students already in Britain in 1907 was Cheng Tien-hsi, who was studying law in London. The ambassador befriended Cheng, on occasion inviting him to dine at the Legation, but neither could have imagined that the young Cheng would one day follow in Li's footsteps by also becoming a Chinese Ambassador to Britain. Cheng's astute diplomatic skills were already apparent when he was still a student. A friend, whose family were one of the richest in Macau, operated a London antique shop and wished to move to a more fashionable district. He asked Cheng to use his legal knowledge to help with the lease and the two young men went to meet the owner who, self-evidently dubious about the two young Orientals, advised them to find somewhere a lot less expensive and dismissed them. Cheng and his friend were too taken aback to say anything at the time but, on reflection, were affronted. On arriving home Cheng picked up the phone and rang the estate agent. 'Look here! My friend and I met the owner and he spoke to us in such a way, as if he is the only person who has money. Tell him that my friend's father owns half a Portuguese colony and that my ancestor was Governor of two Chinese provinces, three times the size of the UK.' Cheng's irritated phone call did the trick and the lease was agreed. Cheng also helped many of the students who began arriving from China, assisting those with limited English to find accommodation and providing coaching to others studying law.

Ambassador Li was replaced in 1910 by Lew Yuk Lin and it may be that the new ambassador's priorities did not extend to the well-being of

Chinese students, for he repeatedly refused requests for a meeting from one student, Yen Sun Zuian. However, given what later transpired, it may be that the ambassador avoided Yen as he knew something of the young man's temperament. Yen, a law student, wished to meet the ambassador to examine documents he claimed were in the ambassador's possession but was rebuffed on four occasions. On Yen's fifth visit to the Chinese Legation, Wen Hsien Chien, the Superintendent of Students, happened to be entering the building. Yen grabbed his arm and demanded that he take him in to see the ambassador. When Wen refused, Yen produced a Mauser pistol and told the Superintendent that he would shoot him if he refused. Wen, clearly believing the student to be bluffing, refused again, at which point Yen pointed the gun at him and pulled the trigger. Fortunately the gun did not go off and a porter managed to disarm Yen, who was swiftly arrested. Wen decided not to press charges so Yen was spared imprisonment, though he was bound over to keep the peace and stay away from the ambassador.

A newspaper article in 1909 reported that one of the few genuine Chinese cafés in London was in the Chinese Students' Social Union. In addition to the café, the building provided social activities, regular debates and lectures, and a billiards room. Other student support organisations included the British Students' Christian Movement that accommodated both Chinese and British students at its hostel in Hampstead, London, to encourage understanding and future contacts, and The Chinese Girl Students' Aid Committee, which arranged for female Chinese students to be paying guests in British homes and for British households to invite students to their homes to see something of their family and social life.

The work in China to promote Britain's educational opportunities was successful and the number of Chinese students rose to 350 by 1913. Most came to study at university but there were others who came to attend vocational training courses, such as twenty-three who arrived in 1919 to study weaving. The subjects being studied were diverse and included agriculture, chemistry, engineering, mining, wireless technology, natural science, nursing, medicine and law. Students attended institutions throughout the country. Chinese students fared as well as British students, with many winning academic prizes and becoming successful members of university sports teams.

Younger boys were sent to boarding schools in Britain.

In the case of nearly all young Chinese who come to this country, great attention will paid to sports, since there is a notable movement in China in favour of open-air pastimes. Indeed, there is hardly a game in which the modern Chinese youth is not interested. Football is very popular, and so cricket, while the best player of lawn tennis at any treaty port is a Chinaman. Nowadays Chinese athletes are quite ready to pit themselves against Europeans, and it is quite likely that they will be in evidence at the 1916 Olympic Games in Berlin. The son of the present Chinese Minister,

Academic Achievements

who is being educated at Bexhill, is outstanding at cricket, while he is almost as good at other games. His father is a first-class tennis player, and so are his two young daughters. All the family, oddly enough, are good billiard players.

In 1912 Yuan Keding and Yuan Kewen, the two eldest sons of Yuan Shi Kai, the then provisional Chinese President, attended a school in Bexhill and, in 1915, when their father proclaimed himself Emperor of China in an attempt to restore the Empire, Yuan Keding became Prince Yuntai. But his period as Crown Prince lasted less than ninety days as his father was ousted, and his future life was undistinguished. His brother, Kewen, was more successful, becoming an expert in Chinese traditional literature and a master of calligraphy and Chinese ink painting, while also gaining a reputation for promiscuity.

In 1911 Ding Wenjiang graduated from Glasgow University with a degree in both geology and biology, going on to become one of China's most eminent geology experts, mapping the geological resources of the whole of China. Around the same time Tseng Yee-king studied mechanical engineering at Durham University and after a period in America, worked for the Ministry of Navy organising the Naval Air Establishment and establishing a course in aeronautical engineering.

One of the few Chinese women to study in Britain in the early part of the century was Zeng Baosun. She had converted to Christianity while attending the Mary Vaughan High School for Girls in Hangzhou. In 1911 the school's headmistress, Louisa Barmes, travelled to Britain on a year's leave, and took the nineteen-year-old Zeng with her to learn English. Zeng attended Blackheath High School for a year and then decided to stay to study at Westfield College, at the time a women's college associated with the University of London. Though Barmes was supposed to return to her job in China and work for a further five years in order to receive a pension, she decided to stay in England as Zeng's unofficial guardian. She told Zeng, 'I feel very firmly that to educate you, a Chinese girl, to return to China and do God's work is ten times more important than my retirement.' When Zeng protested, Barmes replied, 'Don't worry, the Lord will take care of us. He will not allow us to sink into an impossible situation.' While at Westfield College Zeng studied science, botany, chemistry and maths, and was the first Chinese woman to gain a Bachelor of Science degree with honours. Zeng decided that on her return to China she would open a Christian school in Hunan and Westfield College arranged for the Canon of Westminster to help raise funds, and selected three teachers to return to China with her. In 1918, Zeng, accompanied by Barmes and the three teachers, travelled back to China and established Yifang Girls' Collegiate School in Changsha, the capital of Hunan.

The prestigious reputation of Edinburgh University Medical School continued to attract many Chinese and in 1922 there were forty Chinese studying there, including a small number of women. One was Dr Hoashoom who, after graduating, worked at the War Hospital in Edinburgh during the First World War. In 1918 she returned to Hong Kong and became the colony's first female doctor. Dr Ping Win also worked at a military hospital after completing his studies at Edinburgh but he decided to remain in Britain. He took the English name of William Phillip Lamb and in 1927 moved to London and opened a surgery in West India Dock Road. There he provided medical services to the local Chinese community and visiting Chinese seamen. He also acted as the doctor for many of London's Chinese restaurant owners and for the Chinese ambassador and his staff. He married a Scottish woman in 1939 and they set up home in Hampstead Garden Suburb where they welcomed many of the Chinese visiting London. In 1940 Lamb's surgery was bombed but, determined to remain, he moved to another house in the street and continued to run his surgery throughout the Blitz, often staying in the district overnight in spite of the bombing.

In 1912 Lim Boon Keng, who studied medicine at Edinburgh in the late 1880s, became the physician and confidential secretary to Sun Yat-sen. He was married to Margaret Tuan-Keng Wong, one of the first Chinese women to be educated in the United States, and the couple decided to send their eldest son, Robert Kho-Seng Lim, known as Bobby Lim, to be educated in Edinburgh. Although Bobby was just eight years old he was dispatched to Scotland in 1905 to board at George Watson's School. His father was keen for his son to study medicine at Edinburgh University and so, in 1914, having completed his secondary school education, Bobby Lim began his training at the Medical School. However, at the outbreak of war Bobby Lim put his studies on hold and volunteered for the Indian Army. His job was to drill recruits and the young sons of Maharajas who had joined the army objected to being ordered around by a young Chinese. After two years, he returned to Edinburgh and completed his medical studies and in 1923 was elected a Fellow of the Royal Society of Edinburgh. After a period in America, Lim returned to China where he became Head of the Chinese Red Cross and Surgeon General of the Republic of China.

The Chinese students who were in Britain during the First World War were required to register as 'friendly aliens' and their movement was restricted. As some had limited English and the regulations were complicated, a few, such as Weitsen Hsu, inadvertently found themselves in trouble. Weitsen had travelled to Aberdeen University from London and was arrested when he unintentionally entered a prohibited area of the city without any identification. His plea that he was unaware of the restrictions was dismissed by the Sheriff: 'I wish even friendly aliens would be alive to the fact that the country is at war, and that these regulations are made for the express object of safeguarding the interests of this country.' Weitsen was fined 10 shillings.

In 1917 Lee Hysan, a wealthy Hong Kong businessman nicknamed the 'King of Opium', sent two of his sons to Britain to study. Richard was twelve

Academic Achievements

and his brother, Harold, just ten, and the two boys were looked after by a governess in the home of their British guardian and tutor, Mr Churchill. Later, two of their sisters, Shun Wah (Doris) and Shun Ying (Ansie), also attended English boarding schools. Richard went on to study Engineering Science at Pembroke College, Cambridge, and while there acted as the president of the Central Union of Chinese Students of Great Britain and Ireland. In her book, *Profit, Victory and Sharpness*, Richard's daughter, Vivienne Poy, recounts her father saying that his father told both his sons that if they married non-Chinese women while in Britain they would be disinherited. Unsurprisingly, both obeyed their father's stricture. Richard Lee returned to Hong Kong where he became a successful businessman and a significant public figure. His brother, Harold, co-founded Hong Kong's first television channel with Run Run Shaw.

It is not known if Shih-yu Gao's father also prohibited his son from marrying a non-Chinese woman while studying in Britain, but if he did, Shih-yu Gao must have known he would disobey as soon as he met Margaret Scott at a dance in 1934. The couple immediately fell in love and spent time together throughout Shih-yu Gao's four-year course studying textiles at Leeds University. In the summer of 1938, following Shih-yu Gao's successful graduation, they married, and in September set sail for Chungking to settle. Nothing is known of their fate although one fears the worst, for they would have arrived a few months before the city suffered a series of Japanese terror bombing raids, the first of which in May 1939 caused more than 5,000 civilian deaths.

From 1925 to 1930 Teng Hiok Chiu studied painting at the Royal Academy of Arts. He had studied at the Anglo-Chinese College of the London Missionary Society in Teintsin and then spent some time in America studying art history and painting. In Britain he was influenced by the French Impressionists and in his later work combined this influence with Chinese traditional techniques. During his period of study he won many awards, including becoming the first foreign artist to be awarded the Turner Gold Medal and the Royal Academy Scholarship for Landscape Painting. His paintings were shown widely and the queen attended his first solo exhibition at London's Claridge Gallery. As his interest in Chinese art grew, he returned to China in 1930. For the next decade he travelled widely, before settling in New York. He became a close friend with the American artist Georgia O'Keeffe. In 1950 she wrote to Chiu, 'It seems to me that some of the most beautiful things man has created have come from there (China).'

In 1927 Luke Him Sau, who had been working as an architectural apprentice in Hong Kong for four years, travelled to London to become the first Chinese to study at the Architectural Association. This was a period when there was an ideological clash between a conservative approach to architecture and those with a more progressive approach, and Luke assimilated ideas from both camps. His graduation show in 1930 caught the attention of the Bank of China and it sent the young architect on a Grand

Tour of Europe, to look at bank buildings and other architectural models that could potentially be useful for the design of bank buildings in China. His best-known building, constructed in the mid-1930s, is the iconic Bank of China Headquarters in Shanghai.

For their part in the crushing of the Boxer Rebellion, Britain, the US and other countries received compensation from China in respect of damage to its citizens and property. For a number of years America used part of the compensation payments to support Chinese students to travel to America to study and, in 1925, the British Government decided to initiate its own Boxer Indemnity Scholarship Programme. This led to an increase in the number of students arriving from China and Hong Kong. From 1933 to 1939 around 100 British Boxer Indemnity Scholarships were awarded and these were one of the most coveted and competitive scholarships at the time. 'Competition is keen, with 300 or more candidates for the annual twenty awards – a fact which says much for the progress of modern education already underway in China since every candidate must already have a degree from a Chinese university and have had two years' practical work in his subject. Women are eligible as well as men.' While in 1929 it was reported that 'there were two women among last year's scholars and, at a reception given on the students' arrival, one girl made a little speech which for delicacy of thought and grace of phrasing could not have been excelled,' there continued to be significant prejudice within China against women studying certain subjects. Although Ming-chen Wang, who later became a significant figure in modern physics, earned the highest score in the qualifying exam for the Boxer Indemnity Scholarship Programme to the UK, the person in charge of the scholarship programme in China turned her down. He thought that it would be a waste of money to send a female student to study physics abroad and, instead, convinced the committee to award the scholarship to a male student who had earned the second-highest score. The subjects studied by recipients included engineering, medicine, mathematics, chemistry, agriculture, economies, law, history and literature.

In 1935 Qian Zhongshu, a writer who was teaching at Kwanghua University in Shanghai, gained one of the prized scholarships to study literature at Exeter College in Oxford. He had recently married Yang Jiang, also a respected writer and translator, and she travelled to Britain with him. They spent two years in Oxford and had a daughter there in 1937. Qian applied for a lectureship at one of the Oxford universities but was unsuccessful so after a year in Paris the couple returned to China. Both became significant literary figures, Qian's best-known work being the satirical novel *Fortress Besieged*. Yang said of her husband, 'His foolishness could not be contained in books, but just had to gush forth.' Yang became an outstanding translator and is best known for her translation of *Don Quixote*, having taught herself Spanish in order to do justice to the original, although she had to undertake the work twice as her first almost complete version was confiscated by Red Guard militants in 1966.

Academic Achievements

There were also bursaries for engineering students to attend university courses, and work placements organised by the Federation of British Industries. Most of the recipients spent one year in Britain, although a few had their study period extended. Although the scheme came to an end at the outbreak of war, a similar scheme was established in 1943 by the British Council and ten students arrived, including Shao Xianghua, who attended Imperial College, London. On his return to China he became Chief Engineer of the newly founded Anshan Iron and Steel Group and a pioneer of modern Chinese metallurgical engineering. By the 1940s the engineering students included a small number of women. Maria Liu, who studied at Birmingham University in 1944, was featured in *The Birmingham Mail*: 'This is typical of young China's eagerness to learn what the West has to offer in scientific thought and achievement. Miss Liu, who speaks and writes perfect English – a sign of the remarkable efficiency of Chinese language teaching – is passionately eager to assist in the rebuilding of her country.'

This desire to learn from Western technology brought the twenty-four-year-old Xia Peisu to Edinburgh in 1947. In China she had studied Electrical Engineering and had proven an outstanding student and she arrived in Scotland to undertake advanced study in electric circuit theory and automation. After earning her Doctorate she stayed for a further year and while living in Edinburgh married a fellow student, Yang Liming, who was studying physics. On her return to China in 1952, Xia was asked to join a group developing new computer technology and it was she who designed China's first computer.

Two of the first artists to receive British Council scholarships to study painting were Fei Cheng-Wu and Chang Chien-Ying who had jointly previously established the China Institute of Fine Arts in Chongking. They both came in 1946 to attend the Slade School of Art in London. By the time they completed their three-year course the Communists had taken power in China and so they decided to remain in Britain. In 1953 they married and one of the guests was their friend, Stanley Spencer, the British painter, who painted portraits of both Chang and Fei. Although Cheng continued to paint, he primarily concentrated on academic work, whereas Chang focused on painting, exhibiting her work widely. Many of these were executed on silk and special Chinese drawing paper, demonstrating traditional painting techniques. Her artistic work led her to design costumes for a number of films, including *The Inn of the Sixth Happiness*, and textiles for Christian Dior. She performed in amateur Peking Opera productions, singing both male and female roles, and appeared demonstrating Chinese cooking on Kenneth Lo's television programme *The Taste of China*.

It was art that Deh-Ta Hsiung wished to study but his father, the successful playwright, Hsiung Shih-I, objected, telling his son that he doubted anyone could make a living as a painter. So instead Deh-Ta studied Modern Languages at Magdalen College, Oxford, from 1949. However, after getting his degree, Deh-Ta went on to study painting, also at the Slade School. At that time he was living with his parents in Oxford and recalled that his parents' house 'was where the Chinese met. Any person stepping off a train in Oxford looking even vaguely Chinese was brought to the house by the insistent local taxi drivers – regardless of whether it was their destination of choice.' After completing his art course he worked in film, but then took up a career as a cook and writer on wine and food. His first Chinese cookbook, *The Home Book of Chinese Cooking*, was published in 1978.

Although there were a number of scholarships, the majority of those who came to Britain to study were financed by their families. *The Times* estimated that in 1935 there were 400 self-funded students at British universities.

> Many are distressingly ignorant of English – a point which ought to be impressed upon Chinese parents far more strongly than it is. Some have too much money, many are miserably poor; and for all there is the overwhelming strangeness of everything, from the food they eat to the beds they sleep in. In the college life of Oxford and Cambridge a Chinese student soon finds friends and congenial surroundings, for the Chinese are the most likeable people on earth. In some provincial universities special efforts are made to prevent the young Chinese from being left too much to his own resources. But the majority gravitate to London, and with the best will in the world the authorities can do little for them. Their knowledge of English life is limited to the dingy boarding house to which their resources condemn them. It is not surprising if they tend to shrink into themselves, and to fall into that commonest of errors of the foreigner abroad, of measuring the country he is in by himself and not himself by the country.

Most of those who came to study returned to China, but one who decided to stay after graduating was Robert Ya Fu Lee. After studying history at Trinity College, Cambridge, he took jobs at various Chinese and Japanese restaurants before being encouraged by friends to become an actor. Lee played supporting roles in many films and television programmes throughout the 1960s, '70s and '80s, and was frequently called upon whenever a production required an East Asian character. He appeared in television and films, his best known role being Tarō Nagazumi, the Japanese business executive and English language student, in the sitcom *Mind Your Language*.

Throughout the 1950s and early '60s the political turbulence within the People's Republic of China meant that few individuals were allowed to study abroad and in 1967, those that were received orders to return to China. The Chinese from Hong Kong and other areas outside Communist China were unaffected and in the mid-50s there were around 400 individuals from Hong Kong studying in Britain. Among them were Paul Lau Chia Yu and Lam Wai Pui, who were studying at the School of Aeronautical Engineering just outside Perth in Scotland. When the director of the local theatre sought help with a play that required a Chinese servant to speak some Chinese phrases, the two students came to the rescue. They taught the actor appropriate phrases and one can only hope they were not mischievous enough to have the Chinese servant speak about aeroplanes or worse. Another student of aeronautics, Lim Kok Kah, met and married a young English secretary and for their honeymoon they sailed to Singapore and Hong Kong, where the new bride had the unusual experience of meeting four mothers-in-law, as Lim's father had four surviving wives.

In 1959 one Hong Kong newspaper wrote 'that fear of having young minds contaminated by Communism in Britain has prompted many parents to send their children to Australia or the United States for their education.' This stemmed from a report brought back by the Chinese editor of a pro-Nationalist newspaper that Chinese Communists were offering subsidies of £20 to £50 month to Hong Kong students in Britain. Whether the story was true is not known, although it is hard not to think that such an offer would have been welcomed by many impoverished students. In spite of this warning many Hong Kong parents were content to continue to send their children to study in Britain.

Charles Kao was born in Shanghai but moved to Hong Kong with his family in 1948. He wanted to study electrical engineering and as the facilities in Hong Kong in the early 1950s were still disrupted following the war, he boarded a P&O liner for Britain. 'I was nineteen years old and had never before left my family to be on my own. Everything was a new experience. The British Council staff met me in London and arranged lodgings with a landlady in Plumstead Common, near Woolwich Polytechnic.' It was there he had enrolled to sit for the British A-level exams that he required before he could study for a degree. 'Food was still scarce after the war and the slices of meat served for dinner were so thin, they were transparent when held up to the light! I and the other lodgers would go off to buy fish and chips, which we scoffed down hungrily on the walk back.' After successfully passing his A-levels he decided to stay on at the Polytechnic to take his degree, although as he recounted: 'I spent more time on the tennis court than with my books, so my degree was a Second.' His father had been financing his studies but Kao realised he needed to earn money of his own so after graduating took a job with Standard Telephones and Cables (STC) in North Woolwich in London, working on microwave projects. While working for SLT he studied for a PhD at the University of London. At the time there were only a handful of students from Hong Kong studying engineering in London and they would meet during the holidays to cook up a feast. One was a female student, Gwen, who later recalled meeting Charles: 'I first saw him, and I thought he was a handsome looking guy, but I didn't think he noticed me because he was busy with his fried rice then.' However, by chance she also was employed by STC and, although on a different floor from Charles, they met again: 'There was only one other female engineer at my department, and I guess that was the time he noticed me. I was pretty surprised he made a beeline for me. I remember going "oh my gosh!" all the time because my colleagues would be looking at me.' Charles and Gwen married soon after and decided it was time for a move so Charles successfully applied for a lectureship at Loughborough University. They bought a house in the town and prepared to move, but when SLT received their resignations the company convinced the couple to stay by offering them jobs at the company's research centre in Harlow. 'The offer was too good to pass up. Loughborough had to be pacified and the lawyers got to work on that, and to get the house deposit refunded.' While working in Harlow on pioneering work in fibre optics as a telecommunications medium Charles published his ground-breaking paper that helped lead to the development of the internet. He wrote: 'Ideas do not always come in a flash, but by diligent trial-and-error experiments that take time and thought.' The Kaos had two children in the early 1960s. In 1967 Charles' parents, both in their late 60s, came to Britain to live with them. In 1970 SLT gave Charles and Gwen leave of absence to return to Hong Kong so that Charles could found the Department of Electronics at the University of Hong Kong. Charles' parents remained living in Britain but when his mother died, his father joined them in Hong Kong. There Charles served as Vice-Chancellor of the Chinese University of Hong Kong from 1987 to 1996. In Hong Kong, Charles's father began to suffer from Alzheimer's disease and Gwen cared for him until his death in 1996. His ashes were taken to Harlow Cemetery to be spread next to his wife's grave. The Kaos then moved to live in America and, sadly, in the mid-2000s Charles also began to suffer from Alzheimer's. Due to her experience of caring for her father-in-law, and then her husband, Gwen established a foundation to raise awareness of the disease. In 2010 Sir Charles Kao was knighted. In 2015 Lady Kao visited the Harlow Enterprise Zone, between London and Cambridge, where Kao Park has been named in her husband's honour. Harlow was where fibre optic cable was invented by George Hockham and Sir Charles Kao, for which they won the Nobel Prize for Science.

By 1972 the disastrous Cultural Revolution in China, which had led to schools and universities in the country being closed and study abroad banned, began to wane and the British Council were able to negotiate for the introduction of a Student Exchange Programme with the People's Republic of China, and 200 Chinese arrived in Britain to study English at Ealing College. In 1974, one of the students went missing and the police were called. It turned out that Tsui Yen Ming had fled the college to claim asylum in Britain. When the British authorities agreed he could stay, the PRC Government's fury brought the Exchange Programme to an abrupt end. When Deng Xiaoping became leader following the death of Chairman Mao in 1976, he recognised that highly trained people were required to rebuild China. Not only had the closure of almost all educational establishments blighted a generation, but many of those who had been allowed to go abroad to study had decided not to return. Thus in 1978 the Chinese negotiated with Britain for 1,000 undergraduates, 100 post-graduate and 100 post-doctoral students to be sent annually to Britain, all financed by the Chinese Government.

Before 1981 the cost of study at British universities for international students was relatively inexpensive but that changed when the British Government introduced full-cost fees for international students. This coincided with a period when there was reduced funding available from the British Council for scholarships for overseas students and so the number of Chinese and Hong Kong students in Britain fell significantly. In 1982, Dr David Kwok-po Li helped to establish The Prince Philip Scholarships to support students from Hong Kong to study at Cambridge University. One of the first to be awarded a scholarship was Wong Yan-lung, the son of an ice-cream vendor in Hong Kong. He recounted that when he was young he lived with his family in a tiny flat that had no space for study and so outside school spent all his time studying in the Hong Kong Arts Centre. His scholarship enabled him to study law at Magdalen College, Cambridge, and on his return to Hong Kong he became a barrister and served as second Secretary for Justice of Hong Kong.

In 1985 it was estimated that of the 18,000 Chinese students studying abroad, only about 600 were in Britain, but in the thirty-plus years since then, the annual number studying in Britain has increased to more than 100,000.

23

Diplomacy in Troubled Times

> I cannot sleep, the future weights my mind,
> The calls of office – cares of every kind –
> Oppress me with a sense of coming woes –
> A forlorn hope against unnumbered foes!
>
> Tao Qian (365–427),
> translated by Charles Budd

The Chinese Ambassador Quo Tai-chi, playing golf at Sandy Lodge, 1939. (Public domain)

Diplomacy in Troubled Times

In May 1902 Chang Ta-jen arrived in London to take over as ambassador and a week later was at Victoria Station to greet Prince Tsai Chen and his large retinue, who had arrived from China to represent the Emperor of China at the Coronation of Edward VII. The prince was not a popular choice in British Government circles: 'He is twenty-six years old, without personal distinction, and is quite unknown. It is regrettable that China should be so inadequately represented at the great pageant.' Unsurprisingly, Prince Tsai Chen did not share this view although he perhaps saw himself as being of greater importance that he actually was, for although not a crown prince, he had photographs published under that designation. One suspects that all Chang's diplomatic skills were required to deal with the young prince whom he escorted to a number of events in the days before the Coronation, including a dinner given in his honour by the Lord Mayor. A few days after the prince's arrival, soldiers from the Hong Kong Volunteers, the Hong Kong and Singapore Royal Artillery and the First Chinese Regiment disembarked after a lengthy sea voyage and prepared to participate in the Coronation parade. Unfortunately, the overweight fifty-nine-year-old Edward became ill and the Coronation was postponed until August. Most of the significant dignitaries who had travelled from all around the world, including Prince Tsai Chen, had to leave before the coronation. This included almost all the Chinese soldiers, whose long journey was in vain.

Chang was a successful and popular ambassador. When his term came to an end, one newspaper wrote:

> Most genial of Chinese diplomatists, Chang Ta-jen, whose three years' term as Chinese Ambassador to the Court of St James's expires shortly has become thoroughly Europeanised, and indeed has more than once found his life in danger through his barbarian sympathies. Chang had the misfortune after a visit to London to return to Peking just after the outbreak of the Boxer uprising and the fact that he could speak English being regarded by the enlightened patriots a damnatory token he was seized and carried off to a temple outside the city, where he expected that every moment would his last. But he was brought before Prince Chwang, who found nothing against him, and gave him his liberty.

In 1906, Chang's replacement, Wang Tahsieh, travelled to Liverpool to welcome three high-ranking Chinese who were in Britain as part of a Chinese Imperial Commission visiting to study methods of government, commerce and education. Much to the delight of the local Chinese the dignitaries, dressed in their beautiful robes, drove through the streets.

Yung Hsi Hsiao, who had studied English in Peking, arrived in Britain in 1901 to serve as one of the five attachés at the Chinese Legation in London. As he lodged in Norwood in South London, he led a relatively solitary life outside of work but one day, by good fortune, he was invited to tea by friends of his landlady. A young woman poured him a cup of tea and he instantly was smitten. The young woman, Mina Tomalin-Potts, the eldest daughter of a widow of a wholesale druggist, was equally taken by the exotic young man and in 1905 the couple married. When Yung arrived at the church for the wedding, accompanied by two colleagues from the Legation, the only on-looker was 'a German gentleman who explained that he was touring England and that while at Madame Tussauds had heard that a Chinese wedding was about to take place at the nearby church'. If he had expected to see the bride and groom dressed in flamboyant Chinese silk outfits he would have been disappointed as the groom and his two supporters were dressed in frock coats and the bride in white. 'But where is the bridegroom's pigtail? the German inquired, in tones perhaps too loud to be comfortable for Mr Hsiao and his Chinese friends.' Later that year Hsiao was called back to Peking to take up an appointment on the Board of Foreign Affairs, but Mina remained in London as she was pregnant. After she gave birth to their daughter, Muriel, it is likely that she and her daughter then joined Hsiao in China. He had a successful career, including appointments as Chinese Chargé d'affaires in Sweden and Norway, and Director of the Department of Navigation. Although there were some negative articles in British newspapers decrying mixed-race relationships, particularly in the London and Cardiff Chinatown areas, the British coverage of Hsio and Mina's wedding was positive. A report in a San Francisco newspaper report was radically different and underlines the more blatant racism towards Chinese in America at the time:

> Miss Tomalin-Potts may think it very romantic to wed a slant-eyed youth whose language is so peculiar as to make his endearments sound like a kettle falling down a winding stair. Her mamma may fancy that she has attained an unique prestige in uniting her daughter to a man whose pedigree, if translated, would mean nothing to us; but when a yellow baby comes, that infant will be just a Eurasian, a mongrel, a creature with the weaknesses of two races and the strength of neither.

The next ambassador, Li Ching Fong, was one of China's aristocrats, a known reformer and one of the wealthiest men in the world. He had been taught English by his father's American physician and had visited Britain in the 1880s to work with the then ambassador. Li was described as being

> ... of middle age, of medium height, and not quite so stout as is usually the case with southern Chinese gentlemen. In appearance a typical Celestial he invariably wears Chinese costume, including the queue. Similarly he favours the long tapering fingernails of the Chinese upper classes. He is widely read in European literature, well versed in Western sciences, and even able to appreciate Occidental music. At the same time, although the Minister may be imbued with a new spirit, there will be no change in the character of

the Chinese Legation. Thus, when entertaining, his Excellency will wear the usual beautiful robes of Chinese officials, ornamented on the back and chest with the large figures of embroidered swans that denote the difference between civil and military rank.

Two years before Li's arrival the Chinese had taken a lease on 51 Portland Place, the house next-door to the existing legation building, and work had begun on expanding the Legation. At the time newspapers announced that the interior was to be designed in Chinese style and Li ensured no expense would be spared, for it was reported that 'the new Ambassador is having the Legation furnished and upholstered by a first-class West End firm. As his Excellency has plenty of money, the Chinese Legation in time should be one of the handsomest diplomatic interiors in London.'

In late 1909, Prince Tsai-Chen again came to Britain, accompanied by Admiral Sah Chen-Ping and sixteen members of the Chinese Naval Commission who were in Europe to explore commissioning new warships for the Chinese Navy. As well as being wined and dined by British shipbuilders, the Chinese dignitaries, including Li, were received at Windsor Castle where they lunched with Edward VII and Queen Alexandra. At the end of the meal rice was served in the king's royal blue tureens and gold chopsticks provided. A special brew of Chinese tea was also served. In an interview with *The Morning Post* the admiral said they were all delighted with their visit.

> Everybody, from King Edward downwards has been most kind. It is too early to say what Prince Tsai-Chen thinks of England, for we have been out very little yet. However, he is very much pleased with everything. He was much struck by the guard of honour of the Grenadier Guards at Charing Cross station, and remarked that the ceremony of presenting arms was a very pretty sight. During his stay here he conforms to English habits, eating the same sort of food as others visitors in the hotel. Above all he is delighted with the London climate.

While in Britain, Admiral Sah Chen-Ping was knighted by King Edward and six months later, when the king died, it was the admiral who came with Prince Zaixun, China's first Minister of the Navy, to represent the Emperor at Edward's funeral. For the Coronation of George V Prince Tsai-Chen was again chosen to represent China, perhaps as he had missed out on the grand occasion in 1902. Once more his exaggerated sense of his status caused friction as he was upset at not being given higher precedence at the coronation ceremony.

The next ambassador, Lew Yuk Lin, arrived in post at a critical time. By 1911 the internal revolution in China threatening the empire was reaching a crucial stage and Lew was so taken up with the crisis that he had to miss a number of engagements. One was a dinner in Sheffield but in his place he sent his two daughters, Amy and May, who were studying in Brighton. The local press reported that the two young women were 'dressed in European costume' and 'attracted much attention'. One paper added, 'The Ambassador's two charming daughters are representatives of the New Women movement in China, and are devoted to athletics of various kinds. But they are not Suffragettes.'

China's crisis came to a head and on 1 January 1912 the Republic of China (ROC) formally replaced the Qing Empire. Lew must have felt a sense of dislocation as he no longer was the representative of the Chinese Empire with full diplomatic status, but instead the representative of the newly established ROC that was not recognised by the British for two years. However, he continued to represent China and, although no longer recognised as China's representative by the British Government, undertook a number of unofficial visits. The businessmen of Sheffield were certain that the new Republic still would need British goods and were more than happy to welcome Lew to the city and provide a tour of a number of major manufacturing plants. Lew also was busy raising millions of pounds in loans for the new government and in spite of British Foreign Office objections, British banks were happy to provide the loans as they trusted the new Republic Government to repay the loans when due.

In 1914, on the eve of his return to China, Lew expressed sadness at leaving. 'I am sorry to go, I like London. I have been very happy here, and would have liked to stop on, but I have already exceeded the usual term of office by a year. It took my daughters and myself two years to get to know people. Now that we have got used to the English climate and English ways we must go.' His daughter May added, 'I like the English girls. They are so sporting and I have very many friends to say goodbye to. I learned to drive a motor car here; but, then, there is nothing like home, and we have not seen mother for four years.'

Lew's replacement, Alfred Sao-ke Sze, was the first ambassador to swop the traditional Chinese dress for Western style clothes, although he and his wife still dressed in Chinese style on formal occasions. A magazine report of his wife's visit to the Duchess of York pointed out that 'Madame Sze invariably wears her native costume when she is at the Legation and social functions in London, although she wears English clothes for street wear.' The inconsistency between the appreciative coverage of the fashionable Chinese Ambassadors and their families and the negative reporting about Chinatowns was particularly noticeable in 1920 when Sze's replacement arrived. While much of the popular press and popular fiction was portraying the Chinese as devious and immoral, London society and the fashionable magazines were glowing about the new ambassador, Wellington Koo. He had come from America where he had been ambassador, and earlier a student, and was young, debonair and already reputed to be an astute diplomat. He spoke perfect English, and had a sharp sense of humour. It is alleged that a society lady who had read about a Chinese having committed suicide by eating gold leaf asked Koo how this could have caused the man's death. Koo replied with a grave face, 'I suppose that it was the consciousness of inward guilt.' To add to his glamour Koo had just married Countess Hoey Stoker, the recently divorced wife of Beauchamp Caulfield Stoker. She was described in one paper as being

> ... a member of London's smartest set, and a daughter of Count Oei Tyong Han, one of the richest men in China and known here as the Rockefeller of that country. She occupies a big house in fashionable Grosvenor Street and entertains lavishly... In society the countess is a great favourite. She speaks French, English, German and Italian almost as easily as she does her own language, and is also a brilliant pianist. Her great chum is Lady Drogheda, who is so keenly interested in aviation. Countess Hoey Stoker is almost as keen on aviation as Lady Drogheda. She was one of the first society women to avail herself of the permission for civilian flying after the war, and has made several ascents from the aerodrome at Cricklewood.

The elegant, wealthy couple regularly appeared in the style and society magazines of the day, often with photographs of their young children, and were on the invitation list for every fashionable event. As Madame Koo later recounted:

> We went everywhere, I in my jewels and couturier clothes and full-length mink or ermine coats, Wellington in his British-made white tie and tails. We had our Rolls, with a chauffeur, a wedding present from Mamma. I was able, because Mamma had trained me to be a woman of the world, equal to Europeans, to mingle in society as few Chinese women could have.

In 1921 it was announced that a court ball was to be given at Buckingham Palace to honour the visiting King and Queen of Belgium and there was great excitement as this was the first ball since the First World War. Madame Koo instantly ordered a magnificent gold lamé ball gown to wear.

In 1929 Alfred Sao-ke Sze replaced Koo for a second period as ambassador. One official event that must have tested all his diplomatic skills was a theatre visit in 1932. Aggressive Japanese incursion into China was a source of political tension and when Sze discovered that one of the other guests at the premiere was the Japanese Ambassador he must have been discomfited. As the play's subject matter was anti-war, Sze must have been tempted at the interval to suggest that the Japanese would do well to take note of the playwright's message, but no doubt diplomacy meant that he kept any such thoughts to himself.

The first theatre outing for the next ambassador, Quo Tai-chi, was a jollier affair, as he was invited to the first night of Noel Coward's musical revue,

Words and Music, and no doubt particularly enjoyed the lines of one song in the show: 'Mad dogs and Englishmen go out in the midday sun... The Chinese wouldn't dare to... It seems such a shame, When the English claim the Earth, That they give rise to such hilarity and mirth.'

Ivan Maisky arrived in Britain to take up the post of Russian Ambassador in the same year as Quo and they became good colleagues. Maisky wrote of Quo: 'How many times during our conversation did I fly into a rage, become irritated or indignant at one or other action by the British Government. But Quo Tai-chi always preserved an imperturbable calmness and merely observed; "It will pass...." "It will change...." "One must not lose one's patience." I was always impressed by a kind of subconscious sense of the venerability of his race, a kind of majestic serenity nurtured by the thousand-year history of his nation. A Chinese, speaking about the most recent events, will let slip: "There was an incident at the time of the T'ang Dynasty ..." Or "Poet so-and-so said two thousand years ago."'

In 1934 Madame Quo Tai-chi travelled to Glasgow to launch the newly built ship, *Hai*, a cargo and passenger steamer specially designed to repulse attacks by pirates. After Madame Quo Tai-chi completed the ceremonial naming of the ship, the vessel slid down into the river to the accompaniment of exploding firecrackers, the first Chinese launching ceremony ever to take place on the Clyde. In 1935 Quo Tai-chi became the first formal Ambassador of the Chinese Republic to the Court of St James, as in that year the British Government raised the status of the Chinese Legation to an Embassy. Two years later Anna A. L. Huang arrived in Britain to become the third secretary to the Chinese Embassy, the first Chinese woman to take part in diplomatic service abroad.

At the Coronation of George VI in May 1937, the Republic of China was represented by Dr Kung Hsiang-hsi, the Government's Finance Minister, and his wife, the sister of General Chiang Kai-shek. Dr and Mrs Kung had travelled from China by liner and brought with them 100 cases filled with coronation gifts. Unfortunately, when just a few days out at sea, Kung discovered that missing from the mountain of luggage was the suit that he had had made specially to wear at the coronation. It was reported that, 'A British missionary is now travelling post haste to London, via Siberia, bringing with him the elaborate gold-braided Coronation suit left behind by Mr Kung.' To the relief of whoever in his staff had been responsible for not packing it, the suit arrived in time.

As with all foreign ambassadors in London, Quo's schedule included receptions at Buckingham Palace, ministerial dinners, fashionable garden parties, political lunches and semi-official weekends in the country. Yet amid all the diplomatic social events he worked assiduously to draw attention to Japan's continued aggressive expansion in northern China. He lobbied the Government to end British arms sales to the Japanese, whose airplanes, armed with British guns, were killing countless civilians in China even before war was declared, but the British Government was more concerned with fascist acts of war on the Continent. So Quo changed tack and facilitated the creation of an alliance between those who were concerned at Britain's assistance to Japan. This led to the creation of the China Campaign Committee (CCC) that vigorously campaigned against Japanese aggression within China, including for a boycott of Japanese goods. The CCC's 'No Oil for Japanese Bombers' campaign was strongly supported by Communist-led British dockers who blocked Japanese cargoes in several ports, and the solidarity actions spread to France and Australia, where dockers also carried out embargoes. The boycott campaign continued until late 1938 when the shadow of war with Germany shifted focus away from China. A few weeks after Britain declared war on Germany Quo's wife and son sailed to America for safety, but Quo remained in Britain. In spite of the news being dominated by the war in Europe, he continued to strive to ensure the situation in China was not forgotten and to counteract Japanese propaganda. 'In an interview today the Chinese Ambassador emphatically repudiated a Tokyo suggestion that China was in danger of Communist domination. This, he said, was but a renewed attempt of Japanese propaganda by invoking afresh the Bolshevik bogey to confuse world opinion regarding the real issues involved in the Sino-Japanese conflict.' Quo refused to move the legation to the country for safety in spite of the bombing of London and was one of those who understood that the war was a global conflict. Speaking at the London Liberal Club in 1940 he said, 'There is no European war: there is no Asiatic war: there is world war. Whether here, where you have hardly started fighting, or in Asia, where we have already drained our blood and resources, it is the same war, waged against the same opposing forces.' In February 1941 he was proven right when Japan bombed Pearl Harbor. As a result, America entered the war and began to support China. Quo voiced the thoughts of all Chinese: 'After having fought for so long in somewhat lonely fashion, we now know we are no longer alone.' A few months later he was appointed to be the country's foreign minister and returned to China. It was he who, on 8 December 1941, confirmed that the Republic of China was officially at war with Nazi Germany and Italy, in addition to Japan.

In July 1941 Wellington Koo arrived back in London to take up the post of ambassador and his wife joined him a few months later. Events called on all of Koo's well-developed diplomatic skills but amid his busy round of meetings and visits, he and his wife again became part of London's fashionable society. Mrs Koo participated in a number of organisations, including as chairman of the Chinese Women's Association in Britain. Although Germany had surrendered in May 1945, bringing to an end the war in Europe, the fighting in the Far East continued. On 24 July 1945 Koo commented:

To those millions of the brave soldiers, airmen and sailors of the United Nations fighting gallantly in Okinawa, in New Guinea, in Burma, in

Borneo, in Honan and in Kwangsi, the war does not seem to be over. Until the war against Japan is actually over, until the day when Japan surrenders unconditionally like her German partner in crime, all of us should remember that our boys fight and win and die today just like any other day.

He recounted how few people outside China had believed the country could resist Japan beyond a few months, including a Far Eastern expert of a European delegation in 1941 who had bet him that China's resistance would not hold beyond the end of that year. 'After four years the Chinese Army is still in the field. In another six weeks the war in Asia will have surpassed the First World War duration.' Throughout the war years, Koo had been one of those working to establish the League of Nations and in 1945 was one of the founding delegates of the United Nations. He later returned to be the Chinese Ambassador to the United States and worked to maintain the alliance between the Republic of China and the United States when the Government lost power to the Communists and was forced to move to Taiwan. In April 1946, one of Koo's last acts as ambassador in Britain was to unveil a plaque on 8 Gray's Inn Place, the house where Dr Sun Yat-sen had lodged in London while he was a political refugee. Although the house was a ruin owing to wartime bombing, the plaque was attached onto the shell, and fixed on the new building that was erected on the site.

When Koo's successor, Cheng Tien-hsi, met the press one newspaper reported that 'there was no formality about chain-smoking Dr Cheng, the new Chinese Ambassador. "Make yourselves at home," he said, instead of handing out a long official statement. Then, still smoking, he answered a barrage of questions. He ended by saying "England is tops for me."' Cheng of course knew Britain well as in 1907 he had lived in London with his wife while studying law at the University of London. While in London Mrs Cheng had given birth to their second child, a daughter, and as they were about to leave the country to return to China named the baby Ying-Wan, Chinese for 'Return from England'. As Cheng brought his daughter with him to Britain 'Return from England' returned to England. In October 1947 Cheng welcomed the British Prime Minister Clement Attlee and 1,200 other guests at the Legation to celebrate the anniversary the foundation of the Chinese Republic thirty-five years before. Such was the crowd that squeezed into the Portland Place building that even the ambassador's private offices had to be converted into reception rooms. *The Tatler*'s diarist described the scene:

There were several buffets with delicious food. Many guests proceeded up the stairs, where an immense green Chinese Buddha sits imposingly, to the fine drawing rooms. Here I was enthralled by the exquisite Chinese pictures hanging on the walls, some of them beautifully painted on finest Chinese silk. The Prime Minister and Mrs. Attlee, the latter looking charming in black, arrived with their daughter Felicity. A little farther on the Nepalese Minister and his lovely wife in national costume were chatting to Miss Cheng, the Chinese Ambassador's daughter. I met Mrs. Miller, who last year flew with Lady Cripps to China at the invitation of Generalissimo Chiang Kai-shek to visit hospitals and clinics where the money raised by the British Aid to China Fund was being spent, with her husband. Monsieur and Mme Cheng were assisted in entertaining their guests by their son, Mr. Bing Cheng, who is studying International Law in London. Among the guests was Harold Wilson, the new President of the Board of Trade.

On 5 March 1948 Cheng picked up his phone and spoke to the Mayor of Shanghai to launch the first direct telephone link between Britain and China. No doubt the phone was much used in the following months as the battle raged for control of China between Mao's communist forces and the Republic's army under the command of Chiang Kai-Shek. In the face of the threat of defeat, Cheng met with the British Government in an attempt to get aid for the Republic's army but the request was rejected. By the beginning of 1949 the situation for the ROC looked bleak. One newspaper wrote:

Deep in dejection, head bowed, hands clasped behind his back, a little man in the sombre clothes of the traditional diplomat reluctantly walked the high, arched corridors of Whitehall's Foreign Office this evening. It was Dr Cheng Tien-Hsi, the Chinese Ambassador. His lively features, usually ready to acknowledge either a jest or a friend, seemed established in depression. I understand that he had pleaded, even though it was such busy day at the Foreign Office that Mr Bevin should spare him a few minutes. His errand was urgent – and bitter. Dr Cheng expects to stay in London as Ambassador when another Government, probably Communist-dominated coalition, is formed, but he is personally disturbed by the grave news.

Yet even by the middle of that year when it seemed the Communists were likely to gain control, Cheng told a journalist that he did not believe Communism could prevail for long. 'The basis of social life in China is the family,' he says, 'and Communism cannot thrive as long as that tradition exists.' To add to the complicated situation, the Republic's forces began attacking British merchant ships in the ports that had been taken by the Communists in an attempt to blockade shipping. Cheng was summoned to the Foreign Office and informed that such attacks were an illegitimate and unfriendly act, though it is doubtful there was anything Cheng could do to cease what was a last desperate attempt to hold onto power by the government in China. By October, two years after Cheng's great party of celebration, the majority of the Kuomintang army and ROC government officials had taken refuge in Taiwan, and by the end of the year the People's Republic of China (PRC) was in power. Yet Cheng later wrote in his account of 1949, 'In spite of the fact that this was an anxious year, my social engagements continued to grow.

Of these social festivities the most notable was when Princess Elizabeth and the Duke of Edinburgh honoured us with their presence at the Embassy. Chinese food was served and Chinese music played.'

One of Cheng's last acts as ambassador was in December 1949. He could see that British recognition of the PRC was near and so tried to persuade the British Foreign Secretary, Ernest Bevin, to maintain *de facto* relations with the Nationalist Government in Taiwan, but he was unsuccessful. In January 1950 Britain formally recognised the new People's Republic of China and so Cheng and the other staff in the Chinese Legation no longer had any official status. The Foreign Office informed the diplomats that they could remain in the country as private citizens or travel to Taiwan to join the Kuomintang there. Cheng and his wife decided to stay. Chiang Kai-Shek was keen to try to retain relations with Britain as he hoped that the PRC might be seen as an ally against the Communists and thus, although Cheng had no formal position, he was instructed to continue to negotiate with the British. In 1950 he managed to persuade the British Government to recognise Lee Yun-min, who had been a First Secretary at the PRC Chinese Legation in London, as an unofficial liaison officer between the PRC and the British Government. Amid his unofficial political duties Cheng had the pleasure of seeing his son, Bin, marry Foo Kam-Pui, the daughter of the Chinese Ambassador in Russia, who had retired to Paris when he, too, lost his post.

Late in 1950, Chiang Kai-Shek sent his trusted aide, Hollington Tong, to London to try to alert the British authorities to the dangerous situation in South East Asia and enlist moral and material assistance. Although the British Foreign Office was not prepared to meet Tong officially, informal meetings were arranged and it was agreed to keep the unofficial channels of communication open. In 1951, with Britain at war with China in the Korean War, Chiang Kai-Shek believed that there was an opportunity to convince the British Government to change tack and recognise his government instead of the Communists. This time he dispatched Han Lih-wu, his presidential adviser, to London to talk to the British authorities. Han had attended university in London and been leader of the British-Chinese Educational Association in Hong Kong, so he had many friends in high places. One was Robert Scott, then the Assistant Under-Secretary supervising Far Eastern affairs at the Foreign Office. As the British Government was still unwilling for any formal meetings to be seen to be taking place, in December 1951 Scott invited the Foreign Minister, Selwyn Lloyd, to lunch at his house. The only other guest was Han and it is unlikely Lloyd was surprised that the subject of conversation was British policy in regard to China rather than plans for Christmas. Han argued the case for Britain to review its China policy, and requested the Minister to ensure that Taiwan was not treated as a pawn in the course of negotiations to end the Korean War, as it could involve the survival of the ROC Government and the question of Chinese representation at the United Nations. Han's entreaties were in vain. By 1953 the PRC had to accept that Britain would not change its China policy and no further discreet visits from PRC officials took place. Cheng's unofficial diplomatic role was at and end, but he remained with his wife in Britain, collecting Chinese porcelain and writing books, including *Musings of a Chinese Gourmet*.

Although Britain was unwilling to switch its diplomatic recognition from the PRC to the ROC, the fact that Britain and Communist China were on opposing sides in the Korean War brought a temporary freeze to diplomatic relations and trade. In 1954, when Lei Yen-min, the PRC's Minister for Foreign Trade, attended the Geneva Conference to settle outstanding issues resulting from the war, the director of the Federation of British Industries met him to discuss the re-opening of trade between the two countries. This led to a visit later that year by a Chinese trade delegation that visited a range of companies, including the Austin Motor Company and Massey Ferguson tractor works. A few years later, the PRC appointed a Commercial Counsellor in Britain, one of only two in Western Europe at this time; the other being in Bern. However, Anthony Dicks, of the Institute of Current World Affairs, pointed out that the Chinese chose to locate the Commercial Counsellor's office far from the business centres of London: 'It lurks in semi-seclusion in a residential area to the North of Regent's Park, almost discouraging people, one feels, from leaving their offices to go up there.'

In the same year that the Chinese trade delegation visited, the PRC reinstated a form of diplomatic relationship by appointing Huan Xiang, a senior diplomat and a prominent expert in international affairs, as its chargé d'affaires in Britain. One of his roles was to undertake negotiations on the question of establishing full diplomatic relations and re-establishing an ambassadorial post. Xiang had been a Communist spy in the 1940s and, arguably, single-handedly responsible for the Communists taking power. He had secretly joined the Communist Party and then managed to join the staff of the Kuomintang leader General Chiang Kai-shek, serving as the General's confidential secretary for ten years. Xiang decided to leave China to study in America but as he was about to leave, was intercepted by Chiang's secret police. Fearing he was unmasked and would be executed, Xiang was astonished to discover that instead he had been brought back to assist in preparations for a Kuomintang attack on Mao's base. Xiong managed to inform the Communists and Mao later said that Xiong's information was 'worth several divisions'. It was the turning point in the civil war: two years later, the People's Liberation Army entered Peking.

It was not until 1963 that Britain welcomed another high-level visitor from the PRC. Lu Hsu-Chang, the Vice-Minister for Foreign Trade, came with a delegation on a three-week visit and the British Government was hopeful that this would lead to increased trade and keen to ensure the visit went well. It had been made clear that Lu Hsu-Chang had to be described as coming from the People's Republic of China, and not from 'Communist or Red or Mainland China' but, of course, the press kept getting it wrong. When the Chinese complained British officials had to point out that they had no control over the press. Anthony Dicks wryly added in his report that this was in spite of Britain having no constitutional guarantee of press freedom 'unlike China where the Chinese Constitution provides freedom of speech and freedom of press'. The delegation, which included Hsieh Shou-tien, managing director of the China National Metals and Minerals Import and Export Corporation, visited a range of companies including Courtaulds, English Electric Co., the Steel Company of Wales, Bradwell nuclear power station, Glasgow shipyards and the planned new town of Crawley. Dicks reported, 'They showed almost total indifference to such aspects of English life as they came across. I heard no complaints about the food in the English provincial hotels, of which the delegation made extensive use; it may be that the older members had perhaps been schooled in the "English restaurants" of which one sometimes hears from those familiar with Shanghai in former days. It was after all, the first time anyone in Mr Lu's position had been allowed out of China.'

Towards the end of Xiong's time as Chargé d'affaires in Britain, Mao launched his infamous Cultural Revolution. Embassies were attacked, including the British Embassy in Peking, which was set on fire and its staff assaulted. In response, the Government posted Special Branch officers near the Chinese Legation in Portland Place in London. One day, in August 1967, about twenty Chinese Legation staff armed with baseball bats, machetes and dustbin lids poured out of the building and attacked the policemen. Fortunately only minor injuries resulted and the situation was calmed down. Just a month later *The Times* reported:

> It was all smiles when Mao's men in London received guests at the Chinese Legation last night. There was none of the uncomradely scenes of last month when the same Chinese diplomats wielded axes. Last night they handled nothing sharper than a cocktail glass. For two hours about 150 guests drank and talked with the Chinese diplomats at a reception to mark the 18th anniversary of the Chinese Communist revolution. Police surrounded the legation in case of trouble, but none was needed and it was all handshakes by the Chinese as the guests left.

Although the attack on the British Embassy in Peking and what became known as 'The Battle of Portland Place' caused friction, the main barrier to reinstating diplomatic relations between China and Britain was the major issue of China's seat on the United Nations. China had been one of the founding members of the United Nations and although the Communist Party had forced the Republic of China (ROC) to leave the mainland, the ROC continued to hold China's seat at the United Nations and, as there was only one seat per country, the PRC was not admitted. The exclusion of the PRC was led by the United States, with support from other countries, including Britain but in 1971, after secret negotiations between America and China, the USA and other countries agreed that the PRC should take the place of the Taiwan-based ROC.

Diplomacy in Troubled Times

One of the first steps to re-establishing normal diplomatic relations involved table tennis, an unexpected route that came to be known as 'ping-pong diplomacy'. In the 1920s Ivor Montagu, a British banker and devoted Communist, codified the rules of table tennis that had originated in Victorian Britain and created the International Table Tennis Federation, as he was convinced that the sport could spread Communism throughout the world, because the toiling masses could play it during the workday. When, following the establishment of the People's Republic of China in 1949, diplomatic relations with the West became awkward, Montagu decided that table tennis was just the thing to help reconnect China to the rest of the world. So in 1951, twenty years before the PRC joined the United Nations, Montagu invited the communist regime to join his International Table Tennis Federation and enter the world championships. After a Chinese player won the world championship in 1959 Mao congratulated him personally and called ping-pong China's new 'spiritual nuclear weapon' and decreed table tennis to be the national sport of China. Although Montagu's plan that table tennis would improve relations between China and the West began to bear fruit, the Korean War meant that ping-pong's full healing power did not come to fruition for twenty years. It was not until 1971 that Britain welcomed a Chinese table tennis team, an event of such diplomatic importance that the players were given a reception at Downing Street by the Prime Minister, Edward Heath.

The only other stumbling block in Britain's relations with the PRC was Britain's continued trade consulate presence in Taiwan and when Britain closed this, the way was open for an exchange of diplomats with the PRC and a return to formal diplomatic relations. Thus in 1972 the PRC appointed Song Zhiguang as its British Ambassador. In advance of his arrival in London, the British establishment began a charm offensive. Song dined at the British Embassy in Peking and during the dinner conversation it was discovered that he and his wife were keen swimmers. So when Song and his wife arrived in Britain the Foreign Office arranged for them to be admitted to London's Lansdowne Swimming Club. Song's first-rate diplomatic skills and sense of humour helped restore normal relations and he reinstated a programme of official business, including trips to various parts of Britain. A significant one, as it was a sign of the restoration of trade between Britain and China, was a visit to the Ipswich factory of Ransomes & Rapier to announce a Chinese order worth more than £1 million. This was appropriate as it had been Ransomes & Rapier that had built the first locomotive to run in China. Song and his wife managed less formal trips, including being shown round Inveraray Castle by the Duke and Duchess of Argyll while visiting Scotland. It also was in 1972 that Queen Elizabeth visited Hong Kong, the first-ever visit there by a reigning British monarch; but it would be some years before the Queen set foot in the People's Republic of China.

Song was interested in developing sporting and cultural exchanges and to facilitate this the British Government established the Great Britain China Committee, later the Great Britain-China Centre, to facilitate exchanges. One of the most significant cultural events that Song helped arrange was the hugely successful exhibition, 'Genius of China', held in London in 1973, which stimulated renewed interest in China's outstanding cultural legacy. He also worked to get planning permission to enable the Portland Place Legation to be completely rebuilt. Since inheriting the building when it took power, the PRC had wanted to demolish the two buildings and rebuild it as a single building. As the two houses dated from 1785 and had been co-designed by the famed Adam brothers, the planners were resistant. Song gained planning consent by agreeing to ensure the new building's facade was sympathetic to the Adams' design, and the transformation into a single building was completed 200 years after the original construction.

Ke Hua was ambassador during the ground-breaking visit in October 1979 of Chairman Hua Kuo-Feng, the first Chinese leader to visit Britain. This was a coup for the British Government as it was his first visit to a non-Communist country and he was welcomed at Heathrow airport by Prime Minister Margaret Thatcher, who paid tribute to China as a 'great and historical nation which has a crucial role to play in world affairs'. Chairman Hua lunched with the Queen at Buckingham Palace and was taken on a tour of the state rooms, and also had a tour of the Tower of London. There were visits to a number of companies, including Rolls-Royce as discussions were underway about the purchase of military aircraft. As it was known that Chairman Hua had spent twenty years of his life in the Chinese agricultural sector, the Chinese leader was taken to a farm in Wallingford, Oxfordshire, where he was presented with a cow and treated to green tea in one of the barns. The fate of the cow is not known. One agreement made during this visit that paved the way for the huge increase in Chinese visiting Britain from the mid-1980s onwards was an agreement to inaugurate a regularly scheduled airline service between the two nations. However, the major diplomatic issue of Hong Kong's future remained unresolved. Although Hong Kong Island had been ceded to the British in perpetuity after the First Opium War, the larger New Territories on the mainland were on ninety-nine-year leases running from 1898. The British and Hong Kong Governments sought an extension to the leases but the Chinese Government refused. Ke Hua was the ambassador during some of the informal early negotiations and he later praised Margaret Thatcher, who as Prime Minister led the negotiations on the British side, calling her 'an outstanding stateswoman ... who will go down in history as the leader who ended British colonial rule in the Far East'. Formal discussions began in 1984 on the process of Hong Kong reverting to Chinese sovereignty, which it did in July 1997.

In 1985 China's Prime Minister, Zhao Ziyang came to London to meet Margaret Thatcher and before his arrival, the Prime Minister and her ministers discussed a number of key issues concerning the visit. One that caused much debate was the gift the Chinese guest should receive. Thatcher smacked down one minister's suggestion of a watercolour painting of a scene in London and when someone suggested a bolt of suit fabric, Percy Cradock, Thatcher's foreign affairs adviser, responded, 'The tortuous Chinese mind might conclude you think he dresses badly!' So this idea was also rejected and in the end Margaret Thatcher settled on a Scottish cashmere travel rug and a fine piece of Royal Worcester porcelain. The latter was possibly a strange choice as a gift for the Prime Minister of the country that invented the technique of making what is now known as china.

In October 1986, almost 300 years since Britain's King James II met the first Chinese visitor to Britain, the first-ever visit by a British monarch to China took place. With a smile and a wave of her gloved hand, Queen Elizabeth II, wearing a wide-brimmed white hat and a lemon-yellow dress, descended from her plane to be welcomed by China's Foreign Minister, Wu Xueqian. In reply to his welcome the queen simply said, 'I'm very glad to come to China.'

24

Taking up the Pen

Perverse by nature, I'm addicted to fine lines
If my words don't startle people, I won't give up till I die.

                Du Fu, translated by Mark Alexander

Chen Yuan and Ling Shuhua, *c.* 1940. (Public domain)

Taking up the Pen

A number of Chinese began their writing careers while in Britain. One of the most renowned was the Chinese poet Xu Zhimo, who became interested in poetry while studying at King's College, Cambridge, in 1921. Xu previously had read economics and politics in Peking and New York, but during his time in Cambridge discovered the poetry of Hardy, Keats, Shelley and others, and was inspired to begin writing his own poems. When he left King's College in 1922 to return to China he wrote a poem about leaving Cambridge and, following a return visit to Cambridge in 1928, wrote a further version known as the *Second Farewell to Cambridge*. This poignant love letter to the town is one of China's best known and favourite poems, and is a fixture in the Chinese school curriculum. On his return to China Xu became a leader of the modern poetry movement, but, sadly, died in 1931 in a plane crash. In 2008, a white Peking marble stone was engraved with the first and final lines of Xu's poem and sited in Cambridge, and large numbers of Chinese visitors, academics and students visit the memorial every year.

Another young man whose writing flair emerged while studying at King's College was Leslie Charles Bowyer-Yin. He was born in 1907 in Singapore and his father, Dr Yin, claimed to be able to trace his lineage back to the emperors of the Shang Dynasty. Leslie's parents spilt up when he was in his early teens and his mother brought him and his brother to England where they attended boarding school. On leaving school Leslie had a brief try at being a painter in Paris, but as his father insisted he should study for the law, he went to Cambridge in 1926. Leslie's heart was not in studying the law and he legally changed his surname to Charteris, a name that his daughter later claimed he chose at random from a phone book, and spent his first term writing a thriller that was published the following year. *X Esquire* features a mysterious hero, hunting down and killing businessmen who are trying to wipe out the British by distributing free poisoned cigarettes. On the back of this early success Charteris left university after his first year, much to the displeasure of his father who considered writers 'rogues and vagabonds' and warned his wayward son he would end up in the gutter. Although Charteris continued to have his books published, this did not bring in enough money to keep the gutter at a comfortable distance, so he worked at a range of jobs, including as a pearl diver and a fairground roustabout.

Charteris was invited to contribute to a new mass-market weekly magazine and submitted a series of short stories featuring a character he had invented for his third thriller, *Meet the Tiger*. This character, Simon Templar, better known as The Saint, became his most famous and lucrative creation. From 1930 onwards, almost all of his books featured The Saint; a debonair and swashbuckling character who spectacularly robbed the rich and the villainous and gave the proceeds to the out-of-luck, the swindled and the oppressed. The Saint gained iconic status when it became a 1960s television series starring Roger Moore. Although the stories are diverting and fun, there is a subversive side to the character that enabled Charteris to vent his distaste at the money men, arms merchants and the unelected governing elite. In the early 1930s a solicitor pursued the author down Farringdon Street in London waving his stick and remonstrating at the young man who 'didn't look British' for having a fling with his daughter, and perhaps Charteris took his revenge by portraying many of the lawyers in his later Saint books as crooks or men of dubious morality. In 1932 Charteris decided to move to live in America but discovered that he was excluded from permanent residency because of the Chinese Exclusion Act, a law which prohibited immigration to America for persons of '50 per cent or greater' Oriental blood. As a result, Charteris was forced continually to renew his six-month temporary visitor's visa. Although he spent almost all of his working life in the US, writing and working on films, he continued to have visa problems:

> The 'Oriental blood', or any other kind of blood definition, seems to have been pretty well washed out during the last war's campaign for blood donors; but the racial distinction never does seem to have been settled, since I still get a form inviting me to state my 'race', and I still don't know the answer, because there are no stock names for a 50-50 split and in the case of a tie it seems that no prizes are awarded.

It took an Act signed by President F. D. Roosevelt in December 1942 to bestow permanent residence on Charteris and his daughter.

In the same year that Charteris was writing his first novel in Cambridge, Lao She arrived in London to teach Mandarin Chinese at the School of Oriental Studies in London. During his time in Britain, Lao wrote his first two novels and later said that he had begun writing as a result of his loneliness as a Chinese living in London. To pass the time, he read British novels and became particularly fond of the works of Charles Dickens. Inspired by the great writer Lao decided he would populate his imaginary world with characters from his homeland and so alleviate his homesickness. His first novel, *The Philosophy of Lao Zhang*, is modelled on *Nicholas Nickleby*, although set among students in Peking. The influence of Dickens is apparent in Lao's exuberant language, plotting and an assortment of grotesque characters. It also mirrors Dickens' comic satire on society, in Lao's case casting a sceptical, humorous eye on a China changing from its traditional past into a new society. Lao describes the central character, Lao Zhang, whose philosophy is simply to grab as much money as he can, as 'the most important figure in town! If Lao Zhang unfortunately passed away, it would be a disaster worse than the loss of a saint. After all, which saint could be as versatile as Lao Zhang, who masters both the pen and the sword, and who befriends the living and the dead?'

When he returned to China in 1929 Lao published *Mr Ma and Son: Two Chinese in London*, a comic novel that he had begun in London and one that provides a unique account of what life was like for Chinese people in 1920s

London. Early in the novel, the Reverend Ely, an elderly minister who had served as a missionary in China in his younger days, visits Mrs Wedderburn, one of his parishioners, to enquire if she would be willing to let her two spare rooms to two Chinese soon to arrive in London. Lao describes Mrs Wedderburn's uncertainty and Ely's attempts to win her round:

'You can't imagine that I would allow two Chinese to cook rats in my house?' 'The Chinese do not ... Of course I shall enjoin them not to eat rats.' 'And they don't smoke opium?' 'No, no,' the Reverend Ely reiterated. She proceeded to pose countless questions based on the Chinese things she'd learned from rumours fostered by novels, films, plays and missionaries. Going right to the bottom of everything, she left no stone unturned. When she'd exhausted all her questions, she suddenly regretted ever having asked them. Didn't asking questions like that show quite clearly that she already intended letting the rooms to them? 'Thank you Mrs Wedderburn,' said the Reverend Ely with a smile. 'We'll leave it at that then. Four pounds five shillings a week, and you'll see to their breakfast.' 'I can't allow them to use my bath.' 'No, no, of course not. I'll tell them they must go out for their baths.' With these words, the Reverend Ely snatched up his hat and coat, and hastened off. He rushed along the street and when he found himself in a quiet secluded spot, exclaimed in pent-up tones. 'Bloody hell! All for two Chinese!'

Yet Mrs Wedderburn's ambivalence towards her Chinese tenants begins to wane, as shown delightfully in a later passage. It is Christmas and Mr Ma is standing below a bunch of mistletoe hanging from the light in the living room in the lodgings, a glass of wine in his hand:

As Mrs Wedderburn came back into the room, he hastily put his wine glass down. She glanced at him, glanced at the mistletoe on the light, blushed, stepped back two paces, then suddenly stiffened her dainty neck, went even redder, and flew over to him, clasped his face in her hands, and kissed him plonk on his lips. Mr Ma's face immediately went purple, and his whole body quivered. He gave her a numb, gawpy smile and rushed upstairs. Mrs Wedderburn waited a moment, then she too went upstairs.

Given that Lao would later be one of the many artists and intellectuals who were maltreated during the Cultural Revolution and, as a result, committed suicide, this passage from his novel is poignant: 'Ice skating rinks, circuses, dog shows, chrysanthemum shows, cat shows, leg shows, car races, grand contests and special competitions... The English could never have a revolution as with so much to look at and talk about, whoever's got the time for a revolution.'

In 1939 Hsiao Ch'ien also came to teach Chinese at what was now (from 1938) the School of Oriental and African Studies (SOAS). Although he had trained in journalism in China and co-founded the English magazine *China in Brief*, it was while living in Britain that he also wrote his first novels. Hsiao first lived in a London boarding house that catered especially to Asians and he shared the ground-floor flat with a Tamil named Rajarantu, who later became the first deputy premier and foreign minister of Singapore. Hsiao also got to know associates of the Bloomsbury Group, including E. M. Forster with whom he became close friends. In a letter to Forster written in in 1943 Hsiao mentions the prejudice of many landlords against Chinese. 'I experience the colour bar,' Hsiao wrote. 'Civil Liberties are taking up the question of the Colour Bar in Flats, and getting a question asked about it in the House. My landlord will probably connect me to this and get rid of me if he can, so we may all be in the street together.'

Hsiao wrote five books while living in Britain. In the second, *The Dragon Beards versus the Blueprints*, he describes the extraordinary impact many modern inventions had on Chinese people. 'The London buses of today are a development of your Victorian horse-omnibus, and who knows, perhaps the next development will be air transport over London, with aerial conductresses shouting "Hold tight, we're taking off!" But the motor buses in Hong Kong or Shanghai have no tradition behind them. Your wireless sets are, in a way, the successors of your pianolas and your musical boxes but the wireless sets in China seem just like miracles dropped from heaven.' George Orwell, reviewed the book for *The Observer* and in reference to this passage wrote, 'Mr Hsiao is too polite to mention that for some decades the Chinese experienced the benefits of Western civilisation chiefly in the form of bullets.' Hsiao worked at the BBC with Orwell, broadcasting to China on the war in Europe and the war effort of the British. He also created a series of weekly programmes about life in China for BBC Schools' radio. 'He was one of the best broadcasters to children we ever discovered,' his producer said. 'He had the Corporation's blessing because by then the Chinese were wartime allies. More to the point, children loved them and his radiant personality.' In June 1944, Hsiao was appointed the foreign correspondent for the Chinese newspaper *Ta Kung Pao* and set up an office in Fleet Street. Soon afterwards he was sent to France and other parts of Western Europe as a war correspondent, including attending the Potsdam Conference in July 1945. Hsiao remembered wartime London as the period when Britain was 'spiritually the greatest'. Perhaps he was influenced, as many were, by the intense relationships the war seemed to engender for he was reputed to have a complex – and stormy – romantic life in London.

Another Chinese who became friends with the Bloomsbury Group was Ling Shuhua who came to Britain in 1942 with her husband, Chen Yuan. She had published her first novel, *Temple of Flowers*, in China in 1928 and was a well-regarded painter. Her husband, who earlier had studied at the London School of Economics, was a historian and literary editor and had been appointed China's representative at UNESCO in Europe. Before coming

Taking up the Pen

to Europe he had been Dean of the University of Wuhan and Ling was living there with him when, in 1935, the young English poet, Julian Bell, arrived to take up a post teaching English. Bell was the son of the painter Vanessa Bell who, with her writer sister Virginia Woolf, were founding members of the influential Bloomsbury Group of associated English writers, intellectuals, philosophers and artists. Ling was attracted to the young Englishman and they began an affair. During this time Bell asked his aunt, Virginia Woolf, to send copies of her books for Ling to read as his lover was beginning to experiment with writing in English. Bell was supportive of Ling's writing and arranged for three of her stories to be published by *The London Mercury* in August 1936. In a letter to his aunt, Bell described Ling as 'a Chinese Bloomsburian', believing that she, and her husband Chen Yuan, were 'international in spirit and mind, at a time when China was not'. However, while the Bloomsbury set were relaxed about extra-marital relationships, Ling's husband was not. When the affair was discovered Bell was forced to break off the relationship and leave China. In March 1937 Chen wrote to Bell in London; 'I am very much pained, but still more surprised by your conduct... I thought that whatever might be your moral principles in some matters, an Englishman still had to keep his word and to consider his honour. I did not know that in throwing overboard some moral principles, such as loyalty to one's friends, you threw away all. No faith, no honour, no word to keep – nothing would prevent you to seek your selfish gratification.' Later that year Bell enlisted as an ambulance driver in the International Brigade which fought on the Republican side during the Spanish Civil War. A month after Bell arrived in Spain, he was killed.

Ling, who had been upset at the end of the affair and Bell's leaving China, was distraught at the news of her former lover's early death. She later recounted that during this difficult period she 'came across Woolf's *A Room of One's Own* and I was quite carried away by her writing, so suddenly I decided to write and see if she were in my situation, what she would do.' Virginia Woolf replied, urging Ling to work. 'Think how you could fix your mind upon something worth doing in itself. I have not read any of your writing but Julian often wrote to me about it. He said you have lived a most interesting life.' Inspired by Woolf's words, Ling began work on an autobiography, written in English, and up until Woolf's death in 1941 she corresponded with the English writer, who offered advice about the work in progress. Ling completed her autobiography and it was published in 1953 as *Ancient Melodies*. However, the book avoided any mention of her relationship with Julian Bell. Vita Sackville West wrote an introduction in which she praised it for its 'delightful sketches of a vanished way of life on the other side of the world'. It was one of the first books written in English by a Chinese woman. Ling moved to America for a time but returned to London in 1947. As well as continuing to write, Ling exhibited her paintings in London and internationally, to great acclaim. She also lectured on modern Chinese literature, painting and calligraphy. She returned to live in China shortly before her death in in 1990. Her daughter, Chen Xiaoying, worked for the BBC's Chinese service and married John Chinnery, Head of the Department of Chinese at Edinburgh University. He was one of the first Britons to befriend Communist China after the Second World War and worked assiduously to overcome the public ignorance of Chinese culture.

In August 1937 when Japan began its attack on Shanghai, thirty-two-year-old Lu Gwei Djen, a biochemist teaching at the university, decided to escape. She boarded a small boat and after managing to reach a British destroyer, was transferred to a Blue Funnel Line ship and taken to Liverpool. Lu had trained as a chemical pathologist and on arriving in Britain was employed as a research assistant by the distinguished biochemist Dorothy Needham at the Hopkins Laboratory in Cambridge to assist in research into the biochemistry of muscle. Dorothy's husband, Joseph, also an eminent biochemist, worked in the same laboratory, and in addition to being an outstanding scientist was a keen Morris dancer, played the accordion, was interested in nudism, and sympathetic to the politics of the far left although he was also a devout member of the High Anglican Church. A few months after Lu's arrival she and Joseph began an affair. The evening after the two had first consummated their passion, Needham was enjoying a cigarette and asked his new lover to teach him how to write the Chinese characters for cigarette. Lu drew the characters xiang and yan, being 'fragrant' and 'smoke', and in that moment the direction of both their lives shifted dramatically. Needham was entranced by Lu and her calligraphy, and within a short time decided largely to set aside his scientific research and launch into an intensive study of Chinese language, history and culture. Lu became a willing helper, as did Joseph's wife, who appears to have accepted her husband's affair with her assistant, a relationship that lasted for fifty years. The Cambridge professors that were the acknowledged China experts were dismissive of Needham's sudden passion for Chinese history. They did not consider it appropriate for a renowned biochemist to move into their academic territory. Yet such professional jealousies did not affect Needham. The more he studied, the more enamoured he became of Chinese civilisation and culture.

He discovered that printing, gunpowder and the compass – what Francis Bacon in his *Novum Organum* of 1620 had defined as the three things that 'have changed the whole face and state of things throughout the world' – had all been invented in China. Thus he decided to begin work on a book that would illustrate the significant role China had played in science. Although Lu was keen to help, she was about to leave for America to attend the Chinese Academy of Sciences Conference and so they agreed she would begin work with him on her return. She travelled to America in 1939 and when war was declared was unable to return to Britain until 1945, so worked in America as a biochemist researcher. In 1942 the British Royal Academy sent Joseph Needham to China to assist with the country's war effort and Dorothy went

Taking up the Pen

with him. At the end of the war the Needhams were still in China and Lu travelled there to join them. Two years later Needham moved to Paris to establish the UNESCO Sino-British Science Co-operation Office and when he returned to Cambridge to begin writing the planned book, *Science and Civilisation in China*, Lu took over his UNESCO post. She worked in Paris until 1957 and then moved back to Cambridge to assist Needham in what had become a monumental project. Rather than just one book, it had become a series, and Lu was directly involved in researching and writing a number of the volumes, including *Physics and Physical Technology* and *Biology and Biological Technology*. In 1989, when Dorothy died, Needham and Lu, now both in their 80s, married. Lu died in 1991. She often said, 'Joseph has built a bridge between our civilisations. I am the arch which sustains the bridge.' At the time of Needham's death in 1995 the series was unfinished although he had already written more than six million words. The project was completed by the Needham Research Institute at Cambridge.

One of the first Chinese students allowed to travel to Britain for study following the Cultural Revolution was Jung Chang. She was twenty-six when she arrived in Britain in 1976. Her father had been a high-ranking member of the Communist Party and Chang grew up in a guarded, walled compound, with a maid, chauffeur and a nanny for the children. This was the period of Mao Zedong's Cultural Revolution and 'Great Leap Forward' and she became a Red Guard while she was a teenager, although she later quit as she was upset by attacks on teachers and others. Her parents also became disenchanted with the Government's policies and their opposition led to their losing all their privileges. They were publicly humiliated, including having ink poured over their heads and made to wear placards around their necks denouncing the error of their ways. Finally her father was imprisoned and the family forced to leave their home. During this troubled period Chinese universities were closed and Chang, instead of going to university, spent several years working as a barefoot doctor, a steelworker and an electrician. When the universities were eventually re-opened she gained a place at Sichuan University and studied English, later becoming an assistant lecturer.

After Mao's death and her father being politically rehabilitated, Chang was given permission to travel to the West to study. Chang recounts that before leaving Peking, she and the other female students about to go overseas were sent to a special shop known as 'The Clothes Provider For Personnel Going Abroad' where they were issued with new blue suits. 'I was wearing mine when we landed at Heathrow.' Chang recounts how everything about London dazzled her. As Mao had proclaimed that grass and flowers in Chinese parks should be prohibited, London's flowery parks entranced her, as did the sight of women in floral dresses strolling through the streets. She, however, could not afford a dress so had to continue to wear her baggy suit.

In London Chang studied linguistics at Thames Valley Institute but her life continued to be under the control of the Chinese Government. She was housed in a property belonging to the Embassy, required to attend weekly indoctrination meetings and not allowed to travel anywhere or meet anyone without permission. Any wavering from the regulations would have meant her being sent back to China in disgrace. Fortunately, by the end of 1978 the political mood in China was changing and Chang began to sense the regulations were being less strictly enforced. She had always desired to go to a London pub, imagining them to be exotic places, so one day she took the risk but was disappointed only to find a few old men drinking their pints. Over the next months the enforcement of the regulations continued to ease and, although still fearful, Chang began to explore London and meet non-Chinese friends. She felt a great sense of release at being able to be part of a crowd without feeling every eye was on her, assessing her behaviour. One day she even risked applying make-up for the first time.

She was offered a scholarship by the University of York and received permission to accept it from the Chinese Government. While she was studying in York Chang began to consider writing a book about her life, although the idea remained dormant. When Chang completed her studies in 1982 she was the first person from the People's Republic of China to be awarded a PhD from a British university. She then met and married Jon Halliday, an Irish historian specialising in modern Asia, and in 1986 they co-wrote *Mme Sun Yat-sen*, a biography of Sun Yat-sen's widow. In 1988 Chang's mother visited her in London and began to recount her life and that of Chang's grandmother. Chang was fascinated as her mother poured out details of these past lives and when her mother returned to China Chang, with her husband's support, began work on *Wild Swans*, a biography of three generations of Chinese women in twentieth-century China. It was published in 1991 and became the highest-selling non-fiction paperback book ever published, selling more than 20 million copies and being translated into thirty-eight languages. However, *Wild Swans* was banned in China; a potent reminder of the power books can have in exploring an alternative history to the one those in authority wish to promote.

25

Other Travellers

A mysterious whole unites the vast emptiness.
The wholesome wind of heaven tosses and twitches my coat.
I watch the early sun rising from the ship
And feel as if I were reading an unfamiliar book.

Chiang Yee (1903–1977)

Although the majority of Chinese who travelled to Britain came to study or to work on ships, in laundries or restaurants, the twentieth century also saw visitors arrive for other reasons. While large numbers now travel to Britain as tourists, few came simply for sightseeing before the mid-1980s. One of the earliest mentions of a group of tourists appeared in 1908:

Lotus Fragrance (Rebecca Ho Hing Du) in the 1937 film, *The Wife of General Ling*. (Public domain)

The Chinese in Britain

The first organised group of Chinese gentlemen to be taken on a tour of the world are due to reach Scotland. The party, which left Hong Kong, are travelling under the auspices of Cook's (the well-known tourist agency) at a cost per head of £400. The trip – which was advertised in the ordinary way throughout China – is intended to be annual and the tour from beginning end will average five months. The party has already visited the principal cities of Canada and the United States and will travel to Scotland via the beauty spots of Ireland.

Whether the tour became annual is not known, though it seems unlikely as no similar groups were reported in later years. The most ill-fated Chinese tourist to visit Britain was Wai Sheung, the new wife of Chung Yi Miao. In 1928 the recently married couple arrived in Britain from the US at the start of a two-month honeymoon tour of Europe. Chung was a twenty-eight-year-old lawyer and Wai was from a wealthy family. After a couple of days in Edinburgh they arrived at the Borrowdale Gates Hotel in the Lake District. On the following morning the couple went for a walk and returned in time for lunch. The afternoon saw them leave the hotel again, hand in hand, but when Chung returned later he was alone. He told the staff that his wife had gone shopping in Keswick to buy warmer underwear and retired to his room. That evening, Wai's strangled body was discovered beside a riverside footpath. When the police told Chung his wife had been found strangled he cried out, 'It is terrible, my wife assaulted, robbed and murdered.' As the police had not mentioned robbery they were suspicious and searched the couple's bedroom. There they found, hidden in a film carton, Wai's jewellery, including her wedding ring. Also it was discovered that the cord around his wife's neck was the same cord as those on the hotel blinds. Chung was found guilty of the murder of his wife and hanged in Strangeways Gaol, Manchester.

Understandably, many visitors who were in Britain on official business took the opportunity for a little sightseeing while in the country, even when not necessarily planned. In 1929 Mr Yang, the Commissioner of Education in Manchuria, was in Britain to look at educational establishments and travelled to Scotland to visit a school in Edinburgh. The winter that year was especially long and icy and Carsebreck Loch in Perthshire froze over, allowing a curling match to take place. As this was the first time for a number of years the loch had been sufficiently frozen for curling to take place, a large number of curlers descended on the site. Mr Yang, hearing of this unusual event, abandoned the scheduled school visit to go to watch the sporting event. Yang who spoke excellent English recounted to the players that there was a similar winter game in China, though there the stones were pushed by the feet rather than released by hand and, intrigued by the Scottish version, he requested and received a copy of the Royal Curling Club's Rule Book to take back home.

Professor Fong, Dean of the West China University at Chengtu, who was in Britain in 1936 to carry out research into mysticism at Birmingham

Other Travellers

University, spent a holiday in Derby as the guest of former missionaries in Chengtu. When asked what had impressed him most in Derby it was not the sixteenth-century cathedral that he highlighted, but the city's central bus station which he 'thought very good indeed'. For five legal experts who came from China in 1909 to study Britain's approach to policing and punishment, the building that impressed them the most was Wormwood Scrubs.

Chang Kia Ngau, the Governor of the Bank of China, travelled to Britain in 1929 to attend the wedding of his sister, Chia-jui, to Wen Hsiung-Chu, the son of a Chinese merchant. This was the first of a number of weddings to take place in the Chinese Legation. By this time most Chinese weddings in Britain had become partly Europeanised, although aspects of the traditional Chinese wedding ceremony usually were included. So Wen wore a frock coat and Chia-jui, rather than the traditional 'good-luck' red gown, wore 'a white gown and veil fastened with a coronet of orange blossom and diamante, and carried a bouquet of Madonna lilies'. Chang Kai Ngau's words to the couple were translated for a newspaper report: 'Hear no slanders, see no evils; act as your soul dictates; speak fearlessly, and yield not to temptations. Then you will strike the true course of life's ideals. If the bride and bridegroom can attain this virtue they will be loyal to their country, benevolent to their fellow-beings, filial to their parents, and kind to their brothers and sisters – in short, they will bring harmony and happiness to their home circle, and will be a model husband and wife, and worthy parents of their future generation.' Afterwards when asked about the Chinese format one of the witnesses told a reporter, 'There is no honeymoon in China.' Then added with a smile, 'This is a good custom we have copied from the West.' While in Britain Chang Kaa Ngau fitted in both business and sightseeing. He was reputed to be one of China's youngest and most brilliant bankers and when interviewed about his speedy rise in the Bank of China Chang replied, 'I began in a branch of the bank when it started after the Republic eighteen years ago. Then I climbed quickly. Vice-Governor after four years and Governor for the last eleven years. You think I was young? Perhaps I was. But our country is becoming a country of young people nowadays.' He was then asked about his impressions of London.

> So big a city ... Such mighty traffic! I never thought London was so great a place! But so low a building your Bank of England. Our Bank of China is almost bigger. But we are young compared with England in money matters. We have much to learn yet – and what a lot I have learned during the last few days. And then your beautiful countryside. I have visited the Isle of Wight and driven round the South Coast – so green, so fresh. England is a wonderful place.

As well as his sightseeing, Chang met the Governor of the Bank of England and London's Lord Mayor.

In 1934 Alfred Sze, who was the Chinese Minister in America, came to attend the marriage of his eldest son to Bessie Yioh Chung Li, who was studying music London. Bessie, like many other Chinese women marrying in Britain, wore a white bridal gown but Polly Yung was determined to wear a traditional red dress at her wedding that took place in 1962. Polly had met Liu, her husband-to-be, in Hong Kong but as he was a waiter at The Lotus House restaurant in London she agreed to marry in Britain. Well in advance of travelling Polly packed her trousseau and sent it by sea freight. The outfit consisted of a traditional red ankle-length skirt, a black and gold embroidered bodice and a pair of lucky Chinese wedding shoes. A week before the wedding Polly flew to Britain and when she went to claim her box discovered to her distress that she had mislaid the necessary papers. 'The honourable Customs men have put it in a warehouse as sealed as a Chinese tomb,' reported *The Daily Mirror*. 'Those lucky shoes are very important at a wedding,' said a distraught Liu. Fortunately, the paper's coverage led to the release of the precious shipment the following day, and Polly was happily married wearing the traditional red and her lucky shoes. When, in 1969, Esther Yuk Chun Cheng married George Fu Yan Fong Hong, the owner of the Yangtze River Restaurant in Aberdeen, Esther's mother travelled from Hong Kong for the wedding and was thrilled to see snow. Esther was less keen, 'Although I like Aberdeen very much, I think it seems like summer for two months and the rest of the time is winter, compared to the warm climate of Hong Kong. Unlike my mother I hate going out when it is very cold and the snow has been falling.'

In 1939 the baby of George and Wu Chang was baptised Susie Ellen in Christ Church, Gloucester. Mr and Mrs Chang, who had married in Hong Kong, had come to Britain the previous year and while living here had their first child. George, who was working in the local aircraft factory, had become a Christian in Hong Kong and his wife had decided she too would become a Christian so was baptised along with their baby daughter as *The Gloucester Citizen* reported: 'The unique ceremony aroused tremendous interest, extra seating accommodation having to be provided for the congregation of fully 500 people. The oriental decoration of the font, and banner extending across the entrance to the chancel and a scroll hanging from the pulpit, both of oriental appearance, and both setting forth Chinese testimonials in the Chinese lettering, all gave an eastern touch to the ceremony, while the bright oriental colouring of the baby's robes stood out in striking contrast amid the white surplices of clergy and choir.'

This large number of on-lookers was far surpassed at a baptism of a Chinese baby in Bristol six years earlier. The baby was the daughter of two Chinese acrobats who were in Britain performing with the touring Bertram Mills circus. Around 4,000 people turned up at the church to view the event and police were stationed outside the church doors to keep back the eager crowds. Although the parents wore Western clothes, the colourful parade of other performers from the circus provided a brilliant display:

Other Travellers

The members of the Yung Dsai Troupe wore silken robes of patterned brocade all colours of the rainbow, glittering with sequins, and elaborate headwear hung with silk tassels. One six-foot member of the troupe wore a beret, contrasting strangely with his Oriental tunic and pigtail. Animal tamers, jugglers, Russian equestrians, Negro performers, acrobats, clowns, ring masters and chorus girls all entered the church and stood round the font awaiting the arrival of the Bishop of Mahnesbury. When the Bishop entered he had to appeal to the crowded congregation, who stood in the aisles and on pews, to allow him to reach the font and it was only after he had warned them of the solemnness of the service and earnestly asked them to remain in their seats, that the Bishop was able proceed with the baptismal service. The godmother of the child, Miss Rena Jacques, a circus chorus girl, nursed the infant during the service, and the godfather, George Stafford, a member of the circus orchestra, stood by her side. Sucking an English comforter and solemnly watching the Bishop in his white and scarlet robes from the arms of her godmother, the infant was the centre of all eyes. The western side of the ceremony over, the family went back to the circus ring at Arnos Vale, where the Oriental celebrations awaited them. On tables in the centre of the ring stood a Chinese feast and 38 bottles of wine! Margot, the Chinese baby, was presented with a silver christening cup by Bernard Mills.

Many of those who visited Britain were government officials wishing to study British methods, or to visit factories and industrial plants with an eye to making orders. In 1906 Duke Tsai Tse and members of the special Chinese Imperial Commission visited Birmingham and placed a large order for railway carriages with the Metropolitan Amalgamated Railway Carriage & Wagon Company of Saltley. Later, in London, Duke Tsai Tse gave a speech outlining China's ambitions from such visits:

> In times past foreign countries have borrowed from China. I may say they have borrowed the germ, and in their keeping the germ fructified and acquired growth. We therefore feel no compunction in claiming that the debt should be repaid. It is well known that the mariner's compass was invented in China. Gunpowder and guns had also their origin in China – a very harmless beginning – and there it might have stayed. But on the occasion of our recent visit to Woolwich Arsenal we noticed how greatly our germ had developed, and the idea suggested itself whether we had benefited mankind in making the discovery. Our object is to study at the fountain head such foreign methods as may be applicable to our country, and in the pursuance of this object we have the advantage of profiting by your mistakes and of making a start at the point you have reached after many expensive experiments. We may have lost something through our tardiness, but we shall gain by the experience of others.

While China's change from an empire to a republic caused certain diplomatic difficulties in Britain, companies were unfazed and were more than happy to treat the trade representatives of the Chinese Republic as royally as they had those of the Emperor. Thus in 1914, when Yuan Shin Ch'uan, a first cousin to the President of the newly formed Government, led a trade delegation to Britain, Edgar Allen & Co., Sheffield's largest steelworks, ensured that flags of the new Chinese Republic were flying on all three of their buildings. The company, which produced large guns and shells, also laid on a special treat for Yuan, who was invited 'to personally fire a projectile.... So well did he perform the operation that the shell passed through the armour plate and could not be recovered within the brief time at the disposal of the party.'

Those who came to study British systems were expected to report on their findings on their return to China and relate whether or not the system was appropriate for adoption in China. In 1936 Nadine Hwang was chosen to head up a mission to Britain to study the country's financial system. Hwang had an unusual past as she had been born in Spain to a Chinese father and Belgian mother, and served as a colonel in the Chinese Army in the 1920s before becoming one of only two women lawyers in China at the time. Being one of the first women to be sent to Britain on official business, it is possible that there were some who thought it inappropriate for a woman to be entrusted with such an important official visit. If so, the doubters would have felt vindicated, for Hwang never returned to China, although while in Britain she carried out her official schedule of appointments and may well have been planning to report her findings on her return. However, before leaving to return to China, Hwang decided to visit Paris and there she became part of the city's artistic community that included Pablo Picasso, as well as the lover of the author Natalie Barney. Thus Hwang never used her return ticket to China. She was still living in Paris in 1940 when the Germans entered the city and she was imprisoned in a concentration camp, but fortunately survived and afterwards lived in South America.

Britain also offered opportunities to train in new areas of expertise. In 1910 one of the first flying schools was established on Salisbury Plain by the British and Colonial Aeroplane Company, who made Bristol planes, and in that year the Royal Aero Club in Britain became the first organisation to issue Aviators Certificates. As China had begun buildings planes in 1911 it required someone to train pilots and sent Zee Yee Lee to Britain to learn to fly. In October 1911 Lee successfully flew a Bristol biplane and thus gained his Aviators Certificate, Number 148, and on his return to China began training Chinese pilots. The following year Tsoe Wong also gained his Aviators Certificate at the Salisbury Plain flying school. He had come to Britain to study engineering and, having become fascinated by aeroplanes, set out to build a biplane that could be made in China, partly using bamboo for the structure. Wong built a prototype at Shoreham Aerodrome in Sussex although, as he explained, the prototype did not use bamboo. 'You see, in

England there are probably less than a dozen men who know how work with bamboo, which is nature's own tubing. In China, on the other hand, there are countless skilled artificers in bamboo work, and gliders on bamboo frames were made there many centuries ago.' By mid-1913, the Tong-Mei (Chinese for Dragonfly) biplane was ready and after several successful test flights Wong went into partnership with two British men and advertised shares for sale in their company as 'Manufacturers of and dealers in aeroplanes, balloons and airships'. In mid-1914 the Tong-Mei was packed and shipped to Kuala Lumpur, where two days of demonstration were planned. Wong and his partners were convinced that demonstration of the power of flight would lead to many orders for their aircraft throughout East Asia. The city's racecourse served as a makeshift airfield and on 11 July, before any onlookers arrived, Wong flew several successful trials of his plane. In the afternoon, in front of a large crowd, Wong took off. Although the flight went fine, the plane overshot the limits of the field on landing and hit a fence. Wong was able to repair the damage overnight and the next day took to the air again. Unfortunately, after flying for twenty minutes the engine suddenly stopped and the plane crashed. While Wong was uninjured his plane was a write-off. The potential buyers were unimpressed and the growth of aviation in China and other Eastern Asian countries was set back for a number of years.

In spite of Zee Yee Lee returning to train Chinese pilots it was not until the 1920s that the Chinese authorities began to consider developing an air force. To do so required planes, and in 1928 the Chinese Government sent Chen Wen-ling, who had trained as a pilot in Germany, to Britain to buy fourteen Aero-Avian single propeller light aeroplanes. Chen decided to fly one back to China, in spite of this being a flight of some 14,000 miles and no trans-continental flight between Europe and China had ever been attempted. Accompanied by a co-pilot, Christian Johannsen from Denmark, Chen took off from Croydon Aerodrome on 2 March 1929. Unfortunately, the pilots had only reached the English Channel when the plane's power began to fail and they had to turn back towards Dover. The plane only just cleared the cliffs and after it landed a strong gust of wind tipped the plane over and damaged the propeller. A new propeller was fitted and the intrepid pilots took off again on the Monday. This time there were no mishaps and they flew via Amsterdam, Berlin, Prague, Vienna. Budapest, Adrianople, Basra, Calcutta and Hanoi, reaching Canton on 12 May. There they were greeted by 'a tumultuous welcome on the occasion of the greatest long-distance flight in Chinese history'. After a two-day rest Chen flew on to Nanking to receive an official Government welcome.

In 1926 Qui Sing Wong came to London to gain a skill of quite a different kind. Many of the male Chinese who had studied in Britain were so taken by British girls' fashionable hairstyles that on their return to China they were 'eagerly encouraging their female compatriots to be bobbed, shingled, or Eton-cropped'. *The Sphere* reported that Qui

... has settled down as a serious student at the Gallia Institute where she is being trained in the deft wielding of the guillotining shears to luxuriant locks and the application of the permanent wave to give seductive ripples to the straight black hair so characteristic of her people. With the optimism of nineteen summers, Miss Wong expects that the majority of young Chinese women will discard the bun, decorated with its characteristic gold pins arranged fanwise, in favour of the modern hair fashion, just as her Chinese friends in London have done.

With few hairdressers in China able to meet the mania for new hairstyles, no doubt Qui was successful in her ambition to open a beauty parlour and hair salon in Hong Kong. The Chinese actress, Anna May Wong, commented on the new fashion:

I had to bob my hair because of my job. I do like it but it took a lot of thought before I made the decision. A Chinese woman's hair is her chief ornament in life. Chinese women never wear hats, but they put all their ideas of decoration in their hair. As a race, we use hair for head covering instead of hats, so we could not possibly approve of bobbed hair. Some Chinese women think bobbed hair is dangerous to the femininity and beauty of woman!

When Dai Ailian travelled to Britain to train she was an unusual Chinese visitor as she spoke no Chinese. This was because her parents had moved from China to Trinidad before she was born. As a young girl, Dai watched the ships come and go to the island and dreamed of becoming a sailor, but her mother's dream was for her daughter to become a ballerina. So, in 1931, at just fourteen years of age, Dai, with her two sisters, travelled to London to take ballet lessons. As Mr Dai was a wealthy merchant, his wife was able to arrange for Dai to be given lessons by two notable dancers, Marie Rambert and Anton Dolin, both former dancers with Sergei Diaghilev's famous Ballet Russes. Unfortunately, Dai's father lost all his money gambling and the regular allowances to his daughters in Britain ceased. Dai, now passionate about dance, decided to stay in London and, like many other impoverished dance students, took temporary jobs to make ends meet. Her financial position was eased by winning a scholarship to study at the Jooss-Leeder Dance School at Dartington Hall in Devon. There she worked with Kurt Jooss, an avant-garde choreographer, and in her later work Dai fused her classical ballet training with Jooss's experimental theatrical approach. While working at Dartington she met an Austrian-British sculptor, Willi Soukop, and lived with him in London for a year. Although they never married she later said she loved him all her life. Soukop later became Master of Sculpture at the Royal Academy. In the late 1930s Dai choreographed a number of ballets, including *Flower Girl in a Persian Square*, based on the life of the Tang Emperor Xuanzong's

Other Travellers

favourite concubine. Dai befriended Chinese students in London so she could begin to learn some Chinese and learn something about Chinese culture, of which she knew little. After China declared war on Japan in 1937 she created dance works that celebrated the spirt of the Chinese people's resistance, including *Awakening*. She also performed at concerts to raise money for the China Campaign Committee.

During this time Dai read *Red Star over China*, Edgar Snow's account of the Communist Party of China when it was a guerrilla army, and was so enthused she decided to go to live in China, although she still understood little Chinese. In 1940 Dai travelled to Hong Kong and was surprised to discover that ballet and modern dance were almost unknown in China. When she told people that she was a dancer, people thought she meant she was a dance hostess in bars, a label for a prostitute. Dai was determined to create a dance company in China and realised it was important that new dance works should draw on the traditional folk dances and those of the Chinese Opera. She spent many years travelling China researching these and in 1954 became Principal of the newly created Beijing Dance School and, in 1963, Artistic Director of the Central Ballet of China. She was one of many artists who suffered during the Cultural Revolution, being exiled to the country to work on a pig farm, but later was able to return to dance, becoming director of the National Ballet Company. In 1981 Dai visited London to unveil a bust that had been made of her, in honour of her work, at the Royal Academy of Dance; the bust had been sculpted by her Dartington lover, Willi Soukop. Dai visited London again in 1986 when her company, the Central Ballet of China, made its debut in London to great acclaim. In China, Dai is known as 'the mother of dance'.

Although less frequently than in the nineteenth century, missionary societies continued to arrange visits by Chinese individuals and groups who had benefitted from their work to help raise funds in Britain. In 1922 the Church Missionary Society brought the Blind Boy's Band from Foochow to Britain for a tour and audiences enjoyed the band playing a number of hymns and Chinese airs. The tour helped raise funds for The Missionary Society's Blind School, which had been established in 1897 to provide religious instruction and training to help the blind be self-supporting. The creation of the Chinese Republic in 1912 had removed the persecution of the Christian religion and by the 1920s a significant number people in positions of power were Christian, including many in General Chiang Kai-Shek's government. Chiang Kai-Shek's wife, Soong Meiling, tried to convince him to convert but the General was resistant. But in 1930, when Chiang was in the midst of a battle, he became surrounded and faced capture and death. Seeing a Christian chapel nearby, the General went in and made a pledge that if God helped him survive he would become a follower of Christ. When he emerged a heavy snowstorm impeded his enemy's advance, allowing him to escape and his forces gained the victory. In honour of his pledge he was baptised by Bishop Kaung in 1930.

Thus at many of the major Christian conferences and other events in Britain, China was represented by senior Chinese figures. Reverend Professor Ting-fang Lew who travelled to Britain to attend the World Conference on Faith and Order in 1937 was one of China's most important Christian leaders and one of the few psychologists working in the Republic of China. At any other time his first visit to Edinburgh would have been pleasurable, as his father has studied medicine at Edinburgh University and Lew would have heard stories of his father's student days in the city. However, soon after he left China, the country had gone to war with Japan and he was concerned about the fate of his wife and teenage daughter. *The Scotsman* reported:

> Three times a day he searches the letter rack at the Conference post office in the Assembly Hall. Dr Lew stated last night that his wife saw him off at Shanghai on June 4 when he sailed for Britain Her last letter to him was dated July 12, and since then there has been no word from her.

He was particularly worried as his wife, a Professor of Education, had been about to go to Japan to attend a world conference on education and it had been planned that their daughter would be left in Beijing in the care of friends. When asked if he thought his wife and daughter might have sought refuge in the safety of Shanghai Dr Lew replied: 'No place can be safe. It is like sitting on a powder magazine.' At the conference Lew spoke about the crisis and declared that the Church could not be indifferent to the tragedy taking place in China.

> The Far East had been driven to learn from the West the arts of destruction and to acquire from them a mentality of political and economic imperialism. As we sit here and discuss reports in peace and security, remember that there are four hundred thousand Protestants and a million Catholics who are facing the threat of a titanic struggle which may determine their freedom or even their existence.

Fortunately, Lew's wife and his daughter, Grace, survived the war and in 1942 the family left China and moved to America to try and cure Lew's tuberculosis, but he died in 1947. Grace, like her father and grandfather, studied medicine and became an outstanding scientist in a range of fields.

Another key figure in China's Christian community was Dr Tz-Zeung Koo, the General Secretary of the World's Student Christian Association, and he also attended the 1937 conference. He was perhaps the most travelled Chinese at that time, being reputed to have travelled to forty-five countries in the 1920s and '30s. Koo visited Britain on a number of occasions and was renowned as a motivational speaker. In 1925 and 1929, he spoke at the Student Christian Movement Conferences, each attended by almost 2,000 delegates from forty countries At the first in Manchester, his speech was greeted with 'a storm of applause, the audience completely disregarding the Conference rule forbidding such expression of appreciation'; at the second in Liverpool, it was reported that the delegates were kept 'merry and bright' by Koo's witticisms. 'Wearing a deep blue gown surmounted by a short close-fitting jet black tunic, Dr Koo referred to the many misunderstandings between East and West. "Take the simple matter of my dress," he said. "When I put on a black gown some people ask me to what religious order I belong. When I put on a blue gown, as today, many people address me as *Madame*. (Laughter) You see, you have so many preconceived notions about dress to overcome before the very simple obvious explanation that this is my national dress occurs to you."'

In the early 1930s Koo presented a number of talks on BBC radio and, in one, performed on the Chinese flute. He had a keen interest in traditional Chinese music and collected many folk songs; in 1943 a book of these was published in Britain with translations by the highly regarded Chinese translator, Arthur Waley. At the book launch some of the songs were performed but unfortunately Koo was unable to attend as at the time he was imprisoned by the Japanese in Hong Kong. After his release Koo was chosen to be one of the advisors to the Chinese delegation at the San Francisco Conference in 1945 that established the United Nations.

Given the cost of travel, and the time it took before air travel, it was not always possible for someone from China to attend conferences, so students in Britain often represented China. In 1924, the World's Ninth Sunday School Convention, a gathering of those interested in promoting Sunday Schools worldwide, was held in Glasgow, and Fu Shang-ling, a postgraduate student, attended as China's representative. Fu spoke at many other meetings and at one, organised by the London Missionary Society, Fu said 'If science, economics the philosophy of religion are all that the West has to offer China, then China would be better without them; but the West can bring the spirit of sacrifice into the realm of Chinese life, there is nothing which (is needed) more.' From 1925 to 1926 Fu also served as an Honorary Secretary of the Central Union of Chinese Students in Great Britain and Ireland and of the Union of Chinese Associations in Great Britain, and was editor of *The Chinese Student* magazine in London.

In 1938 Cheng Su, who had recently arrived in Britain on a British Council scholarship to research into the translation of Shakespeare into Chinese, was invited to give one of the lectures at the Third Meeting of World Religions held in Cambridge. His talk was on the subject of Confucianism as a religious influence in Chinese life.

> As a Chinese called upon to talk on religion I can but feel somewhat diffident about the task, for the simple reason that in China religion is regarded as either too personal or too remote from the realities of daily existence to be discussed in public. There are over a million Christians in China, but to the

masses of the people, religion is to be lived and felt and not to be discussed. So much so, that the Chinese are considered a non-religious people... It depends on what you mean by religion. If by religion is meant the reunion of man and God, the Chinese people, I dare say, have no religion. But if by religion is meant communion with the unknown through appreciation and reverence and the salvation of man by a high moral life, the Chinese have a religion. In this respect Confucianism may well be regarded as the Chinese religion.

Cheng Su's fiancée, Yao-Kun, followed him to Britain, and they married in October 1938 and settled in London. In 1941 the Foreign Office pressed the BBC to employ staff who could broadcast to the Far East and Cheng and four other Chinese living in London were employed to work for the newly established BBC's Far East Services section. The first section head, until 1943, was Rushbrooke Williams, formerly a Professor of Modern History in India. One of the other members of the section, John Morris, a former army major, British mountaineer and anthropologist, and later controller of BBC Radio's Third Programme, moved up to head the section when Williams left. Another influential member of the team was William Empson, the English literary critic and poet, who in the 1930s taught at Beijing University. Empson later described the Far East Services section as 'this very queer organisation'. The section transmitted twice-weekly news broadcasts in Mandarin and Cantonese and by February 1942, this was increased to seven a week. There also were short commentary pieces that followed the news and included subjects such as 'Education and World Order' and 'What the Common Man thinks about War,' with both British and Chinese participants. Readings of contemporary English poetry were also broadcast.

The role of Cheng and his fellow Chinese was to translate and broadcast the material that had been submitted in English. A regular Chinese contributor was George Kung-chao Yeh, who had arrived in London in May 1942 to take up the post of London Director of the Chinese Ministry of Information. In the 1920s Yeh had studied in the US and at Cambridge University, where he read Indo-European linguistics, and then became Professor of English at universities in Beijing and Shanghai. William Empson was aware that it was important to ensure Yeh was not only broadcasting to China and so arranged for him to make a series of talks under the title, 'If you were Chinese', for the BBC's Home Service. The BBC were particularly keen to work with the Central News Agency of China to break the 'intellectual blockade' of Free China by broadcasting scientific and other academic material to support the universities that were continuing to operate, and so help scientists in China to remain in touch with new developments. To support the talks, descriptive material was flown out to Chunking on microfilm. An impressive array of experts was commissioned to write these technological and intellectual talks and this created translating challenges for the Chinese team. The matter was raised at a section meeting in June 1943:

Other Travellers

The meeting discussed the merits of broadcasting in English talks on highly technical subjects. It was felt the Chinese service should use the Chinese language as much as possible, but in certain cases the listeners might find it easier to understand the talk if it went out in English. It is hoped that modern Chinese technical dictionaries from China will assist in translation.

At another meeting that year the need for clarity given the poor sound quality of receivers was raised and Cheng's colleague, Miss Sam, 'emphasised that only by constant rehearsal and careful reading can satisfactory reception of short wave transmissions be guaranteed. She mentioned the usefulness of the Staff Training School lectures on presentation, microphone techniques, etc.' Unfortunately, transmitters in China were not powerful enough to carry the BBC's long-range transmissions and the section attempted to have the talks rebroadcast by Chinese radio stations. The programmes were regularly relayed by the radio station in Chengtu, in Western China that was controlled by the Chinese Minister of Communication, but the Chinese Central Broadcasting Authority (CBBA)'s station in Chungking was controlled by the Chinese Minister of Propaganda and he demanded that the BBC broadcast some of their programmes in Britain in exchange. As the BBC were reluctant to do so, few of the BBC's output to China was re-transmitted by the Chungking station. This caused frustration in London and the section staff were further depressed to learn that there were probably no more than 250 to 500 radio receivers capable of picking up the BBC long-range transmissions in all the Free China territory. Also, electricity often failed. However, a number of students, scientists and academics, and others managed to listen to the BBC output and it gained a reputation for its intellectual content and quality. Even though it was known the number of people listening in China was small, the BBC recognised that it was essential to be seen to be supporting China's war against Japan by making programmes in Chinese to transmit to China.

Those working in the section tried to have material about China's fight against Japan, and Japanese aggression, included on the Home Service within Britain. In 1942 Empson, with input from other members of the section, wrote a four-part anti-Japanese series, *Japan Wants the Earth*, which presented a forceful account of the aggression and viciousness of the Japanese. One part recounted the Japanese invasion of Nanking and pulled no punches:

> Chinese soldiers who gave up their arms were roped in batches of one hundred and shot – or bayoneted, as were all men of military age. Of women from ten years to seventy, approximately ten thousand were raped.

The section also provided material for broadcast within Britain on the war in China and Asia, but in the latter stages of Britain's own war, particularly when London was being attacked by V-1s and V-2s, Chinese news was squeezed out to a large extent. In his account of the BBC, Lord Briggs stated:

'China, the ally, one of the Big Four at most of the wartime international conferences, played almost as small a part in the pattern of BBC wartime broadcasts as Japan, the enemy.' Following the communists gaining power, the Chinese part of BBC's Far East Services section became to a large extent focused on anti-communist propaganda, as did the BBC's Russian section. Yet this fact brought an increase in the section's output; between 1950 and 1960 the BBC's broadcasts to China rose from sixty hours a year to 690 hours. For the Chinese speakers employed in translating, and possibly creating, propaganda-style material, it must have been a relief when they were commissioned to create *Miss Wang's Diary*, a straightforward fictional account of a young female student in Britain, Wang Kwei Ying. The first episode included Wang visiting the student fair and being enlisted into the university student dramatic society. By Episode 42 Wang had become an established member of the drama society and at a meeting to discuss the next play, it is she who suggests that a nativity play would be appropriate with Christmas approaching. However, an alternative suggestion of Shakespeare's *Anthony and Cleopatra* receives the majority vote, though Wang admits she is not disheartened as Shakespeare's play is a favourite and she is keen to have a part. On New Year's Day 1962 the exhibition, 'BBC Window of the World', opened at Charing Cross underground station to highlight the various BBC services and Doris Cheong, who played Wang, was one of those who attended the opening.

For a number of Chinese who had come to Britain to study in the late 1930s the war in China and Europe made it impossible for them to return to China as planned. One was Wai Szeto who had arrived in 1938 on a bursary from the Federation for British Industries to study engineering at a number of Scottish firms. His planned stay of one year ended up being six. He thus had to find work after completing his year's study and so worked in Scotland on water supply schemes and railway engineering. In his spare time, he gave English lessons for Chinese seamen at The Seamen's Hostel in Glasgow so that they had enough language to get around more easily. 'It's difficult at times,' Wai recounted to *The Daily Mail*. 'Often I have a class well advanced when they have to sail again. But many others come along, and sometimes we have an ex-pupil popping in on a return voyage from the East.' He also helped arrange outings for the seamen. 'Visits to Edinburgh and its historic haunts, to Stirling Castle, and to Loch Lomond are favourites,' he explained. 'Scotland's ancient history stirs a chord in the Chinese – he knows what oppression is.' When Wai Szeto finally returned to China he became an architect and designed many of the buildings of the new Chinese University of Hong Kong.

Possibly the first Chinese to compete in any official sporting competition in Britain was Cheow Kim, an army sergeant, who, in 1910, was selected as the first Chinese to be part of the Singapore team taking part in the Empire Shooting Match at Bisley against teams from Britain, Canada, Australia and

Other Travellers

India. The weather was fair when the competition began and at the halfway point, although Singapore was second last, Cheow had scored a total of forty-six out of a possible fifty points. He continued to score well but the final outcome was undetermined as heavy rain scattered the spectators and washed out the scores from the register-keeper's boards.

A number of Chinese tennis players participated in British competitions. The first player of note was Wei Wing Lock, who, in 1920, played in both the men's singles and doubles at Wimbledon. Wei, the son of Sir Boshan Wei Yuk and who had studied at Dollar Academy in Scotland, became the Chinese national tennis champion in 1914. He then studied engineering in America and at Cambridge. Also studying at Cambridge, and another previous tennis champion in China, was Kenneth Lo who would go on to find fame as the writer of Chinese cookery books. In 1925, Wei Wing Lock captained China's first Davis Cup team when it played Australia in America. He afterwards stayed in the US, where he tragically drowned aged just forty. Another skilled tennis player who came to Britain to study at Cambridge was Wai Chuen Choy. After winning his blue playing tennis for Cambridge in 1935, Wai Chuen Choy went on to play in major tournaments. Kho Sin-Kie was also playing in Britain at this time. He had always had a dream to compete at Wimbledon but as he came from a poor family in Java, travelling to Britain seemed an impossibility. However, after winning the Chinese national championships in 1933, local people raised money to send him to Britain. In 1936 he was given a job at the Chinese Embassy in London and his tennis was sponsored by the Dunlop Rubber Company. Both Wai and Kho played in various British tournaments and in 1938 they met in the quarter-finals of the British Hard Court Championships in Bournemouth. Kho looked favourite to win but Wai began brilliantly, winning the first two sets and the first game of the third. Although all looked over for the Chinese Champion, in a remarkable comeback Kho won every game from that point on to take the match. Kho won his semi-final and in the final faced the British player, Bunny Austin. The British player was the clear favourite and the crowd's preferred winner. The conditions were difficult as it was extremely windy and it was Kho who coped best, crushing British hopes and becoming the first Chinese winner of a major British tennis title. This was no flash in the pan, for Kho retained the title the following year. Unfortunately, the war intervened and brought a temporary end to tennis competitions in Britain. In 1940 Kho married Jane Balfour, the daughter of a judge in Ceylon, whom he had met while practising at the Queen's Club. During the war both Wai and Kho played exhibition tennis matches in various countries to raise money for China's war effort and when the war ended, both returned to competition. Sadly, both Wai and Kho died in their thirties while living in London; Kho in 1947 and Wai in 1951.

In 1936, when both were playing at Wimbledon, a diminutive fifteen-year-old Chinese girl, Gem Hoahing, armed with a bright red autograph book, was busily collecting signatures from the tennis stars. Her father was a highly successful Hong Kong businessman and her mother a doctor, having studied medicine in Edinburgh and Dublin. The family moved to Britain in the late 1920s and settled in Twickenham in a large house that had a tennis court where Hoahing learned to play. On a holiday in France the family happened to pass a tennis club which had a sign saying: 'Tennis tournament starts tomorrow.' The fourteen-year-old Gem said: 'Why don't I enter it?' So she did and, using a borrowed racket, won. In Britain in the next few years Hoahing emerged as one of the most promising tennis juniors and in 1937 made her Championship debut, winning three matches in qualifying before losing in the first round. At just under 5 feet, Hoahing remains the shortest female player ever to have played in the Championships. She swiftly became the darling of the public and the press and had a number of nicknames including 'Little Gem' and 'The Mighty Atom'. She also was a medal-winning ballroom dancer and a very good tap dancer. Hoahing continued playing in the Wimbledon Championships up to 1961, her highest place being in 1949 when she reached the fourth round of the Ladies' Singles. When she retired from playing professionally, Hoahing opened a flower shop near Kensington Gardens, supplying flowers to the great and the good. Although she did not regularly work in the shop, when Frank Sinatra ordered flowers for Ava Gardner, Hoahing personally delivered them. Unlike the two Chinese male players, Little Gem lived into her mid-90s.

In 1900, Tommy Dewar, owner of the famous Scottish whisky firm and a keen sportsman, decided to bring a Chinese football team to play in Britain. His plan was scuppered by the football authorities, who argued that having Chinese play football in Britain might make a laughing stock of the game – although one newspaper suspected the reason might have been a fear that the Chinese team would prove too good for the British. So it was not until 1936 that the first Chinese footballers played in Britain. The team, which had travelled to Europe to represent China at the Olympic Games in Berlin, played in Britain under the name the Chinese Soccer Stars and was mainly made up of University students. At the Olympics, the Chinese had been beaten by England in the first round although their captain, Wai-Tong Lee, a centre forward, was reported to have played brilliantly.

On their British tour the team played a number of amateur sides, including Islington Corinthians at the Arsenal Stadium, losing by five goals to two. Of course many Chinese and British Chinese living in Britain played football and among them were the four sons of Quan and Beatrice Soo, who owned a laundry in Liverpool. Of the four, the most talented was the aforementioned Frank Soo who, in 1933, became the first British Chinese to play for a professional football club when he signed for Stoke City. The signing was widely reported, including in Singapore's *Straits Times*:

> Frank Soo, Stoke City's Chinese footballer, is the most romantic personality in the potteries at the moment... Frank is 19. Oriental looking, but

handsome. He has a flashing, dazzling smile... The crowd admire him for his sunny disposition and for his cleverness as a footballer. He is a player of above average intelligence, with a deceptive swerve, amazingly clever ball control, and a deadly shot with both feet. He should go far.

He did. He was one of the top players of his day and played for England on a number of occasions.

The outbreak of war in China and, later, in Europe, reduced the number of Chinese visiting Britain. In 1939, Mrs Holt in Scunthorpe, who had a deep interest in missionary work in China and had two adopted Chinese girls, reported, 'This is the first time for many years that we have not had Chinese visitors to our home.' A small number of officials did manage to travel to Britain in spite of the war. In 1942 Tang Pao-Huang, a soldier in the China Nationalist Army, was sent to Britain as China's Military Attaché. In a newspaper interview he called for a co-ordination of planning:

The United Nations need more than the pooling of their resources and manpower. They need a pooling of brains for the central direction of the war, with joint planning. All the Allies should share equal responsibility, and have an equal opportunity of making their contribution in technique, planning, and experience, towards the winning of the war. China would be equally happy at an Allied victory on any front, and considers no sacrifice too great to achieve victory for the Allied cause as a whole.

His wife, Han Suyin, had remained in China but travelled to London to join him in 1944. She was a Eurasian whose father was a Belgian-educated Chinese engineer and her mother was Flemish. As Han was discriminated against for being Eurasian at university in China, she had studied medicine in Brussels. On her return to China she worked as a midwife in an American Christian mission and in 1938 married Tang, and two years later they adopted a girl, Tang Yungmei. During the time she was in China separated from her husband, Han Suyin published her first novel, *Destination Chungking*. When she arrived in London with her daughter to join Pao-Huang she began further medical training at the Royal Free Hospital. Han and her daughter remained in London when Pao went abroad, first to Washington, and later to fight at the Manchurian front, where he died in action in 1947. The widowed Han graduated as a doctor in London and in 1949 went to Hong Kong to practise medicine at the Queen Mary Hospital. There she met and fell in love with Ian Morrison, a married Australian war correspondent based in Singapore, who was killed in Korea in 1950. Her second and most successful novel, *A Many-Splendored Thing*, published in 1952, portrayed their relationship.

As the war drew to a close the number of visitors from China increased again. In 1945, four women, including Colonel Mei-yu Chow, head of the Chinese Nursing School; and Priscilla Huang, head of the Relief Department of the

The Chinese in Britain

Chinese Women's Advisory Council, arrived to study methods of rehabilitation for disabled ex-servicemen. They were investigating what resources would be required when China finally was liberated after nine years of war and invasion. Mei-yu Chow recounted how important women were in the country's struggle: 'Vast numbers of Chinese women are in uniform, working shoulder to shoulder with the men. They nurse the sick and wounded soldiers, strive to do something for the countless thousands of refugees, care for war orphans and work on farms – China's food problem is acute – and in war factories.'

In 1949 Diana Kan, a Hong Kong artist, arrived at Southampton by flying boat as a member of a party of Chinese businessmen and women who had come for the British Industries Fair. She brought with her eighty paintings and expected to sell some in London before going to Paris at the end of June. 'Most of my pictures are of women,' she explained. 'Many are in ancient Chinese costume. I painted the costumes from memory after seeing them in Chinese opera.' She was very taken by British clothes, although as she explained to *The Daily Mirror*:

> Chinese women can't wear Western clothes because their figures are so small. This is a great pity. The designs you have on some of your English dresses are marvellous. I always feel more attractive in Chinese clothes because I am so tiny. But I am sure many Chinese women would be glad of the opportunity of wearing their national costume incorporating some of the delightful Western patterns. When I return to Hong Kong I shall try to introduce some of your designs into our clothes.

While in London Kan dined at 10 Downing Street with the Prime Minister Clement Atlee and Sir Winston Churchill. She later lived in New York but her work continued to be exhibited in London and Princess Margaret purchased some.

Following the end of the war in Europe and Asia, sporting visits resumed. In 1947 the Sing Tao Sports Club of Hong Kong became the first Chinese football club to visit. The squad of eighteen players was captained by the forty-one-year-old Fung King Cheong, and they played a number of matches during their month's stay. The first was against Dulwich Hamlet and a large crowd, including the Chinese Ambassador, watched them play, as did the football correspondent of *The South London Press*:

> Though the Chinese footballers who met Dulwich on Saturday were beaten 5–2 the score was very far from being a true indication of the strength of the two teams. On most occasions the Hong Kong boys did things with the ball that had Hamlet all at sea. Time and again their uncanny anticipation and short passing split the home team's defence wide open, but not one Chinaman had much in the way of shooting power. Sing Tao Sports Club, once they improve their shooting powers, will be a hard team to beat.

Other Travellers

In 1948 London hosted the Olympic Games and the People's Republic of China sent a team of thirty men and one woman. As Britain was still suffering from food rationing, the Government decided special rules were required for the competitors from around the world. Thus all the athletes were allowed extra rations, equivalent to the additional amount received by workers in heavy industries. The competitors were housed in colleges, schools and army camps that had been hastily converted and the Chinese team ended up in Willesden County School. A canteen was temporarily created and to ensure the Chinese were fed properly Ley On provided chefs from his Soho restaurant to cater for the team, with bean sprouts being specially grown in wheelbarrows. The Chinese competed in eleven events in six sports but won no medals. The football team played their first match against Turkey on Monday 2 August at Walthamstow Avenue's Green Pond Road ground in front of a crowd of 3,000 and as Turkey won 4–0, China was eliminated. Although the basketball team, captained by the lanky Singapore-born Wee Tian Siak, won their first match against Great Britain 54–25 it failed to qualify for the quarter-finals. When the Games were again held in London in 2012, one of the basketball team of 1948, Wu Chengzhang, then aged eighty-eight, travelled to Britain to support the Chinese basketball players. Despite his inspiring presence, China lost all its basketball matches.

As recounted in the chapter on diplomacy, in 1972 one of the first visits by any group from the People's Republic of China since 1949 took place as a result of 'ping-pong diplomacy'. The Chinese table tennis team played a number of matches around Britain and while the Chinese men won all their matches, the British women beat their Chinese opponents against all the odds. Following that visit, other table tennis teams from Communist China visited. However, if the Chinese players who came had been hoping for some sightseeing of British beauty spots between matches, most were sadly disappointed. One player, Kong Quingwen, who came in the early 1980s, told *The Times*, 'It has been very tough. The players are not happy. We play every night, every day we must travel, rest one or two hours, and then play again.' Not that their itinerary necessarily would have provided much in the way of historic sightseeing as it included Sunderland, Halifax, Oldham, Bletchley and Gillingham. Nor at the time did such places offer much in the way of quality Chinese food. 'The players are dying for a real Chinese meal,' Kong continued. 'Sweet and sour pork at a suburban restaurant is not proper Chinese food.'

Britain's formal recognition of the People's Republic of China in 1950 paved the way for a number of official visits such as that by Lin Ning, Vice Chairman of the Chinese Trade Union movement. He led a trade delegation to Britain, but the outbreak of the Korean War later that year, in which China and Britain fought on opposite sides, brought an end to almost all visits to Britain from Communist China for almost twenty years, although visits by Chinese from Hong Kong, Singapore and other non-Communist countries were unaffected. One positive aspect of the Korean War in terms of Chinese-British relations was that a number of British soldiers who travelled to and from the war via Hong Kong returned with Chinese wives. These included Bandsman William Smith and Bill Griffiths of the King's Shropshire Light Infantry. Griffiths met Nancy Kong on a blind date in Hong Kong. During the Second World War Nancy served as a naval Rating and became an expert rifle shot, winning many trophies. At one competition she was firing next to a British Army Colonel who disparagingly remarked that it was ridiculous to allow girls to compete against experienced riflemen. He was noticeably absent when Nancy was presented with the trophy. In 1952 she became the Hong Kong Ladies Champion. She and Bill married in Hong Kong in September of that year, and sailed for the UK. Later the newspapers hailed the six-week sea voyage as a 'Troopship Honeymoon' although as Bill recounted: 'I was housed in the Troop Deck with hundreds of hairy seasick squaddies, whilst Nancy was up in a cabin shared with three other ladies.' One newspaper recounted that the morning after the foursome had arrived back at the Griffiths home in Swainshill, Herefordshire, their new wives stood by the gas stove watching Bill's mother cook their first English breakfast of bacon and baked beans on toast. '"My mother-in-law is going to teach us how to cook English food," said Wai Kong – now Mrs Nancy Griffiths. "We have only got ten weeks to learn, because soon the battalion goes to Germany and we hope to go with our husbands."' Wai Kong was very taken the Griffiths' pig that was in the sty being fattened up for Christmas. 'Ours in China are small and short-legged,' Wai Kong said. 'but him, he is so big.'

In the early 1960s Hong Kong was being flooded by refugees fleeing the conflicts in Communist China and many struggling families placed their babies into already overcrowded orphanages. To ease the problem, the authorities arranged for a number of the foundlings to be adopted by Asian American families but the primary demand was for boys not girls, and so British families were recruited to adopt 104 Hong Kong foundlings, aged between eight months and six years of age. The arrival at London's Heathrow Airport of almost every one of the Chinese babies and infants was greeted by widespread press coverage, with photographs of the new arrivals in the arms of their adoptive mothers regularly published. *The Birmingham Post* published a photograph of Sheila Jones, wife of the Rector of South Normanton, Derbyshire and their adopted child and captioned it:

The eighteen-month-old orphan girl from Communist China is living at the Rectory after having been flown from Hong Kong. Mr and Mrs Jones intend to adopt the child, Wong Pik Ha, which means 'clear and beautiful cloud'. The Rector said today that for a long time he and his wife had been concerned about the plight of deprived children all over the world and they felt that by taking Wong Pik Ha into their home to join their two children they would be helping in a practical manner. They intend to christen Wong Pik Ha and call her Anna.

All but one of the couples who adopted children were non-Chinese and although all adopted with the best of intentions, many had little understanding of Chinese culture. Yet, fifty years after the children had arrived in Britain, the British Association for Adoption and Fostering interviewed seventy-two of the adopted children and the findings were generally positive, with the majority reporting they had enjoyed loving relationships with their adoptive families. On the negative side all reported having experienced racism at times and a sense of feeling neither Chinese nor British. One recounted that it was not until she was a teenager that she met anyone else of Chinese origin. 'Even then, it was in Chinese restaurants. I'd dread them speaking to me in Cantonese because I wouldn't have a clue what they were talking about.' Lucy Sheen, who trained as an actress and was one of the leads in the 1986 British Chinese film, *Ping-Pong*, was just eleven months old when she was brought to Britain. In an interview she recounted her experience:

> I was brought up like any other British child; there was no reference for me to my cultural or ethnic origin. It was a strange one, because I'd spent the majority of my formative years being told I could neither call myself English nor British because I wasn't white. Then I discovered this whole other Chinese side – not the majority – but quite a vociferous section that were basically unwilling to accept me as Chinese because I didn't speak the language. That was a head-scratching moment: so what the hell am I then? This thing, stuck between two very, very different cultures and backgrounds, neither of which were particularly willing to accept me.

In 1963, Gordon, a four-year-old Chinese, visited Britain with his adoptive mother, Gladys Aylward, who had travelled from Taiwan to undertake a lecture tour. Aylward was by this time famous as her remarkable life had been portrayed in the film *The Inn of the Sixth Happiness*, released five years before. Aylward, who was born into a London working-class family, worked as a parlour maid and in her late teens became a devout Christian, and increasingly concerned about the spiritual state of the millions of people in China who had never heard the gospel. She went on at length to everyone she met about the need for more missionaries in China and her younger brother, Lawrence, perhaps irritated by his sister's continued dwelling on the subject, suggested that if she was so interested in the country's plight maybe she should go there. Gladys took up her brother's challenge and applied to work for the China Inland Mission but was rejected as it did not consider her qualified enough. Undaunted, in 1930 she travelled alone by railway to China and began assisting an elderly, widowed missionary named Jeannie Lawson in the village of

Yangcheng, in the mountainous Shanxi province of northern China. When Mrs Lawson died, Gladys worked on alone, opening an inn in the village. She became the mandarin's official foot inspector, helping to put an end to the cruel custom of foot-binding girls and women, taught Bible stories to muleteers who passed through the village, and cared for a large number of orphans, adopting several. Aylward became a Chinese citizen in 1936. In 1938 the region was invaded by Japanese forces and Aylward led more than 100 orphans to safety over the mountains, despite being wounded. She was repatriated to Britain at the beginning of the Second World War and taught young children at Basingstoke Preparatory School for several years. After ten years she applied to return to China but the Communist Government refused her application. Instead, she settled in Taiwan in 1958 and founded the Gladys Aylward Orphanage, where she worked until her death in 1970. On her visit to Britain in 1963 Aylward stayed with her brother, Laurence, in Birmingham, and he was interviewed about the visit by his famous sister: 'She is staying until Monday and we have tried to keep Saturday free, but she is bound to have to go to a meeting or to see someone. She is such a lively busy person that we rarely have time for more than a few minutes together. She does not talk about her life in China very often. We have to wait until she lets bits drop.' While in Britain Aylward was often asked to preach and at one service the four-year-old Gordon relieved the solemnity of the occasion by running his toy cars up and down the pulpit.

Another notable Christian woman to visit was the Reverend Florence Li-Tim Oi, who came in 1984 to be honoured in a special service held in Westminster Abbey. After studying theology in Hong Kong in the 1930s Li was ordained as a deaconess in the Anglican Church in 1941 and sent to Macau to assist refugees. Due to the Japanese occupation of Hong Kong Macau was without an Anglian priest and, as none could reach it, Li was ordained, the first female to become a priest in the Anglican church – and the only one until 1971, when the church finally agreed to the ordination of women, although it was not until 1994 that women were ordained in the English Anglican Church.

As the twentieth century progressed the number of British households employing servants dwindled and while there doubtless were Chinese working as domestic servants in Britain, details are hard to find. An entry in the 1911 census records Azon as working as valet for Ernest Guinness at 17 Grosvenor Square in London. Guinness was a senior member of the brewing family and at the time a handsome society playboy. He married Marie Clothilde Russell in 1904 and by 1911 they had three children. To house his family and his extensive social life, Guinness built two large houses on the Chapelizod estate, near Dublin. One house he used for his family life and the other for society parties, fine dining and entertaining.

Other Travellers

In 1919 Jehangir Mody, a wealthy Indian shipbroker, and his family came from India to live in Torquay and with them came their Chinese servant, known as Miss Lucy. She lived with and served the family for thirty years and when Mr Mody died in 1949 he left her a significant annuity 'in appreciation of her honest and faithful service to the family'.

Shin Hong Ma was the son of a wealthy Shanghai financier and came to Britain around 1930 to take charge of his father's London office. In 1932 Rebecca Ho Hing Du, whom had been betrothed to Shin from childhood, arrived in London to marry. She was a renowned beauty and the wedding in St Martin in the Fields Church was a glittering society event, attended by hundreds of guests. Many of the Chinese women who attended dressed in brilliant colourful satin tunics and heavily embroidered trousers, with elaborate dress ornaments and jewels in their hair. The couple had two children and lived a luxurious life in London. In 1936 Rebecca's striking looks caught the eye of talent scouts and she was contracted to play the part of a Chinese maid in the film *The Wife of General Ling*, under the stage name Lotus Fragrance. She also performed in the play *The Old One Smiles* at the Q Theatre in Kew and sang in the film *Incident in Shanghai*. In 1937, the Japanese attack on Shanghai resulted in Shin's father's office being bombed and a run on his finance house. As a result, the London office had to close and Shin was out of work. The war in China also meant that he could not get any financial assistance from his family in Shanghai to help with his substantial family bills. Although Rebecca was earning a fee from her film role and Shin cut down on their lavish London life style, this was insufficient to pay their bills, and Shin was forced to take a job as a butler to a stockbroker in Mayfair. His new employment came to an end soon after, but it was not his lack of experience that caused his dismissal. Shin had continued to run up debts, hoping that the war in China would end and he would get bailed out by his father. As his financial position worsened he began pawning articles he had obtained on approval and forging cheques. It was not long until he was arrested and appeared at the Old Bailey. When sentencing him to nine months imprisonment the judge said: 'It is sad to see a man of your family and education in your position. I have no doubt your position was made acute by what has taken place in the East. The reverberations of war reach far and wide and penetrate even into the silence of this court.' It was reported that Rebecca was not in court but heard the news by telephone. 'His wife, who has been described as one of the loveliest women in China, will keep their home together by doing film work.' While her husband was in prison, Rebecca, under her stage name, took whatever work she could get to make ends meet: 'Lotus Fragrance, the Chinese film star famous for her perfect complexion, in conjunction with Ann Frankel Continental Beauty Specialist, will give Demonstrations, Treatments and advice on "Sylkys" Facial Fashions of 1940 in the Southsea Spa.' She also was employed to sell goods on a Chinese Industries Stand

and sang in *The Chinese Follies*, a revue that toured Britain in 1939. In 1941 she decided to leave Britain, and most probably her husband, and she and her two children boarded a ship for China. En route they survived the torpedoing of the ship in the Atlantic. For a time she lived in Bombay where she established a fashionable beauty salon and then, in late 1946, went to live in America, by which time her marriage to Shin had ended. There she became a translator, interpreter, and office associate for a private immigration lawyer specialising in Chinese clients. What became of Shin when he left prison is not known.

In 1938, the press reported that a Chinese servant employed by Muriel Martin was trained to answer the door to callers and pretend that he could not speak English. Martin's reason for not wishing to take callers became clear when she appeared in court charged with various offences. Martin was an undischarged bankrupt and had illegally obtained credit, including leasing a shop in Mayfair and filling it with stock paid for by worthless cheques. When the police called at her house and asked to examine her attaché case she threw it down the stairs and called out 'Lee', and when her Chinese servant appeared told him to run off with the case. Whether Lee sensibly refused or was caught is not recounted. The prosecuting counsel told the court that Martin 'had described herself as a film actress and the wife an Army officer, and was known by a variety of names chosen for their picturesqueness rather than their accuracy'.

Tee-Ha was another Chinese who worked for someone with a false name, although his employer, Justin de Villeneuve, had retitled himself to impress rather than deceive. Born Nigel Jonathan Davies in Hackney in London, he became a hairdresser at the fashionable Vidal Sassoon salon and it was then he decided he needed a more stylish name – 'a nom de perm', he later quipped. In 1964 Justin de Villeneuve met a skinny fifteen-year-old called Lesley Hornby and within six months had changed her name to Twiggy, and as a model she instantly became one of the icons of London's Swinging Sixties. She appeared on the front cover of every fashionable magazine, often snapped by Justin himself, who began passing himself off as a fashion photographer. In a short space of time Villeneuve became immensely wealthy and employed a cook, butler, chauffeur and a Chinese manservant, named Tee-Ha. At Justin's house there were lavish parties attended by the celebrities of the day and if Tee-Ha had written an account of his time there it would make for a fascinating read. Villeneuve said of him:

> We were abroad a lot and while we were away Tee-Ha, my Chinese manservant, would look after the studio. Tee-Ha was a fabulous character. Once when I was away my younger brother, Tony, moved in without my knowledge. He got the Rolls-Royce out of the garage, drove round to the Speakeasy, picked up four girls and brought them back to the studio. When Tee-Ha told me about it afterwards, his little slit eyes were practically

popping out of his head. Still, he got out of rid of Tony by waving a huge carving knife from the kitchen under his nose.

For many who could afford servants, the first-rate reputation of Chinese in such positions was an attraction, as one newspaper reported in 1966:

> The Vere Harmsworths have talked it over and made up their minds to engage some Chinese servants for their penthouse home in Chester Square. The Hon Vere is, of course, Lord Rothermere's son and vice-chairman of Associated Newspapers, and the idea came to him and his vivacious wife when they visited Charles Clore recently. 'We were so impressed by his Chinese staff,' says Mrs Harmsworth. Other friends of theirs, the Danzigers, also have Chinese help: 'their cleanliness and efficiency struck us,' Mrs Harmsworth explains. 'Accordingly,' Mrs Harmsworth says, 'we are going to take the opportunity to go to Hong Kong in two or three weeks' time and see a number of girls, to interview them for the jobs. We only need about three for our London home.'

One employer who deeply cared for his Chinese servants was Captain George Wright. He had run away to sea when he was fifteen and spent thirty years sailing the seas around China before retiring to Britain. He was interviewed by *The Daily Mirror* in 1963 as he had recently bought the racehorse, Gay Navaree, for £5,000 and was hoping it would win that year's Grand National. He recounted that when the Japanese invaded Singapore in 1942 he had to abandon all his oriental treasures but smuggled out the six things of most importance to him; his two Chinese servants, their baby, two boxer dogs and a kitten. His two servants were still working for him at his home near York and Wright had paid for both their children to be educated. The boy who had been smuggled out was studying at Trent College, preparing to join the RAF, and another boy, born in Britain and named Chong Shing, was at Gordonstoun School, where at the time he was studying alongside Prince Charles thanks to Wright paying the significant annual fee. One hopes that Chong had a better time at the school than the Prince, who famously described his former school as 'Colditz in kilts'. Sadly, Gay Navaree fell at the last fence in the Grand National and Captain Wright sold it to the holiday camp owner, Fred Pontin, who renamed the horse, Pontin-Go.

In the 1970s, as more people began to seek out alternative forms of medicine, especially for illnesses that Western medicine seemed to struggle to treat, there arose opportunities for Chinese living in Britain to provide acupuncture and other forms of Chinese treatments, and to open shops selling Chinese medicinal herbs. Previously, traditional Chinese medicine had not been regarded as a valid form of medicine by the medical establishment and so practitioners of Chinese traditional medicine had almost solely been confined to the Chinatowns. British Chinese children who grew up in Liverpool recounted that they were given only Chinese medicines, such as herbs boiled into liquids or Tiger Balm, for their ailments. The majority of those who began offering acupuncture treatment were non-Chinese practitioners, but Chinese doctors who had trained in traditional medicine in China started to travel to Britain to practise. One was Professor Song Xuan Ke who arrived in 1986. He had begun training when just thirteen, as an apprentice to herbal masters in his home province of Hubei, and then studied both Chinese Medicine and Western Medicine at Canton University in 1982. In Britain he helped found the Association of Traditional Chinese Medicine and later established the Asante Academy for Chinese Medicine in London that introduced the use of acupuncture into a number of London hospitals. In 1988 it was estimated that the number of individual practitioners of Chinese Traditional Medicine was around 200, although the majority remained non-Chinese. However, the next decades would see traditional Chinese medicine grow in popularity and create new business opportunities for Chinese practitioners and specialist Chinese medicine shops.

Van Cuong Truong, a Chinese teacher living in Vietnam, and his family were among the thousands forced to flee the country because of the Vietnam War. Truong paid for his family and himself to be transported in a small crowded boat on a perilous sixty-hour journey across the South China Sea, arriving in Malaysia with little more than the clothes they were wearing. Britain had agreed to accept a number of refugees and in 1979 the Truongs arrived in Folkestone, where they spent their first months, before moving to a small flat in London's Surrey Docks, not far from the vanished old Chinatown. The year after arriving, Truong was interviewed for an article on recent immigrants in *The Illustrated London News* and told the journalist, 'My children speak with cockney accents. We are happy to be British now, but I want that my children should not forget their 5,000-year-old heritage.' So concerned were the Truongs that their children might not learn to speak Chinese they fundraised to establish a Chinese Community School in the borough that, within two years, had 200 pupils. Over the following years they raised sufficient funding to build a brand-new school, including an Indo-Chinese Community Centre that expanded to employ fifty staff delivering a wide range of services for the Chinese and Vietnamese immigrants. In 2010 Truong's remarkable achievements in the twenty years since he had arrived as an almost penniless immigrant was marked by the award of an MBE, and in 2012 he was one of those selected to be an Olympic Torch Bearer in the run-up to the London Olympics. In that same year, Truong was invited to attend the Queen Elizabeth's Diamond Jubilee Anniversary Luncheon, where he was seated next to the Queen.

26

Portraying Britain

> Afar in the ocean, towards the extremities of the north-west,
> There is a nation, or country, called England;
> The clime is so frigid, and you are compelled to approach the fire;
> The houses are so lofty, that they may pluck the stars.
>
> Unknown Chinese poet in London (1813)

Two of the earliest Chinese to write about Britain in English were Min-ch'ien T. Z. Tyau and Chiang Yee, and their accounts provide an intriguing view of the country as seen from a Chinese perspective, and fascinating scenes of a bygone Britain. Min-ch'ien T. Z. Tyau arrived in Britain 1909 to study law. He attended the University of London and then St John's College in Cambridge, where he was awarded a prize in International Law. While in London he edited the *World's Chinese Students' Journal*, and was the London

Chiang Yee,
c. 1940s.
(Public domain)

correspondent of the *Republican Advocate* (Shanghai) and contributed articles to *The Times* and other publications. In 1910, he represented China at the Universal Peace Congress at Stockholm and at the Anti-Opium Conference in Paris in May 1914. Later in life he became a journalist and lecturer on International Law in China.

While living in Britain Min-ch'ien T. Z. Tyau began work on a book describing aspects of British life from a foreigner's perspective, and after returning to China in 1916 completed it. However, there was a delay in its publication as he explained in the book's foreword: 'The continuance of the submarine warfare has also been responsible for this delay: we sent off the first half of our MS to the publishers in December 1917, but their letter of acknowledgment never arrived in Peking until November 1918 although it was dated February of that year!' The book was eventually published in 1920 as *London through Chinese Eyes*. In the preface Sir John Jordan, Britain's Envoy Extraordinary in China, wrote:

> China, it must be remembered, has always been a literary nation and when the masses of this people turn their attention to foreign learning and become imbued with foreign ideas, the Chinese problem, which is now so little understood, will compel worldwide attention. The Author of this Book, who has turned his journalistic adventures in London to good account and who is now the Editor of one of the most influential newspapers in the Capital, is perhaps foremost amongst those who are educating public opinion in China and preparing it for the wise assimilation of Western thought and ideas. In heartily commending his Work to British readers, I venture to hope that the interest which the Author shows in all things British may stimulate some of them to take an equal interest in things Chinese and in the Chinese people.

Min-ch'ien T. Z. Tyau begins his book by relating how he had imagined the city before he came.

> Aided and coloured by a fertile imagination, I pictured London as the embodiment of all the wealth and luxury that were so vividly portrayed in the Arabian Nights or as Peking was painted by Marco Polo in his remarkable Travels. To be able to visit it would be the height of human happiness, and to be privileged to live therein, for even just a few days, would be to dwell in an earthly Paradise... But I was soon disillusioned. The streets were far from being paved with rich marble or precious stones; nor did the inhabitants use or drink from vessels of gold and silver. As a matter of fact, London or Paris or Berlin is no more a fairy palace than is either Peking or Canton ... but my respect for the city increased nonetheless with the lapse of years. In fact, before I finally bade it a long farewell, I had also come to regard it as the 'dear old London town'.

The topics he focuses on are beguilingly diverse – the weather, cockney dialect, football, royal events, the social position of women, street vendors and afternoon teas all feature. One chapter eulogises the British 'Bobby'. In the days before traffic lights, policemen controlled the traffic from the middle of the road with nothing but a waved hand, pointed finger or expressive look to control the traffic flow. Min-ch'ien T. Z. Tyau sees the Bobby's traffic control as a metaphor for Britain's recognition that:

> True freedom is to know where that liberty ends and begins. Cars and drays may lumber past him, or taxicabs and motor omnibuses may tear past him, but like the Roman sentinel in the supreme hour of trial, he seems glued to his post. He is neither excited nor flurried, but is as cool as a cucumber in the performance of his duties. He does not waste words or time unnecessarily; nevertheless, his sphinx-like silence compels universal obedience, and, consequently, ensures perfect smoothness in the running of the traffic machinery.

One chapter explores the differences between English and Chinese food and in it he admits 'the trifle, diplomatic pudding, or treacle pudding with plenty of golden syrup are certainly appetising'.

Min-ch'ien's account of London before 1914 is fascinating, but his book has few personal accounts of meetings or experiences. Quite different are Chiang Yee's books about Britain written in the 1930s and '40s, and published as the series, *The Silent Traveller*. As well as observations on life in Britain, these contain personal anecdotes, jokes, poems, illustrations, and musings on Chinese culture. Chiang Yee was born into a wealthy middle-class family in Jiangxi province, south-west China. His father was a successful portraitist and encouraged his son's early interest in painting and calligraphy. After graduating with a degree in Chemistry from South Eastern University in Nanjing in 1926, Chiang taught for a short period before joining his elder brother in the National Revolutionary Army. He was appointed to various posts in local government, eventually becoming a local magistrate in his native city of Jiujiang, in 1929. Chiang held a highly respected post, with a contingent of soldiers guarding his office and house. He employed six servants and lived the comfortable life of a traditional scholar official. In 1924, he married a first cousin, Zeng Yun, and they had four children. Yet in 1933 Chiang decided to abandon his Chinese life and family and travel to Britain, with no job in prospect and speaking almost no English. His reasons appear to have been a combination of frustration with the corruption rife in local politics at the time, apprehension at the volatile situation in China, compounded by the persistent threat of Japanese aggression, an unhappy relationship with his wife, and a desire for a fresh start. It is unlikely that he could have imagined when he sailed away from China, and his wife and children whom he placed in the care of his elder brother, that it would be forty years before he would return.

Once in London Chiang began learning English, and after a few months shared a flat in Hampstead with the Chinese author and playwright Hsiung Shi-I, who introduced him to other Chinese living in Britain and notable figures in London's art and literary circles. Chiang began producing paintings and illustrations and, to help him establish a reputation, Hsiung arranged for his friend to illustrate the published version of his successful play, *Lady Precious Stream*. As with any artist, finding places to exhibit work was difficult and Chiang's first was in a fundraising exhibition organised by Richard St Barbe Baker to raise money for his environmental organisation, 'Men of the Trees'. By chance, one of Chiang's works in the exhibition, a painting depicting trees in a Chinese style, was reproduced in the *London Evening Standard*. This led to his first solo exhibition at a commercial gallery in Knightsbridge, and his 1935 book on Chinese painting, *The Chinese Eye: An Interpretation of Chinese Painting*, brought him further acclaim. By 1937, although Chiang was established as a successful painter and commentator on Chinese art, he struggled with depression, anxiety, loneliness and guilt from having abandoned his family, negative emotions that continued to plague him throughout his life.

Chiang decided to write a travel book and chose the Lake District because of its historical associations with a number of Britain's literary and artistic elite, including Turner, Wordsworth and Constable. It begins:

There are numbers of books on travel and scenery published every year, some of them written from the geologist's special point of view, some to dilate upon peculiar racial differences, and some purely for the sake of an unusual piece of scenery, or of some loveable romantic incident that happened there. But the book I am about to write is unlike any of these!

Indeed it was not, and the many publishers he sent the book to rejected it on the grounds that its inclusion of musings on Chinese culture, poetry and illustrations were 'too Chinese' and the book unlikely to find many readers. Fortunately, *Country Life*, decided to publish *The Silent Traveller: A Chinese Artist in Lakeland* and the publishers who had rejected it were proven wrong, for the book sold out in its first month and was republished in nine subsequent editions. This was the first of six British 'Silent Traveller' books, including Oxford, London and the Yorkshire Dales, and the series brought him wide popularity and acclaim. These illustrated travelogues provide a unique perspective on Britain, through the eyes of a Chinese exile at a time when books about the West by a Chinese author were exceptionally rare. Although Chiang's grasp of English was good, he relied on the editorial assistance of Innes Jackson, who assisted with many of Chiang's books. Chiang's illustrations for the books drew on the techniques and principles of Chinese painting, though he emphasised that he did 'not set out to turn the British scene into a Chinese one', rather 'to interpret British scenes with my Chinese brushes, ink and colours, and my native method of painting'. He explained:

> Most people nowadays know something about the general appearance and subject matter of Chinese paintings. Unfortunately, they are apt to be biased. If they see a picture with one or two birds, a few trees or rocks piled together, they will certainly say that that is a lovely Chinese painting. But if they see anything like Western buildings or a modern figure there, they will suddenly say 'that is not Chinese.' In this book I have painted from the surroundings in which I have lived these last few years, and I hope my readers will not be so biased as to say that they do not like the paintings because they are not 'Chinese'. And I also hope some of my readers are not biased in another way and will not say that they like this painting because it has a Chinese flavour. I should like them to criticise my work without preconceptions.

The books' charm comes from Chiang's exploration of ostensibly trivial subjects such as the weather, teatime, children, books and the theatre. 'My most vivid impression is of Gracie Fields singing Lancashire songs. Though I could not understand the dialect, I found the greatest pleasure in her voice and gestures.' He delights in small details of everyday life. 'I am diffident of fixing my eyes on big things, I generally glance down at small ones. There are a great many tiny events which it has given me great joy to look at, to watch and to think about.' Although Chiang became friendly with many cultural luminaries, it is clear from his books that he was as happy meeting ordinary people including coalmen (and their horses), porters, butlers, policemen and landladies. He is generally flattering about Britain and any criticisms are wryly couched, such as his comment on the fashion for wearing historic Chinese garments:

> I was once struck by a lady who wore an old Chinese robe at a party. She was very proud of her gown ... but I am inclined to wonder what English people would think of a small and short Chinese lady wearing an Elizabethan type costume picked up from the drawer of a repertory theatre. I can almost imagine the head of the lady would not even emerge from the huge skirt.

There were times when his self-styled title, 'the silent traveller', was apt. For example, he writes that when he visited the painter and critic Roger Fry: 'I did not talk to him at all.' And on a second visit recounts that Fry 'beckoned me near him and said he had got one brushstroke right. I thought I ought not to disturb him and went away.' Perhaps Chiang was simply overawed, as he records that meeting the painter was one of his greatest experiences.

All Chiang's travelogues are interwoven with references to China and reflections on Chinese cultural history and traditions. Thus they provide fascinating insights into Chinese life, culture and ways of seeing. Yet the writing reflects the ambivalent state of most individuals who become resident in a country that is not their homeland, as it mingles fascination with the new culture with wistful longing for home. His writing was a way to stay connected to China, though possibly an idealised view of a past China, free of the internal and external conflicts that continued to plague the country. His 1940 autobiographical account of growing up in China, *A Chinese Childhood*, confirms that he believed that China's cultural life and its heritage had suffered from the introduction of social reforms. Yet, its account of Chiang's early life, with its anecdotes and stories about life in China, enabled many British readers to gain an insight into daily life there.

Throughout the 1930s and '40s, Chiang was recognised as an authority on Chinese culture and invited to contribute to BBC radio programmes, and speak to societies and at literary festivals. He hosted a number of Chinese artists who visited London at his house, and offered encouragement when needed, as well as hospitality. He helped a young female artist, Xiao Shufang, by collaborating on a book, *Chinese Children at Play*, and she recalls him as 'reticent, extraordinary diligent, yet very warm-hearted'. In 1942, Robert Helpmann, the illustrious Australian choreographer, commissioned Chiang to design the set and costumes for his new ballet, *The Birds*, to be performed by the Sadler's Wells Ballet company. Chiang recounts going to an early fitting of his costumes: 'In the afternoon Moira Fraser and Beryl Grey (two of the dancers) came to be fitted for the costumes of the hen and the nightingale respectively. I had been anxious about the execution of the elaborate hen costume, for the hen is an important character in the ballet, and her costume had to be perfect in every detail... The nightingale costume, I admit, was not very good in my original design. Happily, however, after much discussion and numerous suggestions from everyone, the costume turned out to be very pretty.' *The Spectator*'s dance critic agreed:

> It looks as if Mr. Robert Helpmann, of the Sadler's Wells Ballet may turn out to be the English Diaghilev, for he has now followed up his amazing success in his *Hamlet* with a new ballet in quite another genre, *The Birds*, in which a similar complete unity of style in music, choreography and decor is achieved... The music has an intricacy and delicacy which are matched and repeated in the fascinating, slightly Chinese character given to the English woodland and birds. The costume of the Hen is a brilliant chef-d'oeuvre of caricaturing fancy, while those of the Dove and the Nightingale are quite lovely.

Audiences were equally delighted as Beryl Gray recounted: 'An enchanting little ballet, it was well liked. On the first night, to everyone's astonishment, we took fifteen curtain calls.'

In 1938, Chiang was commissioned by Peter Johnston-Saint, then head of the Wellcome Historical Medical Museum, to arrange its section on Chinese medicine. Chiang was determined to provide an accurate picture of China, for he recognised that China and its culture was often misrepresented or only partially understood in Britain. He wrote accepting the commission, 'Yours is the first and best medical museum in the world, so it must be adequately arranged. We Chinese have suffered sometimes from the inadequate and not proper arrangement of our things in some museums in Europe.' Chiang came up with a plan for four sections: Folklore in relation to sickness and death, Chinese conception of the human body, Chinese Pharmacology, and Medical and Surgical practice. He envisaged the sections featuring not only objects collected by Wellcome, but also specially commissioned models and illustrations, which he would produce to contextualise the exhibits.

The plans, however, never came to fruition. Work slowed on the project following the outbreak of the war in 1939 and in June 1941 Johnston-Saint wrote to Chiang that the Chinese Section had 'suffered rather severely' through bomb damage. Thus the planned project was never completed. Johnston-Saint recalled their early meetings:

> I often think of our pleasant and enjoyable monthly Chinese dinners when we used to foregather all together. They were very enjoyable evenings and I still recall the numerous cups of wonderful tea that we used to consume in the course of the evening. I don't mean tea in the British sense, that is to say a cup of dish water with a faint flavour of cabbage, but a lovely scented orange-pekoe drunk out of little semi-transparent miniature cups. That was tea in those days.

In 1955, Chiang moved to America to take up a teaching post at Columbia University. One of his students recalls Chiang being asked how he had liked Oxford, and him replying in a perfect London East End accent, 'Not 'arf.' He subsequently published further *Silent Traveller* books about Boston, Dublin, New York, Paris and San Francisco. In the 1930s, Chiang wrote a New Year resolution that challenged him to try his very hardest to develop his writing and his painting while in Britain, for 'the world is so big that one can surely find a place to survive.' Chiang more than fulfilled his resolution, for he played a significant role in improving the understanding and appreciation of Chinese culture through his work as an artist, writer and educator. Yet in spite of his having a full and successful life, a poem written by Chiang in the 1950s (translated by Da Zheng) shows that he experienced moments of discontentment at his emigrant life.

> Monkeys and birds have long been my companions;
> Amongst ghosts and monsters I dwell and mingle.
> Using the barbarian language is but means for survival;
> As the Silent Traveller, I simply manage to get by.
> My appearance is here and there;
> And my body travels to and fro.

The poem alludes to his experiences of Sinophobia and a general sense of dislocation while living in the West; sentiments no doubt felt by many of the Chinese travellers to Britain since 1687.

Chiang once explained to a friend, 'I have been working diligently because I believe that a man leaves a name behind him just as a tiger leaves a skin behind.' This book includes only some of the names of the Chinese who have come to Britain, but their endeavours clearly underline the significant and lasting impact Chinese travellers have left on Britain's cultural life.

Index

Page references in *italic* refer to illustrations.

Aberdeen University 106, 107, 217
Acton, Harold 170–171
actors 170, 199, 201, 205, 206, 209, 210, 211, 220, *249*, 256, 269, 271
Admiral Sah Chen-Ping 227
Admiral Ting Ju-chang 36
Aeronautics 220–221, 254–255
Albert, Prince 92, 94
aliens
  Aliens Act 1793 22, 25
  Aliens Act 1905 139
  Aliens Restriction Act 1914 142, 178
  Aliens Restriction (Amendment) Act 1919 142
  Bank of Scotland Act 1695, court case 25–28
  definition of 22
  friendly aliens 216
  illegal aliens 164–166
  status of alien's wife 139, 144
Ambassadors, Chinese 79, *109*, 113–117, *118*–133, 213, *224*, 225–239
Amherst Embassy 111
Ancient Melodies 245
Anglo-Chinese College 70, 100, 105, 217
Anthony, John 31–33

Architectural students *146*, 156, 206, 217, 262
Architectural Association 217
artists *see* painters and sculptors
associations, Chinese 142, 150, 158, 174, 193, 231, 234, 259
political asylum 139, 174, 222
attacks on Chinese 32, *138*, 140, 142, 162
Authentic account of the Chinese commission sent to report on the Great Exhibition 93
authors *see* writers
Aylward, Gladys 269–270
Bank of Scotland court case 25–28
Barnum, P. T. 58, 92, 94–95
Battle of Portland Place 236
ballet *see* dance
BBC Far East Services 260–262
Bell, Julian 245
Bennett, Arnold 153
Beresford, Lord Charles *38*, 40–41, 43
Better maintenance and care for Lascars and other Asiatic seamen Act 33

Bin Chun *109*, 113, 114, 115
Birds, The 280
Birmingham University 131, 219, 250
Black Narcissus 170
Blackheath High School, London 215
blind children 101, 257
Blue Funnel Shipping Line 35, 142, 145, 147, 156, 246
Bodleian Library 12
Boshan Wei Yuk 103, 263
Boswell, James 15, 20
Bowra, Edward 113, 115
Boxer Indemnity Scholarship Programme *212*, 218
Boxer Protocol 132
Boxer Rebellion 131–132, 197, 218, 225
British Council 143, 219, 221, 222, 223, 259
British Empire exhibition 200
British Navigations Act 30
British Royal Fleet Auxiliary (RFA) 185–186
Broken Blossoms 200
Broomhall, Benjamin 74–75

Buckingham Palace 36, 96, 114, 129, 130, 183, 229, 230, 238
Burford, Thomas 13
Burke, Thomas 153, 196, 200
Burlingame, Ansom 103, 115
Canton, British in 11, 30, 60, 61, 81, 111–112
Cardiff Chinatown 46, 138, 140, 142, 149, 154, 162, 163, 178
Central Ballet of China 209, 257
Chairman Hua Kuo-Feng 238
Chang Chien-Ying 219
Chang Gow, the Chinese Giant 43, 56–59
Chang Kia Ngau 251
Chang Polka 57
Chang Ta-jen 225
Chang Yen Hoon 128–130
Charteris, Leslie 241–242
Cheltenham College 107
Chen Yuan 240, 244–245
Chen Zhanxiang 146, 156
Cheng Su 259–260
Cheng Tien-hsi 213, 232–234
Cheng Wu-Fei 219
Chiang Kai-shek 136, 143, 180, 230, 233, 234, 235, 257
Chiang Yee 171, 202, 249, 275, 277–282
Chih-chen Lo-Feng-Luh 104, 127–128, 129, 130–133, 173
China Campaign Committee (CCC) 180, 231, 257
China Inland Mission 74, 75, 269
China Week 184
Chinese Childhood, A 280
Chinese Children at Play 280

Chinese Communist Party in Britain 68, 143, 158, 168, 231
Chinese Detective, The 211
Chinese Exhibition, The 92
Chinese Eye, The 202, 278
Chinese food 97, 121, 122, 154, 157, 158, 159, 164, 167, 166–176, 193–194, 197, 200, 220, 252, 267, 277
Chinese Giant *see* Chang Gow
Chinese Girl Students' Aid Committee 214
Chinese Honeymoon, A 196
Chinese in Britain 1800-Present 7
Chinese Labour Corps 142, 170, 179, 189, 190–191
Chinese Legation 107, 119, 123, 132, 135, 172, 214, 225, 227, 230, 231, 232, 234, 236, 238, 251
Chinese Life and Art 196
Chinese Seamen's Union 141, 143, 158, 173, 181
Chinoiserie 12
Chinque, Samuel 158
Chiu Yiu Nam 177, 186–187
Christianity *see* religion
Chu Chin Chow 198
Chun Yee Association 150, 158
Chung Hwa School 154–155
cinema 170, 185, 199–201, 203, 206, 207, 209–210, 219, 220, 249, 269, 271
Classical Theatre of China 208
compensation for seamen 141, 143, 181
Confucianism *see* religion
Cooking the Chinese Way 173
Cultural Revolution 206, 208, 236, 243, 247, 257

Dai Ailian 256–257
dance 72, 120, 197, 198, 206, 208, 209, 256–257, 280
Dartington Hall 256
Deh-Ta Hsiung 169, 171, 219
Deng Xiaoping 222
Destination Chungking 265
Dickens, Charles 49, 91, 196, 242
Diplomatic Journal of Four Countries 122
diplomatic relations
 Britain and Chinese Empire 11, 96, 110–117, 118–133
 Britain and People's Republic of China 234–239
 Britain and Republic of China 228–239
discrimination *see* racism *and* negative views of Chinese
doctors *see* medicine
Dollar Academy 103
domestic service *see* servants
Dragon Beards versus the Blueprints, The 244
Dragon of Wrath, The 197
Duchess of Gordon's School, Huntly 100
Du Halde, Jean-Baptiste 13
Durham University 215
Ealing College 222
East India Company (EIC)
 seamen employed by 30–31
 see trade with China
East of Suez 199
Edinburgh University Medical School 105, 119, 215, 216, 258
Edward VII 225, 227
Elizabeth II 155, 172, 208, 234, 237, 238, 239, 274
Elphinstone, John Fullerton 80–88
Empson, William 260–261

Index

Engineering students 215, 217, 219, 220, 221, 254, 262, 263
Epsom College 87
Eurasian children 23, 46, 58, 59, 60–67, 85, 86–87, 145, 150, 154, 155, 163–164, 183, 184, 192, 242
executions of Chinese 151, 250
exhibitions
 Chinese art objects 90, 92, 95–97, 196–200, 201–203, 209
 Chinese artists 15, 217, 278
 Chinese people as 'curiosities' 52–54, 56–58, 89, 93–95
 horticultural 86
 Keying, Chinese junk 90–94
 Salvation Army 78
factory visits 114, 115, 237, 253
Falklands War 177, 186–188
Federation of British Industries 219, 235
films *see* cinema
first Chinese immigrant 18–28
First World War 141–142, 178–179, *189*, 190–191, 216
Flame of Love, The 170, 201
football 184, 214, 264, 266, 267
49th Parallel 170
Fou Ts'ong 210
Fry, Roger 279
Fu Manchu 196, 200, 201, 205
Fu Shun 116
Fuk-Tong 105
funerals 33, 36–37, 50, 59, 133, 151
Fung Siu Ng 164
gambling 32, 151–152, 153, 162

General History of China, The 13
Genius of China, The 209, 238
geologist 215
George II 13
George III 15
George IV 53
George V and Queen Mary 155, 207
George VI 183, 230
George Watson's School, Edinburgh 216
Gladstone, William 125–126
Glasgow University 107, 108, 215
Gordonstoun School 273
Great Britain-China Centre 238
Great Exhibition 84, 92–93
Great London Exposition 95
Guo Songtau 104, 118–121, 127
hairdressers 158–159, 255–256
Han Lih-wu 234
Han Suyin 265
Hart, Robert 96, 113, 123
Ho Kan 182
Hochee, John 80, 82–88, 102
Hollington Tong 234
Holt Ocean Steamship Company *see* Blue Funnel Shipping Line
Home Book of Chinese Cooking 220
Home for Lascars and Chinese Seamen 34
Hong Kong colony status 112, 140, 238
Hope, Charles 61–67
House of Commons *see* Parliament
Hsiao Ch'ien 204, 243
Hsiung Shih-I *195*, 203, 204, 219, 278
Huan Xiang 235
Huang Kuan 99, 105–106
Hyde, Thomas 12

Imperial College 219
Inn of the Sixth Happiness 205, 209, 219, 269
International Exhibition of Chinese Art 201–202
International Health Exhibition 97, 121
International Sea Fishing Exhibition 96, 168
interracial relationships, 61, 62, 144
 see also marriages
James II 12
Johnson, Samuel 13
Jottings from Carefree Travel 71
jugglers and acrobats *51*, 51–52, 54–55, 197, 205, 208, 209
Jung Chang 247–248
Kai Ho Kai 106–107
Kao, Charles 221–222
Ken Hom's Chinese Cookery 174
Kenneth Lo 143, 171, 173, 180, 219, 263
Keying, Chinese junk 90–94
Kneller, Sir Godfrey 12
Knole House 16, 129
Korean War 234, 235, 237, 267, 268
Kua Hua 238
Kung-chao Yeh, George 260
Kung Chao-Yuan 123
Kung Hsiang-hsi 230
Kuo Teh-lou *167*, 174
Kuomintang 136, 143, 155, 158, 180, 233, 234, 235
Kwan, Nancy 206
Kwouk, Bert 209–210
Lamb, William Phillip (Ping Win) 216
Langtry, Lillie 41–42
language test for foreign seamen 140
Lao She 153, 242–3
laundries *138*, 140, 147, 148, 149, 154, 156,

160, 161–166, 171, *183*, 191–194, 264
law
  court appearances 26, 28, 32, 33–34, 37, 39, 41, 55, 65–66, 90, 162, 165–166, 197, 271–272
  law students/lawyers 25, 106–107, *212*, 213–214, 223, 232, 241, 250, 254, 272, 275
  oath-taking in court, Chinese form 32, 39
Lee, Robert (Ya Fu) 220
Leeds College of Dramatic Arts 108
Leeds University 217
Legend of the Willow-Pattern Plate 201
Legge, James 6, 70–71, 100–101, 103, 105
Lew Yuk Lin 213–214, 227–228
Ley On 169–170, 201, 267
Li Ching Fong 213, 226
Li Hongzhang 99, *118*, 123–126
Liao Zilan 210
Life in the London Streets 46
Lim, Bobby 216
Limehouse Blues: Looking for Chinatown in the London Docks 7
Limehouse Chinatown, London 31–33, 35, *45*, 46–50, 146–158, *160*, 184
Limehouse Nights 196
Ling Shuhua *240*, 244–246
Liu Ruifen 122
Liu Xihong 118–120
Liverpool Chinatown 35, 46, 47, 142, 144, *145*, *146*, 146–158, 163, 171, 180, 181
Liverpool University 144, 156
Lo, Anna 157
Lock Ah Tam 150–151
lodging houses, Chinese 46, 147, 148, 149

London Blind School 101
London Chinatown *see* Limehouse and Soho
London Missionary Society 69, 70, 103, 217, 259
London School of Economics 244
London through Chinese Eyes 152, 276
Looty, Pekinese dog 96
Lotus Fragrance (Rebecca Ho Hing Du) *249*, 271–272
Loum Kiqua *10*, 13–14
Lu Gwei Djen 246–247
Lu Hsu-Chang 235
Macao, William 17, 18–28
Macartney Embassy 110–111
Macartney, Halliday 119, 136
Madame Koo (Countess Hoey Stoker) 229, 231
Madame Mao's Memories 206
Magniac, Daniel 60–67
Many-Splendored Thing, A 265
marriages
  Chinese 251, 252, 271
  interracial 23, 32, 43, 46, 55, 58, 62, 63, 82, 85, 106, 108, 147, 148, 150, 154, 157, 161, 163, 165, 179, 181, 184, 192, 206, 210, 216, 217, 221, 226, 247, 248, 263, 267, 268
  arranged 164
Maugham, Somerset 199
medicine
  medical students/doctors 64, 87, 99, 105–108, 122, 135, 152, 216, 247, 258, 264, 265, 274
  traditional Chinese medicine 16, 122, 200, 273–274, 281
Memorabilia domestica 18

Min-ch'ien T. Z. Tyau 152, 275–277
Ministers to Britain *see* ambassadors
Miss Wang's Diary 262
missionaries *see* religion
Mr Ma and Son 242–243
Mr Wu 198–199
Morrison, Reverend Robert 69–70, 105, 111
music
  bagpipes, Chinese accounts of 91, 124
  Chinese music *10*, 14, 49, 56, 91, 94, 97, 121, 201, 210, 211, 259
  Chinese opera *see* theatre
  Pu Tian Le, composition of Chinese national anthem, 121
Nadine Hwang 254
National Sailors' and Firemen's Union (NSFU) 139, 140, 141, 142
Naturalisation 46, 107
  Act of Parliament 33
  Bank of Scotland Act 1695, nationality clause 26
  Commonwealth Immigrants Act 1962 175
  denization petition 62, 83–84
  illegal immigrants 139, 165, 191
  Macao versus Officers of State 26–28
  Nationality Act 1948 172
  residency permits 173
Needham, Joseph 246–247
negative views of Chinese 91, 94, 131, 139–140, 141, 142, 152, 153, 162, 182, 196, 198–199
Ng Choy 106
Nobel Prize 222
Oi, Reverend Florence Li-Tim 270

286

Index

Olympic Games 170, 214, 264, 267, 274
opera, Chinese *see* theatre
opium
  illegal trade 30, 61, 110, 112
  opposition to trade 75, 112
  usage 47, 152–153
Opium Wars 34, 70, 89, 112, 238
orphans 34, 59, 77, 100, 210, 268–270
Orwell, George 147, 244
Oxford University 218, 219
Pageant of China 198
painters and sculptors 14–15, 163, 202, 217, 219, 220, 245, 254, 266, 278, 279, 280
pandas 206–207
Pandemonium 207
Parliament 19, 25–28, 31, 33, 75, 76, 110, 115, 139, 140, 196
  Chinese visitors to 36, 58, 119, 124, 126, 129
  Member of Northern Ireland Assembly 157
  Parliamentary candidate 168
Philosophy of Lao Zhang 242
Piccadilly 170, 201
pilots *see* aeronautics
Ping-Pong 210, 269
Place I Call Home, The 157
plays *see* theatre
political asylum 139, 174, 222
Poon Lim 183
Poon, William 175–176
population statistics 6, 31, 35, 110, 156–157, 159
Prince of Wales 40, 49, 114, 129, 130
Professor from Peking, The 204

Profit, Victory and Sharpness 163, 217
prostitution 31, 32, 42, 76, 162
protests against Chinese workers 139, 142, 162
Queen Mary College, London 203
Quo Tai-chi 224, 229–230
racism 122, 139, 140, 142, 157, 158, 161, 162, 193, 204, 226, 242, 269, 282
radio 184, 201, 244, 259, 260–262, 280
religion
  Chinese missionaries 70, 78, 101, 257–259
  Christian baptisms of Chinese 19, 31, 252–253
  Confucianism and Chinese religious beliefs 50, 78, 79, 116, 259–260
  converts to Christianity 12, 77, 131, 135, 215, 257
  Edinburgh Medical Missionary Society 105–106
  Macao, William, 23–24
  missionaries in China 11, 12, 69, 70, 74–75, 269–270
  prohibition of Christianity in China 54, 69
  Salvation Army 68, 75–78, 156
  translation of the bible into Chinese 69, 70, 74, 102
repatriation of Chinese workers 142, 144, 145, 154, 178
restaurants *see* Chinese food
Reynolds, Sir Joshua 16
Rohmer, Sax 153, 196, 200, 201
Royal Academy 15, 52, 201, 209, 246

Royal Academy of Dramatic Arts 205, 256
Royal Academy of Music 210
Royal Ballet School 206
Royal encounters 12, 13, 15, 36, 58, 89, 91, 94–95, 97, 114, 119, 125, 127, 128–130, 133, 155, 174, 187, 207, 208, 225, 227, 229, 230, 237, 238, 274
Royal Naval College, Greenwich 104
sailors *see* seamen
Salisbury Plain Flying School 254
Salvation Army *see* religion
Sao-ke Sze, Alfred 228, 229, 252
Science and Civilisation in China 247
seamen 30–37, 139–145, 178–188
  Chinese Merchant Seamen's memorial 188
  Chinese Merchant Seamen's Pool 181
  Chinese navy in Britain 29, 35–36, 104
  employed by Blue Funnel Line 145
  employed by East India Company 30–31
  employed by Royal Navy 19, 35, 178–188
  life in port 31, 47–48, 147, 149, 150, 156, 262
  maltreatment of 31, 35, 142, 144, 182
  opposition to 139–142, 178
  strikes 140, 142, 143
  unions 141, 143, 158, 173, 181
Second Farewell to Cambridge 241
Second World War 142–143, 155, 173, 180–185, 192, 270
servants 19, 39–44, 81–88, 128, 270, 271, 272–273

Sevenoaks School 16
Sheen, Lucy 210, 269
Shen FuTsung 11–12
Shin Hong Ma 271–272
ships
  Automedon 182
  Benlarig 178
  Benlomond 183
  Chaoyong 37
  Conway 34
  Cyclops 181
  Empress of Scotland 182
  Flowery Land 33
  Glencoe 35
  Keying 90–94
  Royal Yacht *Victoria and Albert* 34, 40, 130
  Sir Galahad 186–187
  Sir Tristam 186
  Strathnairn 178
  Zhiyuan 29
shops, Chinese 44, 45, 46–48, 147, 172, 180, 194, 273
Silent Traveller books 171, 277, 278–279, 281
Sinophobia *see* racism *and* negative views of Chinese
Slade School of Art 219, 220
Social & Political Reminiscences 124
Soho Chinatown 154, 158–159, 168, 169, 201
Song Zhiguang 237
Soo Yow 189, 190–194
Spencer, Stanley 219
Staunton, Thomas 39, 110, 111
Story of Ming, The 207
students 35, 99, 100–108, 157, 163, 180, 212, 213–223, 247, 256, 259, 262, 275
Sun Yat-sen 73, 106, 107, 134, 135–136, 141, 149, 150, 185, 216, 232, 248
table tennis 237, 267
Tan Chitqua 14–15
Taylor, Hudson 74

television 203, 205, 207, 211, 217, 219, 220, 241
Ten Thousand Chinese Things 90
tennis players 173, 214, 221, 263–264
Thames Valley Institute 247
Thatcher, Margaret 218, 238–239
theatre
  British plays with a Chinese theme 196, 198–200, 204, 205, 208, 211, 230, 271
  Chinese opera 97, 98, 176, 193, 203, 204, 207–208, 210, 219
  Chinese plays 197, 203–204, 208
Thomas Cook tours 153, 250
Tom Fat 40–41
trade visits 36, 116, 120, 124, 129, 228, 235, 236, 237, 238, 253, 254
trade with China 11, 30, 35, 81, 110, 111
travel abroad from China, negative views on 11, 14, 110
Tsai Chen, Prince 225, 227
Tsai Chin 205–206
Tsai Tse, Duke 253
Tz-Zeung Koo 258–259
United Aid to China Fund 185
University of London 102, 203, 209, 215, 221, 232, 275
Van Cuong Truong MBE 274
Victoria, Queen 36, 40, 89, 91, 92, 94, 96, 97, 113, 114, 118, 119, 125, 127, 128, 129, 130, 133
Waley, Arthur 38, 203, 259
Wang Laiquan 74
Wang Tao 6, 39, 68, 70–73
Wang-y-Tong 16, 129

war in China 143, 180, 185, 217, 231, 234, 261
weddings 128, 226, 250, 251, 271
Wedgewood, Josiah 16
Wellington Koo 228–229, 231–232
Westfield College 215
Whistler, James McNeill 161
Wife of General Ling, The 249, 271
Wild Swans 248
Wong, Anna May 201, 204, 256
Wong Yan-lung 223
Woolf, Virginia 245
Woon Wing Yip 176
World of Suzie Wong 205, 206
writers
  autobiographical 157, 245, 248–249
  cookery 173, 220, 235
  fiction 152, 218, 241–244
  painting and calligraphy 202
  plays 203–204
  poetry 241
  portrayals of Britain 71, 275–282
  science 247
Xia Peisu 219
Xinhua, People's Republic of China news agency 158
Xu Zhimo 241
Xue Fucheng 79, 117, 122
Yan Fu 104
Yang Hui-min 185
Yang Jiang 218
Yellow Jacket, The 198
Yip, David 210, 211
York University 248
Yuan Shin Ch'uan 254
Zeng Baosun 215
Zeng Jize 39, 121
Zhang Deyi 73, 113, 115
Zhao Ziyang 238
Zoffany, Johann 15